THE ADVANCE TECHINCAL PROJECT MANAGEMENT PROGRAM

1st Edition

Idris Parks, PMP, MBA, CISSP, Six σ Green Belt, CCAI, CompTIA CTT+,CCIE Voice & Security Qualified
I'LL Show U Technologies
70 W Madison St
Three National Plaza Suite 1400
Chicago IL 60602
1-855-ILL-SHOW
iparks@isutech.com

THE ADVANCE TECHNICAL PROJECT MANAGEMENT PROGRAM, 1st Edition

To arrange bulk purchase discounts for sales promotions, events, training courses, or other purposes, please contact I'LL Show U Technologies at the address listed on the previous page.

Book URL: www.isutech.com
13-Digit ISBN: 978-0-615-61437-3
10-digit ISBN: 061561437X

Distributed worldwide for I'LL Show U Technologies through CreateSpace, LCC

For general information on I'LL Show U Technologies, including information on corporate licenses, updates, future titles or courses, contact I'LL Show U Technologies at 1-855-ILL-SHOW or send email to iparks@isutech.com

For authorization to photocopy items for corporate, personal or education use, contact I'LL Show U Technologies at email to iparks@isutech.com

Limit of Liability/Disclaimer of Warranty. The author and publisher have used their best efforts in preparing this book and the related materials used in this book. I'LL Show U Technologies make no representations or warranties or merchantability or fitness for a particular purpose. I'LL Show U Technologies assume no liability for any damages caused by following instructions or using the techniques or tools listed in this book or related materials used in/for this book. I'LL Show U Technologies make no representations or warranties that extend beyond the descriptions contained in this paragraph. No warranty may be created or extended by sales representatives or written sales material. The

I'LL Show U Technologies
70 W Madison St
Three National Plaza Suite 1400
Chicago IL 60602
1-855-ILL-SHOW
iparks@isutech.com

Purpose of this Book

The Advance Technical Project Management Program, herein referred to as the "atPMP", objective is to provide Project Managers with the technical & conceptual knowledge required to manage large scale complex technology projects within the Networking, Telecommunication and IT Security field by using a Project Management Framework, Microsoft's ePMO solution: SharePoint/Project Server and a Cisco VoIP Infrastructure approach. Included with this book are Project Management "How To" videos & templates covering all functional areas of project management showing step-by-step tricks, tips and trade-secrets on creating, using and publishing all templates for most high impacting stakeholder and project scenarios. The objective is to teach Project Managers the technical side of Project Management through the Business Case surrounding the PLAN for TRANSFORMATION for the XYZ Company.

Intended Audience

This handbook is intended to assist team leads or project manager as they participate in technology projects. Specifically, The ITS PMO Senior Management are recommended to review this handbook to ensure that consistent methodologies are used across all technology projects.

Structure of this Handbook

The remaining chapters of this handbook either focus on particular the Project Management Office processes. Each chapter is organized as follows:

- Each chapter begins with an overall process overview containing the following information:
    - Reason process is important
    - Summary of inputs and outputs associated to the XYZ Housing Authority PMO processes and the tools/techniques recommended to achieve the outputs
    - Heads up on overall resources and timeframe necessary to complete process
- Each process is split into various stages. Each stage has its own section containing the following information:
    - Overview and main highlights of stage
    - Inputs and outputs associated to stage and the tools/techniques recommended to achieve the outputs
    - Resources and timeframe necessary to complete stage
    - Stage description in step-by-step detail, including tips for success and examples
- At the end of each chapter, any additional reference materials are listed

The Inputs and Outputs of the Initiation Chapter will show what items, task or documents are to be considered in completing the three stages of the Initiation framework. The inputs can be described as what work needs to be done which as a result will lead to the actual output which can be described as the final deliverable for that particular stage.

Accompanying any resource recommendation is a RACI matrix. All matrices will resemble the example below.

Step	Resource 1	Resource 2	Resource 3	Resource 4	Resource 5
Step 1	C		R	C	A
Step 2	A/R	R	C		I

and identify the following:

- R - Who is RESPONSIBLE? - The person who has to do it
- A - Who is ACCOUNTABLE? - The person who makes the final decision and has ultimate ownership
- C - Who is CONSULTED? - The person who must be consulted *before* a decision or action is taken
- I - Who is INFORMED? - The person who must be informed that a decision or action *has* been taken

Key Terms Used

Key terms used throughout this document are listed below with their definitions.

Key Terms	Definitions
Business Department	Any department which The ITS PMO services - e.g. Asset Management, Communications, Procurement, Relocation
Business Owner	The principal representative from the department or departments represented in the project, capable and authorized to make decisions regarding the business aspects of the project.
Executive Decision Team (EDT)	Executive Decision Team – the governing body of "C" level executives responsible for overseeing and collaboratively deciding the ITS PMO project portfolio
Executive Business Sponsor (EBS)	Managing Director responsible for technology initiative
The ITS PMO Owner	CIO or ACIO for Infrastructure or Applications depending on project nature and complexity
The ITS PMO Senior Management	Consists of Chief Information Officer, Assistant Chief Information Officers, and Senior Portfolio Manager
Portfolio Dashboard	A reporting mechanism used by the Department of Information Technology Services to systematically and consistently report on the status of its project portfolio. Typically updated on a monthly basis, the Dashboard is distributed to the EDT, Managing Directors, Directors, Business Owners and the ITS PMO Project Managers.
Project Initiation Document (PID)	Documents a request for a Technology Initiative - After traversing through the Project Initiation Process, a request contained within a Project Initiation Document is either approved or rejected to become a Technology Project
Project Initiation Process (PIP)	The process with which a Technology Initiative is formally requested, evaluated, and eventually approved or rejected - All Technology Initiatives must go through this process in order to become a Project
Project Portfolio	Terminologies used to refer to the collection of all projects currently in planning or in progress that have been approved by the Executive Decision Team (EDT).
Project Team	Members from XYZ Company (The ITS PMO and Business) as well as vendor who are assigned to deliver the work of the project on a day-to-day basis
Resource Capacity Model	A tool used by The ITS PMO senior management to allocate its available resources (human) across the project portfolio as well as daily operations and maintenance tasks. The tool shows, based on an annual number of work hours in a 12-month period, the number of hours each staff member can devote to particular projects and operations.
Technology Initiative	A discrete set of activities designed to achieve a desired change to the current technology environment
Technology Project	Also referred to simply as "Project" - A technology initiative that has been approved by the EDT and funded
Managing Directors (MD)	Senior Management Team
Project Management Office (PMO)	

Icons Used in this Book

Strategies. Used to note the strategies used inside this book. There are a total of 33 strategies included in this book.

Notes. Additional information given for topic at hand.

Project Manager Technical Studies. Technical topics that are linked to Videos and Template solutions available on CD.

Business Case Scenario – The Strategy for XYZ Housing Authority

The Renovation

The HQ Move

The Plan for Transformation

The Plan for Transformation, herein after known as "the Strategic Plan", began in 2000 under the leadership of Mayor Richard M. Daley with approval from the U.S. Department of Housing and Urban Development (HUD). It is the largest, most ambitious redevelopment effort of public housing in the United States, with the goal of rehabilitating or redeveloping the entire stock of public housing in Chicago.

By the end of the Plan, 25,000 units of housing will be renovated or built new. The Plan for Transformation functions under a Moving To Work Agreement with HUD.

The Plan for Transformation goes far beyond the physical structure of public housing. It aims to build and strengthen communities by integrating public housing and its leaseholders into the larger social, economic and physical fabric of Chicago.

XYZ Company, through various City of Chicago departments and non-profit partners, offers leaseholders a comprehensive array of supportive services that lead to self-sufficiency, such as job training, job placement, substance abuse treatment, education, summer programs, day care, and more. Mixed-income communities break down the social barriers that formerly segregated public housing residents from the larger city of Chicago. Where there were once isolated superblocks, the street grid is being recreated to seamlessly integrate the new developments into the surrounding neighborhoods.

In addition to transforming the culture and structure of public housing, the Plan also improves the administration of XYZ Company. Since the Plan's inception, XYZ Company has streamlined its staff from more than 2,600 to fewer than 500 today. XYZ Company now focuses on its primary responsibility as an asset manager and contracts with private professional property management firms to manage properties. For a more detail overview of *the PLAN FOR TRANSFORMATION VIDEO* for XZY Housing Authority, look at the Business Case Overview Video on the atPMP CD.

Project Requirements:

- Provide project management oversight over The Plan for Transformation Project from a PMO perspective from project start to project completion-using SharePoint as the team collaborative tool.
- In addition to the renovation of various housing units, XYZ Company has also decided to move it's corporate headquarters from the South Loop Chicago Area to the CNA Insurance building in an effort to save money. Two major project initiatives will come from this physical move:
    1. Relocation of all WAN data circuits (OC48) to the new home location while maintaining current data communications for all services during the transitions. This will involve implementing a parallel network. All departments will move in a phase migration over 30 days.
    2. Redesign of all LAN IP addresses to accommodate dual migration to new LAN environment. All data servers are located at the South Loop campus location and will be moved to the new CNA Insurance location.
    3. Transition from existing AT&T Centrex Bases Telephony solution to a Cisco VoIP Premise based Solution in an effort to streamline unified communication cost.

Terms and Project Understanding

- Provide project management oversight over The Plan for Transformation Project from a PMO perspective from project start to project completion-using SharePoint as the team collaborative tool. **What does this means?** PMO or Project Management Office is a term used to describe the alignment of the organization with the purpose of providing management over multiple projects. A PMO consist of multiple project managers working together to complete individual projects in a uniform fashion. For example, each Project Manager within the PMO may be assigned one or two projects to complete a strategic plan set by company objectives for that year. The PMO provides project oversight & strategic direction ensuring that all project deliverables; goals and objectives stay consistent with management's goals & objectives. In addition, the PMO should use SharePoint

as the team collaboration Tool. **What does this means?** Use SharePoint as a resource tool for all the team collaboration. Using SharePoint create a site, list, libraries, workflows and InfoPath Web Forms as a tools & method for streamlining all project documentation, issue reporting, etc. Below is a snapshot of a SharePoint team site. A SharePoint site is a typical web site used as the basis for all communication inputs. A list and/or library are attribute (Fields) used to store data. Similar to fields in table of a database (i.e. Microsoft Access or SQL Server) . The different between a list and library is that a library can hold physical documents along with field attributes i.e. Excel, Word, etc documents stored in with create date, modified date

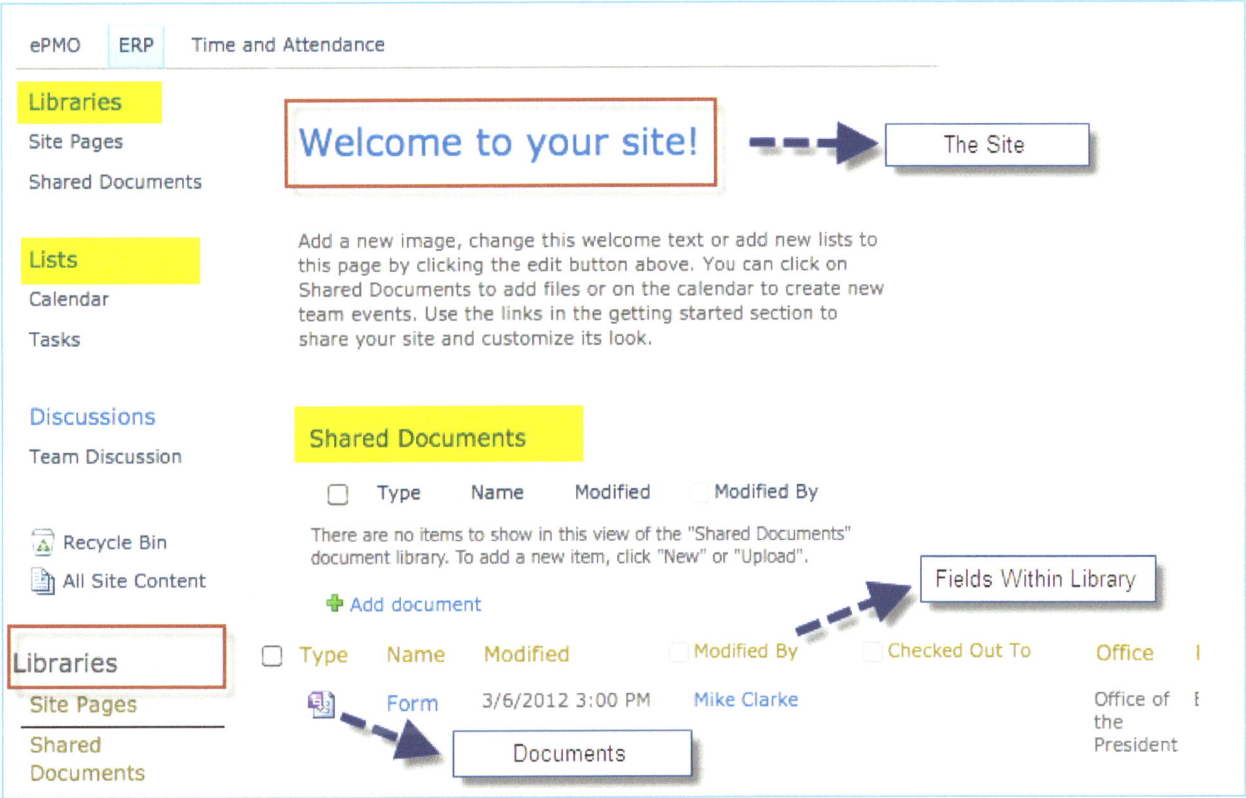

- ❖ Relocation of all WAN data circuits (OC48) to the new home location of the CAN Insurance location while maintaining current data communications for the South Loop campus for all services during the transitions. This will involve implementing a parallel network. Please refer to *Figure 1* for a detail network topology overview. **What does this mean?** Implement a project plan to achieve this deliverable. Use any tools deemed necessary to achieve desired deliverable.
- ❖ Redesign of all LAN IP addresses to accommodate dual migration to new LAN environment. **What does this mean?** Since XYZ Housing Authority must still be able to received data services (email, internet, etc) located at the South Loop campus while moving by departments over 30 days onto the CNA Insurance campus, design a IP Scheme and routing design that will enable achieve this desired result.
- ❖ Transition from existing AT&T Centrex Bases Telephony solution to a Cisco VoIP Premise based Solution in an effort to streamline unified communication cost. **What**

does this mean? Implement a Cisco VoIP system for phone service for the CNA Insurance campus Area, Branch 1 and between Branch 2. Departments that move into the CNA campus location should be able to dial the same number as before to reach other users at Branch 1 or Branch 2. All current phone capabilities like ACD routing for Call Center Agents, & Voicemail resource be available at all campus locations.

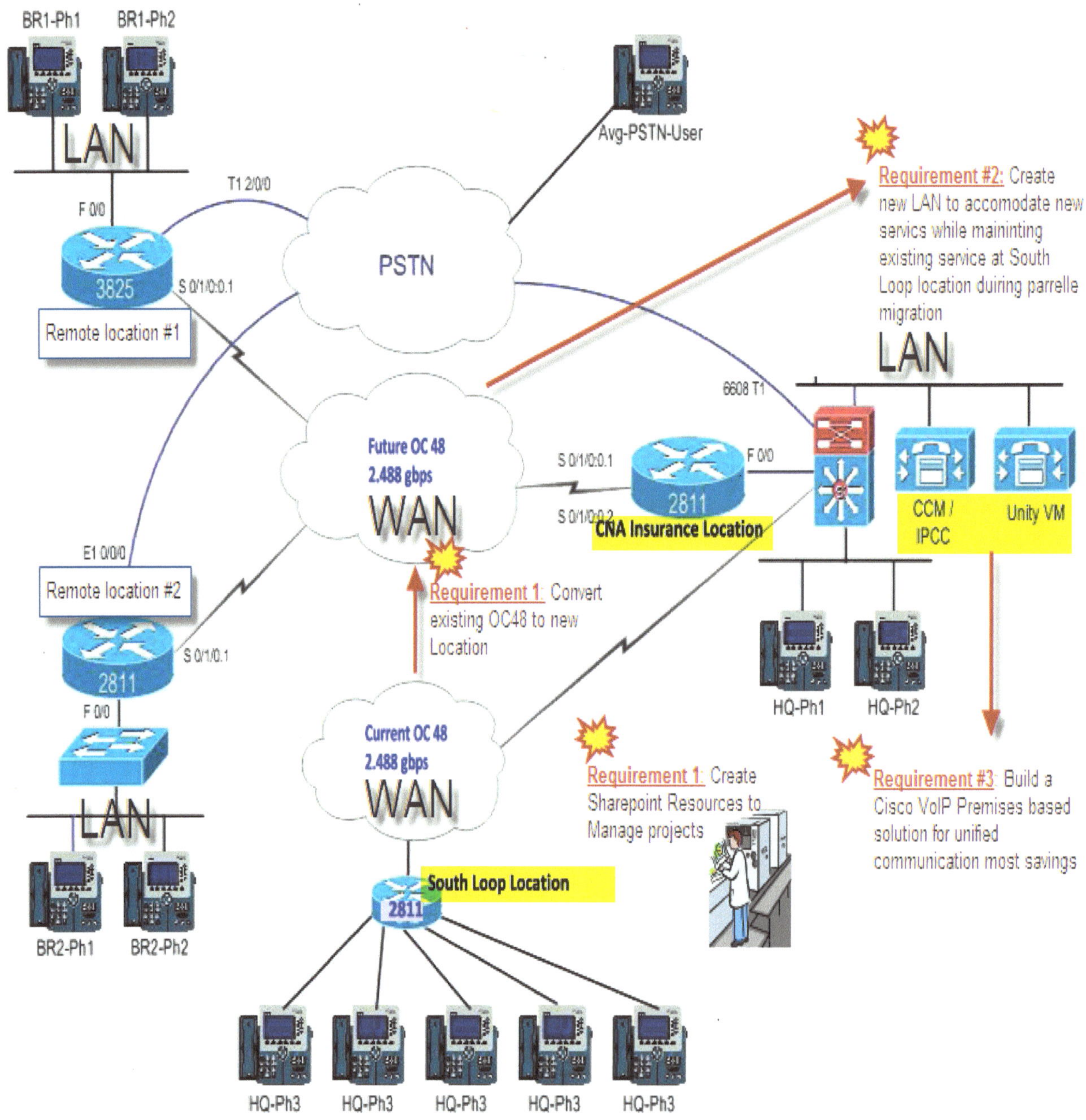

Figure 1: Network Topology

Table OF Contents

1 Project Initiation

Topics Covered:

- Process Initiation Process (PIP)
    - Generate Idea
    - Develop Scope
    - Validate Need
- Process Initiation Document (PID)
- Understanding of Strategies 1-7
- InfoPath Web Forms
- SharePoint List, Libraries and Workflows for PIP Process
- Designing your project approach
- Understanding of Networking Infrastructure

How To Videos & Templates on CD :

- Walk through of the Project Initiation Process
- Understanding SharePoint List, Libraries, web parts, content types and Workflows for PIDS
- Creating InfoPath Web Forms
- Understanding of SharePoint PIP Process

STRATEGY For Initiation:

- ✓ Overview of the Project Initiation Process (PIP)
- ✓ Understanding and Following the Strategic Plan of the Organization
- ✓ Understanding the Authority of the Project Manager
- ✓ Understanding the Politics and Power of the Stakeholder
- ✓ Estimating Qualitative Benefits and Cost of a Project
- ✓ PID Scoring Framework
- ✓ EDT Presentation Meeting

Project Initiation Overview

Project Initiation is the first in a series of phases comprising the Project Management Lifecycle. The ITS PMO has established a Project Initiation Process (PIP) derived from the Project Management Body of Knowledge (PMBOK) Core Process Group and tailored for the XYZ HOUSING Authority's technology projects. This process improves The ITS PMO' ability to plan for the long term and better support their customers' (Business Departments) needs.

Any technology-related initiatives that a Business Department wishes to undertake must follow the PIP Process in order to be considered by The ITS PMO. If The ITS PMO recognizes a technology initiative that may benefit a Business Department, the Business Department must be convinced of the need and take the request through the PIP Process as well.

The ITS PMO initiatives should also follow the PIP Process. These would tend to be initiatives that may affect the systems that Business Departments use but not how they do their business.

The PIP process consists of three main stages - 1) Generate Idea, 2) Develop Scope, and 3) Validate Need. Each stage is described in greater detail in the next three sections of this chapter.

PROJECT INITIATION

2.2. Stage 1 – Generate Idea	2.3. Stage 2 – Develop Scope	2.4. Stage 3 – Validate Need
Steps 1. Draft Qualified Idea within PID 2. Review Qualified Idea 3. Approve Qualified Idea 4. Send Electronic and Initialed Copies of Qualified Idea to The ITS PMO Management and PMO 5. Review Qualified Idea 6. Assign The ITS PMO Owner and PMO Resource	Steps 7. Refine Idea with Key Stakeholders 8. Draft Estimated Benefits 9. Draft Estimated Costs for Project and Maintenance 10. Consolidate Results into PID 11. Review Completed PID with Key Stakeholders 12. Approved Completed PID 13. Send Electronic and Signed Copies of Completed PID to PMO 14. Input IT "Non Personnel" Initiative Request into BIS System	Steps 15. Apply PID Scoring Framework 16. Analyze Budget and The ITS PMO Resource Capacity 17. Evaluate Prioritization Results and Generate Recommendation 18. Prepare Formal Presentation 19. Present to EDT 20. Update The ITS PMO Project Portfolio

Objectives and Benefits

Prior to the establishment of the Project Initiation Process, technology initiatives were often scoped by the ITS PMO with minimal Business Department/ End User involvement or pushed upon the ITS PMO with minimal notice and justification. The use of a standardized, repeatable process ensures consistency and efficiency from year to year when allocating resources to technology initiatives.

The PIP process was established to meet the following objectives:

- Create standardized process to define and qualify Information Technology initiatives
- Ensure link to XYZ Company Strategic Objectives (Plan for Transformation)
- Force consideration of comprehensive cost estimates and benefits behind initiatives
- Formalize organizational (MD) buy-in

Some benefits that have been realized through utilizing this process are as follows:

- Initiatives prioritized by
    - Strategic alignment
    - Payback to XYZ Company
    - Technological importance
    - Mandate
- Organizational support
- Assurance that scarce resources are allocated properly to mission critical initiatives

Tools

The following tools support the Project Initiation Process:

- Process flow diagrams for each of the three main stages - visual representation of the steps in each stage
- PID template - the Project Initiation Document consists of two parts; PART ONE must be completed in order to begin the process; PART TWO must be completed in order for the initiative to be considered for approval

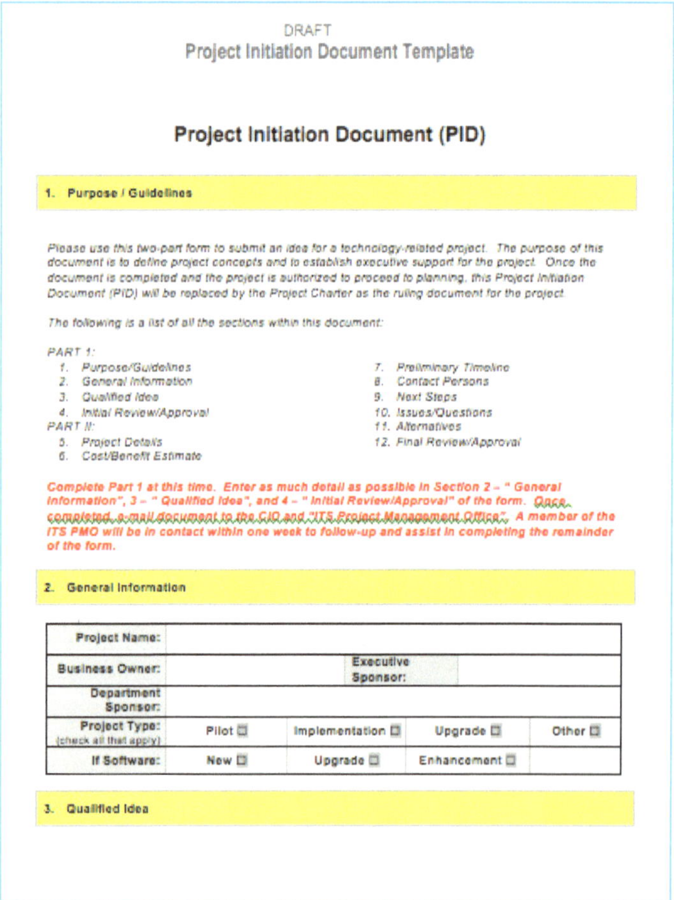

DRAFT
Project Initiation Document Template

Project Initiation Document (PID)

1. Purpose / Guidelines

Please use this two-part form to submit an idea for a technology-related project. The purpose of this document is to define project concepts and to establish executive support for the project. Once the document is completed and the project is authorized to proceed to planning, this Project Initiation Document (PID) will be replaced by the Project Charter as the ruling document for the project.

The following is a list of all the sections within this document:

PART 1:
1. *Purpose/Guidelines*
2. *General Information*
3. *Qualified Idea*
4. *Initial Review/Approval*

PART II:

5. *Project Details*
6. *Cost/Benefit Estimate*
7. *Preliminary Timeline*
8. *Contact Persons*
9. *Next Steps*
10. *Issues/Questions*
11. *Alternatives*
12. *Final Review/Approval*

Complete Part 1 at this time. Enter as much detail as possible in Section 2 – " General Information", 3 – " Qualified Idea", and 4 – " Initial Review/Approval" of the form. Once completed, e-mail document to the CIO and "ITS Project Management Office". A member of the ITS PMO will be in contact within one week to follow-up and assist in completing the remainder of the form.

2. General Information

Project Name:				
Business Owner:		Executive Sponsor:		
Department Sponsor:				
Project Type: (check all that apply)	Pilot ☐	Implementation ☐	Upgrade ☐	Other ☐
If Software:	New ☐	Upgrade ☐	Enhancement ☐	

3. Qualified Idea

- PID tracking worksheet - assists in keeping track of PID status throughout the process

PID Worksheet
2006 PIDs

As of 6/14

#	Name	Description	2005 Resubmiss	Date Receive	App /Infr	Submitter/ Owner	Exec Spons
PID06-17	Lowden Technology Center	Development of residents' computer center and security component	N	6/3/05	INFRA		
PID06-24	Altgeld Gardens/Murray Homes Neighborhood Network	Duplicate of PID 06-17	N	6/6/05	INFRA		

- Project costs and benefits worksheets - assists in estimating costs and benefits for the initiative
- PID Scoring Framework - assists in prioritizing amongst initiatives
- Resource Capacity Plan - assists in determining the ITS PMO resource capacity to execute initiatives

PID Number:
PID Name:

		Month 1	Month 2	Month 3	Month 4	Month 5	Month 6
(A)CIO	John Doe						
	John Doe						
	John Doe						
PMO-Apps	John Doe						
	John Doe						
	John Doe						
PMO-Infra	John Doe						
	John Doe						
	John Doe						
Vendor	John Doe						
	John Doe						
ITS PMs	John Doe						
	John Doe						
	John Doe						
	John Doe						
PMO	John Doe						
	John Doe						

Project Management Office
Portfolio Resource Leveling Plan

Portfolio Manager: Idris Parks, PMP

Targeted Week: 03/08/04 – 07/31/04

PMO Status Definition

1. Monitor (M)
2. Counsel (C)
3. Assist (A)
4. Participate (P)

PORTFOLIO RESOURCE LEVELING PLAN

- These hours reflect the demanded hours by the infrastructure projects for the week of 3/8/04 – 7/31/04

Project	Status	Monday	Tuesday	Wednesday	Thursday	Friday	Utilization
Metro WAN	P	3	3	3	3	3	38%
CHAC	P	2	2	2	2	2	25%
BIO Mouse	A	1	1	1	1	1	5%
PMO	P	2	2	2	2	2	25%

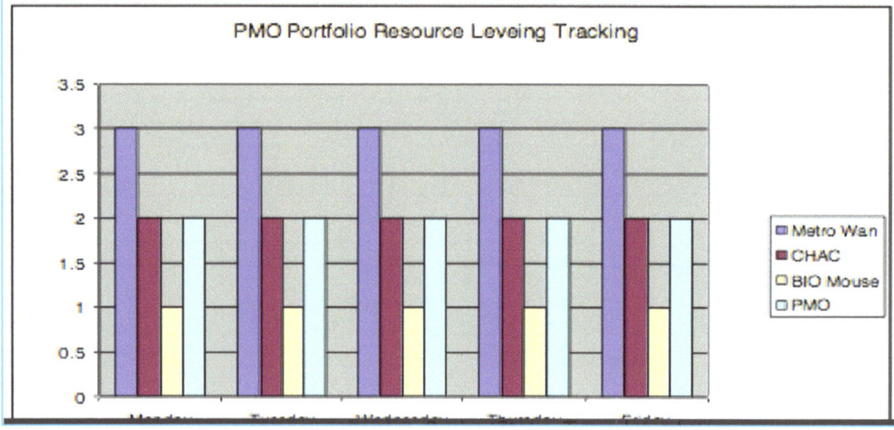

- PID communication templates -
- The ITS PMO Project Portfolio - visual representation of timeframes for approved PID's alongside pre-existing technology projects

Sections 2.2, 2.3, and 2.4 describe when and how to use each tool and provide examples.

Inputs and Outputs
The primary inputs to the Project Initiation Process are various sources that dictate the direction in which the XYZ Company is heading. The primary outputs from the process are documentation on the scope, benefits, costs, resources, and timeline for an approved technology project. The outputs will flow into the Project Planning phase of the project. The primary inputs and outputs are listed below, with further detail on how they are used, how they are created, and/or any interim work products described in Sections 2.2, 2.3, and 2.4.

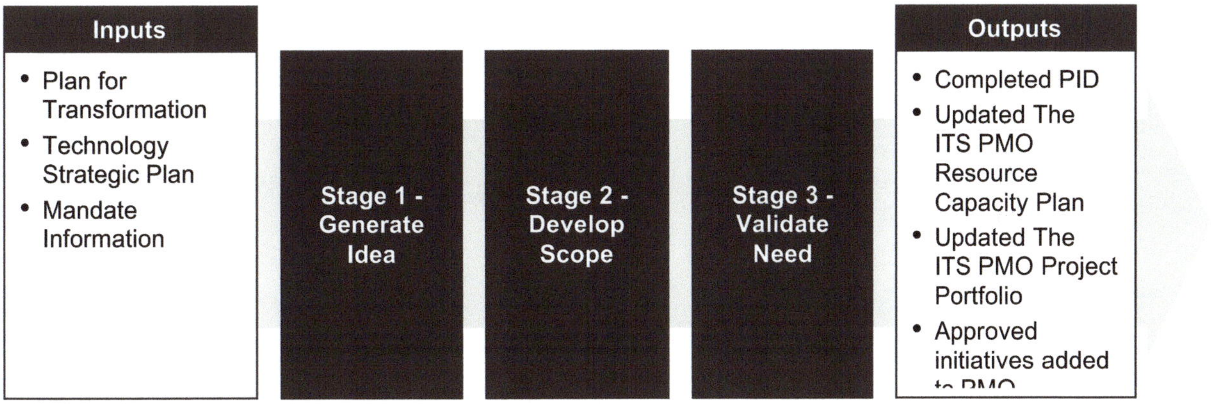

Timeframe/Total Duration

There are two main timeframes for the Project Initiation Process depending on whether or not the process is occurring in correspondence to the Annual Budget Process. Whenever there is a difference, the two timeframes are distinguished throughout the remainder of this chapter as 1) Annual Budget Submission Process and 2) Ongoing PID Requests.

<u>Annual Budget Submission Process</u>

- 16 weeks
- The Project Initiation Process plays an important role in requesting technology-related projects, which require budget allocation in the upcoming fiscal year.
    - The schedule for this yearly event should be determined in mid-April. This includes conversations with the Budget Department to ensure activities are in synch.
    - Communication of the schedule to the Business Departments in the form of MD Workout presentations, DSAR presentations.
    - An email memo from the CIO officially kicking off the start of the event should occur at the end of April.
    - PID PART One should be due into The ITS PMO by the end of May.
    - PID PART TWO should be completed and results entered into the Budget Information System by the end of June (based on the Budget Department's submission schedule).
    - Prioritization and capacity assessments should be completed by early August.
    - Presentation to the EDT and Budget Director should occur mid-August.

<u>Ongoing PID Requests</u>

- 6 weeks
- The Project Initiation Process must still be followed even if a technology project is being requested outside of the Annual Budget Process, even if budget can be pulled together to fund it.
    - Any PID PART ONE submitted up to one month prior to an upcoming EDT meeting will be eligible to be considered for that meeting.
    - PID PART TWO completion, prioritization, and capacity assessment should be performed during the month leading up to the EDT meeting.
- Please note that at the current time, the Project Initiation Process had not been fully executed for technology-related project requests outside of the Annual Budget Process. The material presented for these events are recommendations and have yet to be tested.

Resource Participation

The following resources participate in the Project Initiation Process:

- <u>Business Owner</u>
- <u>Dept Director</u> – primary Business Department Director sponsoring initiative

- Executive Sponsor
- The ITS PMO Mgmt – Chief Information Officer and/or Assistant Chief Information Officers
- Senior Portfolio Manager
- Other Key Stakeholders - departments in addition to the primary Business Department that will be significantly impacted by the initiative
- Dept BIS Resource - resource in primary Business Department responsible for entering requests into Budget Information System
- Executive Decision Team – Managing Directors with large stake in technology investments
- Budget Department – primarily the Budget Director

Sections 2.2, 2.3, and 2.4 go into further detail as to when and in what capacity each resource participates.

Understanding & Following the Strategic Plan of the Organization.

The strategic plan or otherwise known as and referred to as management objectives are the goals that senior management set for the upcoming year for the organization. Most objectives are set as short-term goals those make-up long-term cost savings opportunities, federal mandates or provide the organization as competitive edge for increasing cash flow or bottom line return on investment. Each year, a meeting or document is published to the organization explaining the goals/objective of the organization so that everyone can

become knowledgeable about the direction of the organization. The Strategic Plan contains usually contains quantitative metrics and/or deliverables that are push "top down" (CIO → Team) vs "bottom up" (Team → CIO). It is imperative that as a Project Manager you are fully aware of the strategic direction of the organization and upper management expectation especially at the city, county, state or federal level this is extremely important due to the hidden silos that exist for political interest which are many times tied to user votes. Understanding, the organization direction will often time help you to keep the overall project scope and deliverables closely aligned with your planned baseline schedule because you will be better able to understand management objective or the end game which will allow you to strategic always be ahead of your planned schedule vs you building a bridge to nowhere.

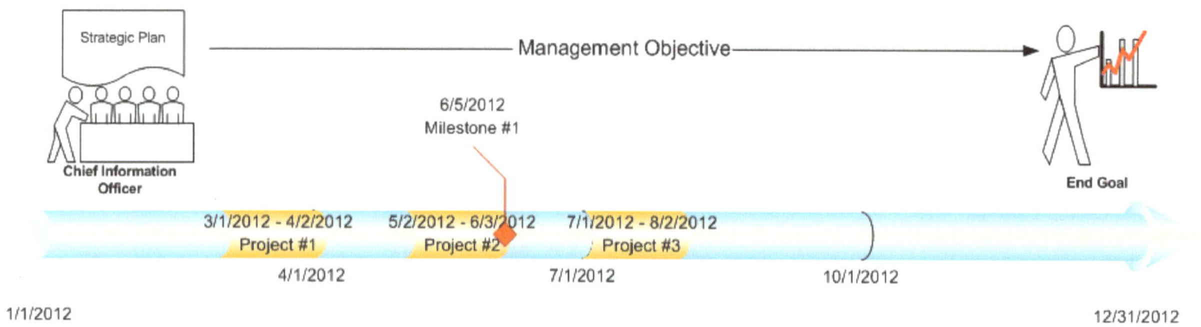

1.1 Stage 1 - Generate Idea

Overview

The Project Initiation Process begins with Business Departments coming up with ideas for technology initiatives to support their business objectives and operations. In this first stage, Business Departments formally submit a request for a technology initiative to The ITS PMO in the form of a Project Initiation Document (PID). This begins the documentation trail of what a particular technology initiative is, who originated it, and who approved it. The Project Initiation Document is the business case for project justification. The total portfolio of PIDs is equal the opportunities of all management objectives usually in the form of Information Technology Projects.

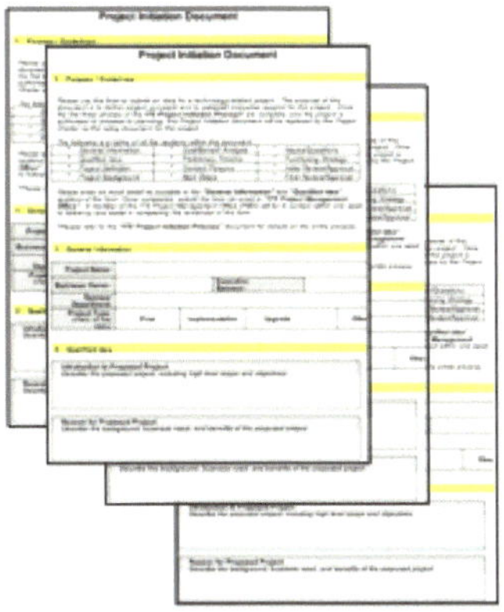

TOTAL PIDS = MANAGEMENT OBJECTIVE

Ideas for initiatives internal to The ITS PMO should also be submitted using this process. Initiatives that fall into this category include the technology strategic plan, network build out, systems security policies, etc.

PROJECT INITIATION

2.2. Stage 1 – Generate Idea

Steps
1. Draft Qualified Idea within PID
2. Review Qualified Idea
3. Approve Qualified Idea
4. Send Electronic and Initialed Copies of Qualified Idea to ITS Management and PMO
5. Review Qualified Idea
6. Assign The ITS PMO Owner and PMO Resource

2.3. Stage 2 – Develop Scope

Steps
7. Refine Idea with Key Stakeholders
8. Draft Estimated Benefits
9. Draft Estimated Costs for Project and Maintenance
10. Consolidate Results into PID
11. Review Completed PID with Key Stakeholders
12. Approved Completed PID
13. Send Electronic and Signed Copies of Completed PID to PMO
14. Input IT "Non Personnel" Initiative Request into BIS System

2.4. Stage 3 – Validate Need

Steps
15. Apply PID Scoring Framework
16. Analyze Budget and The ITS PMO Resource Capacity
17. Evaluate Prioritization Results and Generate Recommendation
18. Prepare Formal Presentation
19. Present to EDT
20. Update The ITS PMO Project Portfolio

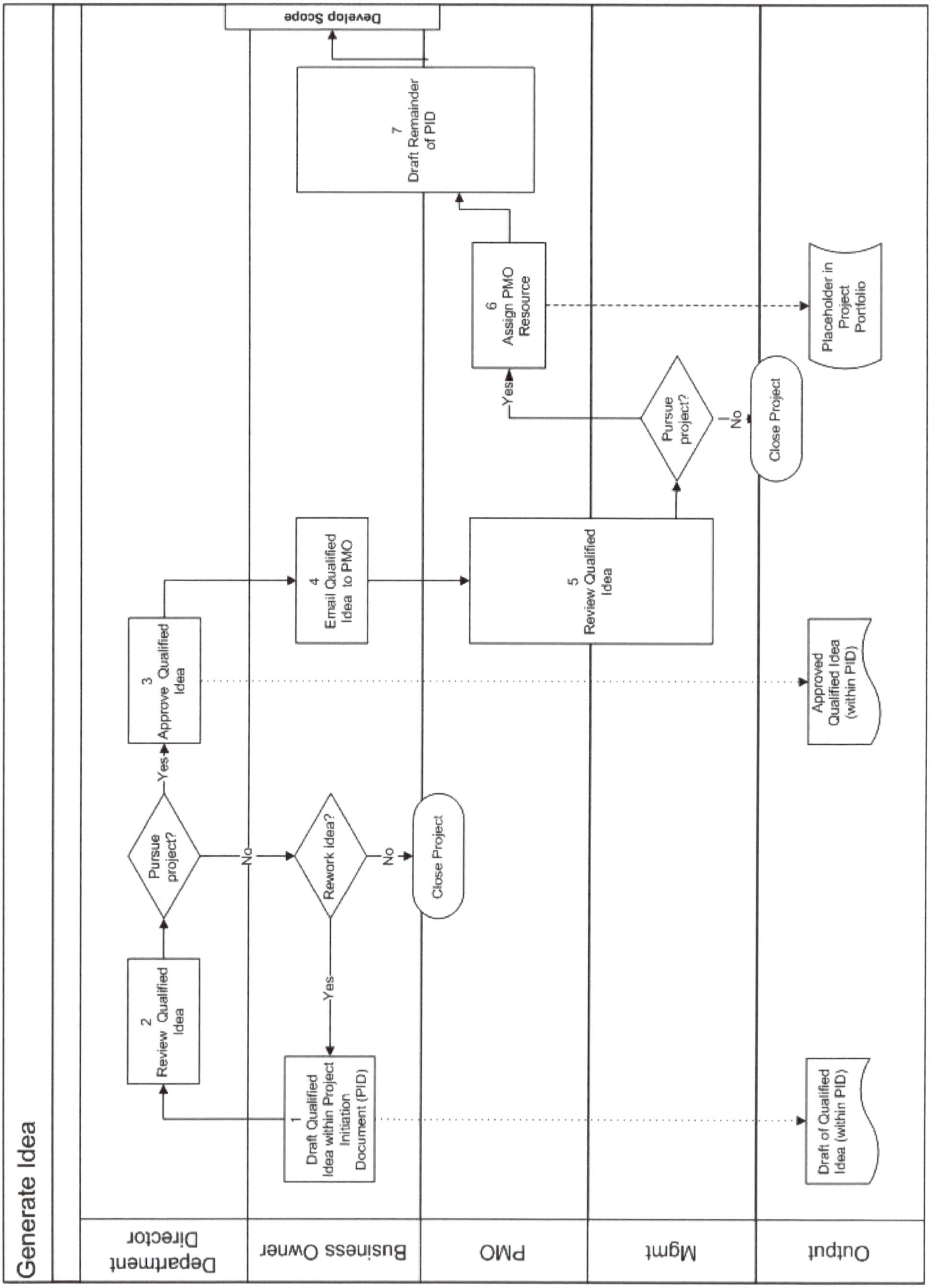

Generate Idea
Department Director
Business Owner
PMO
Mgmt
Output
1 Draft Qualified Idea within Project Initiation Document (PID)
2 Review Qualified Idea
Pursue project?
Yes
3 Approve Qualified Idea
No
Rework Idea?
Yes
No
Close Project
4 Email Qualified Idea to PMO
5 Review Qualified Idea
Pursue project?
Yes
No
Close Project
6 Assign PMO Resource
7 Draft Remainder of PID
Develop Scope
Draft of Qualified Idea (within PID)
Approved Qualified Idea (within PID)
Placeholder in Project Portfolio

Inputs, Outputs, and Tools

Business Departments can utilize the Annual Plan for Transformation, herein after known as "the Strategic Plan", to determine how technology may assist them to meet their goals. Internal The ITS PMO initiatives utilize the Technology Strategic Plan. The Project Initiation Document template assists in structuring what information needs to be documented. At this stage, only PART ONE of the document needs to be completed. Requests moving on after the end of this stage have had their PID PART ONE reviewed and initialed by the associated Department Director, the Managing Director, and The ITS PMO senior management.

Inputs	Tools & Techniques	Outputs
• Annual Plan for Transformation • Technology Strategic Plan • Mandate Information	• Stop Work Notice • Project Budget • Consultation (Legal, Procurement, Senior & Executive Mgmt) • Issue/Risk/Change Log • Meeting Minutes • Statement of Work • Scope Changes • Updated Payment Schedule • Updated Statement of Work • Updated Project Schedule	• Completed PID PART ONE (Qualified Idea/ PID 2-pager) • The ITS PMO Owner identified

Timeframe/Total Duration

Time	Description
One Month	Generate Idea
Four Days	Business Days of actual work effort per Qualified idea
Budget End Window	June
PID submission Window to PMO	May

One (1) month duration allotted for the "Generate Idea" stage. Four (4) business days of actual work effort per Qualified Idea.

This stage should communicate begin and end dates as follows:

- Annual Budget Submission Process
    - If the Qualified Idea is being submitted in correspondence to the Annual Budget Window, The ITS PMO should establish and communicate a deadline for Qualified Idea submissions that is approximately one month before the Budget Window closes. Typically, the Budget Window closes at the ***end of June*** so the deadline for submissions should be around the ***end of May*** or the beginning of June. This would correspond to a stage begin date around the end of April or the beginning of May
    - The ITS PMO should look for information regarding the dates of the Budget Submission Process around *mid-April*. There is a chance that the Budget Department will not have determined exact dates until late-May in which case the ITS PMO should contact the Budget Department around mid-April to get an idea of dates to begin establishing the PIP schedule.
- Ongoing PID Request

- If the Qualified Idea is being submitted at any time other than in correspondence to the Annual Budget Window, The ITS PMO should establish a schedule whereupon submissions by a certain date will be considered in time for a given Executive Decision Team (EDT) meeting. Recommendation would be to set a deadline one (1) month prior to an EDT meeting. This would correspond to a stage begin date of two (2) months prior to an EDT meeting.

Resource Participation

The following resources participate during the "Generate Idea" stage:

- Business Owner – primary Business resource assigned to initiative. This is often the person most impacted by the business problem that the technology project is intended to solve. This person can be any level within the department but most importantly should have detailed knowledge of the problem and the processes impacted and should be empowered to make decisions regarding the solution.
- Dept Director – primary Business Department Director sponsoring initiative; may also be the business owner.
- Division MD – Managing Director over primary Business Department; may also be the business owner.
- The ITS PMO Mgmt – Chief Information Officer, Assistant Chief Information Officers, and Senior Portfolio Manager
- The ITS PMO – The ITS PMO Project Management Office

The matrix below shows in what capacity each resource participates throughout the stage.

Step	Executive Sponsor	Dept Director	Business Owner	The ITS PMO Mgmt	Sr. Portfolio Manger	The ITS PMO Owner	Budget Director	Other Key Stakeholders	Dept BIS Resource
1 - Draft Qualified Idea within PID	A/C	C	R	C	C	C			
2 – Review Qualified Idea	A/R	R	R						
3 - Approve Qualified Idea	A/R	R	R						
4 - Send Electronic and Initialed Copies of Qualified Idea to The ITS PMO Management and PMO	A/I	I	R	I	I	I			
5 – Review Qualified Idea			C	A/R	R				
6 – Assign The ITS PMO Owner and PMO Resource			I	A/R	R	I			

Stage Description

The "Generate Idea" stage consists of 6 primary steps. This section provides detailed instructions for each of those steps.

Step 1 – Draft Qualified Idea within Process Initiation Document (PID)

- **Instructions**
  - The Qualified Idea corresponds to Sections 1-4 of the PID template, also known as PID PART ONE.
  - Each Qualified Idea must specify the following:
    - Business Owner – primary business resource assigned to initiative
    - Department Sponsor – primary business department sponsoring initiative
    - Executive Business Sponsor – Managing Director over primary department
    - Overview of request – what is needed
    - Reason for request – why is it needed, e.g. a regulatory mandate

- Desired completion date – when is it needed

Note *that the Business Owner, Department Sponsor, and Executive Business Sponsor may all be the same person for Authority-wide projects. Likewise, the Business Owner and Department Sponsor might be the same person. The Business Owner should intimately know the nature of the business problem to be solved by the technology solution as well as the time to work with the project on a day-to-day basis. The Department Sponsor/Executive Business Sponsor should have the authority to change the people, processes, and policies involved in implementing the solution.*

- It is preferred that the overview, reason, and desired completion date is filled out as detailed as possible. This will only assist resources further down the road in understanding what the initiative being requested is all about, or a historical view of what form the initiative first started. It is important that this idea can be tied back to the overall goal of the department and eventually up to the overall Authority goal, currently known as the "Plan for Transformation". It is also important to be able to articulate what types of benefits are expected to be achieved with the requested initiative.

- **Estimated Time Duration**
  - 8 hours.

- **Resource Participation**
  - The Qualified Idea is primarily the responsibility of Business Departments to draft.
  - The ITS PMO senior management may be contacted in order to assign The ITS PMO resources to assist in formalizing the idea.
  - Oftentimes, The ITS PMO resources may be involved in helping to trigger the idea. This is often through communicating with Business Departments to introduce them to potential new technologies or enhancements to existing systems that might be beneficial for them.
  - Despite The ITS PMO resources assisting in formulating the idea, an official PID PART ONE affecting specific Business end users must be generated by the Business Department in order to be considered a valid request.

- **Tips for Success**
  - The better a Business Department understands what its goals are and how technology will assist it, the less time it will take to complete the document. A fully developed Qualified Idea typically takes less than 8 hours to document, after the idea has been thought through.
  - To avoid the hassle in Step 5 of having to return a PID PART ONE to the Business Department, The ITS PMO resources should assist the Business Owners in formulating the idea. The PID tips document and/or a sample of a completed PID PART ONE can also be used to assist Business Owners in developing a good Qualified Idea

Step 2 – Review Qualified Idea

- **Instructions**
  - The Qualified Idea must be reviewed with Department Director and Managing Director listed as Executive Business Sponsor.

- Both persons must agree to the scope of the requested initiative before the Qualified Idea moves on to the next step.
- If either persons is dissatisfied, the Qualified Idea can either be returned to the Business Owner for modifications (return to Step 1), be shelved for later when the idea can be better formulated, or closed out such that the process completely ends.

- **Resource Participation**
  - It is the responsibility of the Business Owner to review the Qualified Idea with the Business Department Director.
  - Either the Business Owner or the Department Director must review the Qualified Idea with the Division Managing Director.

- **Estimated Time Duration**
  - 2 hours.

Step 3 – Approve Qualified Idea

- **Instructions**
  - Once the Qualified Idea has been reviewed and no more modifications are needed, the Department Director and Executive Business Sponsor must formally confirm that they have reviewed the document and approve its contents.
  - There are two methods of confirmation – 1) date and initial in Section 4 in the space provided or 2) send an email memo with the version reviewed attached to the Business Owner.

- **Estimated Time Duration**
  - 30 minutes.

- **Resource Participation**
  - It is the responsibility of the Business Owner to obtain the initials of the Business Department Director.
  - Either the Business Owner or the Department Director must obtain the initials of the Division Managing Director.

-  **Tips for Success**
  - Obtaining formal confirmation from the Executive Business Sponsor is frequently a challenge. The ITS PMO management must firmly enforce the requirement of appropriate reviews and approvals from the Business departments before a Qualified Idea can be accepted into The ITS PMO.

Step 4 – Send Electronic and Initialed Copies of Qualified Idea to The ITS Management and PMO

- **Instructions**
  - Once the Qualified Idea has been approved by the necessary parties, it can be submitted to The ITS PMO for review.

- The ITS PMO will require both an electronic copy to store in an online repository (i.e. SharePoint) for version control purposes and an initialed copy for their records.
  - Electronic documentation should be sent via email
  - Paper copies should be directed to the PMO manager.
- Annual Budget Submission Process
  - If the Qualified Idea is being submitted in correspondence to the Annual Budget Window, steps 1-5 must be completed by the deadline established and communicated by The ITS PMO.
  - Typically, the deadline for submissions should be around the end of May or the beginning of June.
- Ongoing PID Request
  - If the Qualified Idea is being submitted at any time other than in correspondence to the Annual Budget Window, The ITS PMO should establish and communicate a schedule for submissions.
  - Recommendation would be to set a submission deadline one (1) month prior to an EDT meeting.

- **Estimated Time Duration**
  - 30 minutes.

- **Resource Participation**
  - It is the responsibility of the Business Owner to provide copies of the approved Qualified Idea to The ITS PMO.
  - It is recommended that the Department Director and Managing Director by carbon copied on this communication.

Step 5 – Review Qualified Idea

- **Instructions**
  - Each Qualified Idea is assessed using the following criteria:
    - Is the PID **Complete**? – portions identified above are completed
    - Does the initiative involve a **Discrete Change to the Status Quo**? – a project with a defined beginning and end (e.g. process evaluation and improvement) not an operational request (e.g. request for standard computers/printers)
    - Is the initiative **Unique**? – does not duplicate another previous or planned initiative
    - Does the initiative have **Dependency on Other Initiative's Completion**? – is not constrained by an initiative that has yet to be completed for year of request (e.g. a 2005 website project requiring a given platform that will not be complete until 2006)
  - Based on the amount of information provided in PID PART ONE, the Business Owner may need to be contacted to fill in some additional details.
  - If the Qualified Idea passes all criteria, The ITS PMO senior management must approve of continuing with the PID. This is done by initialing the hard copy or sending an email memo.
  - If the Qualified Idea fails any of the criteria, The ITS PMO senior management must concur and the Business Department is notified via the Rejection Communication form.

- **Estimated Time Duration**
  - 8 hours.

- A response to the business owner is expected within five (5) business days of submitting a Qualified Idea to The ITS PMO.

- **Resource Participation**
    - The ITS PMO is responsible for a timely initial review of the Qualified Idea and following up with the Business Owner if any questions arise.
    - The appropriate ACIO will then review and agree or disagree with the PMO's assessment.
    - If the Qualified Idea is rejected for any reason, the Business Owner, Department Director, and Managing Director are notified.

- **Tips for Success**
    - The ITS PMO should place the approved version of the Qualified Idea in a designated central location.
        - The electronic copy should be placed in a central electronic repository (SharePoint) and appropriately labeled. The "Develop Scope" stage will work off of the electronic copy.
        - Currently, the paper version, or a printout of the electronic copy accompanied by approval email memos, should be place in a PID 3-ring binder. The assumption is that eventually paper will be phased out of this process and all approvals provided electronically.
    - A tracking spreadsheet should be maintained in the central electronic repository.
        - Anytime a Qualified Idea is received, it is recorded in this spreadsheet and tracked throughout its lifetime.
        - This log will provide a single point of access to see all PID's requested and what happened to each one. Section ... provides a link to the template and Section 2.2.5.6.4 provides an example of how to fill one out.
    - Immediately upon receipt of a Qualified Idea, the ITS PMO should formally communicate status to the Business Owner that the Qualified Idea has been received and what to expect for next steps. Section 2.2.5.5.5 provides and example of the communication.
    - If a Qualified Idea has been rejected, the ITS PMO should formally communicate status to the entire Business Department with the reason for rejection and available options. Section 2.2.5.5.5 provides an example of the communications

<u>Step 6 – Assign The ITS PMO Owner and PMO Resource</u>

- **Instructions**
    - If The ITS PMO approves the Qualified Idea, the Chief Information Officer must initial the PID PART ONE. An email memo will also suffice.
    - An ITS Owner is assigned as the primary The ITS PMO resource to work with the Business Owner in completing the rest of the PID. The ITS PMO will assist in providing technical assistance and ensuring consistency across all PID's.
    - This is the final step in the "Generate Idea" stage.
        - After this step, a Qualified Idea has been documented, reviewed, and approved by the Business Department Director, Managing Director, and CIO.
        - In addition, a team of the Business Owner, The ITS PMO Owner, and The ITS PMO has been assigned to complete the remaining portions of the PID using the process outlined in the "Develop Scope" stage.

- **Estimated Time Duration**
    - 4 hours.

- **Resource Participation**
    - The appropriate ACIO is responsible for assigning an ITS PMO resource as the ITS PMO Owner.
    - The ITS PMO is responsible for getting all parties up-to-speed on the contents of the Qualified Idea.
    - The ITS PMO Owner will coordinate to follow-up with the Business Owner on completing the rest of the PID.

- **Tips for Success**
    - The tracking spreadsheet in the central electronic repository should be updated with assignments.
        - Any status changes to a PID are recorded in this spreadsheet and tracked throughout its lifetime.
        - This log will provide a single point of access to see all PID's requested and what happened to each one. Section 2.2.5.6.4 provides an example of how to fill one out.

Project Initiation Document

1. Purpose / Guidelines

*Please use this form to submit an idea for a technology-related project. The purpose of this document is to define project concepts and to establish executive support for the project. Once the first three phases of the **ITS Project Initiation Process*** are complete, and the project is authorized to proceed to planning, this Project Initiation Document will be replaced by the Project Charter as the ruling document for the project.*

The following is a listing of all the sections within this document:

• *General Information*	• *Cost/Benefit Analysis*	• *Issues/Questions*
• *Qualified Idea*	• *Preliminary Timeline*	• *Purchasing Strategy*
• *Project Definition*	• *Contact Persons*	• *Initial Review/Approval*
• *Project Background*	• *Next Steps*	• *Final Review/Approval*

*Please enter as much detail as possible in the **"General Information"** and **"Qualified Idea"** sections of the form. Once completed, submit the form via email to **"ITS Project Management Office"**. A member of the ITS Project Management Office (PMO) will be in contact within one week to follow-up and assist in completing the remainder of the form.*

Please refer to the **"ITS Project Initiation Process" document for details on the entire process.*

2. General Information

Project Name:				
Business Owner:		Executive Sponsor:		
Sponsor Department:				
Project Type: (check all that apply)	Pilot ☐	Implementation ☐	Upgrade ☐	Other ☐

3. Qualified Idea

Introduction to Proposed Project *Describe the proposed project, including high level scope and objectives.*

Reason for Proposed Project *Describe the background, business need, and benefits of the proposed project.*

Is the proposed project in response to a regulatory mandate?	Yes ☐	No ☐

Desired Project Implementation Timeframe *Describe when the proposed project needs to be completed or available by and why.*

1.2 Develop Scope

Overview

The Develop Scope phase begin after The ITS PMO has received the two-pager and a project manager has been assigned to work with the business sponsor in completing pages 5-11 of the PID (Process Initiation Document). Some items that must be considered during this phase as each project manager continues to work with each business sponsor:

- Scope – expand on objectives and hi-level requirements of initiative
- Previous actions – specify any efforts already expended towards initiative
- Involvement levels – identify how stakeholders will be impacted during implementation of initiative
- Assumptions – identify aspects assumed to be true but still to be verified
- Dependencies and constraints – identify aspects which affect initiative but are outside of its control
- Costs – identify items to be procured (more details to follow)
- Benefits – evaluate how initiative will positively impact stakeholders (more detail to follow)

- Funding allocation – specify if a source for funding has already been established
- Hi-level timeline – expand on desired timeframe for beginning initiative
- Contact persons – specify key individuals involved in scoping initiative
- Next steps – track and begin working towards project planning activities
- Issues – track and begin working to resolve any issues that can already be identified
- Potential alternatives – evaluate other possibilities for achieving same objectives

PROJECT INITIATION

2.2. Stage 1 – Generate Idea

Steps
1. Draft Qualified Idea within PID
2. Review Qualified Idea
3. Approve Qualified Idea
4. Send Electronic and Initialed Copies of Qualified Idea to The ITS PMO Management and PMO
5. Review Qualified Idea
6. Assign The ITS PMO Owner and PMO Resource

2.3. Stage 2 – Develop Scope

Steps
7. Refine Idea with Key Stakeholders
8. Draft Estimated Benefits
9. Draft Estimated Costs for Project and Maintenance
10. Consolidate Results into PID
11. Review Completed PID with Key Stakeholders
12. Approved Completed PID
13. Send Electronic and Signed Copies of Completed PID to PMO
14. Input IT "Non Personnel" Initiative Request into BIS System

2.4. Stage 3 – Validate Need

Steps
15. Apply PID Scoring Framework
16. Analyze Budget and The ITS PMO Resource Capacity
17. Evaluate Prioritization Results and Generate Recommendation
18. Prepare Formal Presentation
19. Present to EDT
20. Update The ITS PMO Project Portfolio

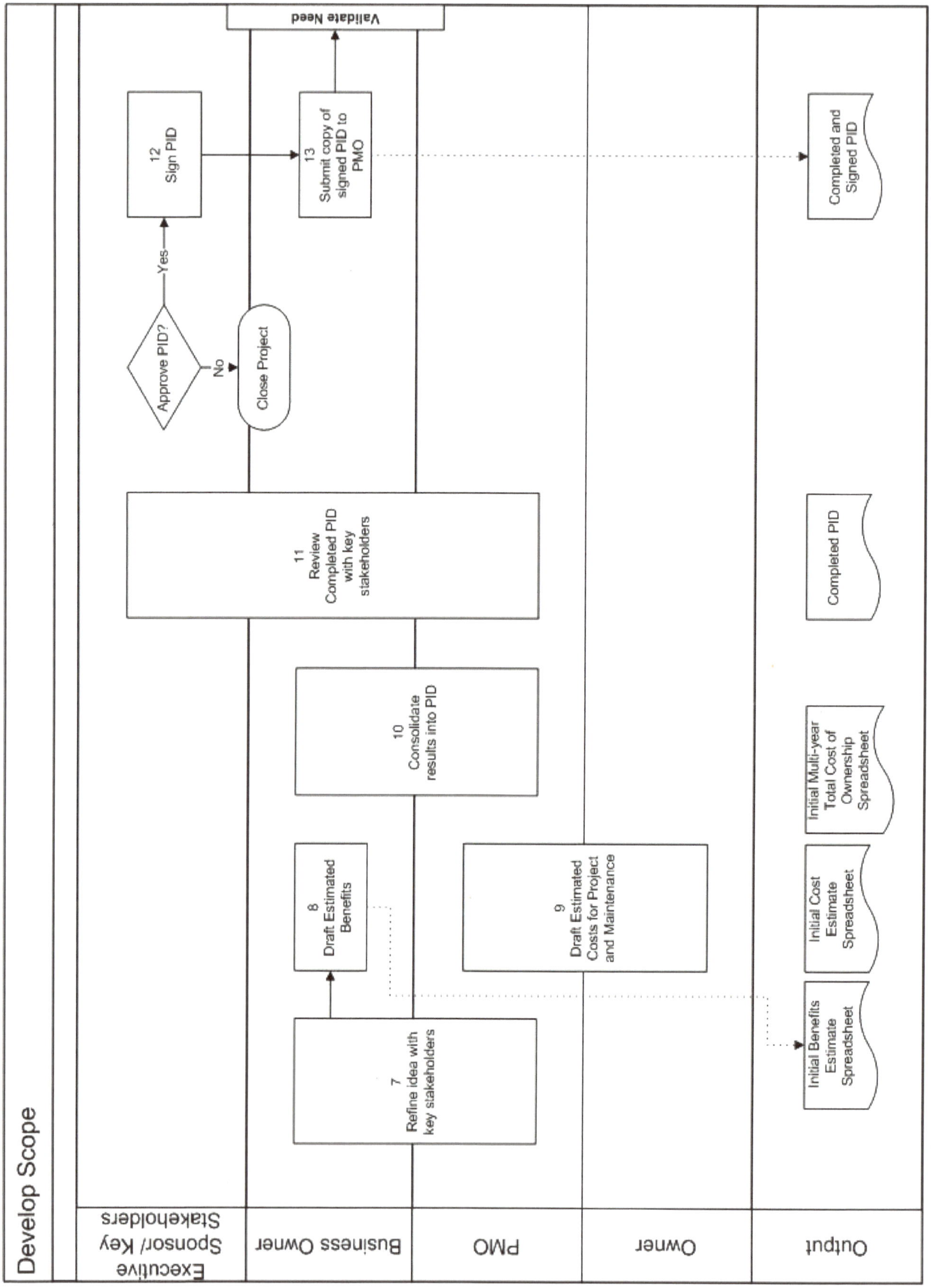
Develop Scope
Executive Sponsor/ Key Stakeholders
Business Owner
PMO
Owner
Output
7 Refine idea with key stakeholders
8 Draft Estimated Benefits
9 Draft Estimated Costs for Project and Maintenance
10 Consolidate results into PID
11 Review Completed PID with key stakeholders
Approve PID?
No
Yes
Close Project
12 Sign PID
13 Submit copy of signed PID to PMO
Validate Need
Initial Benefits Estimate Spreadsheet
Initial Cost Estimate Spreadsheet
Initial Multi-year Total Cost of Ownership Spreadsheet
Completed PID
Completed and Signed PID

Inputs, Outputs, and Tools

After all two-pager PIDS have been received by The ITS PMO, a project manager will be assign to work with the Business Sponsors to complete the remaining 5-11 pages which include: Project details, project assumptions, known dependencies and constraints, cost/benefit analysis, preliminary timelines, contact persons, next steps, critical issues and questions.

Inputs	Tools & Techniques	Outputs
• Completed Qualified Idea (PID 2-pager)	• Process flow diagram for Stage 2 - Develop Scope • PID template • Project benefits worksheet • Project costs worksheet • Support costs worksheet • PID tracking worksheet	• Completed PID • IT Non-personnel Initiative request in BIS

Three of the main tools that will be used in Stage 2 (Develop Scope) are: Benefit Worksheet, Project Estimating Worksheet and the Project Support Cost Worksheet, which should help when completing pages 5-11.

The benefit worksheet is a tool that should be used to calculate the project's hard and soft benefits. The total of a project's benefit will be subtracted from its cost using the Project Estimating Worksheet (below) to determine its value. A positive number would suggest that there is positive return on investment from the project. A negative return would suggest that there is no return on investment (ROI). Projects with negative return should only be pursued if it is a HUD regulatory mandate.
The Project Estimated Worksheet shows the total cost of labor hours and all other Bill of Material (BOM) that will sum up the total project cost. The Project Estimated Worksheet should be derived from the Work Breakdown Structure (WBS) and task sequencing process, which will be outlined in the Planning Section of this book.

The Project Support Cost Worksheet will sum up the operation cost of ownership for a project. Cost will vary depending on contractual agreements and time limits.

Timeframe/Total Duration
The typical timeframe to complete the "Develop Scope" stage is 5 business days.

Resource Participation
The following resources participate during the "Develop Scope" stage:

- Business Owner – primary Business resource assigned to initiative
    - The business owner should take lead on creating the business case of the project.
- The ITS PMO Senior Mgmt & Senior Portfolio Manager
    - The assign project manager should be used to research past project archives for supporting information/documentation that will help in scoping out the project. The project manager should a assist in creating the benefit/cost analysis section or any other section that may seem unclear to the business owner.

The matrix below shows which steps within the stage and in what capacity each resource participates.

Step	Division MD	Dept Director	Business Owner	The ITS PMO Mgmt	Sr. Portfolio Manager	The ITS PMO Owner	Budget Director	Other Key Stakeholders	Dept BIS Resource
7 - Refine Idea with Key Stakeholders	A	A/C	R		R	R		C	
8 - Draft Estimated Benefits		A	R		C	C			
9 - Draft Estimated Costs for Project and Maintenance		A	C		C	R			
10 - Consolidate Results into PID		A	R		C	R			
11 - Review Completed PID with Key Stakeholders	C	A/C	R		C	R		C	
12 - Approve Completed PID	A/R	R	R			R		R	
13 - Send Electronic and Signed Copies of Completed PID to PMO	I	A/I	R		I	R			
14 - Input IT "Non Personnel" Initiative Request into BIS System		A	R			C			R

Stage Description

The "Develop Scope" stage consists of 8 primary steps.

<u>Step 7 – Refine Idea with Key Stakeholders</u>

<u>Instructions</u>

- Primarily responsibility of Business Owner and The ITS PMO Owner
- Corresponds to sections 5-11 of the PID template
- Identify other Key Stakeholders

Understanding the Authority of the Project Manager

At this point in the process, the Project Manager is the eyes, ears and voices of the stakeholder. It's imperative that the project manager knows how to guide the stakeholder toward reasonable objectives that are aligned with the Strategic Plan of the organization so that their PID has a greater chance of ranking high in relation to the corporate objectives. Those PID that are usually scored high during the PID scoring process are the ones that have the greatest chance of becoming strategic initiatives for the next budget cycle. At this point it is extremely important that the project manager document the ideas of the stakeholder into measureable functional requirements that are measureable and stays aligned with the overall corporate strategy. Ideas that have tangible cost savings, regulatory mandates and high return on investments typically make good business cases for senior management. At this stage of the PID process, it is important that you stakeholder has trust that you, the Project Manager, are capable of moving their ideas toward not only corporate goals and strategies but also toward their interest.

The Project Charter

The Project Charter is a high level formalize document created giving the Project Manager authority over the project. It is usually a business case like document signed by Senior Management and is used by the project manager as tool for managing the communication flow and strategic direction of the project and members of the team. Below is a example of a Project Charter.

PROJECT CHARTER

Project Title: ITS Relocation Project

Purpose: The purpose of this Project Charter is to set the authority level of the Portfolio Manager and Project Manager(s) for the ITS Relocation Project. In addition, this charter will present a high level scope of work for all key stakeholders. A more detail scope of work will be detailed in the ITS Relocation Project Plan.

Assignment of Authority Level

Authority Level of *Portfolio Manager*:

1. Coordinate and manage all project resources, work plans and sub-project schedules as it relates to the scope of work necessary to complete the ITS Relocation Project.
2. Keep overall Program in line with approved budget, time, quality and scope
3. Control all project change orders that are not within project scope, project defined budget or approved project baseline schedule.
4. Coordinate efforts with third-party vendors to complete scope of work. Duties will include weekly project updates and plans for corrective action on issues and risk items as it relates to the XYZ Vendor Management control process.
5. Control configuration management changes that do not add value to the overall program success and take corrective action to mitigate all risk factors.
6. Meet with Project Decision Team (PDT) monthly to give project update, status and project recommendations.
7. Meet with Project Team (PT) weekly to get project update and status on all team activities and deliverables.
8. Act as the single communication channel between all vendors, XYZ and XYZ
9. Provide overall risk assessment to ITS Relocation Program.

Authority Level of *Project Manager(s)*:

1. Coordinate and manage day-to-day resources and WBS tasks as outlined in the approved scope of work document and Project Schedule.
2. Keep all task aligned with XYZ PMO's triple constraint of: Scope, Quality, Time, Budget and overall Customer Satisfaction.
3. Monitor and take corrective action against all work effort and WBS tasks that are considered "Gold-Plating" or Out of Scope to the overall project.
4. Meet with perspective team members as to report daily task, work effort, etc.

Goals and Objectives

On January 6, 2012 it was announced that the XYZ (626 W. Jackson, 500 users) along with five other remote sites (1000 S. Wabash, 4700 S. State, 35 S. Paulina, 600 W. Jackson and 200 W. Adams) would consolidate all data/voice/infrastructure services as a result of the relocation to XYZ's new headquarters, the CNA building located at 333 S. Wabash. Currently, there are two mutually exclusive telecommunication systems at XYZ. The first system is a Centrex based solution that services XYZ's current headquarters (626 W. Jackson) and 64 other XYZ remote sites. The main DMS 100 switch for the Centrex based solution is located at SBC's Central Office. Total users on the Centrex system are approx. 500 users. The second telecommunication system is a premise based PBX Avaya solution staged at XYZ's largest remote site, XYZ (300 users: 6500 inbound calls daily), located at 1000 S. Wabash. XYZ is responsible for managing XYZ's popular Housing Choice Voucher Program (HCVP). As a result of this relocation initiative, there is now an opportunity to consolidate both XYZ & XYZ's telecom service. By taking advantage of this new opportunity, it will allow XYZ the ability to convert many of the their now manual tasks into automatic processes thus overall saving the XYZ money, resource time while at the same time increasing the quality of service to XYZ's main client base: XYZ residents and Landlords. The first location, 200 W. Adams (50 users), is schedule to move into the new location, CNA building, November 1, 2006. Under the given scenario, XYZ is in the need of a third-party assessment of its current *"AS-IS"* voice/data/infrastructure services that will take into account the functional requirements of the relocation project *AND* as an output produce a *"SHOULD-BE"* documented/strategy of the resources/tasks needed to complete the service delivery/execution phase of the relocation project. The scope of the assessment phase will include but will not be limited to XYZ's voice/data/infrastructure services and those objectives that are aligned with the XYZ 2006 Corporate Strategy and goals set by the key stakeholders.

Business Case

As a result of the move, there is now an opportunity to lower XYZ's overall operating cost by consolidating data/voice/infrastructure services onto one common platform. At the moment, it can be qualitatively said that the cost savings will be moderate. A more detailed business case quantifying the Return on Investment (ROI), Cash Flow and Net Present Value will be presented to the Project Decision Team (PDT) during the planning phase of the ITS Relocation Project. The final results will be posted to the approved ITS Relocation Project Plan.

Product Description

After the completion of the ITS Relocation Project the XYZ will have an enterprise wide Telecommunication/IVR/Voicemail solution that will be the common entry point for all inbound calls to both the XYZ and XYZ organization. In addition, all data and infrastructure services will be consolidated onto one common platform to minimize overall operational cost enterprise wide and will provide an increase in the quality of services to all of XYZ's main customers.

Approvals

________________________	________________________
Project Manager	**Chief Information Officer**

Understanding the Politics and Power of the Stakeholder

In this phase of PID process, it is very important that project managers are aware of the "silos" that exist for personal interest groups. Many times, especially within the public sector, projects are often tied to votes, which in turn controls budget dollars for a particular city, state, government agency. Often, elected officials are granted budget dollars for operational cost which in turn will lead to employment for those who have faithfully help in assisting with winning of an election. Getting your stakeholder buy-in is key to winning and will assist with overcoming many of the project constraints and risk that may exist in the future sake of the project. Understanding the politics and sometimes being three moves ahead for a project manager is key. A project manager must be aware of the waters they are swimming in to stay afloat especially in public sector industries. Many times, the objectives and goals of personal silos are not what is best for the project but is a necessity for political gain within the public sector environment. Know and understand those who labor and rest among you. Know the silos that exist and mitigate this risk by staying three moves ahead. Know these stakeholders because they can have a positive or negative impact on the outcome of your project.

Estimated Time Duration

- 3-5 days

Step 8 – Draft Estimated Benefits

Instructions

- Primarily responsibility of Business Owner
- Corresponds to Benefits Estimate Spreadsheet
- Sample categories of hard (quantifiable) and soft (non-quantifiable) benefits provided in spreadsheet
- Research current costs (money, time, etc.) to estimate potential savings

Estimated Time Duration

- 3-5 days

Step 9 – Draft Estimated Costs for Project and Maintenance

Instructions

- Primarily responsibility of The ITS PMO Owner
- Corresponds to Cost Estimate and Total Cost of Ownership Spreadsheets
- Sample categories of costs provided in spreadsheet
- Research market and/or previous projects of similar scope to estimate duration of initiative and numbers/rates of resources required to implement

Estimated Time Duration

- 3-5 days

Step 10 – Consolidate Results into PID

Instructions

- Primarily responsibility of Business Owner and The ITS PMO Owner

- Formalize all conversations with Business Owner/Key Stakeholders and results of estimation spreadsheets into PID

Estimated Time Duration
- 3-5 days

<u>Step 11 – Review Completed PID with Key Stakeholders</u>

Instructions
- Primarily responsibility of Business Owner and The ITS PMO Owner
- Review with Department Director, Executive Business Sponsor, and other Key Stakeholders and determine whether or not to continue

Estimated Time Duration
- 1-3 hours

<u>Step 12 – Approve Completed PID</u>

Instructions
- Primarily responsibility of Business Owner
- Business Owner and The ITS PMO Owner sign completed PID
- Obtain signatures (or email memos) from Department Director, Executive Business Sponsor, The ITS PMO senior management, and other Key Stakeholders

Estimated Time Duration
- 1 hour

Qualitative Estimating Cost and Benefits

Qualitative estimating is the method of assigning high, medium and low metrics to cost and benefits. Qualitative estimating is best done using a four-quadrant matrix showing the relationship between cost and benefit. For example, the cost of this project is estimated to be high vs. Quantitative estimating which is a method of estimating based on more identifying metrics such as actual numerical figures. For example the cost of this project is estimate to be at $1,000,000. Quantitative estimating and cost are more believable and have a better chance of showing the true relationship in aligning with corporate objectives because the results consist of more factual input based on facts and not assumptions. If possible, provide quantitative metrics based on your research for each PID. However, many times due to the resource constraints of the PMO, many companies will settle for qualitative metrics.

Qualitative Measuring:

	Project 1	Project 2	Project 3	Project 4	Project 5
Functionality	431.7	422.63	414.68	404.81	403.9
Cost					
Func. Ranking [1-5]	1	2	3	4	5
Cost Ranking [1-5]	4	1	2	3	5
Total Ranked Score	5	3	5	7	10

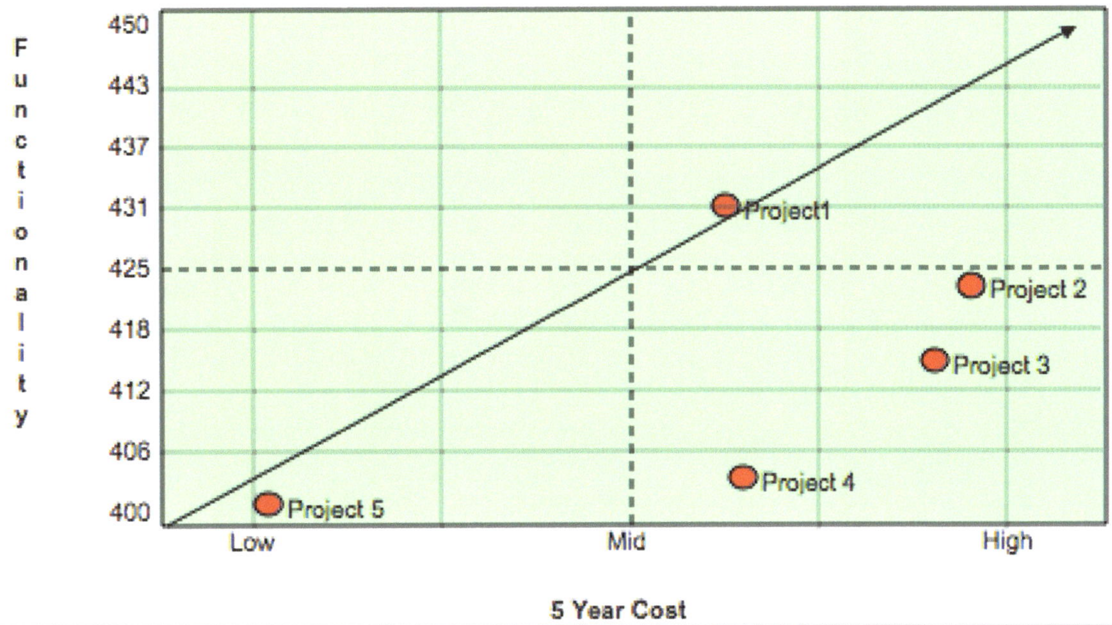

Quantitative Estimating:

GigaMAN Project Cost Summary

Project Cost	$500,000.00
One-Year Operation and Support	$1,200,000.00
Contingency Funding	$170,000.00
Total Project Cost of Ownership	$1,870,000.00

Total Benefit $$	$741,000.00
Net Cost Benefit $$	-$1,129,000.00

Step 13 – Send Electronic and Signed Copies of Completed PID to Sr. Portfolio Manager

Instructions

- Primarily responsibility of Business Owner
- Electronic copies and signed hard copies (or email memos) to be sent to the Senior Portfolio Manager

Estimated Time Duration

- Less than 1 hour

Step 14 – Input IT "Non Personnel" Initiative Request into BIS System

Instructions
- Primarily responsibility of Business Owner
- Any IT "non personnel" request in Budget Information System (BIS) requires a PID

Estimated Time Duration
- Less than 1 hour per PID

4. Project Definition

Description of Proposed Project *Describe the desired outcome of the proposed solution, how the solution will address the business need, and how the solution serves the CHA's Plan for Transformation and/or known MBOs.*

Alternatives to the Proposed Solution *List alternatives to the proposed solution, whether technology-focused or not, and describe in brief why these alternatives might be preferable to the proposed solution.*
•

User Groups and Other Key Stakeholders *List other departments (or constituents) who would be affected by this project. Indicate their level of involvement in the project, and how the project will affect their activities.*
•

5. Project Background

Project Assumptions *List any and all assumptions that have been made with regards to the scope, schedule, and/or staffing of the proposed solution.*
•

Known Dependencies / Constraints *List any and all known dependencies and/or constraints that could affect the scope, schedule and/or staffing of the proposed solution. Include both projects/activities that the solution is dependent on and a dependency for.*
•

Steps Taken Previously to Address the Business Need *Describe any and all previous attempts to address the business need, through technology or other means, including any previous attempts to implement the proposed solution. Indicate whether these attempts were successful, or not successful, and why. Also, describe any efforts to gather information related to this project.*
•

6. Cost / Benefit Analysis

In order to establish that the proposed project provides a net benefit to the XYZ we must provide estimates of the costs that will be required to implement the project and the benefits that the project will generate. Exact numbers are not essential at the Initiation phase, but a clear outline of the cost elements and good estimates will be very helpful in determining the viability of the project.

Cost/Benefit Analysis *Provide a brief description of the primary cost elements, and estimated amounts for each. Indicate whether funding has already been allocated for this cost element for this project, and from what source.*

Costs				
Category	Description	**Amount**	**Funded (Y/N)**	**Funding Source (Capital / Operating)**
Resources	•			
Equipment PurXYZses	•			
Professional Services Contracts	•			
Construction	•			
Other	• (*please specify*)			
TOTAL				

Benefits		
Driver	Description	Amount
Increased Revenues	•	
Decreased Costs	•	
Increase Customer Satisfaction	•	
Enhance Public Image	•	
Other	• *(please specify)*	
TOTAL		

Net Operational Impact		
+/0/-	Description	Amount
	•	

'. Preliminary Timeline

Provide a summary timeline for the initiation of this project through the start of the execution (i.e. contract awarded to and approved by a vendor).				
Task	Owner	Begin Date	End Date	Compl ete
Draft PID				
PMO Review				
Project Development				
Executive Approval - PID				
Consult with ITS				
Consult with Stakeholders				
ITS Approval – PID				
Develop Initiation Workplan				
Develop Business Case				
Develop Full Recommendation				

1.3 Validate Need

Overview

The third and final stage of the Project Initiation Process is the "Validate Need" stage. The entire The ITS PMO Project Portfolio is considered at this point to assess how each completed PID aligns with

XYZ Company and The ITS PMO' strategy. All PID's that are included in the Project Portfolio will have a targeted start of Planning Phase and Execution Phase identified. The completed PID will become very useful as the basis to formulate the Project Plan, including the procurement strategy and development of attendant solicitation document. All PID's that are not included into the Project Portfolio can be retained and reassessed at a later time for further consideration.

PROJECT INITIATION

2.2. Stage 1 – Generate Idea

Steps
1. Draft Qualified Idea within PID.
2. Review Qualified Idea
3. Approve Qualified Idea
4. Send Electronic and Initialed Copies of Qualified Idea to The ITS PMO Management and PMO
5. Review Qualified Idea
6. Assign The ITS PMO Owner and PMO Resource

2.3. Stage 2 – Develop Scope

Steps
7. Refine Idea with Key Stakeholders
8. Draft Estimated Benefits
9. Draft Estimated Costs for Project and Maintenance
10. Consolidate Results into PID
11. Review Completed PID with Key Stakeholders.
12. Approved Completed PID
13. Send Electronic and Signed Copies of Completed PID to PMO
14. Input IT "Non Personnel" Initiative Request into BIS System.

2.4. Stage 3 – Validate Need

Steps
15. Apply PID Scoring Framework
16. Analyze Budget and The ITS PMO Resource Capacity
17. Evaluate Prioritization Results and Generate Recommendation
18. Prepare Formal Presentation
19. Present to EDT
20. Update The ITS PMO Project Portfolio

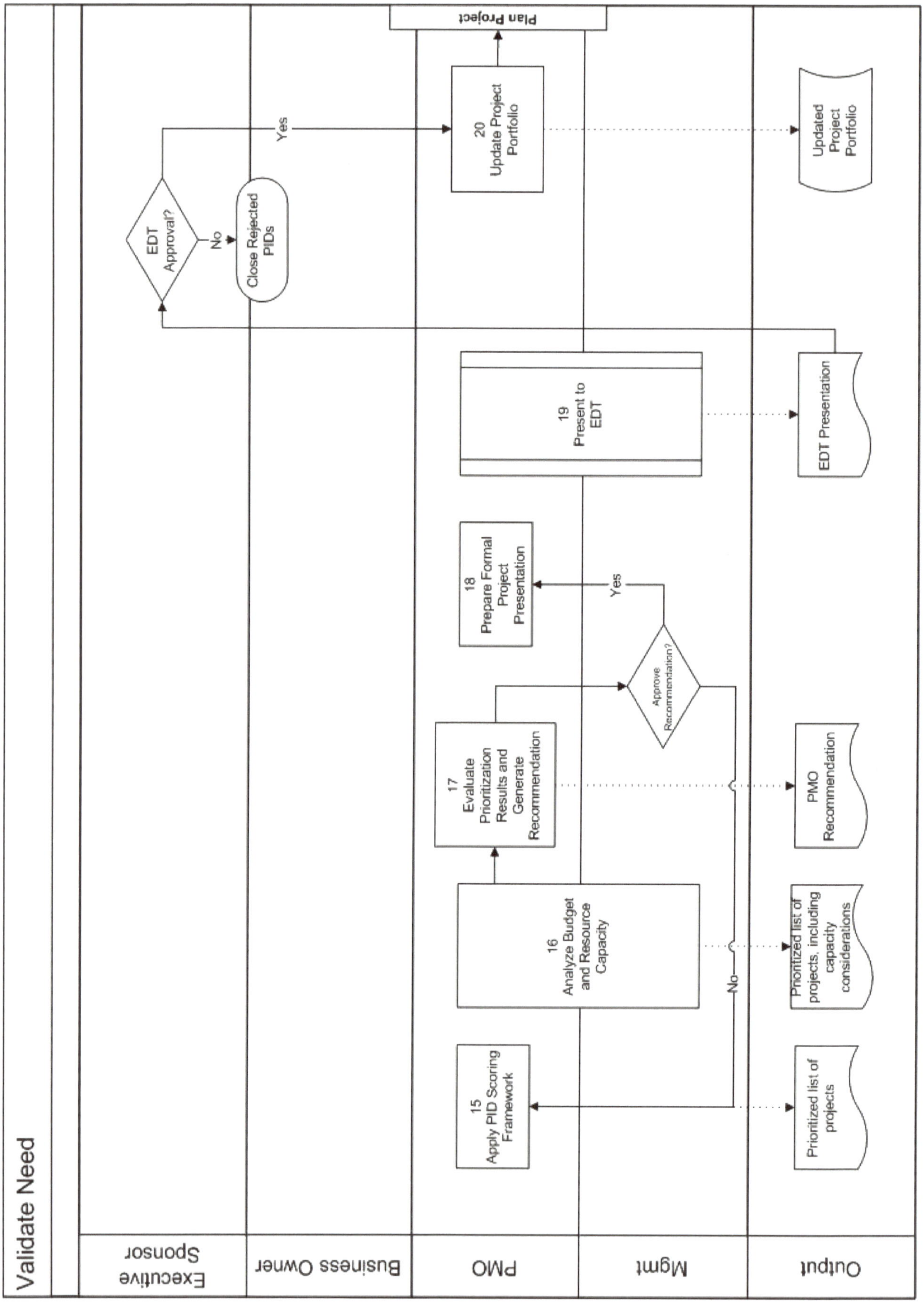
Validate Need
Executive Sponsor
Business Owner
PMO
Mgmt
Output
15 Apply PID Scoring Framework
16 Analyze Budget and Resource Capacity
17 Evaluate Prioritization Results and Generate Recommendation
Approve Recommendation?
Yes
No
18 Prepare Formal Project Presentation
19 Present to EDT
EDT Approval?
No
Close Rejected PIDs
Yes
20 Update Project Portfolio
Plan Project
Prioritized list of projects
Prioritized list of projects, including capacity considerations
PMO Recommendation
EDT Presentation
Updated Project Portfolio

Inputs, Outputs, and Tools

At least one completed PID must be available before entering this stage. As this is a pretty time-consuming stage of the process, it is useful to schedule this stage coinciding with Executive Decision Team meetings. During the course of this stage, the PID Scoring Framework and worksheet will be needed in order to prioritize the PID's, as well as an up-to-date Resource Capacity Model needed to assess whether there is The ITS PMO capacity to take on the PID(s). If this stage is corresponding to the Annual Budget Window, a guideline from the Budget Department of what the following year's budget will allow will be needed. Otherwise, there will be a parallel activity of determining how to fund the PID should it become a project. At the end of this stage, the Project Initiation Process is completed and a determination has been made as to which PID's will be transformed into actual initiatives. The ITS PMO Project Portfolio will be updated to reflect PID's for execution and their timeframes. The ITS PMO Portfolio Dashboard's Initiation tab will be updated to also reflect the resources involved and report out what high level activities have taken place. The updated ITS PMO Project Portfolio will have been approved by the Executive Decision Team and the Budget Department.

Inputs	Tools & Techniques	Outputs
• Completed PID • Most recent The ITS PMO Resource Capacity Plan	• Process flow diagram for Stage 3 - Validate Need • PID Scoring Framework • Budget Capacity Analysis • Resource Capacity Analysis	• Updated The ITS PMO Resource Capacity Plan • Updated The ITS PMO Project Portfolio • Approved initiatives added to PMO Dashboard

Timeframe/Total Duration

Due to the assumption that there will be many more PID's submitted in correspondence to the Annual Budget Window, two time estimates are provided.

- Annual Budget Submission Process - Five (5) weeks.
- Ongoing PID Requests - Three (3) weeks

Resource Participation

The following resources participate during the "Validate Need" stage:

- The ITS PMO Mgmt – Chief Information Officer and/or Assistant Chief Information Officers
- Senior Portfolio Manager
- Executive Decision Team – Managing Directors with large stake in technology investments
- Budget Department – primarily the Budget Director
- The ITS PMO Project Manager
- Business Owner
- Dept Director
- Division MD

The matrix below shows in what capacity each resource participates throughout the stage.

Step	Division MD	Dept Director	Business Owner	The ITS PMO Mgmt	Sr. Portfolio Manager	The ITS PMO PM	Budget Director	Other Key Stakeholders	Dept BIS Resource
15 - Apply PID Scoring Framework				A/C	R	R			
16 - Analyze Budget and The ITS PMO Resource Capacity				A/R	R		C		
17 - Evaluate Prioritization Results and Generate Recommendation	C			A/R/C	R		C		
18 - Prepare Formal Presentation	C			A/R/C	R		C		
19 - Present to EDT	C			A/R	R	I	C		
20 - Update The ITS PMO Project Portfolio	I	I	I	A/C	R		I		

Stage Description

The "Validate Need" stage consists of 6 primary steps. This section provides detailed instructions for each of those steps.

Step 15 – Apply PID Scoring Framework

- **Instructions**
    - Apply the scoring framework to each PID using the scoring tool.
        - The tool will calculate the total score taking into consideration the rating in each category and it's weighting.
        - The PID's should be ordered by total score, with the highest score reflecting the PID with the highest priority.
    - The rationale behind the scoring framework is as follows:
        - Establishing a scoring framework removes much subjectivity from the scoring and approval process and reflects each project initiative against the same criteria based on its merits
        - Reflecting technology projects against categories that model the "business of the Authority" supports The ITS PMO alignment with business departments
    - The framework criteria are listed below and also within the scoring tool.

Framework for Weighing PIDS:

Criteria	Weight	Description	Rating
Plan Alignment	50%	Extent to which this project aligns with or supports goals stated in the Plan for Transformation	0 - does not support Plan at all 1 - can be loosely tied to a goal in the Plan 2 - is indirectly supporting a goal firmly stated in the Plan 3 - is directly supporting a goal firmly stated in the Plan 4 - is firmly stated as a goal in the Plan
Business Benefit	40%	Amount of qualitative (or quantitative) benefits this project provides	0 - provides absolutely no benefit, negative payback, and/or causes detrimental effects 1 - provides very little level of benefits - no quantifiable/hard benefits or savings, and/or low level of soft cost savings 2 - provides low level of benefits - hard cost savings

			payback essentially break-even - modest soft costs savings 3 - provides moderate level of benefits - hard cost payback in 24-60 months, significant soft cost savings and publicity/service benefits 4 - provides high level of benefits - significant, measurable savings - hard cost payback in 0-24 months, compelling soft cost savings and other benefits
Technology Dependency-(Successor) Proven	10%	Extent to which other technology projects are dependent on this project	0 - has no dependency requirements from other projects and/or is an unproven, 'bleeding edge' technology 1 - has low level of dependency requirements from other projects - portions of other projects(s) may need small amount of rework depending on outcome of this project, and/or is a 'beta' technology with few-to-no other organizations of this size known 2 - has medium level of dependency requirements from other projects - other project(s) may need a fair amount of rework depending on outcome of this project, and/or is based on a technology solution that has good general industry awareness, but is from a 3 - has high level of dependency requirements from other projects - portions of other project(s) dependent on outcome of this project before they can start and/or is a proven technology solution which many of the Pre-Qualified Vendor pool have credentials 4 - has critical level of dependency requirements from other projects - entire or most of project(s) dependent on outcome of this project before it can start, and/or is based on a proven piece of technology from which numerous vendors can provide the service
Pre-requisite (Predecessor Dependency)	2 -.05 -.05	Extent to which this project is dependent on ongoing project completion	**Predecessor** project is currently in GREEN status and thus likely to finish

	Defer		according to scope, schedule, and quality requirements and proposed project is clearly tied to predecessor project and part of multiyear phased approach **Predecessor** project is currently in YELLOW status with potential to problems in scope, schedule, and quality **Predecessor** project is currently in RED status but with a workaround whereby the proposed project can be started and finished independent of predecessor project, albeit with additional cost and time impacts **Predecessor** project is currently in RED status with no workaround and has a high probability of completion after Q3 in the next fiscal year
Regulatory Requirement	+3pts	Extent to which this project is necessary to fulfill a regulatory requirement, e.g. will fail audit if not compliant	0 - is not tied to a mandate 1 - is firmly tied to a federal, state, local, or Authority mandated requirement

Final Data of PID Ranking
Green = Projects that are highly aligned with Strategic Plan
Yellow = Projects are aligned with Strategic Plan
Red = Projects are not aligned with Strategic Plan

Scoring Formula = =C2*Criteria!$B$2+D2*Criteria!$B$7+E2*Criteria!$B$12+F2+G2

PID #	Project	Plan	Benefit	Dependency (Successor)	Dependency (Predecessor)	Regulatory	Score
PID06-6	Senior Designated Housing Plan (SDHP) Tracking System	3	3	0	-0.5	3	5.2
PID06-8	Home Visit Survey Generation & Reporting Application Implementation	3	1	0	0	3	4.9
PID06-27	Vendor Disclosure: Phase II	1	1	0	0	3	3.9
PID06-22	E Recruiting	1	1	0	0	3	3.9
PID06-19	Occupancy IVR TTY Upgrade	2	1	0	-0.5	3	3.9
PID06-10	XYZ IVR 2006	4	4	0	0	0	3.6
PID06-12	XYZ Doc Mgmt - Phase 2	4	4	0	0	0	3.6
PID06-3	Data Warehouse - Phase I	4	3	2	0	0	3.4
PID06-16	Intra/Internet Phase 2	4	3	0	0	0	3.2
PID06-1	BOC Doc Mgmt	4	2	0	0	0	2.8
PID06-26	Electronic Storage of Pertinent Property Mgmt Documents	4	2	0	0	0	2.8
PID06-4	ITS Filenet Records Mgmt Module Implementation	4	2	0	0	0	2.8
PID06-14	XYZ Network Migration & Implementation	2	4	0	0	0	2.6
PID06-9	XYZ Event Tracking Log Yardi Implementation	3	4	0	-0.5	0	2.6
PID06-20	Electronic Storage of Closeout Docs	4	1	0	0	0	2.4
PID06-5	Workforce Development Career Tracking System	3	2	0		0	2.3
PID06-7	XYZ Ticket Tracking Software	2	3	0	0	0	2.2
PID06-13	HCV Sec 8 Invoice Processing	2	4	0	-0.5	0	2.1
PID06-17	Lowden Technology Center	2	1	2	0	0	1.6
PID06-23	Web Based Audit Tracking System	2	1	0	0	0	1.4
PID06-25	Facilities Mgmt Reporting System	1	1	0	0	0	0.9
PID06-18	XYZ Network Fax Capability	1	1	0	0	0	0.9

- **Estimated Time Duration**
    - 1 hour per PID.

- **Resource Participation**
    - The ITS PMO is responsible for applying the scoring framework.
    - The ITS PMO and Business Owners should be consulted to ensure that the PID is accurately being considered.
    - The results of the scoring should be shared with The ITS PMO senior management to ensure buy-in.

The matrix below shows in what capacity each resource participates.

- **Tips for Success**
    - The scoring framework is a useful tool to ensure that PID's are evaluated in a consistent and objective manner.
        - If any concerns are raised about how a PID is scored against particular criteria, the PID must be weighed against that criteria.
        - If the criteria are deemed insufficient or inaccurate, the framework should be modified and all PID's going forward evaluated against the modified framework.
    - Request the assistance of the ITS PMO Owner and/or Business Owner while scoring a PID. They have the most knowledge of the scope and benefits of the request and may be able to modify the PID in order to better reflect the criteria.

Final PID ranking that is presented to EDT:

2012 Project Initiation (PID) Process

Ranking of Submitted Project Initiation Requests

Priority	Score	Proposed Initiative	Alignment 50%	Benefit 40%	Predecessor +/-0.5	Successor 10%	Mandate	Cost
H	5.2	Senior Designated Housing Plan	3	3	(0.5)	0	4	$192K
	3.9	Vendor Disclosure: Phase II	1	1	0	0	4	$144K
	3.9	eRecruiting	1	1	0	0	4	$560K
	3.9	Occupancy IVR TTY Upgrade	2	1	(0.5)	0	4	$145K
	3.6	XYZ IVR: Phase II	4	4	0	0		$290K
	3.6	Document Management: XYZ	4	4	0	0		$526K
	3.2	Inter/Intranet: Phase II	4	3	0	0		$571K
M	2.8	Document Management: BOC	4	2	0	0		$328K
	2.8	Document Management: Asset Mgmt	4	2	0	0		$191K
	2.6	XYZ Network Migration	2	4	0	0		$88K
	2.6	XYZ Electronic Tracking Log (ETL)	3	4	(0.5)	0		$200K
	2.4	Document Mgmt: CCD	4	1	0	0		$97K
	2.3	Workforce Development Tracking System	3	2	0	0		$332K
L	2.2	XYZ Ticket Tracking Software	2	3	0	0		$45K
	2.1	HCV Sec 8 Invoice Processing	2	4	(0.5)	0		$19K
	1.9	Home Visit Survey Application	3	1	0	0		$344K
	1.6	Web Based Internal Audit Tracking	2	1	0	0		$84K
	1.4	Facilities Mgmt Reporting System	1	1	0	0		$224K
	0.9	XYZ Network Fax Application	1	1	0	0		$20K
								$4.4M

Plan Alignment – extent of alignment to Plan for Transformation and/or Bronner Strategic Technology goals	**Business Benefit** – amount of qualitative/ quantitative benefit provided	**Predecessor/Successor Dependency** – extent to which critical downstream/upstream dependencies exist	**Mandate** – Initiative is required due to Federal, State, Local or Authority mandate

Key: (0.5)- 0 - 1 - 2 - 3 - 4 -

Source: CHA Interviews, PMO Analysis. See Appendix for details.

Step 16 – Analyze Budget and The ITS PMO Resource Capacity

- **Instructions**
  - Ability to realize a PID is based on budget and resource availability.
  - The Budget Director is the key to determining budget availability in a given year.
    - If this stage corresponds to the Annual Budget Process, the Budget Director needs to be contacted to provide an allocation guideline for technology initiatives.
    - Otherwise, the Business Department may have already secured funds for the initiative or must work with the Budget Director on how to fund the initiative. This is a separate but parallel activity to the Project Initiation Process.
    - The level of funding available dictates which prioritized PID's can be realized and/or how much of the scope can be realized.
  - The Resource Capacity Model is the primary tool used in determining The ITS PMO resource availability.
    - The model includes consideration of operational activities, continuing projects, and the new PID initiatives (Business and The ITS PMO). Several scenarios are created within the model based on adjusting initiative start dates and/or removing initiatives in reverse priority.
    - This activity concentrates on the availability of The ITS PMO resources only.
    - It is assumed that Business Departments have their own separate methods for determining capacity of their resources.
  - Based on analysis of budget and resource capacity, two (2) lines are drawn onto the prioritized PID list – 1) budget line and 2) resource line. The PID's that fall upon the combination of these two lines are considered realizable.

- **Estimated Time Duration**
  - The time duration increases as number of PID's to be considered increases.
    - One to three PIDS - 4 hours.
    - Three to six PIDS - 8 hours
    - Six to nine PID's - 12 hours
    - Ten or more PIDS - 16 hours

- **Resource Participation**
  - Much of the discussions with the Budget Director will emanate from the CIO.
    - The CIO should communicate Budget guidance to the rest of The ITS PMO senior management and the Senior Portfolio Manager.
  - The Senior Portfolio Manager is responsible for leading The ITS PMO senior management in allocating resources into the Resource Capacity Model.
  - The Senior Portfolio Manager then formulates scenarios and presents them to The ITS PMO senior management with recommendations.
    - The ITS PMO senior management will review the scenarios and recommendations and make a decision.
    - This determines the updated The ITS PMO Project Portfolio.

-  **Tips for Success**
  - This activity relies heavily on the Resource Capacity Model. In order to best estimate if The ITS PMO has capacity to include one or more PID's, the model must already accurately reflect the current situation.
    - This model should be reviewed and refreshed on a regular basis, even if a PID is not being evaluated.
    - A reasonable schedule would be in correspondence to the Portfolio Dashboard schedule, or at minimum the EDT schedule.
  - Once budget guidance is obtained from the Budget Department, it is easy to integrate in the evaluation as the priority list has already been established. The challenge is in obtaining an accurate guidance.
    - Several rounds with the Budget Department will be necessary as the guidance may evolve over the course of the Annual Budget Process.
    - A safe bet is that, assuming the Budget Window closes at the end of June, the guidance will stabilize by early August.

Step 17 – Evaluate Prioritization Results and Generate Recommendation

- **Instructions**
  - The results of analysis from steps 15-16 are summarized into a Project Portfolio recommendation.
  - This recommendation is first reviewed within The ITS PMO and then with any Managing Director listed as Executive Business Sponsor of a PID.
  - If during the Annual Budget Process, the Budget Director should also be included in the review.
  - If the recommendation affects any previously approved initiatives (e.g. project timeframe is shifted), the affected Executive Business Sponsor is also consulted.

- **Estimated Time Duration**
  - 1 hour per PID.

- **Resource Participation**
  - The Senior Portfolio Manager combines the results of analysis into an overall recommendation with assistance from The ITS PMO senior management.
  - The recommendation is refined by consulting with affected Managing Directors and the Budget Director.

-  **Tips for Success**
  - When consulting with Managing Directors, use a PowerPoint format.
    - The most efficient manner is to begin creating drafts of the slides that will eventually be used for the EDT presentation.
    - These drafts need not have all details, but should at least provide the results of the scoring framework such that any questions can be answered.

        - In addition, an idea of The ITS PMO resource capacity and budget capacity should be communicated, especially if the Managing Director will need to be concerned about determining other sources of funding.

Step 18 – Prepare Formal Presentation

- **Instructions**
    - Prepare a presentation that highlights PIP activities leading up to the EDT meeting.
        - The EDT presentation template should be used.
        - Include a summary of PID's received, results of prioritization exercise, and recommendation for The ITS PMO Project Portfolio.
    - Review drafts of the presentation with The ITS PMO senior management.
        - If the presentation deviates from the recommendation that was previously socialized in step 17, review with affected Managing Directors.
        - If during the Annual Budget Process, the Budget Director should also be included.

- **Estimated Time Duration**
    - 20 hours.
    - This is assuming the presentation is rolled into whatever will be included in the EDT presentation.

- **Resource Participation**
    - The Senior Portfolio Manager prepares the presentation materials. The presentation is socialized with The ITS PMO senior management, Managing Directors, and Budget Director to collect feedback prior to finalization.

- **Tips for Success**
    - Assuming that the Project Initiation Process does not change drastically, the most efficient manner for developing the presentation is to start with what was created in the previous year. While the PID's submitted and the overall recommendation will be different, most of the process slides should remain pretty much the same.

Step 19 – Present to EDT

- **Instructions**
    - Present highlights of PIP activities and overall recommendation to EDT for decision. Review meeting minutes with The ITS PMO senior management and then distribute to the entire EDT audience.
    - When in correspondence with the Annual Budget Window, approval of the ITS PMO Project Portfolio recommendation from EDT and Budget Director will lead to inclusion of initiatives in Authority-wide budget submitted to the Board of Commissioners at the end of the year.

- **Estimated Time Duration**
    - 4 hours.

- **Resource Participation**
  - As the EDT meetings are the main formal forum for discussion business and technology alignment, The ITS PMO senior management is accountable for the information being presented.
  - For presentation of the Process Initiation Process, the Senior Portfolio Manager will likely present much of the material.
  - The audience is the Managing Directors that sit on the Executive Decision Team.
  - If this stage corresponds to the Annual Budget Process, the Budget Director is also invited.
  - Additional Managing Directors may be invited if they have a PID that is under discussion.

- **Tips for Success**
  - EDT is interested in understanding the sequence of how Qualified Idea submissions led to the final recommendation. However, they want to see the entire story at once so be ready with the final recommendation before presenting to this audience.

PID Scoring Framework, Evaluating and Prioritization of PIDS for PMO Recommendation

Here is where the rubber meets the road. This is the most important step in the PID process. During this phase, all project managers (PMO team) who were instrumental in managing the PID(s) up to this point will meet to rank, evaluate, prioritize and provide a draft for recommendation to the Executive Decision Team of the project portfolio for the upcoming year with projected cost estimates that will be the driving force for the IT Project Budget. This process is extremely cumbersome because each project manager depending on where their PID is ranked on the scoring sheet will have to provide convincing arguments to other project managers and the PMO Director to possibly save a project from being eliminated from the Executive Decision Team recommendation list. This process depending on the list of projects should take no more than a week to discuss, produce the final project list. At this point, the PMO Director will present the recommendation to the EDT for 1st pass approval. This will provide the EDT the opportunity to shuffle the deck with the scoring weights being the final driver. Based on the political interest of the EDT some PIDs will be shifted to lower or higher rankings. The result will be the total project portfolio and budget cost for projects that will be implemented in order to achieve the Strategic Plan and/or objective set by the organization.

Step 20 – Update The ITS PMO Project Portfolio

- **Instructions**
  - Add approved initiatives into Portfolio Dashboard and submit corresponding PID's to Budget Director. Results of the Project Initiation Process are communicated to affected Business Departments.

- **Estimated Time Duration**
    - 2 hours.

- **Resource Participation**
    - The Senior Portfolio Manager is responsible for updating the ITS PMO Portfolio Dashboard with the approved initiatives as well as providing the corresponding PID's to the Budget Director.
    - The ITS PMO senior management informs all parties participating in the Project Initiation Process of the results of their PID's.

- **Tips for Success**
    - Review the updated Project Portfolio on a monthly basis to determine when each approved initiative should begin its Planning Phase.
    - Track end results in the PID tracking spreadsheet. This will assist in the communication to the Business and provide a historical reference.

Technical Case Scenario – The Initiation Phase

- ❖ Walk through of the Project Initiation Process
- ❖ Understanding SharePoint List, Libraries, web parts, content types and Workflows for PIDS
- ❖ Creating InfoPath Web Forms
- ❖ Understanding of SharePoint PIP Process

2 Project Planning

Topics Covered:

- Process Planning Processes
  - Update PID & Finalize Planning
  - Develop & Implement Procurement Strategy
  - Prepare for Execution
- Understanding of Strategies: 8-22

How to Videos & Templates on CD:

- Walk Through of the Project Planning Process
- Review of Lifecycle Approach
- Make or Buy Decision
- WBS Overview
- Earned Value Approach
- Review of Networking Infrastructure
- OSI model
- Routing Protocols
- VoIP Infrastructure Review and Configuration
- IP Subnetting
- Microsoft Project & Publishing to Project

STRATEGY for Planning:

- ✓ Understanding of the PM Life Cycle vs. SDLC
- ✓ Make or Buy Decisions
- ✓ Procurement Process Tips & Tricks
- ✓ Contract Types
- ✓ The Work Breakdown (WBS) Structure Process
- ✓ Network Diagrams
- ✓ The Critical Path – Earned Value
- ✓ Milestone Approach – Earned Value
- ✓ Estimating Project Cost & Resources
- ✓ Designing your PM Strategy
- ✓ The Baseline Project Schedule
- ✓ Change Control Process
- ✓ Quality Assurance Process
- ✓ The Project Plan
- ✓ The Kickoff Meeting

Project Planning Overview

Projects by their definition are temporary and unique work efforts -- temporary in that they have a defined timeframe, and unique in that they have not previously been undertaken. Projects undertaken by the any client are also temporary and unique. Since projects are unique, there may be no "lessons learned" to review and infuse into the implementation of the effort before you. Planning their initiation and execution, therefore, is key to their success. Project planning helps identify what needs to be done to reach a desired outcome, who will do it, how long it will take and how much it will cost.

The amount of planning that is devoted to a single project should mirror the complexity, visibility, and timeframe within which the desired outcome is needed. A small scale project to roll out patches / fixes to the clients on a network, for example, may not need the same amount of planning as when the XYZ Company embarks upon a major enterprise-wide project which impact end users and how they conduct their daily operations. In that there is no perfect plan, and that planning is not a science, the planning exercise described in the pages below may be subject to multiple iterations until the assigned Project Manager (PM) is confident that the planning effort and attendant documents:

1. Represents reasonable critical thinking and background research surrounding the project;
2. Identifies alternate courses of action among various alternative solutions reviewed;
3. Documents information that will provide valuable inputs into any XYZ Company procurement document needed;
4. Identifies all known activities and resources needed to realize the desired project outcome; and
5. Identifies high level deliverables and milestones anticipated for the project.

In thinking through, managing and completing all the activities that comprise "project planning" the Project Manager (PM) may find it helpful to ask and answer the following questions:

1. What are the *objectives* of this project? What do we hope to gain by completing it? How will our customers be better served?
2. What *activities* need to be completed to achieve the desired outcome?
3. What internal and external *resources* are needed to achieve the desired outcome?
4. What is the *cost* estimate to achieve the desired outcome, and
5. Within what *timeframe (schedule)* is the outcome needed?

The Project Planning phase consist of three (3) discrete stages. They are as follows:

Stage 1: Update the Project Initiation Document (PID) and Finalize Planning
Stage 2: Develop and Implement Project Procurement Strategy
Stage 3: Prepare for Execution

Each stage is described in greater detail in the next three sections of this chapter.

Three (3) Stages of Project Planning

PROJECT PLANNING

Stage 1 – Update PID & Finalize Planning

Steps

1. Refine Project Schedule
2. Create and Execute Project Charter
3. Assign Planning & Execution Resources
4. Complete Market Research & Cost Estimate
5. Define Scope
6. Collect Requirements
7. Draft Project Approach
8. Develop Project Plan

Stage 2 – Develop and Implement Procurement Strategy

Steps

9. Development Procurement Document (Scope and Requirements)
10. Procurement and Legal review
11. Solicit Responses
12. Evaluate Responses
13. Conduct negotiations
14. Prepare Contract & Contract Support Documents

Stage 3 – Prepare for Execution

Steps

15. Conduct Project Organization Meeting
16. Develop Statement of Work
17. Develop Work Plan (MS Project Plan)
18. Finalize Engagement logistics

Objectives and Benefits

The primary objectives of project planning are:

- To conduct reasonable, critical thinking with the business owners to identify and document:
    i. The reasons prompting this action
    ii. The underlying business problem(s) to be solved
    iii. How the organization's people and processes will be impacted when the project is completed
- To identify possible solutions or responses to a business need among various alternatives available:
    i. What might be likely solutions offered in the vendor market place? Although a Project Manager may not know available solutions, a quick survey of internal PM's may reveal likely responses, as would a quick review with the requestor.
    ii. Although a particular technology may be optimal, might we achieve similar results with a less expensive approach?
- To document the project scope and requirements which become inputs into the procurement process. Given the probable solution, can we procure the solution within XYZ and HUD's procurement policies and regulations?
- To identify internal and external resources needed
- To identify project management and control methods needed to support the project, and
- To ensure project success: delivery of the solution on time and within budget.

Benefits to be realized by project planning include:

- **Quantification** of all resources – financial and human – that may be required to implement a project
- **Maximization** and **optimization** of limited resources – financial and human

- **Identification** and **authorization** of staff to work on the project during planning and implementation
- **Identification** of requirements to provides clarity and specification to the vendor community about what is sought
- Understanding of management and control strategies to ensure that the project will be completed according to the desired timeline and budget.

Tools

The following list the *primary tools* used to support the Project Planning Process:

- Process flow diagrams -- for each of the three main states – visual representation of the steps in each stage; use this document to guide you through the initiation and completion of discrete activities needed to create a Project Plan, Solicitation Document and ultimately a Statement of Work and executed contract for a project.
- Approved and Updated PID Document – This document, approved by the appropriate Business Owner, Department Director, Managing Director and Chief Information Officer, authorizes the initiation and execution of the project, according to the high level cost and timeframe documented in the PID.
- Project Charter – signed document identifying and authorizing the Project Manager for the work effort.
- Resource Capacity Model -- comprehensive spreadsheet identifying The ITS PMO resource availability. The model, used and maintained by the Senior Portfolio Manager and the ACIO's, factors individual staff members' time assigned to operational needs, continuing projects and new projects.
- Requirements Document – a formal document identifying the functional and technical requirements for the project. This document is prepared to support the procurement process.
- High Level Project Plan – a document fully describing the work to be undertaken, time frame for completion, and high level approach to governing the project:
    - Project Management
    - Issue, Risk and Change Management
    - Scope Management

  (The Project Plan is a separate document from the Project *Work Plan*, which is jointly developed by the awarded vendor, and the XYZ Company.)

There are some *secondary tools* that can be useful to the Project Manager when planning an initiative:

- PMO Dashboard – a "scorecard" for each project, assessing status and likelihood of completion, compiled by the Project Management Office (PMO) on a monthly basis; the dashboard is a compilation of all projects within the PMO portfolio.
- After Action Review Documents (AAR) – AAR's document the outcomes of a project and via a group session with the project team, documents "lessons learned" as a result of implementing a project. The document can be used as a reference when embarking upon a project of a similar scope and nature of one completed.

Inputs and Outputs

The Inputs and Outputs of the Planning Chapter will show what items, task or documents are to be considered in completing the three stages of the Planning framework. The inputs can be described as what tasks need to be done which will lead to the actual output or the final deliverable or series of deliverables for a particular activity in a stage. For project planning, the inputs frequently mirror the "tools" available to those planning a project. The main inputs into planning for any project are primarily:

1. Identifying the timeframe (via an approved PID and Project Charter)
2. Identifying the resources, staff assigned to the project (as initially identified in an approved PID)

3. Estimating the cost (Project Cost)
4. Articulating the requirements for the project (Scope Statement)
5. Thinking through and documenting all known activities, which when completed, will lead to the desired result. (Project Approach Document and Project Plan)

Planning Process, Inputs and Outputs, by Process Stage

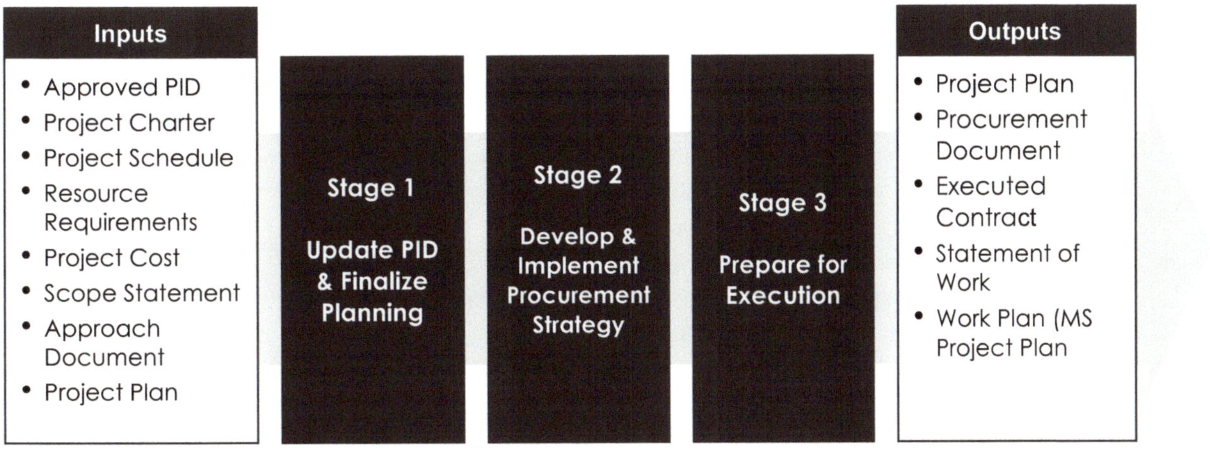

Timeframe/Total Duration

The Project Planning process begins once XYZ Company Board of Commissioners has approved the next fiscal year's budget. Board approval usually is rendered in December of any year. The Authority's annual budget proposal includes the estimated cost of projects (developed using the Project Initiation Process, detailed above) to be implemented during the next fiscal year, by department, as well as operating and maintenance expenses. Once the Budget is approved, the planning process can be initiated.

Importantly, planning for most projects will not begin in earnest until the Board has approved the budget, sometime in mid-December. Check with the ACIO, however, to determine if a project's approval is reasonably certain, and scheduled to begin in the 1st Quarter of the New Year, in which case, it is sensible to begin planning activities prior to Board approval. Once approval has been granted, you may not actually start planning activities immediately, but rather, according to be the planning timeframes identified in the PID document (refer to Chapter 1).

Check the PID to determine the month and quarter that planning begins. Depending upon the number of projects to be initiated in a given year, and the availability of The ITS PMO resources, planning is staggered from December of the current year (after Board approval of the budget), into about the 3rd quarter (October) of the following year. The duration for planning will depend upon several factors such as the size and complexity of the individual project. Another factor affecting when planning is initiated is the availability of resources to plan a project. Resource availability is identified using the Resource Capacity Model. The Model factors in all known projects, about how long both planning and execution will take (duration) and who in The ITS PMO will be assigned to specific projects.

The typical Project Planning cycle begins, then:

1. After BOC approval, and,
2. According to the month and quarter identified in the Resource Capacity Model

Resource Participation

The recommended The ITS PMO and business representatives' resource participation required in the project planning phase of the project life cycle will be outlined in Stage One (Update PID and Finalize Planning), Stage Two (Develop and Implement Procurement Strategy) and Stage Three (Prepare for Execution) of the Planning Process, in the sections that follow. Resource participation requirements are presented using a "RACI" matrix, which identifies, by suggested participant, each participant's specific role, according to the following possible choices:

- **R**esponsible – person(s) who is working on the activity ("the doer(s)");
- **A**ccountable – person(s) with ultimate yes/no authority. This should be pushed down to the lowest level possible;
- **C**onsulted – person(s) involved prior to decision or action;
- **I**nformed – person(s) who need to know of decision or action.

The following resources participate throughout the three (3) stages of the Project Planning Process:

- Executive Business Sponsor – Highest level representative of business unit (usually Managing Director) for which the project is being delivered. The Executive Sponsor retains overall responsibility for project's success
- Business Owner – Business department manager (usually Director or Manager level) who reports to the Executive Business Sponsor and ensures that the project definition and execution meet the business objectives
- The ITS PMO Mgmt – Chief Information Officer and/or Assistant Chief Information Officers
- The ITS PMO Senior Portfolio Manager – Senior The ITS PMO manager who provides guidance and oversight to all projects in the ITS PMO portfolio. She/he is responsible for providing overall status reporting to EDT/PDT for all The ITS PMO projects as well as compliance with The ITS PMO project management standards
- Project Manager – XYZ Company person (usually from The ITS PMO) responsible for delivering the project as defined in project scope and overall project plan, leading and managing the overall project team (incl. any vendor project managers and other XYZ Company staff in The ITS PMO or business departments) on a day-to-day basis. Depending on the size, scope, nature, and complexity of the project there may be an The ITS PMO Project Manager and a Business Project Manager.
- Other Key Stakeholders - departments in addition to the primary Business Department that will be significantly impacted by the initiative
- Project Decision Team (PDT) – Managing Directors, Directors, The ITS PMO management and others with a significant stake in the project. Executive Business Sponsor is typically the chairperson. The PDT is collectively responsible for removing obstacles and enabling any type of change required for the project to be successful

Update PID & Finalize Planning

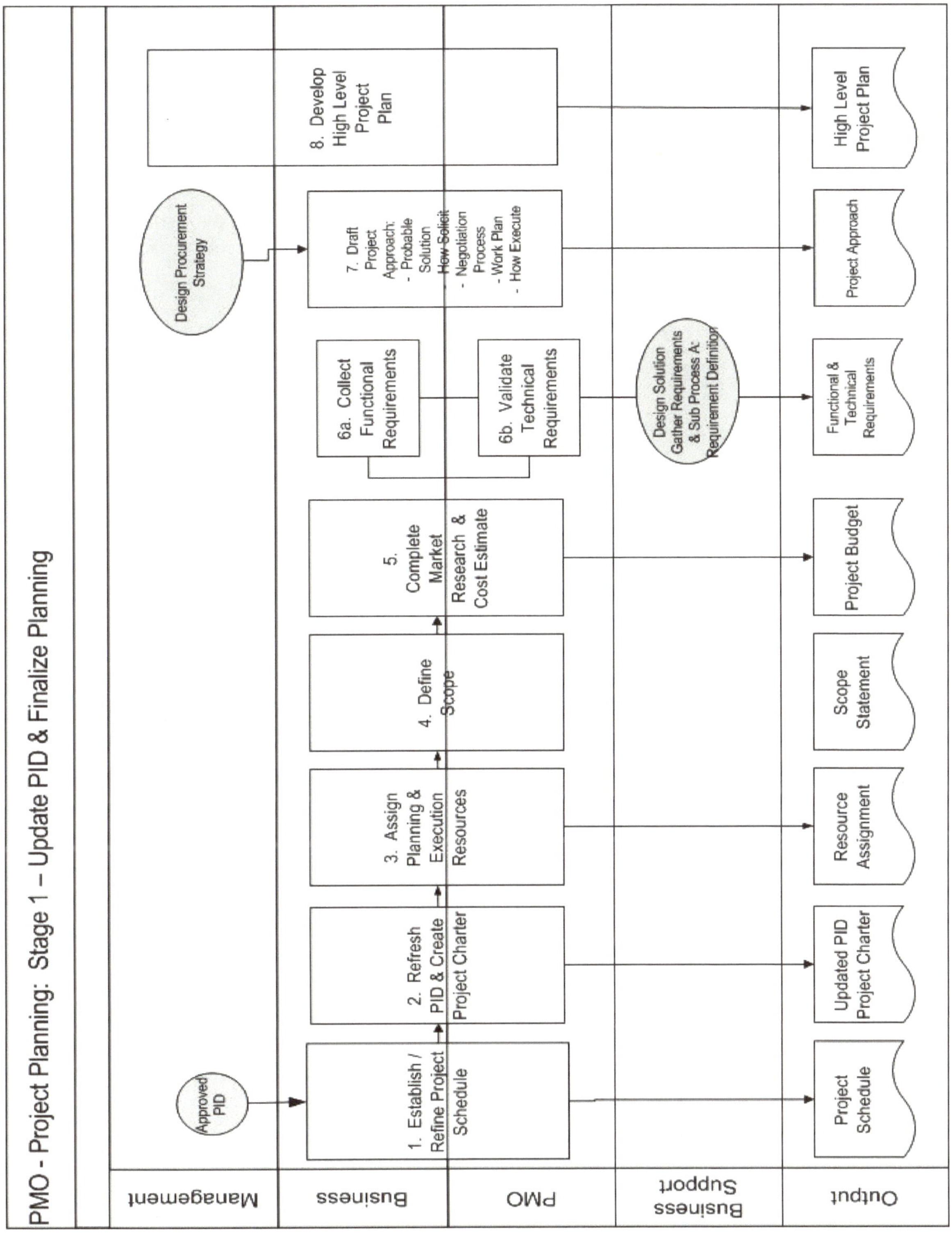

The first stage of the Planning Phase is initiated by the approval of a PID. The PID has been approved by the Business Sponsor, responsible Department Director and Managing Director, the Chief Information Officer, the Executive Decision Team (EDT – a standing committee of XYZ Company executives who provide guidance over the ITS PMO portfolio), and ultimately the Board of Directors (via XYZ Company Budget Review and Approval Process). Once approved, a Project Charter, assigning authority and responsibility to a PM to plan out the initiative, is executed. The process map above indicates that the approved PID is the driver of the project-planning phase. The approved PID defines the key elements of the anticipated project -- who in the XYZ Company will participate in both planning and execution, the expected benefits of the work effort and the estimated cost and timeframe. An updated PID becomes a primary source of information for all activities (steps) in Stage One. As one progresses through the steps of Stage One – described in sections following, one will notice that all of the outputs in Stage One are actually *refinements and expansions of information detailed in the PID*. The project team is now gathering more detail ,and exacting information about project scope, time frame, cost, resources and overall approach. One will also notice that each output in the stage – schedule, charter, resource allocation, requirements, etc., while developed separately, become individual inputs into the ultimate output of Stage One, that being the Project Plan.

The exhibit below highlights the activities comprising the first stage of the Planning Phase.

Project Planning: Stage 1 – Update PID & Finalize Planning

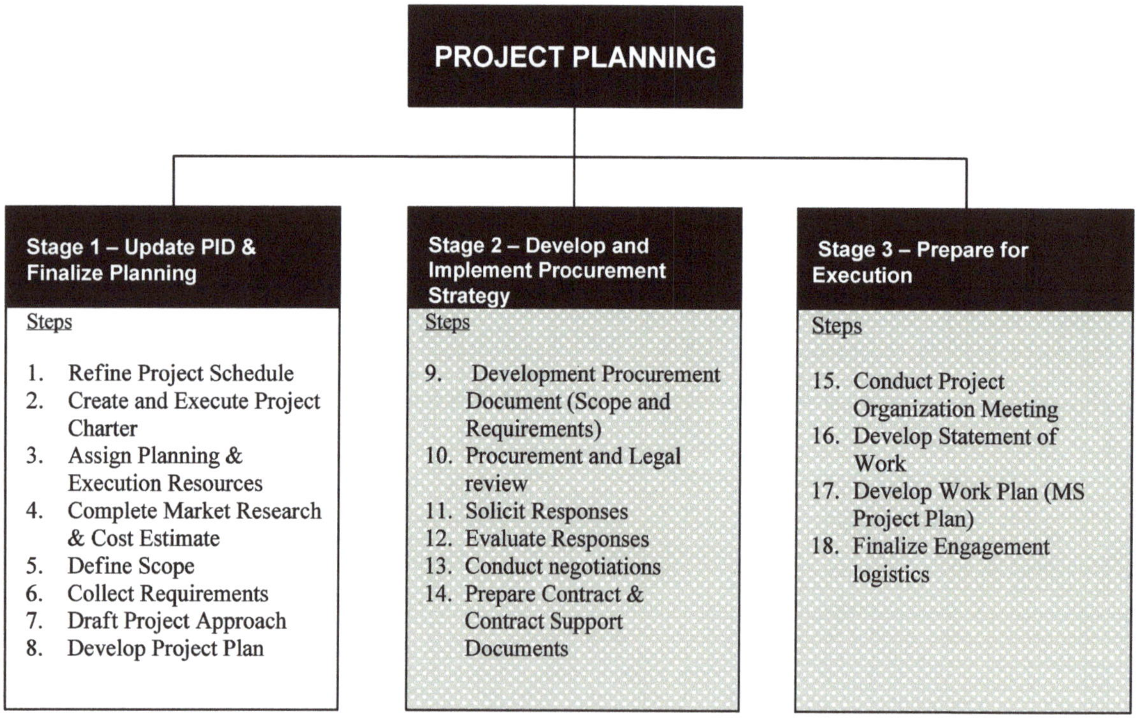

Stage 1: Inputs, Outputs, and Tools

The major inputs into the "Update PID and Finalize Planning" Stage is as follows:

- Project Initiation Document (PID): Captures the initial data gathering efforts that were compelling enough to garner approval: project intent, expected costs and benefits and high-level time line.
- Schedule / Timeframe: A definition and breakdown of the project's overall timeframe, as indicated in the PID
- The Project Charter: Identifies the PM authorized to manage the project

- Resource Requirements: An identification and documentation of all of the resources required to complete the project. Human resources include both those required for planning and for execution.
- Budget: Financial requirements to support the implementation of the project.
- Scope Statement: An understanding of what exactly is the anticipated outcome of the project, parameters of the project and anticipated deliverables
- Approach: An understanding of the most logical approach to resolving the business problem or meeting the described business need.

Stage 1: Inputs, Tools and Outputs

Inputs	Tools	Outputs
• Approved PID • Schedule / timeframe • Project Charter • Resource Requirement	• Process flow diagram for Stage 1 • Resource Capacity Model • PMO Dashboard • After Action	• Project Plan

Tools used to support the Project Planning Process:

- Process Flow Diagram - provides a ready reference for understanding the discrete steps, which when accomplished in total, will drive the creation of the Project Plan.
- Resource Capacity Model - The Resource Capacity Model will indicate the timeframe set-aside for planning and execution of this project. The Resource Capacity Model will help you identify who in The ITS PMO is potentially assigned to the project. However, you will need to work with the business owner to identify who from the business will be assigned to the project and at what rate.
- The PMO Dashboard - provides the PM with information about the status of all projects in the PMO portfolio. It is important to review project status because your project may be dependent upon the completion of another project.
- After Action Review Document (AAR) – as projects are completed, an "After Action Review" session is conducted to discuss lessons learned and determine what may be applied, re-used in future projects. Check the PMO Library for an After Action Review document if undertaking a project similar to one, which has been completed, for example, software development, and check for useful information.
- Available functional requirements – check professional associations, sister agencies, etc. for requirements which may have been developed for a similar project.

The anticipated deliverable or outcome for Stage One is a Project Plan.

External Resources for Technology Information:

While planning the approach to project implementation, you may need additional support to understand how the technology market is currently behaving, what similar agencies may have experienced when looking to procure or implement similar technologies. The following organizations may prove helpful as you continue researching probable solutions to the business need at hand:

- Meta/Gartner (www.gartner.com): a leading information technology research center. The XYZ Company is a member of this service organization, and as such, has access to white papers and consultation around specific technology areas. Ask the CIO and/or the ACIO for and login id and password to this organization
- The Government Finance Officers Association (GFOA) [www.GFOA.org]: a membership / service organization for government entities throughout the United States and Canada, the GFOA conducts mostly financial research, but has a strong technology consulting division. GFOA publishes white papers on how to procure technology in government, how to project manage large technology implementations, etc. Memberships are typically through the Finance Division of the XYZ Company. Ask the CFO, Deputy CFO, Comptroller, Treasurer, etc. for details on accessing this institution and the literature, research results it has on hand.
- Public Housing Authority Directors Association (www.phada.org): this is a professional association for public housing administrators and directors, nation-wide. PHADA hosts regional and national meetings on a quarterly and annual basis. There are typically standing committee on housing policy issues and, technology issues for XYZ Company. Ask a member of the Executive Decision Team (EDT) or the Chief Information Officer for permission to attend these sessions, and/or **login** ids and passwords to its website and research.

Timeframe/Total Duration (ranges from 1 week to 2 months)

It is important to remember that the total time it will take to complete all the activities of Stage One is dependant upon both the size and complexity of the project, as well as how much time has lapsed since the PID was completed. If, for example, the PID was just recently completed, is expected to be short-lived (6-12 weeks), and has a straightforward solution, this stage can be completed in one week. If, however, the PID was completed more than 2 months ago, has Authority-wide implications (is an infusion of technology across the enterprise), and is dependent upon completion of another project, or overlaps resources assigned to another project, it could take from 1-2 months to plan appropriately.

- Attributes of a One – Two Week Planning Effort:
    - PID was just recently completed
    - Project is relatively short-lived, e.g., 6 – 12 weeks
    - Predictable solution

- Attributes of a One – Two Month Planning Effort:
    - PID was completed several months ago, verification of need is required
    - Solution has Authority-wide impact
    - Project depends upon the completion of another project
    - Will have resources overlap which require assessment, consideration

Resource Participation

The following resources participate during the "Update PID and Finalize Planning" Stage

- Executive Business Sponsor
- Business Owner
- The ITS PMO Management
- The ITS PMO Senior Portfolio Manager
- The ITS PMO Project Manager
- Project Team
- Other Key Stakeholders

Step	Executive Sponsor	Business Owner	The ITS PMO Sr. Mgmt	Sr. Portfolio Mgr	The ITS PMO PM	Project Team	Key Stakeholders
1 - Establish / Refine Project Schedule	I	A/R	A/C	C	R	R	C
2 - Complete Project Charter	R	A/R	A	C	R	R	
3 - Assign Planning and Execution Resources	A	R	A/R	C	R		I
4 - Validate and Refine Project Scope		A/R	I	C	A/R	R	C
5 - Complete Market Research and Cost Estimate	I	A/R	I	I	R		I
6 - Collect and Document Requirements		A/R		I	R	C	C
7 - Draft Project Approach		A/R		I	R	C	C
8 - Develop Project Plan	I	A/R	I	I	R	R	C

Key: R – Responsible A – Accountable C – Consulted I - Informed

Stage One -- Update and Finalize Plan – Description; Activities requiring completion to adequately plan for the project

The "Update PID and Finalize Planning" stage consists of eight (8) primary steps. This section provides detailed instructions for the authorized Project Manager (PM) to organize thinking about and execution of each of the steps required to adequately plan for any approved The ITS PMO project.

Stage One Objective: to refine, or update all information contained in the PID document. Key categories of information to be addressed are: project timing (overall schedule), resources (human and financial) and the overall approach to the project.

Understanding of the PM Life Cycle vs. SDLC

The PM Life Cycle consists of what's known as the five process groups: Initiation, Planning, Executing, Monitor/Control and Closing is used to *manage the work*. This is the cycle that the project manager will be in throughout the total duration of the project. The System Development Life Cycle consist of the Planning, Designing, Testing, Implementation, Closing is used for the team when *doing the work*. During the WBS and network diagram (sequencing) stages both the project manager and team will be working together as a team to complete the scope of work in an effort to produce a valid project schedule which will be baseline and reporting against.

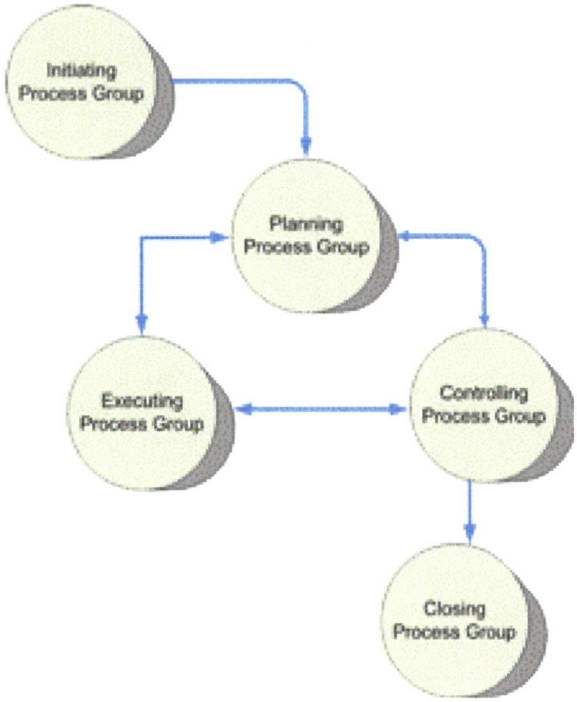

As a project manager you need to understand what life cycle you are in and when it is relevant. There exist two life cycles for every project 1) The Project Manager Life Cycle (project manager life cycle for managing the work) and 2) The System Development Life Cycle (team life cycle for doing the work). Below is a visual of the two life cycles.

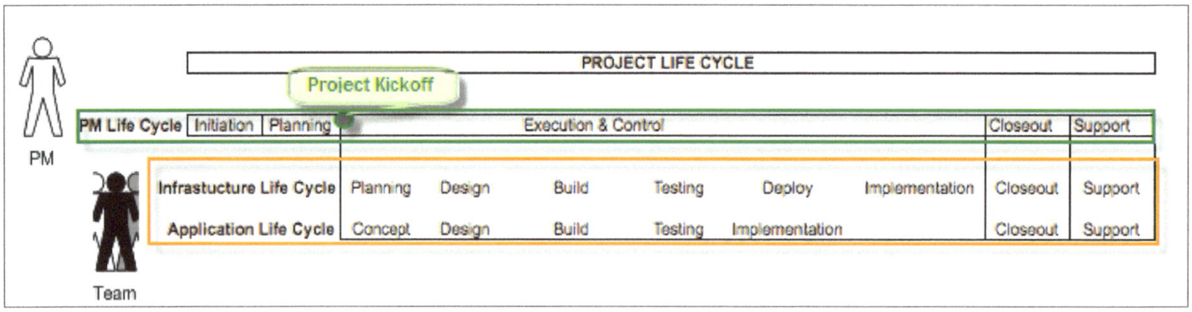

In the above diagram, after Project Kickoff the Project Manger will move the engagement into the "Execution" process group of the PM life cycle. However, the team will then move to the "Planning" stage of System Development Life Cycle". In this phase of the project, the team will be following the planned work plan that was planned during The WBS stage. So for example, if during the WBS stage the team planned for 5 days of documenting functional requirements, during this time is when the team will be actually doing the work of documenting functional requirements. It is very important that the PM understands that two life cycles exist because knowing both is key because the PM is responsible for managing the work and getting all deliverables complete. So while the team is going through Planning, Design, Building, Testing process of the SDCL, the Project Manager will be using the tools in the PM Execution & Control Phase as ways to manage the project. So in short, after the project kickoff meeting the Project Manager will remain at the top level in the PM Life Cycle whereas the team will fall down into a System Development Lice Cycle. Both cycle are required in order to complete the project.

Step 1 – Review, Update Project Schedule (addresses project time / schedule)

- **Objective(s):**
  - To verify that the project objective (PID – Introduction to Proposed Project) has been included in the PID.
  - To verify that the anticipated completion date for the project remains the same or warrants update
  - To review project dependencies that might impact the start date, for example, it may be that another project must be completed, prior to beginning this one
  - To ensure that both the timeframe for planning and executing the project is sufficient enough to achieve the business owner's defined or updated implementation and completion dates

- **Instructions**:
  - Update the PID:
    - Verify the project objectives as stated in the PID; review with the project team members for accuracy and completeness. Objectives should be clear, attainable, specific and measurable.
    - Verify that the initially proposed *schedule and completion dates* remain the same
    - Verify the following schedule drivers:
      - Market Availability: for example, if software is the desired version released, tested and generally available? If hardware, is the desired model released, tested and generally available?
      - Internal Resource Availability – The ITS PMO and Business: is the initially assigned XYZ Company personnel still available to 'work' project planning and execution activities? Are the ITS PMO personnel initially assigned to the project still available for the duration initially projected?
      - Dependence on completion of other projects: if dependent on the completion of another project, what is the status of that project as well as its relative health?
    - Check that *resource* assignments remain the same:
      - Business Owner
      - The ITS PMO Project Manager
      - Department Sponsor
      - Executive Business Sponsor
      - Other project resources
    - Update resources, if needed

- **Estimated Time Duration:**
  - 8-10 hours

- **Resource Participation:**
    - The Business Owner and The ITS PMO PM are jointly responsible for updating the completion date. The Business Owner may be privy to events within his/her organization which require the completion date to be pushed up or back; similarly the ITS PMO PM may be aware of events that require the date to be amended, such as continuation of a project expected to be completed upon which this project is dependant, lack of the requested technology in the market place, etc.
    - The ITS PMO Assistant CIO's and/or the Senior Portfolio Manager will have the most recent status regarding availability of The ITS PMO resources initially assigned to the project.

- **Tip(s) for Success:**
    - Be certain that the PM and project team all can identify and agree upon the project objectives. If the objectives of the project are not clear, incomplete, or not agreed upon, completing all other components of project planning -- determining how long it will take, what needs to be done, and the cost – will be a difficult, if not impossible exercise.
    - For smaller projects and for projects that start relatively soon after PID approval, the PID document will not require extensive review and updating. However, for more complicated project, enterprise-wide projects, projects with a dependency on another effort, and those that have considerable lag from the time of approval, it is imperative to review the document and ensure that assumptions made while completing the PID have not changed as well. Too, in the technology arena, a six-month lag between approval and project planning is sufficient time for the market to have changed and newer solutions to have emerged.

Step 2 – Create and Execute Project Charter

- **Objective**: to assign responsibility and authority for project planning and eventually project execution to a Project Manager. This assignment communicates to the XYZ Company and eventually to the vendor community that the assigned Project Manager is XYZ Company's main point of contact and will be responsible for the execution of all day-to-day activities needed to plan for and execute the project.

- **Instructions:**

    - Complete the "Project Charter":
        - Reproduce a copy of the approved PID
        - Attach the one-page Project Charter template. Indicate the name of both project managers (business and The ITS PMO). As stated above, the Project Charter assigns authority and responsibility for the project to a particular resource(s), specifically a Project Manager from The ITS PMO, a business manager from the involved department or a group of departments, if appropriate.

- Project Management authorization is garnered via signature by both the CIO (for the ITS PMO PM) and the Department Director for the represented business PM.

- **Estimated Time Duration**
  - 4 hours

- **Resource Participation**
  - The Business Owner and The ITS PMO Project Manager are jointly responsible for obtaining the required signatures for the Project Charter.
  - At a minimum, the Chief Information Officer and the Department Director are required to sign the Project Charter, indicating who will be the respective Project Managers

Step 3 – Identify and Assign Project Planning and Project Execution Resources

- **Objective**: to identify resources across the Authority who will be responsible for planning and executing this project and, to assign them roles and responsibilities for carrying out planning and executing activities.

- **Instructions**
  - Use these templates:
    - For Project Planning:
      - PID Document – at a minimum, indicates the Executive Business Sponsor, Business Owner, and Chief Information Officer
      - Resource Allocation Model – an electronic spreadsheet that lists resources in The ITS PMO to be used for project planning and project execution for a given 12-month period. The spreadsheet indicates who is to be responsible by particular role: CIO, ACIO, IT PM, Technology Manager, Data Base Architect, Subject Matter Experts (SME's), etc.
      - Project Organization Chart – just as with any business organization, all projects regardless of size and/or scope should create a project organization chart for both planning and execution phases. The organization chart should detail the hierarchical reporting structure needed to plan and complete the project.

  Note: The ITS PMO Resource Allocation Model is a standard document to be used to support Planning Resource Allocation needed for Project Execution. It is owned by the ACIO's and managed by the Senior Portfolio Manager.
  - Identify and Assign Project Planning Resources
    - Review Approved PID
    - Contact Business PM (if assigned), Business Department Director, and the Department of Procurement and Contracts to request initial meeting to assign resources needed to assist with project planning activities
    - Procurement and Contracts assigns a buyer to this purchase to insure that the procurement approach (incorporated into Step 7 below) conforms with the U.S. Department of HUD and XYZ Company policies regarding competitive solicitations and compliance with M/W/DBE goals and HUD, Section 3 Requirements
    - Confirm The ITS PMO resources allocated to the planning and execution of this project with the Senior Portfolio Manager (as outlined in the ITS PMO Resource Allocation Model)
    - Identify project roles and responsibilities for at least these positions:

- <u>For Project Planning</u>:
    - o IT Project Manager
    - o Business Owner
    - o The ITS PMO Sponsor (CIO, ACIO- Applications, or ACIO-Infrastructure depending on project scope and complexity)
    - o Executive Business Sponsor
    - o Procurement Representative
    - o Business representatives and Subject Matter Experts – needed to define functional requirements for the project
    - o IT ACIO / Infrastructure – needed to define the technical requirements for the project (e.g., security)
- <u>For Project Execution</u>
    - o In addition to all of the above,
    - o Evaluation Committee Members - (representative Stakeholders who will be impacted by the project and will be voting members of the group assigned to review responses to your procurement document)
    - o Evaluation Committee Advisors - (representative Stakeholders who will be impacted by the project, who will not vote, but whose expertise in a particular business function or process will be tapped by the Evaluation Committee to help them make a decision)
    - o Project Decision Team (PDT) – Managing Director and Managers of the impacted departments; the Executive Business Sponsor sits as the chair of this group
    - o Senior Portfolio Manager – who will be charged with reviewing the project for quality, risk, etc.
    - o Team Captains – if the scope of the project involves various functional areas in the Authority (for example – Manager of Buyers, in the Purchasing Department), and dividing the implementation among teams makes sense, a Team Captain will be needed for each area
    - o Technical Leads – depending on the nature of the project, it may be that a technical lead is needed to assist the vendor with product installation and testing
    - o Subject Matter Experts – for any size project, the persons who know most about a particular area and are deeply involved with a particular function or process, will be needed to support the business representatives as they review and implement technology solutions.

- Develop Project Organization Chart depicting the following:
    - Project Decision Team Members – usually Executive Business Sponsor, other Managing Directors, department directors from the key stakeholder departments, and the Chief Information Officer
    - XYZ Company Project Manager
    - Vendor Project Manager – TBD
    - Internal Subject Matter Experts
- ▪ Estimate the number of hours per week that the various project participants will need to devote to the project while in the planning phase
- ▪ Estimate the number of hours per week that the various project participants will need to devote the project while in the execution phase
- ▪ Document resource assignments and estimated time requirements

- Review project "organization" chart, time commitments with The ITS PMO Sponsor, Senior Portfolio Manager, Business PM and Department Director, and, if an enterprise-wide project, impacted Managing Directors and CIO

- **Tip(s) for Success:**
    - Regardless of project size, be sure to review the project team commitment (stated in number of hours per week for the duration of the project) with all participants and their department director and finally, managing director. It is important for staff, managers and managing directors to understand the level of commitment the project will entail. It allows the departments involved to accomplish the planning they need to determine how to relieve resources to work the project and still meet the mission and objectives of their department.
    - The assignment of resources must be a collaborative effort between all impacted departments.

- **Estimated Time Duration**
    - 12 hours

- **Resource Participation**
    - The Business Owner and The ITS PMO PM are jointly responsible for assigning resources from their respective departments for both project planning and execution. The ITS PMO Sponsor (CIO/ACIO's) must approve all The ITS PMO resource assignments.
    - The Director of Procurement and Contracts is responsible for assigning a buyer to assist the business develop the solicitation document
    - The Buyer from the Department of Purchasing and Contracts (DPC) assigned to the project will be responsible for including XYZ Company Corporation Council in various stages of review of the solicitation document
    - The Business Owner will be responsible for identifying all stakeholders who will play the following roles:
        - Requirements Definition Gathering – Planning Phase
        - Evaluation Committee – Planning Phase
        - Subject Matter Experts – Planning Phase
        - Advisors to the Evaluation Committee – Planning Phase
        - Team Captains – Execution
        - Core Team Members – Execution

Step 4 – Validate and Refine Project Scope

- **Objective**: to document all anticipated work required to produce the desired outcome of the project. The scope statement also identifies all XYZ Company data, locations and/or departments to be incorporated into or impacted by the project. The process of scope definition inventories all work that is included in the project and that which is not. It should be descriptive enough to ensure that the project team understands what is to be done, on a high level, when the project moves into execution.

- **Instructions**

    - Use these available templates / documents to support the scope definition refinement activity:

        - Approved PID and Project Charter
        - Critical thinking of the resources, especially subject matter experts involved in planning and execution
        - Existing scope documents. If this project is a follow-on, expansion or upgrade to an existing system, the initial scope document can be used for reference.

    - Assemble the Planning Team identified in Step 3 above

    - Work with your Planning Team (resources) to document or refine the following:

        - The Business Problem or Need / Expected Outcomes

          Refine / review the issues as described in the PID, confirm the business "pain" with the project team. It is imperative to further define/refine the project's goals and objectives. If we are not clear about the objective of the project, why it is to be undertaken, then we will not be able to adequately determine what logical activities might be completed to resolve the problem, what kind of resources we may need, and how much they may cost. This section does not have to be lengthy, but you need to include enough detail to ensure the business needs and expected outcomes are clearly documented, and that at least some of the stated objectives and/or benefits are quantifiable. Without some quantification, the Authority will not be able to assess the relative success of the project.

        - Deliverables

          To the best of the team's ability, identify all products and outcomes that are expected, as project implementation progresses and when the project is completed. For example, if the project is to upgrade our Wide Area Network, some examples of deliverables would be:

            - Survey and report out on the condition of the current infrastructure
            - Recommendation for improvements to the hardware, telecommunication links
            - Implementation of the desired state
            - Certification of the equipment installation

- **Estimated Time Duration**
    - 8 hours

- **Resource Participation**
    - The Business Owner and The ITS PMO PM are jointly responsible for defining the project scope statement.
    - The Business Owner is responsible for identifying the expected benefits of the desired product or solution. Benefits should be both qualitative and quantitative.
    - The Business Owner and The ITS PMO PM are jointly responsible for defining expected project deliverables; however, they will need to be assisted by representatives of impacted groups.

- **Tip for Success**:
  Review other projects of a similar nature for samples of project deliverables.

Designing Your PM Strategy

During the planning stage and at this point it is very important that a project manager at a high level determine what tools he/she will need during the Execution, Monitor and Control phase of the project. Because the scope and complexity of every project is different having a strategy for small, medium and large projects is key. For example, for a project that's only planned to last 30 days would you really need to perform earned value, detailed statistical risk management? That is a project manager judgment call and is dependent on several internal and external key factors and the expectations of your stakeholders. In the previous section we talked about the PM life cycle, which consist of the five process groups: Initiation, Planning, Execution, Monitor/Control and Closing. Within each process group, there also exist nine functional areas that are aligned with the five process groups: Integration Management, Scope Management, Time Management, Cost Management, Quality Management , Human Resource Management, Communication Management, Risk Management, Procurement Management .

Functional Area	Function
Integration Management	The process of managing the high level aspects of a project
Scope Management	The process or work to be done to create the finish product. Managing time, qualities, cost are critical aspects of scope management.
Time Management	The process of outlining the details of the project through task sequencing, resource leveling, plan scheduling using various task estimating models
Cost Management	The process of costing out in detail all aspects of the scope of work, project schedule, resources using very cost models and strategies.
Quality Management	The process by which requirements are fulfilled and accepted as outlined in the scope of work document.
Human Resource Management	The process of managing human capital according to the scope of work, project cost and project task requirements.
Communication Management	The process of establishing a channel for all communication for all project deliverables.
Risk Management	The process of managing any aspects that can have a negative or positive impact on the project.
Procurement Management	The process of buying services, software or anything to meet project demands.

Knowing the scope of your project whether small or large in scope, a project manager should design a managing strategy that consist of what tools he/she will use, how he/she will use them and when he/she will use them. The resulting tools are inputs into the project manager's communication plan for how he/she will report on project performance, issues, etc.

Step 5 – Complete Market Research & Cost Estimate

- **Objective**: to ensure that all knowable costs have been identified and updated, if more that a few months have transpired since the PID was approved. In the technology sector, external variables can impact costs very quickly. New providers enter the marketplace, there may have been mergers, and acquisitions between or among key players, of newer technologies or higher versions of software might be available since the PID was approved. Marketplace variables may warrant a review and update of the PID's cost estimates.

- **Instructions**:

    - Use available templates / documents to support the market research and costing step:
        - Cost Estimate and Total Cost of Ownership Spreadsheets used to develop cost / benefit estimate for PID
        - If this project is a follow-on, expansion or upgrade to an existing system, the existing contract can be used for reference to scope and price.
    - Review the costs estimated in the approved PID, evaluate the market to identify and understand factors which may impact the estimate as prepared
    - Contact comparable Housing Authorities to determine price points for recently procured products/services of a similar nature
    - Ensure that a contingency line item of at least 15 – 20 % is included
    - Use XYZ Company memberships/subscriptions in professional organizations that track technology costs:
        - Meta / Gartner - for their knowledge of recently procured products / solutions of a similar nature, particularly software
        - Government Finance Officers Association (GFOA) - includes a research and technology consulting practice that tracks technology costs
    - Check current Authority contracts to assess market rates for technical and management consultants
    - Review costs provided by vendors in XYZ Company Pre-Qualified pool for Information Technology Services
    - Review vendor costs as specified in the Government Services Administration (GSA) schedule. The GSA prepares price schedules for vendors to use when bidding on government contracts (typically for equipment). Vendors will honor these prices when bidding on state and local government projects.

- **Estimated Time Duration**
    - 4 -12 hours

- **Resource Participation**
    - The Business Owner and The ITS PMO PM are jointly responsible for reviewing the market and updating costs.

- The Business Owner should tap all of its existing resources and contacts with product, service providers; similarly The ITS PMO should tap its existing resources, contacts with product providers
- The ITS PMO can request the services of Meta / Gartner to review costs, particularly for enterprise-wide solutions for which they may have a consulting specialty
- The Budget Director must be informed and is ultimately responsible for approving an increase in the cost estimate

- **Tip for Success:**
  Keep in mind that the market costs do not reflect more favorable rates that may be obtained through a competitive process and contract negotiations.

Step 6 – Collect and Document Requirements

- **Objective(s):** to compile functional and technical requirements that:
  - Clearly and succinctly relay to the vendor community, what it is the Authority wishes to procure
  - Describe expected functionality, use for the desired product or solution

- **Instructions**
  - Use these Templates/Documents:
    - A Microsoft Visio process flow for requirements development. Please refer to Exhibit 6 below, for a high level understanding of how requirements are gathered.

Process Flow: Requirements Definition

- Gather/verify The ITS PMO technology requirements: The ITS PMO Department maintains technology requirements pertaining to it hardware, operating system and data base platforms to provide to the vendor community. Technology requirements speak to:
  - What can meet, compliment or competes with XYZ Company chosen technology investment
  - What hardware and software *must* be used, and/or *cannot be* used
- Develop functional requirements: functional requirements are statements that identify attributes of the product so that it has value and utility for the user. It is the responsibility of the business to develop functional requirements. Functional requirements state what the system is to do, but not how it is to do it. To help the business start gathering requirements, here are some suggestions for resources:
  - Review existing literature for:
    - Comparable organizations that may have developed requirements for a similar need, for example:
      - Contact the sister agencies (City of Chicago, Chicago Transit Authority, etc.)
      - Contact public housing professional associations
    - Extract very high level specifications from industry literature
    - Search the web for system / product requirements
    - Contact governing federal agencies for requirements such as:
      - The Government Accountability Office (GAO) for financial system requirements

        - The U.S. Department of Housing & Urban Development
        - Others
    - Talk with Stakeholders (internal & external)
        - Ask strategic questions about what is the business problem, what are the "pain" points? Problem statements can usually be turned into functional requirements
        - Ask Meta / Gartner for sample requirements
        - Understand what functionality may be required by the U.S. Department of Housing and Urban Development
    - Map the business process and identify distinct phases within the process
        - On a high level, create a "picture" of the business process, which your project is addressing, supporting, etc. this will help you understand the business process and its inherent strengths and weaknesses
        - With the map, you can better organize for the requirements gathering exercise and facilitate discussions about what is needed, by the different phases of the process
    - Compile requirements in logical order and sequencing, for example, according to the governing process flow for the business area in question
    - Document, validate & update requirements with end users prior to publishing

- **Estimated Time Duration**
    - Depends upon the complexity and scope of the product / solution sought.
        - For a smaller project with limited duration, limited scope, and applicability to a single department - up to 8 hours
        - For an enterprise-wide project, plan on 3 – 4 weeks to coordinate time with all departments and solicit their needs.

- **Resource Participation**
    - The Business Owner is primarily responsible for developing functional requirements
    - Stakeholders are responsible for meeting with the Business Owner and articulating their specific requirements
    - The ITS PMO PM is responsible for ensuring that the most current technology standards (requirements) are compiled and verified with the Business Owner, as most current.

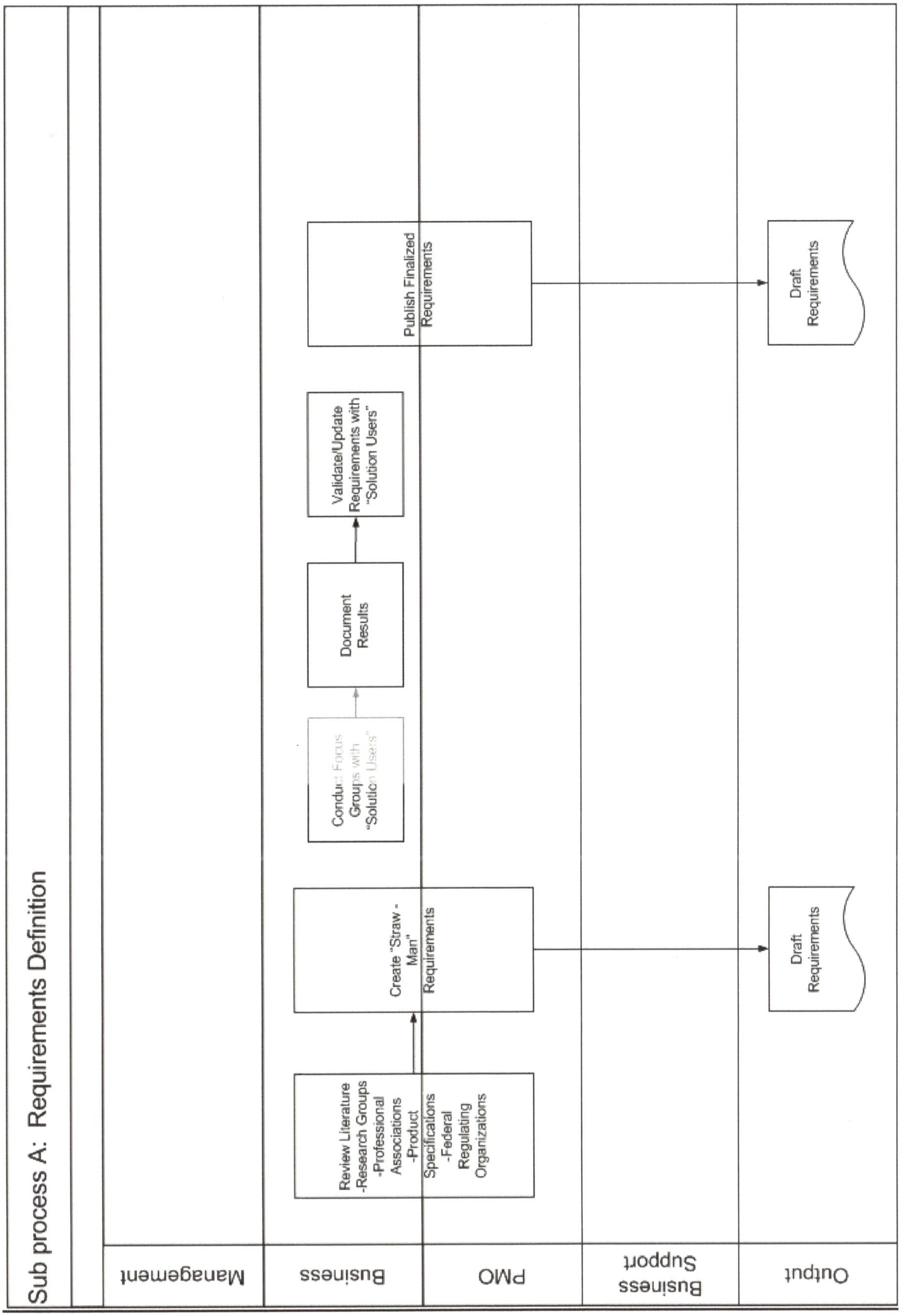
Sub process A: Requirements Definition
Management
Business
PMO
Business Support
Output
Review Literature -Research Groups -Professional Associations -Product Specifications -Federal Regulating Organizations
Create "Straw - Man" Requirements
Draft Requirements
Conduct Focus Groups with "Solution Users"
Document Results
Validate/Update Requirements with "Solution Users"
Publish Finalized Requirements
Draft Requirements

Step 7 – Draft Project Approach

- **Objective:** to identify and document the most likely, logical and proven method of resolving the stated business problem, or achieving the desired result.

In the Authority, the "approach" to the project will encompass some or all of the following considerations:

a. Identification of market structure – the business owner and IT PM should understand how the market is structured, or how the product or solution is most typically offered in the marketplace. Ask and answer questions such as:
   - What major services and products are needed?
   - What is the likelihood that we will be able to obtain the complete product / solution from a single vendor?
   - Will we need to prepare for a "teamed" response? How will that affect contract terms and conditions? **Who will be ultimately responsible for delivery?**

b. Identification of implementation standards and best practices – based on the type of project being pursued. What is the typical implementation approach? How is it typically divided into phases, activities, and tasks to assure success?

c. Internal or External Solutions – the IT PM will need to assess / validate how the desired state can be achieved – either using internal resources or by contracting a third party for resources. If an internal solution, the IT PM will need to identify staff needed and their availability. If an external solution is sought, the optimal procurement strategy needs to be identified and followed. (See below)

d. XYZ Company /HUD procurement considerations – depending on the type of products and services anticipated, the Planning team needs to understand how to procure the desired state using available, XYZ Company procurement tools:
   - Request for Proposal (RFP): if the desired state includes problem solving or delivery of consulting services, a Request for Proposal will be used.
   - Request for Qualification (RFQ) – periodically the Authority releases a RFQ; in The ITS PMO, a RFQ is typically for specific categories (management consulting, web design, database design, telecommunications, etc., to identify companies with specific qualifications, or area of expertise. With an RFQ, there is no purchase, rather, when the Authority identifies a need, a pool of vendors is readily available.
   - Request for Services (RFS) - When a need arises in the categories of service, and if an RFQ is in effect (typically 2 years) the request for services is released only to a pre-qualified pool in the specific area.
   - Invitation of Bid (IFB) – if the XYZ Company requires specific equipment with exact specifications, such as personal computers, servers, routers, hubs, etc., an IFB is used. IFB's are awarded to the lowest bid.
   - Non-Compete – If we are certain that there is only one provider in the marketplace, or if other competitive procurement tools were used and only a single response is received, we may procure using a single source, via justification to the Department of Procurement and Contract's Non-Compete Committee.

e. Payment Method/Deliverables – define on a high level how the solution will be paid for: upfront with warranty (if equipment, software), over time and based on deliverables (if for services)

f. Negotiation Method -- identify who will negotiate the contract, if it will follow typical XYZ Company process, or if competitive negotiations are in order

- **Instructions**
  - Review approach to projects of similar scope and duration undertaken by the Authority, or others, for identification of implementation standards, whether services are provided internally or procured and if procured, what tool was used.
  - Brainstorm with vendors, how do you typically implement this type of product/solution?
  - Conduct research with Meta / Gartner
  - Thoroughly review options for solicitation with the Department of Procurement and Contracts
  - Review and re-use those project phases that are generic to any project, applications, infrastructure, telecommunications:
  - Review of the current state
  - Validation of requirements with client
  - If a system:
    - Installation of various environments
    - Design
    - Testing
    - Training
    - Accept

- **Estimated Time Duration**
  - Depends upon the complexity and scope of the product / solution sought.
  - For a smaller project with limited duration and scope, e.g., an 8-week project within a specific area of the Authority, developing a project approach may take up to 8 hours
  - An enterprise-wide project may require up to one week conducting research, drafting and then validating the approach with the ACIO.

- **Resource Participation**
  - The Business Owner and The ITS PMO PM are responsible for jointly drafting the Project Approach Document
  - The ITS PMO PM may have prior experience planning and executing projects and are familiar with available information repositories, and standard Project Management tools and templates.
  - The Department of Purchases and Contracts must be involved in the "Solicitation" component of project approach to assure that all pertinent regulations and policies are met.

Step 8 – Develop Project Plan

- **Objective:** The purpose of the Project Plan is to establish clear definition of the project and to set expectations for all involved parties. The Project Plan defines scope, schedule and budget for the project, with more detailed documentation (e.g., design documentation, work plan). The Project Plan will incorporate the solicitation strategy (as identified in Step 7) to be employed, should one be necessary, and serve as the basis for drafting the Procurement Document (RFP, RFS, etc.). When complete, the project plan will:

        - Guide project execution
        - Document all assumptions made during planning
        - Document project planning decisions regarding alternatives chosen
        - Define major activities to be undertaken
        - Facilitate communication among stakeholders
        - Serve as the basis for the Statement of Work for the project

- **Instructions**
    - Refer to already completed documents which are inputs into the Project Plan
    - Complete the Project Plan Template, using documents identified below:
        - Introduction: PID and Scope Document
        - Project Scope: PID and Scope Document
        - Project Approach: Project Approach Document; Cost worksheet
            - Major Activities: the intent of this section is to think through as best as you can with your planning team, all the work needed to accomplish the overall project. Resources available to you to inventory high level activities include:
                - Brainstorming with your team members
                - Reviewing completed projects
                - Drawing upon experience in past projects

              Sample Activity List (for System Development)

              Verification of Requirements
              Conceptual Design
              System Development
              System Test
              Data Conversion
              System Test
              System Acceptance
        - Project Resources: Project Assignment Document, Organizational Chart, Project Roles and Responsibilities
        - Project Management: this section incorporates the likely manner in which the project is to be managed and identifies those resources from the XYZ Company that will act in this manner, such as a Project Decision Team (PDT) and the XYZ Company Project Manager, as well as the Vendor's Project Manager. At this point in planning, the vendor's PM will not be known until the award of the contract.
        - Project constraints: factors that limit the options available to the planning team, for example, there may be limited funds for the particular project, or HUD may be requiring that the Authority complies with a particular regulation by a specific date which the project timeline must meet.
        - Project assumptions - factors that are thought to be true, real or certain. For example, we might assume that we need just one server and one load balancer to support a particular software application.
        - Deliverables: Describe all known, tangible outcomes or products to be generated or developed as a part of the successful completion of the project, as well as those that the client wishes for. Gauge the level of description to be documented on your client's need for detail and the complexity of the project. If it is the first time your client is undertaking project execution, for example, be sure that you identify as many deliverables as possible, in as clear and concise manner as possible.

- **Estimated Time Duration**
  - Depends upon the complexity and scope of the product / solution sought.
    - For a smaller project with limited duration and scope, e.g., an 8-week project within a specific area of the Authority, it will take about 6 – 8 hours to complete the Project Plan. Key components have already been documented (refer to steps 1 – 8 above) and are easily incorporated into the Project Plan.
    - An enterprise-wide project may require from 8 – 16 hours to gather together and incorporate previously completed documents (from steps 1 – 7 above) into a single Project Plan template.

- **Resource Participation**
    - The Business Owner and The ITS PMO PM are jointly responsible for completing the Project Plan Document
    - The ITS PMO Management should be consulted when the document is complete, notifying them that it reflects decisions that they have already reviewed, participated in, and the next step is to prepare a solicitation document.

- **Tip(s) for Success:**

The only component of the Project Plan that has not already been developed in prior steps of this Planning Stage is the "Activities Development". For a larger project you may want to develop a Work Breakdown Structure (WBS), which breaks a project down into manageable pieces to help identify all that is needed to be done. The basis of the WBS is the hierarchical organization of activities from the highest, broadest level down to the lowest task that can be identified. For the Project Plan, which is created *prior to solicitation and review of the possible solutions proposed by vendors,* we'll want to limit the breakdown to only two levels. An example of a WBS blown out to the second level might be as follows:

Sample Work Breakdown Structure
Project: Build a Bridge

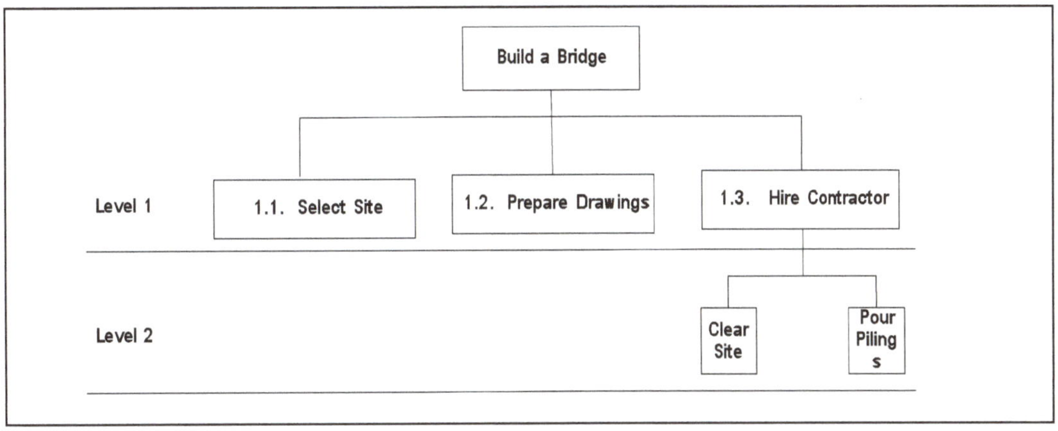

Allocate sufficient time and energy to create your Project Plan document. It will become the basis for not only the solicitation document, but also a Statement of Work (refer to

Planning – Stage 2 for instructions on developing a solicitation document and statement of work) for the project. Once an evaluation committee has selected a solution and awarded a contract, the vendor, XYZ Company business owner (or a designated representative—note: that if it must ultimately be approved by the business owner) and the ITS PMO Project Manger, will collaboratively develop the Statement of Work.

The Work Breakdown Structure (WBS)

The Work breakdown Structure, WBS, is one the most important team functions for project planning. The WBS consist of taking a task and breaking it into smaller manageable parts usually no more than 8hr work effort(s) which are called work-packages then given to a person to complete, along with a WBS Dictionary explaining in detail what the requirements for the work-package. The complete WBS composition makes up the total scope of the project. If any task is outside of the WBS, it is out of scope for the project.

WBS DICTIONARY (Task Description)			
Project Name____	Task No.____	Date Issued ______	Person Assigned ___
Task Description (what work is authorized)			
Quantified goals and objectives			
Goals and Objectives			
Acceptance Criteria			
Resource Assigned			
Duration			
Cost			
Due Date ____________			
Interdependencies: Before this task _______	After this task _______		
Approved by: Project Manger _________________________	Date ___________		

The WBS is created by the entire team, the subject matter experts (SME) . The creation of the WBS is usually done in a class-like environment where the project manager will lead the team into the task at a high level and then depend on the SME to assist in breaking the task down into smaller manageable parts (work-packages) that will then be assigned a duration and then be put into sequence (network diagramming).

Example of WBS:

Work Break Down Structure (WBS)
Metro WAN

1.0 Project Startup
2.0 Planning
- 2.1 Build Project Plan for Metro WAN (PM Team)
  - 2.1.1 Create project initiation plan (PIP)
  - 2.1.2 Create Statement of Work
  - 2.1.3 Obtain approval of Statement of work
  - 2.1.4 Create WBS
  - 2.1.5 Determine Critical Path
  - 2.1.6 Develop baseline schedule
  - 2.1.7 Finalize PIP
  - 2.1.8 Obtain approval of project schedule
  - 2.1.9 **Obtain approval of project plan**
  - 2.1.10 Kick off meeting
- 2.2 Needs Assessment
  - 2.2.1 Site Survey
    - 2.2.1.1 Main Location
      - 2.2.1.1.1 Visit 626 W. Jackson (SBC)
      - 2.2.1.1.2 Visit 50 W. Washington (SBC)
      - 2.2.1.1.3 Visit 1000 S. Wabash (SBC)
      - 2.2.1.1.4 Visit 4859 S. Wabash (SBC)
    - 2.2.1.2 Remote Locations (SBC)
      - 2.2.1.2.1 Visit 82 Remote Locations
      - 2.2.1.2.2 Rack Space Evaluation
      - 2.2.1.2.3 Determine Environmental Eval. (HVAC, Power)
      - 2.2.1.2.4 Determine Cabling Eval.
      - 2.2.1.2.5 Determine Telecommunication Evaluation
        - 2.2.1.2.5.1 Determine Demark Extension
        - 2.2.1.2.5.2 Determine Cable Jumper Requirements
      - 2.2.1.2.6 Determine Physical Security
      - 2.2.1.2.7 Inventory existing equipment
    - 2.2.1.3 **Document Findings and Report** (SBC)

After creating the WBS, durations are assigned to each work-package. The best estimating technique that takes into account risk is the PERT method, which is calculated using this formula: (**Pessimistic Duration + 4(Most Likely Estimate) + Optimistic Duration)/6**

WBS AND PERT ANALYSIS FOR CALCULATING PROJECT DURATION

WBS Element							PERT
Phase	Activity #	Description	Dependencies	O	M	P	DURATIONS
1	1.1.1	Creating Project Documentation	1.1	13	15	20	15.500

Network Diagram

After WBS creation and task estimation performing a PERT Analysis, the next step is to sequence the task and to determine successor task (A task whose start or finish date is driven by its predecessor task) and predecessors (A task whose start or finish date determines the start or finish date of its successor task) based on the following:

Finish-Start – In order for the successor to start the current task must finish first
Start-Finish - In order for the successor task to finish the current task must start
Finish – Finish – In order for the successor task to Finish the current task must finish first
Start-Start – In order for the successor task to start the current task must start

Below is an example of a complete network diagram for a sample project:

Task	Dependency
1	START
2	START
3	START
4	START
5	START
6	START
7	START
8	START
9	START
10	START
11	START
12	START
13	12
14	13
15	13,14
16	6
17	16
18	16,17
19	1,2
20	19
21	20
22	19,20,21
23	START
24	19,20,21
25	24
26	25
27	6,16,17
28	27
29	28
30	29
31	25
32	5,23
33	21,24
34	25
35	34
36	3
37	35
38	37
39	38

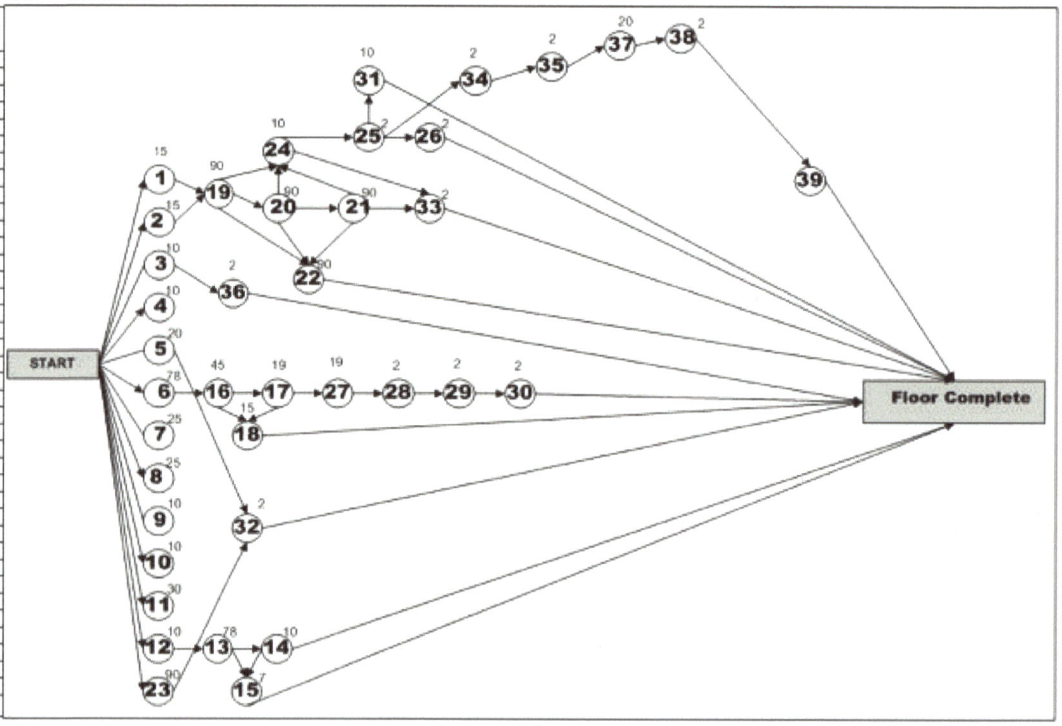

The critical path is the longest path through the network diagram and is the shortest time that the project can be completed. Any delay of a task on the critical path will impact the planned end date. Each task has a early start, early finish, last start and late finish and is used to calculate *total float* (slack) which is the amount of time that an task can be delayed without delaying the planned project date. All tasks that are on the critical path have zero float. *Free float* is the amount of time that a task can be delayed without delaying the early start date of its successor. Project float is the amount of time that the project can be delayed without delaying the expected date of the project. All task on the critical path have zero float. In the above diagram the critical path is 1→19→20→21→33.

ES	EF
LS	LF

Float = LS-ES or Float=LF-EF

Following each task through the network diagram to determine the longest path is critical in order to establish the total duration throughout the project, the critical path. Those tasks that consist of the critical path will be used to report on project performance in the next Earned Value section (The Critical Path – Earned Value).

Estimating Cost and Resources

After WBS creation and sequencing the project manager can then begin assigning resources and cost based on task PERT durations. The total cost of all work-packages in the WBS is the estimated total "resource" cost of the project with a 5% upper/lower variance. Other cost resources such as equipment or other non-human capital should be added to the total resource cost for total "project" cost. An additional 15% should be added to the total project cost to account for contingency funds. Sometimes, for internal projects it may be impossible to get resource cost because salaries are not published within the organization. In this situation, use a generic cost structure for the internal resources because most of the true project cost will be tied to non-human capital i.e. servers, routers, switches, etc. In this scenario generic resources may be estimated at $90.00 per hour. By taking this approach to use a generic cost rate your project performance using earned value will still be relative to the performance of the project for reporting purposes. All work-packages using resource "X" @ $90.00 per hour will lead to a created deliverable "Y" at cost "Z" after a certain amount of time according to the WBS. The total of all deliverables "Zs" and non-human capital will equal the total "project" cost.

The Critical Path to Earned Value

The critical path to earned value reporting is the process of monitoring and reporting on all tasks on the critical path in an effort to track project performance. Since the longest path of the project and earliest completion time for any project consist of the tasks that make-up the critical path, measuring these tasks using earned value to report on the relative success of the project is a good measure. Earned Value is the actual amount of work effort earned based on the planned work effort based on a point on time. Below are the definitions of the component of earned value.

Milestone
Shows graphical representation of estimated milestones or critical path task

WBS

These are the task ids that ***makeup the critical path***.

Task
Description of milestones or critical path task

Date
Date that milestones or critical path task are due

Weight
Weight that each milestone or critical path task will carry

Project Completion
Progressive percentage of work completed over project duration

Act % Com.
Actual percentage completion of milestone or critical path task at due date

Weight Dollar $
Dollar amount of weighted percentage. This value is added to EV amount if milestones or critical path items are completed ahead of schedule

PV (Planned Value)
This is the progressive amount of work that was planned for the given milestone or critical path due date overtime

EV(Earned Value)
This is the progressive amount of work that was actually earned in dollar amount because upon the percentage of actual work being complete overtime

AC(Actual Cost)
This is the actual cost of work that was done to complete the milestone or critical path task

SV (Schedule Variance)
This is Earned Value - Planned Value. If negative then project is behind schedule. If positive then project is on schedule or ahead of schedule

CV(Cost Variance)
This is Earned Value - Actual Cost. If negative then project is over cost. If positive then project is within cost limitations.

SPI(Schedule Performance Index)
This is the percentage that your baseline schedule is executing compared to actual results.

CPI(Cost Performance Index)
This states that for every 1 dollar invested, we are getting the CPI percentage out of every dollar.

EAC (Total Budget at Cost)
This shows how much the project will cost at a given time at the rate of execution (SPI)

ETC(How much more $$ to Spend)
This shows how much more money do we have to spend in order to meet the project at the rate of execution

VAC(How much over budget will I be)
This shows at the end of the project how much money will be under or over budget

Earned Value Graph to Project Schedule
Graphical Representation of planned vs actual completion of milestones or critical path task

History EV
Taken to show history of project progress for Archiving purposes.

Future Completion of Milestones
If some milestones are completed ahead of time. The Dollar Weight of that milestone will be added to the EV amount, thus increasing the SPI Index.

Earned Value Reporting

Actual % Complete:
Targeted Milestone:
Budget: $300,000.00

NETWORK UPGRADE PROJECT

START C | END

Milestones										
WBS	1.2	1.3	1.4.1	1.5	1.6	1.7	1.9.9	5.4	6.0	6.1
Task										
Date	1/1/04	1/2/04	1/3/04	1/4/04	1/5/04	1/6/04	1/7/04	1/8/04	1/9/04	1/10/04
Weight	10	10	10	10	10	10	10	10	10	10
Project Completion	10%	20%	30%	40%	50%	60%	70%	80%	90%	100%
Act % Com.	100%	100%	50%	80%	100%	100%	90%	100%	100%	0%
Weight Dollar $	$30,000	$30,000	$30,000	$30,000	$30,000	$30,000	$30,000	$30,000	$30,000	$300,000
PV	$30,000	$60,000	$90,000	$120,000	$150,000	$180,000	$210,000	$240,000	$270,000	$300,000
EV	$30,000.00	$60,000.00	$75,000.00	$99,000.00	$129,000.00	$159,000.00	$186,000.00	$216,000.00	$246,000.00	$246,000.00
AC	$30,000.00	$60,000.00	$75,000.00	$99,000.00	$129,000.00	$159,000.00	$186,000.00	$216,000.00	$246,000.00	$246,000.00
SV	$0.00	$0.00	($15,000.00)	($21,000.00)	($21,000.00)	($21,000.00)	($24,000.00)	($24,000.00)	($24,000.00)	($54,000.00)
CV	$0.00	$0.00	$0.00	$0.00	$0.00	$0.00	$0.00	$0.00	$0.00	$0.00
SPI	1.00	1.00	0.83	0.83	0.86	0.88	0.89	0.90	0.91	0.82
CPI	1.00	1.00	1.00	1.00	1.00	1.00	1.00	1.00	1.00	1.00
EAC	$300,000.00	$300,000.00	$300,000.00	$300,000.00	$300,000.00	$300,000.00	$300,000.00	$300,000.00	$300,000.00	$300,000.00
ETC	$270,000.00	$240,000.00	$225,000.00	$201,000.00	$171,000.00	$141,000.00	$114,000.00	$84,000.00	$54,000.00	$54,000.00
VAC	$0.00	$0.00	$0.00	$0.00	$0.00	$0.00	$0.00	$0.00	$0.00	$0.00
History EV	$22,500.00	$50,000.00	$80,000.00	$100,000.00	$120,000.00	$180,000.00	$186,000.00	$240,000.00	$230,000.00	$290,000.00
History SPI	0.75	0.83	0.89	0.83	0.80	1.00	0.89	1.00	0.85	0.97

EARNED VALUE GRAPH TO PROJECT SCHEDULE

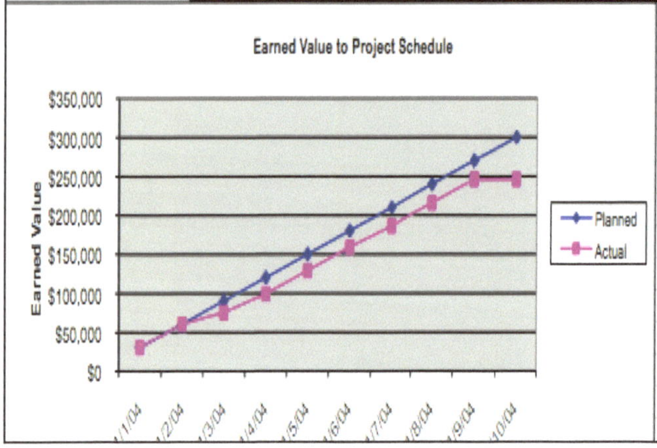

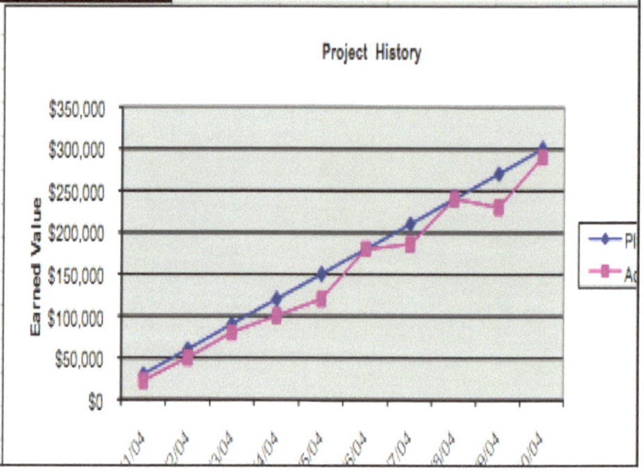

Using this earned value approach, you can measure project performance based on the critical path during the weekly team meetings or review the past performance during lessons learned phase.

Milestone Approach to Earned Value

Same method as the critical path earn value method but the following is different:

WBS
These are the task ids that ***makeup the milestones of the proposed contract***. In the RFP response by the vendor these are the milestones that are in the signed contract proposed by the vendor when the contract is based on a deliverable-based pay schedule. Using this approach will assist in aligning project performance to vendor payment schedule as a method controlling the project. In the diagram below, you can review past history and variance in the project as lessons learned.

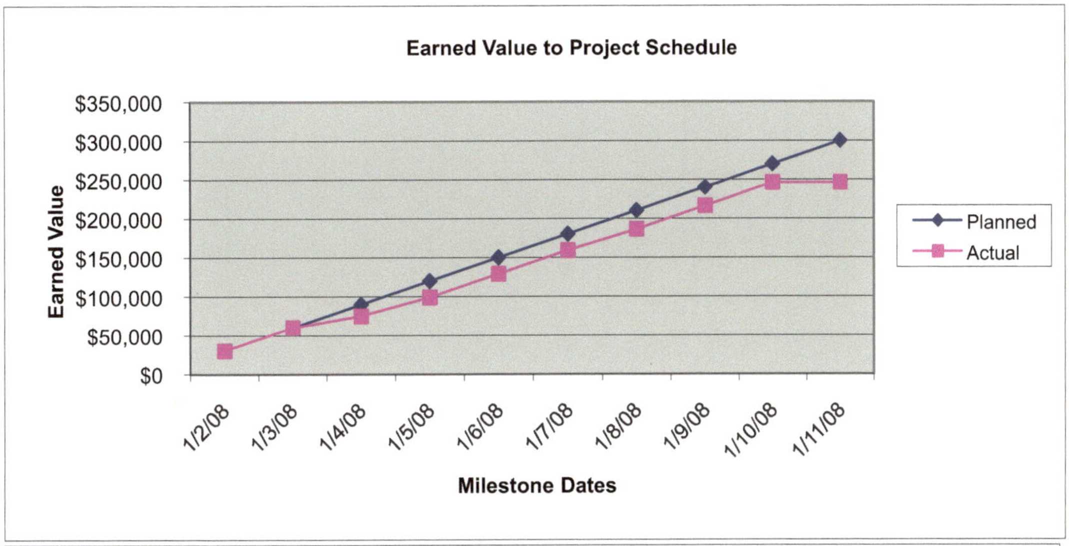

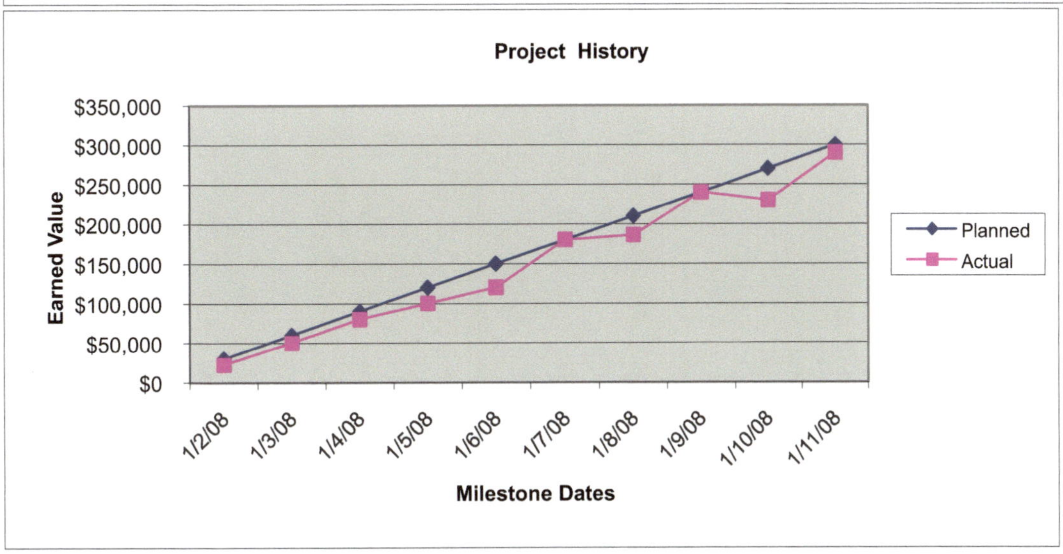

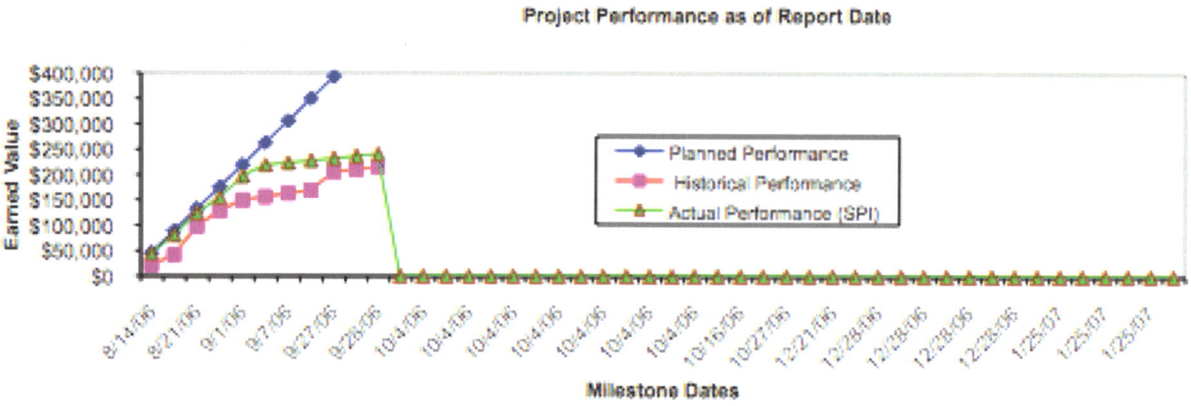

Develop and Implement Procurement Strategy

Planning Process, Stage 2

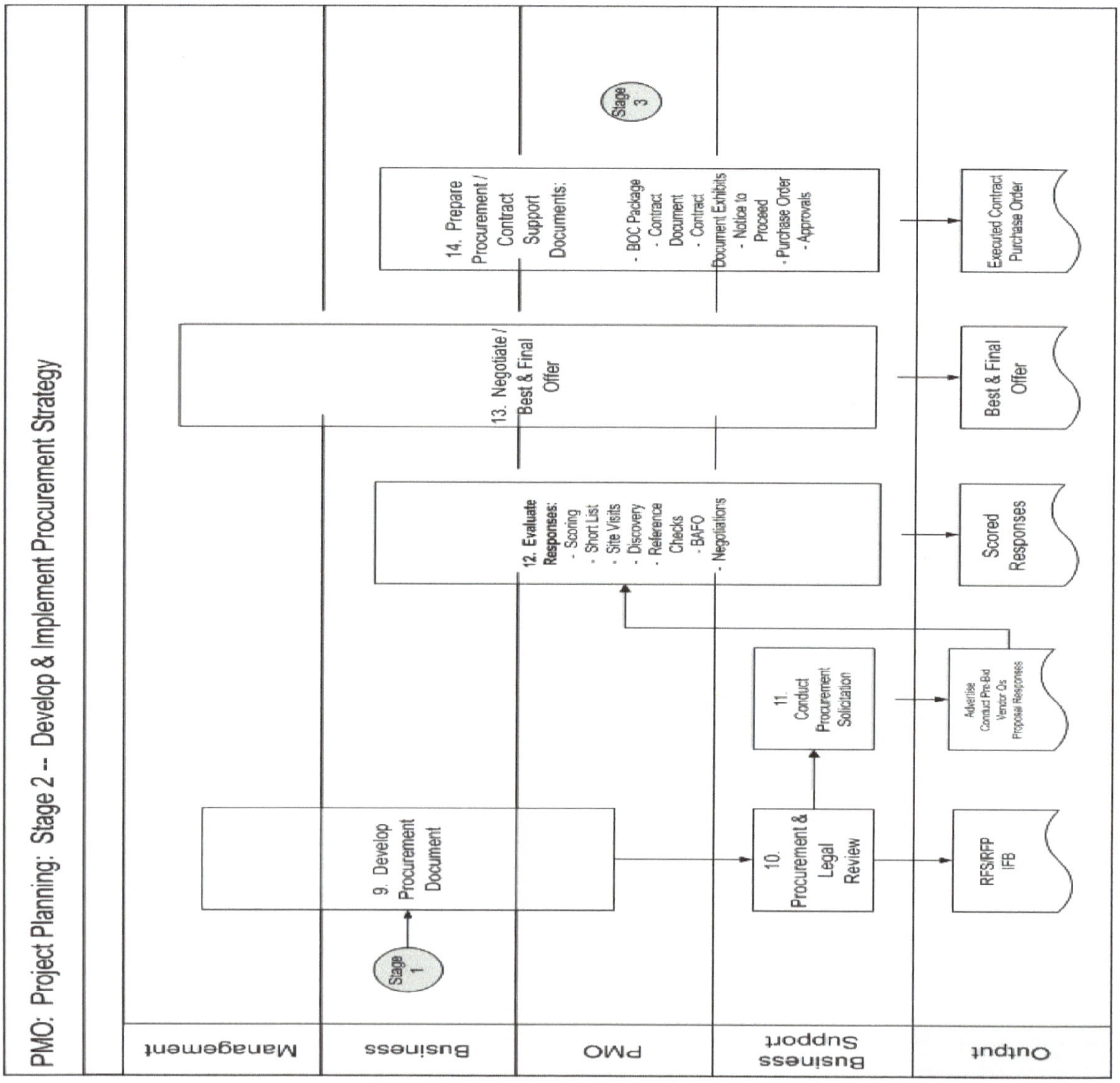

Government agencies invented the Procurement document as a way to determine the lowest bid for products. Government agencies, particularly those that were required to accept the lowest bid, quickly adopted the Procurement document process to itemize the specifications desired in a system. Government agencies continue to justify the Procurement document process as a way to do Needs Assessments, as a way to involve staff, as a tool for negotiating a contract with a vendor, and as the means to appear fair when seeking products and services from competing vendors. The second stage of the Planning Phase is initiated by the completion of a project plan. With the goals and initiatives clearly defined XYZ Company can now engage in the development and implementation of a project procurement strategy. The exhibit below depicts the initiation of Stage 2 of the Planning Process:

The second stage of the Planning Phase is initiated by the development of the Procurement Document otherwise known as Request for Proposal (RFP), Request for Information (RFI), Request for Services (RFS), and Invitation for Bid (IFB).

A Request for Proposal (RFP) is a proven method for increasing competition and leveraging negotiations with vendors. Some of the benefits to be realized through use of the RFP are:

- Informs vendors that an official contract is pending and encourages them to make their best effort. More rapid and responsive vendor responses result.
- Requires the XYZ Company to specify what it proposes to purchase. If the requirements analysis has been prepared rigorously, it can be incorporated quite easily into the RFP.
- Alerts vendors that the selection process is competitive.
- Forces vendors to respond factually to the identified requirements. Vendors know that if selected, they are contractually bound by their previous representations. (It is not uncommon for a vendor to hedge about capabilities of hardware during the contract negotiation. The hedging can be eliminated quickly and effectively when the vendor is reminded about previous representations in the RFP response.)
- Is designed to be distributed to all potential vendors both pre-qualified and non-qualified.

A Request for Qualifications (RFQ) is a document, which is issued by the project team to a wide group of potential suppliers to enable them to register an interest in becoming a preferred supplier for the project. To enable suppliers to formally register their interest, they must provide information regarding their Company, product offering and approach towards satisfying the needs of the project.

A Request for Services (RFS) is a document similar in nature to the RFP but is submitted only to a pool of pre-qualified vendors.

An Invitation for Bid (IFB) is issued to a pool of vendors whose status could be pre-qualified or non-qualified. This form of procurement is used to solicit bids for materials and commodities (i.e. hardware, software, common services). The award under the IFB is generally given to the lowest bidder.

The Procurement document is an essential instrument that enables XYZ Company to solicit the aid of qualified and non-qualified vendors to address their strategic business objectives. The Procurement document also helps define the parameters of evaluation for all respondents. It is up to The ITS PMO management and project team to determine the best procurement option (best suited to meeting project objectives, while providing value for money). They must identify the risks for each procurement model. To determine which Procurement document is appropriate for a given project several factors may need to be considered. The primary factor is the dollar amount required for the specific project.

The exhibit below highlights the activities comprising the second stage of the Planning Phase.

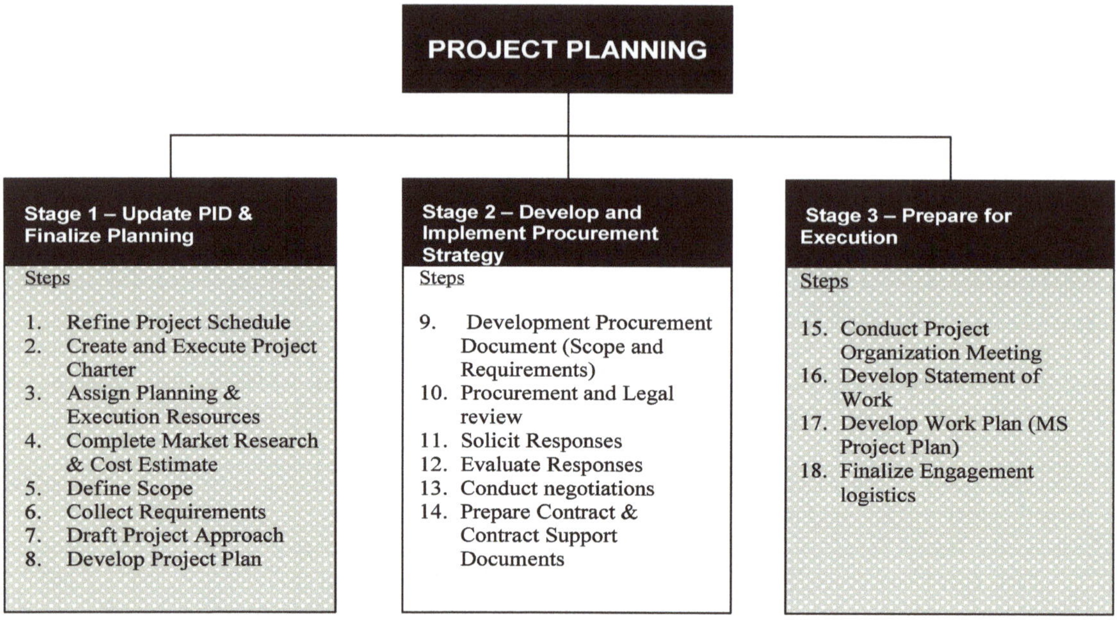

Inputs, Outputs and Tools

The inputs and outputs for Stage 2 are as follows:

- Inputs:
    - Project Plan
- Outputs:
    - Procurement document
    - Executed Contract (Vendor Response)
    - Purchase Order

Timeframe/Total Duration (Ranges from 1 week to 2 months)

The procurement document creation process begins when the approved project time line has been established by The ITS PMO and business stakeholder. They are careful to keep into consideration limitations in human resources and technology infrastructure before deploying projects.

Each procurement document has a range of time parameters associated with it.

- Request for Services averages around two (2) months to complete.
- Request for Proposal must be released to the general public for a minimum of 1 month.
- Invitation for Bid averages no more than 1 month to complete
- Factors that may extend the timeline:
    - Vendor requests for extension to due date
    - Vendor questions may also extend the due-date as they can take a while to answer or they may force a change in the Procurement Document due to errors or conflicting or ambiguous language
    - The evaluation process (internal evaluations of responses can be extremely time consuming or interrupted by existing responsibilities to the XYZ Company)
    - Purchase order creation by Procurement department can be exceedingly lengthy

Resource Allocation

The following resources participate during the "Develop and Implement Procurement Strategy" Stage:

- Executive Sponsor
- Business Owner
- The ITS PMO Management Sponsor (CIO or ACIO for Applications or Infrastructure, depending on project scope and complexity)
- The ITS PMO Senior Portfolio Manager
- The ITS PMO Project Manager
- Key Stakeholders (here includes XYZ Company Procurement and Legal departments)

Step	Executive Sponsor	Business Owner	The ITS PMO Mgmt	Sr. Portfolio Manager	The ITS PMO PM	Other Key Stakeholders
9 – Develop Procurement Document	A	A/R	A	C	R	C
10 – Procurement & Legal Review		I	I	I	R	A
11 – Conduct Procurement Solicitation	I	C	I	C	R	A
12 – Evaluate Responses	I	A/R	A/R	I	R	R
13 – Prepare Contract & Supporting Documents		R	C	C	R	A

Stage Description – Activities requiring completion to adequately plan for the project

The "Update PID and Finalize Planning" stage consists of five (5) primary steps. This section provides detailed instructions for each of those steps.

Make or Buy Decisions

During the Planning Process a company will come to a make or buy decision in producing their project deliverables based on the goal of the initiative. Should we make or use internal resources to complete the project, should we go through the RFP process to complete the project or should there be a mix of both. To determine the answer to that question, a business case is needed to answer that question. Creating a business case for the make or buy decision will give Senior Management. As we previous mentioned, the PID document back in initiation provided us with projects that were aligned with the Strategic Plan of the organization, the business case at this point will decide do we internal make the PID deliverables using our own resources or do we procure the resources external to meet our needs. Also, asking the question of should we lease or buy-networking equipment serves the same purpose. Below are the general sections of a business case that will assist management in making the correct decision as to whether make or buy.

1. Objective of Proposed Project
2. Reason for Proposed Project
3. Regulatory Mandate
4. Description of Proposed Solution
5. Technology Design to Proposed Solution
6. User Groups and Key Stakeholders
7. Project Assumptions
8. Known Dependencies and Constraints
9. Steps Taken Previously to Address the Business Need
10. Financial Metrics

The following methods will be used to represent the financial metrics for XYZ Project

1 **Qualitative Benefit Analysis**
2 **Net Cash Flow**
3 **Cumulative Cash Flow**
4 **Payback**
5 **Return on Investment (ROI)**
6 **Net present value (NPV)**
7 **Internal Rate of Return**

11. Qualitative Benefit

The qualitative benefit analysis outlines at a high level and at its simplest form will provide an indicating of successes over particular measurable categories. This analysis is subjective

(green)	Indicates that high benefit exist or has low impact or is easy to execute
(yellow)	Indicates that a benefit exist or has medium impact or can be a challenge to execute
(orange)	Indicates that a low benefit exist or has high impact or is difficult to execute

Qualitative Benefit Analysis		
Measurable Categories	**Descriptions**	**Benefit/Impact**
Resources	• Are there adequate resources available to complete the project with minimal impact to the user	
Equipment Purchase	• Are there contingency funds available for the project • Is the project properly funded	
Professional Services Contract	• Do we have access to external resources if needed • CHA current Procurement process may be challenge	
Cost Savings	• Are there current and future cost saving opportunities to XYZ Company	
Ease of Use, Flexibility, Scalability	• How does the proposed infrastructure compare against the current network infrastructure	
Success Factor	• How difficult is this project to implement without impact to the users	
Impact to XYZ Company users	• Minimal risk exist with the implementation of proposed solution	
Benefit to XYZ Company organization	• Does the solution provide any benefit to XYZ Company	

12. Net Cash Flow

Cash flow is the fundamental financial metric that will used for the XYZ Project business case. Each important cost or benefit impact leads to an expected cash flow result, or is otherwise assigned value in cash flow terms. Most other financial metrics in the analysis derive from the summary totals at the bottom of the cash flow statement(s). The Following cash flow figures will outline:

1) Source Date
2) Our Proposed Solution
3) Business As Usual (Current Solution)
4) Incremental Cash Flow: Proposed – Business As Usual

The Net Incremental Cash Flow will be the basis for all of the other financial metrics outlined in the continued financial sections.

13. Data quantitative analysis and time analysis:

14. The Proposed Solution

15. The Business As Usual

16. The Incremental Cash Flow Proposal – Business As Usual

17. Cumulative Cash Flow

18. Payback

19. Return on Investment (ROI)

20. Net Present Value (NPV)

21. Recommendation Summary: Make or Buy…Purchase or Lease

Graphical examples of Purchase equipment vs. Lease equipment

Lease Factors

Lease Rate Factors

Enter the standard Lease Rate Factors that will be used for Public Sector and Private Sector Customers

Standard Lease Rate Factors by Customer Type

Public Sector Tax Exempt Lease Term	Hardware Lease Factor	Smartnet Lease Rate Factor	Deployment Lease Rate Factor
36 Months	0.02921	0.02778	0.02921
48 Months	0.02235	0.02138	0.02235
60 Months	0.01825	0.01755	0.01825

Default Assumptions

Default Assumptions

Variable	Default
Enter changes to defaults in yellow area	
Global Default Values	
Cost of Money used in Present Value Calculations	6.5%
Current Cost Default Values	
Monthly Net Centrex Fee per line	$ 25.00
Percent of users that move, add, or change in a year	25%
Cost of Moves, Adds, Changes	$ 90
T1 Costs per month per remote site	$ 150
Long Distance Cost per user per month if remote	$ 5.00
Cisco Cost Default Values	
Number of users per PRI	80
PRI cost per month	$ 400
Number of FXO (POTS) lines per remote site	2
FXO (POTS) cost per month	25.00
Deployment cost default percent of Hardware net cost	25%
Smartnet default percent of Hardware List Price	9%
Blended list cost of IP Phones and User Licenses	$ 425.00
End User Discount	42%
Lease Type and Rate Factors	
Public Sector Lease (Y or N)	Y

Assumptions

XYZ

Voice Comparison Assumptions

Enter changes to assumptions in yellow area

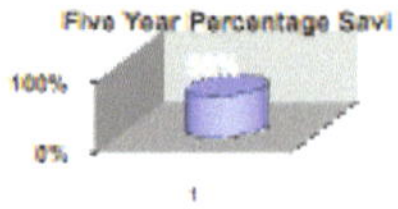

Variable	Assumption	Default	Comments
Current Cost Assumptions			
Customer Name	XYZ	none	Enter Customer Name
# Phones	1500	none	Approximate number of phones
# of Remote Locations	50	0	Number of remote sites
Monthly net Centrex fee per line	32	$ 25.00	Default: Monthly fee per line
Current monthly PBX/Key System lease cost			Default: none
Current monthly PBX/Key System maintenance			Default: none
Current monthly voicemail maintenance	$ 700	$ 2,344	Default 15% of voicemail cost per year
Monthly conference calling expense to be reduced	$ 4,000	$ 7,500	Default $5 per user per month
Percent of users that move, add, or XYZnge in a year		25%	Default users that move per year X $ 90
Monthly cellular expense to be eliminated		$ -	If applicable, estimate $60 per user per month
Monthly local and long distance to be eliminated	$ 1,000	$ 3,750	Default: Per remote user $ 5.00 per month
Monthly savings from Telecom line consolidation	$ 1,000	$ 7,500	Default one T1 line per remote site/mo.
Annual Personnel Savings		$ -	If unsure, leave blank
Other cost avoidance - enter monthly cost & description		$ -	
Cisco Solution Assumptions			
Voicemail or Unified Messaging included? (V, U, or N)	U	V	Default includes voicemail, and not unified msg.
Inline power switches required? (Y or N)		N	Default inline powered switches not included
Conference Connection included? (Y or N)		Y	Defaul includes Conference Connection
Equipment leased or one time purXYZse (L or P)		L	Default finance equipment as operating lease
Deployment leased or one time purXYZse (L or P)		L	Defaul finance deployment as capital lease
Number of PRI's per month		19	Default one for 80 users
Number of FXO lines for remote sites		100	Default per site: 2 if remote
Other costs - enter monthly cost & description			
Approximate hardware list cost		$ 1,057,500	Default calculated based on options selected
Deployment Costs		$ 163,338	Default based on 25% of Hardware net cost
Annual Smartnet List Cost		$ 55,202	Default based on 9% of Hardware net cost
Operating Lease Term in Months (36, 48, or 60)		60	Default 60 months

Cost Comparisons

Description	Assumptions	5 Year Total	Annual Cost	Monthly Cost	60 Month Net Present Value
Current Costs	**1500 Phones**				
Centrex Fee	Monthly Centrex fee including all taxes	$ 2,880,000	$ 576,000	$ 48,000	$ 2,393,671
Current Lease Costs	Current PBX/Key lease cost	$ -	$ -	$ -	$ -
Maintenance	PBX and voicemail maintenance	$ 46,415	$ 8,400	$ 700	$ 38,341
Voice Conferencing	Estimated conference calling	$ 240,000	$ 48,000	$ 4,000	$ 199,473
Moves, Adds, XYZnges	Annual MAC's X $ 90	$ 168,750	$ 33,750	$ 2,813	$ 140,254
Local long distance	Local and site to site	$ 56,506	$ 12,000	$ 1,000	$ 47,144
Cellular Cost	Current Cellular cost to be eliminated	$ -	$ -	$ -	$ -
PSTN, PRI, T1 lines	Savings from line consolidation	$ 56,506	$ 12,000	$ 1,000	$ 47,144
Other Cost Avoidance		$ -	$ -	$ -	$ -
Personnel	Personnel consolidation savings	$ -	$ -	$ -	$ -
Total		**$ 3,448,178**	**$ 690,150**	**$ 57,513**	**$ 2,866,028**
Proposed Voice Costs					
Voice Equipment	Call Manager, Servers, and Phones	$ 443,091	$ 88,618	$ 7,385	$ 161,038
Voicemail, Unified Messaging	Includes Unified Messagins	$ 190,577	$ 38,115	$ 3,176	$ 162,336
Inline Power Switches	Inline powered switches not included	$ -	$ -	$ -	$ -
Conference Calling	Includes conference connection	$ 38,115	$ 7,623	$ 635	$ 32,467
Voice PRI's	PRI's Cost 19 X $ 400	$ 423,798	$ 90,000	$ 7,500	$ 353,583
PSTN Lines	FXO lines 100 X $ 25	$ 141,266	$ 30,000	$ 2,500	$ 117,861
Other Costs		$ -	$ -	$ -	$ -
Deployment Cost	Baseline deployment capital lease	$ 178,899	$ 35,780	$ 2,982	$ 148,689
Maintenance	5 Year Prepaid Maintenance	$ 290,636	$ 58,127	$ 4,844	$ 241,558
Total		**$ 1,706,382**	**$ 348,264**	**$ 29,022**	**$ 1,217,532**
Cost Savings					
Savings		**$ 1,741,796**	**$ 341,886**	**$ 28,491**	**1,648,497**
Percent Savings		**50.5%**	**49.5%**	**49.5%**	**57.5%**

Cash Flow Summary

Year 1 Total	Year 2 Total	Year 3 Total	Year 4 Total	Year 5 Total	5 Year Total	5 Year Net Present Value
$ 576,000	$ 576,000	$ 576,000	$ 576,000	$ 576,000	$ 2,880,000	$ 2,393,671
$ -	$ -	$ -	$ -	$ -	$ -	$ -
$ 8,400	$ 8,820	$ 9,261	$ 9,724	$ 10,210	$ 46,415	$ 38,341
$ 48,000	$ 48,000	$ 48,000	$ 48,000	$ 48,000	$ 240,000	$ 199,473
$ 33,750	$ 33,750	$ 33,750	$ 33,750	$ 33,750	$ 168,750	$ 140,254
$ 12,000	$ 11,640	$ 11,291	$ 10,952	$ 10,624	$ 56,506	$ 47,144
$ -	$ -	$ -	$ -	$ -	$ -	$ -
$ 12,000	$ 11,640	$ 11,291	$ 10,952	$ 10,624	$ 56,506	$ 47,144
$ -	$ -	$ -	$ -	$ -	$ -	$ -
$ -	$ -	$ -	$ -	$ -	$ -	$ -
$ 690,150	**$ 689,850**	**$ 689,593**	**$ 689,378**	**$ 689,207**	**$ 3,448,178**	**$2,866,028**
$ 134,357	$ 134,357	$ 134,357	$ -	$ -	$ 403,070	$ 355,841
$ 90,000	$ 87,300	$ 84,681	$ 82,141	$ 79,676	$ 423,798	$ 353,583
$ 30,000	$ 29,100	$ 28,227	$ 27,380	$ 26,559	$ 141,266	$ 117,861
$ -	$ -	$ -	$ -	$ -	$ -	$ -
$ 35,780	$ 35,780	$ 35,780	$ 35,780	$ 35,780	$ 178,899	$ 148,689
$ 58,127	$ 58,127	$ 58,127	$ 58,127	$ 58,127	$ 290,636	$ 241,558
$ 348,264	**$ 344,664**	**$ 341,172**	**$ 203,428**	**$ 200,142**	**$ 1,437,669**	**$1,217,532**
$ 341,886	**$ 345,186**	**$ 348,421**	**$ 485,951**	**$ 489,065**	**$ 2,010,509**	**$1,648,497**
50%	**50%**	**51%**	**70%**	**71%**	**58%**	**57.5%**

5 Year Cash Flow Comparison

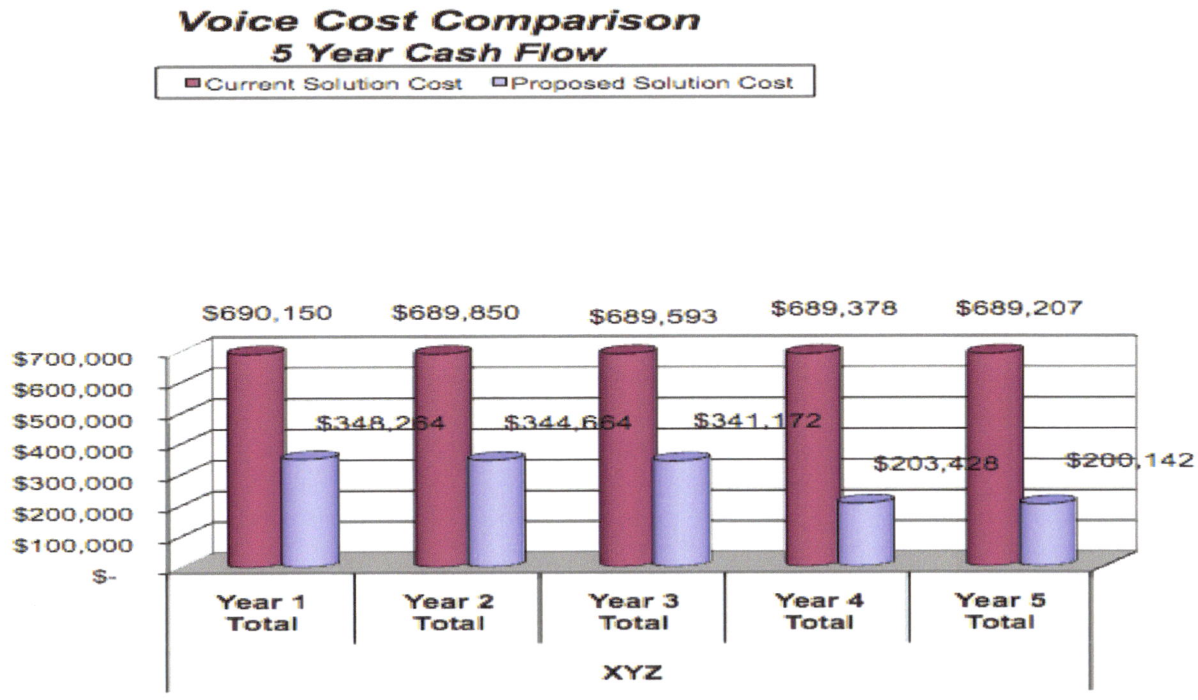

5 Year Cost Comparison

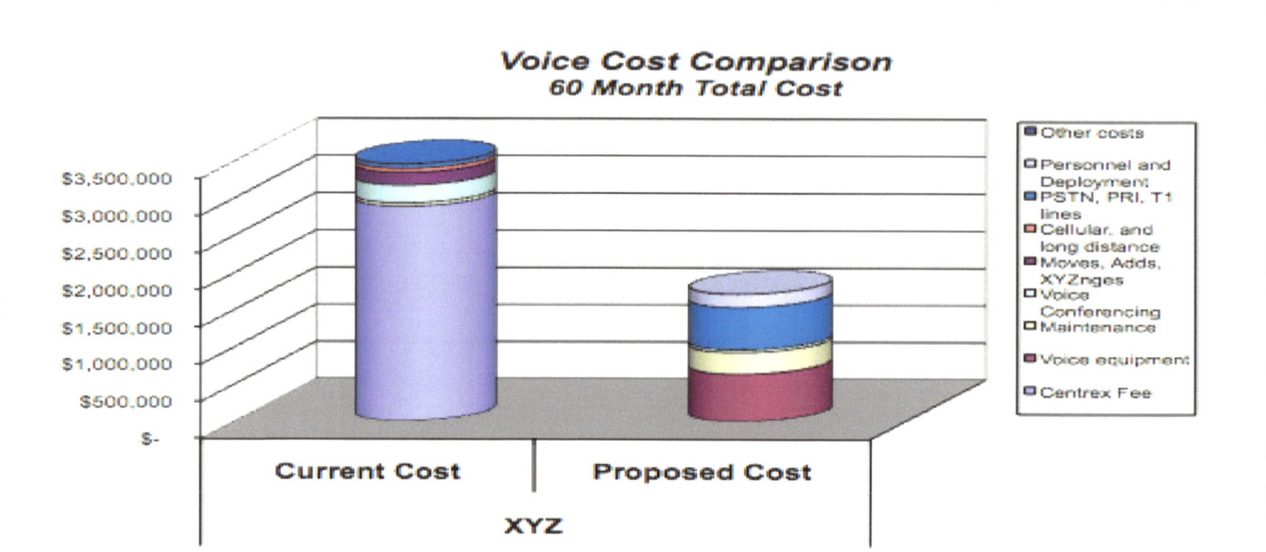

Recommendation: Due to the positive cash flow and high ROI , it is my recommendation to purchase the equipment instead of leasing the equipment given the immediate payback and positive net cash flow within the five-year period.

Step 9 – Develop Procurement Document

- **Objective:** To develop a document that clearly defines the business need and outlines all requirements necessary for evaluation and acceptance.

- **Instructions:**
  - **Determine Procurement document type (RFS, RFP, IFB, and RFQ)**. The determination is based on risk analysis, project complexity, and the timing required for project accomplishment. Review the project scope in light of the nature of the work to be accomplished, the magnitude and complexity of the work, the timing associated with project delivery, and the consideration of the consequences if something goes wrong.
  - **Obtain Procurement document template** (*reference knowledge repository)
  - **Complete the Procurement document**
  - **Submit Procurement document for The ITS PMO management approval**. In order to release the Procurement document to the public it must first go through several levels of approval. First level is The ITS PMO management, second level is department director, and third level is division managing director

- **Estimated Time Duration:**
  - As stated before there are several variables that can impact the duration of the creation of procurement document, however an average time required is one (1) month.

- **Resource Participation**
    - The business owner and The ITS PMO PM are jointly responsible for creation of Procurement document.
    - The ITS PMO Management must review and approve the Procurement document

Procurement Document Template for a Request for Services (RFS)

The following is a detailed listing of the components of a RFS, the most typical procurement document a PM will use:

- Project Overview
- Scope of Services
- Calendar of Procurement Events
- Submittals
- Pre-Proposal Conference
- Evaluation Criteria and Scoring
- Selected Contractual Provisions
- General Instructions
- Addenda to this Request for Services
- Interpretation
- Questions
- Attachments

Project Overview

- Project Overview - An explanation of why the Procurement Document is being issued and a description of the project. Include the purpose of the project and problems that must be addressed (such as the limitations of local access networks, rights of ways issues etc.)
- Response Requirements – An explanation of the rules of engagement for the Procurement Document. Specifically, this section identifies the instructions that respondents must comply with in order for them to be considered for award of the bid. **Note:** An important component of this section of the Procurement Document is the notification that failure to follow these instructions may be considered an unresponsive proposal and may result in immediate elimination from further consideration. For example, if a Procurement Document is created for the procurement of an ERP system the respondents to the Procurement Document could be required to be software providers of financial systems as well as integrators of such systems. Other parameter examples are as follows:
    - All vendor's submitting proposals agree that their pricing is valid for a minimum of 4 (four) months or 120 days after proposal submission to the XYZ Company.
    - All vendor's participating in this process recognize that the vendor finalists shall be required to develop a Statement of Work with the XYZ Company that will be incorporated into the implementation services agreement. Vendors will not be compensated for this or any other part of the procurement process.
    - In an effort to maintain fairness in the process, all inquiries concerning this procurement are to be directed to the XYZ Company Purchasing Agent. Any attempt to contact XYZ Company appointed officials or employees may lead to immediate elimination from further consideration.
    - The XYZ Company reserves the right to reject any or all proposals if it determines that select proposals are not responsive to the RFS or if the proposals themselves are judged not to be in the best interest of the organization. Moreover, the XYZ Company reserves the right to reconsider any proposal submitted at any phase of the procurement. It also reserves the right to meet with vendors at any time to gather additional information. Finally the XYZ Company reserves the right to cancel this

solicitation if that is deemed to be in the best interest of the Authority.

- The XYZ Company expects to sign a joint licensing and implementation services agreement (i.e., one license and implementation contract). This RFS will be let to XYZ Company pre-approved vendor list under the category "Management Consulting". The selected vendor will be considered the primary vendor and engagement manager.
- Integration with and Adherence to XYZ Company The ITS PMO Project Management Standards: The XYZ Company Information Technology Services Department has implemented a set project management standards, overseen by the Senior Portfolio Manager which govern the coordination and delivery of technology initiatives, including this engagement. Pre-qualified vendors will be required to integrate with The ITS PMO project management standards when sharing status, resource-loaded work plans, risks, and issues; as well as to use standardized change control, project initiation, and issue/risk/change escalation procedures. **Utilization of project management standards approved by the Senior Portfolio Manager is mandatory for all projects.**

- **Scope of Services**
  - Purpose - Provide a brief overview of the service(s). Include a brief description of the purpose of the procurement, type of services required, any planning activities, references to data/reports related to the procurement.
  - Scope – Identify the areas impacted by the procurement.
  - Required business Functionality – Describe desired functionality that is required of the vendor's solution or service.
  - XYZ Company Computing Environment - Describe the technology requirements or constraints of the XYZ Company. The XYZ Company is moving towards a more standardized technology environment that emphasizes the use of open technology and provides for more universal access to the XYZ Company's data. The XYZ Company seeks to minimize the technology impact of implementing new application systems. **The XYZ Company requires that any new technology proposed by the vendor be compatible with existing environments and maximizes the use of existing technology platforms and systems.**

Calendar of Procurement Events

The calendar of procurement events highlights the steps from release of the RFS to the award of the bid. The exhibit below is an example.

Sample Procurement Calendar

Key Activity/Event	Event Date
XYZ Company Issues Request for Services (RFS)	April 1, 2004
Pre-Proposal Conference	**April 16 - 11:00 am**
Deadline for Written Questions to be submitted. (If e-mailing, attach a MS Word document.)	April 19; 5:00 pm
XYZ Company issues an Addendum with responses to all vendor questions.	April 26
Deadline for Pre-Qualified Vendors to Submit Proposals	**Wednesday, May 12; 3:00 pm**
Short List of Vendors Developed	May 12

Short listed Vendor Demonstrations of Software	May 26 – June 9
Discovery Sessions (Optional)	May 26 – June 9
Site Visits (Tentative)	June 14 – 25
Final Presentations and Negotiations Vendors in the competitive range will be notified of Final Presentations and Negotiations. Vendors must be able to meet within 48 hours of notification.	June 21 – July 2
Work Plan Approved	July 19
Contract Issued	July 19, 2004

Note: Pre-Qualified Vendors must submit their questions and proposals by the respective dates and times listed above unless the XYZ Company gives prior written notice of a change in such dates and/or times. In such event, the changed date(s) and time(s) set forth in the notice(s) will control. The XYZ Company may send any of its written notices by mail, fax, or e-mail, or by publishing any of them on the XYZ Company's web site. XYZ Company notices that are published on the XYZ Company's web site will be deemed received by all Pre-Qualified Vendors on the date such notices are first published. The XYZ Company's not mailing, faxing or e-mailing a written notice to a Pre-Qualified Vendor when such notice was published on the XYZ Company's web site will not in any way be deemed to prejudice or favor that Pre-Qualified Vendor, even if the XYZ Company mailed, faxed, or e-mailed that same notice to another Pre-Qualified Vendor. For this reason, the XYZ Company strongly urges all Pre-Qualified Vendors wishing to submit a proposal under this RFS to check the XYZ Company's web site frequently for any notices regarding this RFS.

Submittals (Requirements)

- Cover Letter of Intent – Is a signed document authorized by a vendor's principals (i.e. CEO, CFO, COO) that declares their commitment to provide services and deliverables (as such terms are defined in ARTICLE I, Section 1.2 of the Master Agreement) described in the RFS and indicating that the offer is good for at least one hundred twenty (120) days? The cover letter also includes a statement that the vendor understands that XYZ Company will consider all cost and business terms to be negotiable and not artificially constrained by internal corporate polices.

- Profile of Proposed Partners/Sub-Contractors - Pre-Qualified Vendors shall provide information about their company and their respective subcontractors/partners so that the XYZ Company can evaluate financial stability and ability to support the commitments set forth in response to the RFS. The XYZ Company, at its option, may require a vendor to provide additional support and/or clarify requested information. The following information relative to **each** partner and subcontractor (**not**) the Pre-Qualified Vendor) proposed to be used by the Pre-Qualified Vendor:

    - The legal name of the individual or entity, headquarters address, and web site address (if any).

    - If an entity, the entity's legal form of business (i.e. a corporation, partnership, limited liability company, or other entity, if the entity is a corporation, whether it is publicly or privately held; the entity's State of formation, and whether it is authorized to do business in the State of Illinois).

- A brief background and overview of the entity or individual.
- Details of any past, existing, pending or expected litigation, mediation and alternative dispute resolutions facing the individual or entity as it would relate to the products or services provided to existing and/or former customers and as it may affect the Services and Deliverables proposed to be provided to the XYZ Company under the Pre-Qualified Vendor's proposal.
- Names of the principals
- How long the company has been in business.
- A brief description of the company size and organization.
- How long the company has been selling the proposed software or services to public sector clients.
- A list of customer installations both public and private. For each installation identify the number of users. Please categorize the list by: Public Housing installations, current projects, projects anticipated crossing the duration of this request, and the staff assigned to the current and anticipated projects.
- Audited financial statements or annual reports from the previous two (2) years, or the two (2) most recently available, or such other information as is reasonably acceptable to the XYZ Company, for the software vendor and any subcontractors.
- Any material (including letters of support or endorsement from clients) indicative of the vendor's capabilities.
- Brief summary, indicating the specific role for all subcontractor(s) listed in your proposal.
- The Pre-Qualified Vendor shall provide it's most recent, audited financial statement.
- The Pre-Qualified Vendor and Partners/Subcontractors shall submit a Dun & Bradstreet Business Information Report run at the time of proposal submittal.

o Scope of Services - This section of the proposal shall include a general discussion of the vendor's understanding of the overall project, the scope of work proposed, and a summary of the proposal features of the software product and services.

- Proposed Application Software and Computing Environment - The vendor must present the specific products and versions being proposed. The response to this section must also detail the features and capabilities of the proposed application software.
- Project Approach and Implementation - A detailed description of the Pre-Qualified Vendor's project approach and methods so that the XYZ Company can clearly understand the manner in which the Pre-Qualified Vendor would proceed if awarded this engagement. Also described in the section the explicit steps to be taken to mobilize for and perform under a Notice-to-Proceed awarded under this RFS, and the timeframe for completion.
- Database and Technology Architecture - The Vendor shall identify the ideal database platform for the proposed software. In the event there is more than one suitable database platform, list all options indicating the relative strengths and drawbacks (if any) of each.
- Third Party / Optional Products - The vendor shall explicitly state the name of any third-party products that are part of the proposed solution to the XYZ Company list of requirements. For example the ERP Software may not include a module for Contract Compliance. For each third-party product there shall be a statement about whether the

vendor's contract will encompass the third-party product and/or whether the XYZ Company will have to contract on its own for the product

- Business & Technical Requirements – Vendor responds to a list of requirements by XYZ Company indicating how their solution or service addresses those requirements.
- Training - The vendor shall provide a detailed plan for training our users, based on audience type, i.e., end-users and technical support staff.
- Maintenance and Support – This section specifies the on-going support provided by the vendor.
- Past Experience with Similar Scope and Client References – In this section the vendor provides a description of at least three (3) previous, engagements of similar scope and magnitude, including experience in the public sector, which can be used as references by the Evaluation Committee. **Note:** XYZ Company considers references for both the software and implementation vendors to be important in its decision to award a contract. Any vendor who does not provide CLIENT names and phone numbers may be eliminated for non-responsiveness.
- Cost Proposal - Vendors shall submit an estimate of all project costs. The vendor's cost proposal must be presented in the format provided in Attachment C -- Cost Schedule -- of the RFS.
- Sample Documents – This section is used to review any vendor's warranty or service agreement.

  Submittal Forms - The following documents, properly executed and notarized (to the extent required by the specific document's terms):

  - Status of Partnership with Software Vendor (e.g., Training Received, Certification Received, etc.) -- Attachment A
  - Business and Technical Requirements Responses Fee Proposal Form -- Attachment B.
  - Cost Schedule -- Attachment C
  - Software Training Questionnaire -- Attachment D
  - Software Maintenance and Support Questionnaire -- Attachment E
  - Vendor Reference Information -- Attachment F
  - MBE/WBE/DBE Utilization Plan -- Attachment G
  - Section 3 Utilization Plan -- Attachment H

Pre-Proposal Conference

A mandatory pre-proposal conference is scheduled on the date and at the time set forth for it in ARTICLE III "CALENDAR OF PROCUREMENT EVENTS" presented above. The pre-proposal conference will be held at the XYZ Company's Board Room located on the 6th floor of the XYZ Company's Administrative building at 8820 S Stony Island Blvd., Chicago, IL 60661. It is requested that each Pre-Qualified Vendor notify the XYZ Company, via an e-mail addressed to: johndoe@dummies.org of the number of participants the Pre-Qualified Vendor estimates to have in attendance at this pre-proposal conference. **Please note all pre-qualified vendors who submit a proposal must attend the pre-proposal conference.** Failure to attend could lead to disqualification.

Evaluation and Selection Method

The XYZ Company has established a method for reviewing and evaluating each response and refining the list of possible solutions for the XYZ Company. An Evaluation Team representing the various business interests of the XYZ Company has been assembled and will report to an Executive Steering Committee (ESC). The Evaluation Team is charged with completing the evaluation process as described below, refining the list of potential solutions, and reporting their progress and ultimately their recommendation to the Chief Information Officer (CIO) and the ESC.

The ESC, comprised of key XYZ Company executives, will confirm that the recommended solution properly meets the overall goals of the XYZ Company. The ESC will provide a governance role once the resulting software implementation project is established.

The XYZ Company has established the following as the evaluation and selection approach for the financial, procurement, human resources management and payroll system. The chart below identifies key tasks in the evaluation process and the party responsible for its completion. The chart is presented in approximate sequential order:

	Task	**Performed By**
1.	Conduct an initial review of all responses for completeness, adherence to submittal requirements and responsiveness.	Purchasing
2.	Conduct in-depth reviews of all proposals found to be responsive and in compliance with submittal requirements. Responses will be reviewed for qualifications and demonstrated competence.	Evaluation Team
3.	Rank each proposal to establish a competitive range. Competitive range responses will be invited to demonstrate their software and present their services.	Evaluation Team
4.	Evaluate software demonstrations and implementation approach and services.	Evaluation Team and Business Users
5.	Conduct and evaluate optional, "Discovery Sessions" to provide clarification or additional information regarding the response, if needed.	Evaluation Team, Business Users and Vendors
6.	Develop Finalist List and present to Chief Information Officer and the Executive Steering Committee	Evaluation Team
7.	Conduct Competitive Negotiations (optional)	Purchasing/Legal/The ITS PMO/Finance
8.	Recommend Solution to ESC	Purchasing/Legal

XYZ Company reserves the right to use parallel negotiations as a contracting method where discussions will be held with finalists in an effort to secure the best procurement for the XYZ Company.

An award will be made to the most responsive and responsible Respondent whose solution and services are determined to be the most advantageous to the XYZ Company when the evaluation criteria identified below are considered. The Purchasing Director reserves the right to award a contract, accept or reject any and all submittals when it is determined to be in the best interest of the XYZ Company.

Evaluation and Selection Criteria *(sample)*

Below is an example of Evaluation and Selection Criteria used in the selection of a vendor for the implementation of the XYZ Company's Enterprise Resource Planning (ERP) system.
The XYZ Company intends to procure a functionally complete, cost-effective, integrated ERP system. Responses to this RFS will be evaluated and/or selected for further evaluation, according to the following criteria:

1. Responses to business and technical requirements
2. Quality of the proposed implementation plan and services: project management,

implementation approach, training, testing, etc.

3. Quality and relevancy of the proposed team (resumes must be provided)
4. Quality of on-going system maintenance, upgrades, and technical support.
5. Reference able performance of proposed software and implementation services including public sector references (will include site visits and reference checks)
6. Vendor Financial Stability
7. Cost of software and implementation services

The Evaluation Team will evaluate each proposal and will determine in its sole discretion which proposals fulfill the seven (7) evaluation criteria in a way that serves the overall best interest of the XYZ Company. Materials or explanations should be included in each proposal to allow the evaluation criteria to be considered as presented below:

No.	Criteria	RFS Section Reviewed	Max Points
1	Ability to Meet Business and Technical Requirements.	- Business and Technical Requirements -- Attachment B - Site Visits - Discovery Sessions (if any) - ARTICLE IV, Section H -- System Requirements	35
2	Project Approach, Implementation, Understanding of Scope.	ARTICLE IV, Section E and J - Project Approach and Implementation, and Training respectively	20
3	Qualifications and Specialized Experience of Key Personnel	ARTICLE IV, Section E - Project Approach and Implementation	15
4	Maintenance & Support Capabilities	ARTICLE IV; Section K - Maintenance and Support	15
5	Past and/or Current Performance on Similar Engagements and References	ARTICLE IV, Section L – Past Experience with Similar Scope / Client References	10
6	Vendor Financial Stability	ARTICLE IV, Section B 1(x) 2, and 3.	05
7	Cost (evaluated but not weighted)	ARTICLE V, Section M –Cost Proposal	0
	TOTAL		**100**

Participation in XYZ Company's MBE/WBE/DBE and Section 3 Opportunities Plan is mandatory. Although the participation has no numerical weight, the utilization plans are evaluated for responsiveness.

While the proposal's price will not be assigned a specific weight, each proposal must indicate a firm, fixed price for software and maintenance and a "not to exceed" price basis for implementation services. A cost breakdown as identified in Attachment C -- Cost Schedule – must be provided. Your cost breakdown must be reasonable and justifiable and reflect the proposed approach evaluated under ARTICLE IV – Section E. Prior to any face-to-face interview, the XYZ Company may require further information from a Respondent regarding its Proposal and/or request that a Respondent provide other data as required by the XYZ Company. However, the XYZ Company reserves the right to make its decision based solely on the submitted written Proposals without any requests for formal interviews, negotiations or further discussions.

DEMONSTRATIONS/PRESENTATIONS EVALUATION

After the XYZ Company Evaluation Committee has evaluated the Proposals submitted in response to an RFS, the XYZ Company's Contracting Officer establishes a competitive range. Those Respondents determined to be within the competitive range will be notified and unless otherwise indicated shall be required to participate in presentations/negotiations and provide additional information as required by the XYZ Company. Respondents in the competitive range will be provided an agenda detailing what the XYZ Company expects in the demonstrations/presentations in advance of their scheduled demonstrations/presentations. After demonstrations, Respondents in the competitive range will be scored according to a quantitative scale. Below is an example of a 40-point scale used for the ERP implementation project:

CRITERIA	**MAX POINTS**
Degree to which vendor adheres to demonstration script	**10**
Description of proposed Implementation Methodology, feasibility and completeness	**10**
Demonstrated approach to software training	**10**
Degree to which Vendor demonstrates solution meets objectives without customization	**5**
Ease of Use of Software	**5**
Total	**40**

The objective of the presentations/demonstrations is to demonstrate the proposed solution, answer questions, clarify issues, and to provide additional information regarding the vendors' proposals. Presentations are evaluated by the same evaluation committee that originally scored each proposal. Typically, the additional scores are added to the scores utilized to determine the competitive range.

Following the presentations, the evaluation team evaluates and summarizes their findings for each pre-qualified vendor who participates in the presentations, and makes a recommendation to the XYZ Company Contracting Officer. The XYZ Company then makes an award to the responsible Respondent whose offer conforms to the solicitation and is most advantageous to the XYZ Company (i.e., that which represents the best value to the XYZ Company), cost or price and other factors considered.

Selected Contractual Provisions

Procurement documents will often contain a section entitled "Selected Contractual Provisions." The purpose of this component is to explain the terms of the contract for work performed under the Procurement Document. Procurement Document should contain the following stipulations:

A. Contract Award

(i) The term of the work to be performed from an award granted under the RFS shall be until the completion of all services in accordance with the terms of the Master Agreement, this RFS, the Notice(s)-to-Proceed awarded under this RFS, and such other Project Documents that may apply, whichever is sooner.

(ii) The XYZ Company anticipates awarding a firm fixed-price and "not to exceed" contract under each RFS. No award may be made to an individual or entity that is on the list of contractors ineligible to receive awards from the XYZ Company or the United States, as furnished from time to time by HUD.

(iii) The XYZ Company reserves the right to award one or more Notice(s)-to-Proceed in connection with this RFS.

B. Method of Compensation and Payment

Pre-Qualified Vendors must identify distinct phases and Deliverables within their Work Plans and base compensation on the selected completion or delivery of it. Upon completion of the Services and Deliverables, the selected Pre-Qualified Vendor and a XYZ Company representative conduct an examination to certify that the work has been performed satisfactorily and meets Detailed Acceptance Criteria (as such term is defined in ARTICLE III, Section 3.1 of the Master Agreement). The selected Pre-Qualified Vendor will submit a payment request for the work to be certified. The selected Pre-Qualified Vendor shall furnish such supporting documents and additional information as may be required to approve the payment request and the XYZ Company may further request the selected Pre-Qualified Vendor to demonstrate the Deliverables or phase completion pursuant to Acceptance Procedures and Acceptance Criteria (as such terms are defined in ARTICLE III, Section 3.2(A) of the Master Agreement). If the XYZ Company objects to all or any portion of the payment request, it shall notify the selected Pre-Qualified Vendor of its objection and both parties shall make every effort to settle the disputed portion. Notwithstanding the foregoing, the XYZ Company may, at its option, pay the undisputed portion without being deemed to have accepted the disputed portion.

C. Audit and Record Retention Requirements

The XYZ Company retains an irrevocable right on behalf of itself and HUD to independently, or through a third party, review and/or audit the selected Pre-Qualified Vendor's books, documents, papers, and records pertaining to any work awarded under this RFS and disallow any inappropriate billings upon written notice to the Pre-Qualified Vendor. The XYZ Company retains the right to conduct the audit for three (3) years from the date of final payment and all other pending matters are closed in connection with such award.

D. Insurance

The selected Pre-Qualified Vendor agrees to procure and maintain at all times during the term of the work awarded under this RFS the types of insurance specified below in order to protect the XYZ Company from the acts, errors and omissions of the selected Pre-Qualified Vendor and his, her or its officers, officials, subcontractors, joint venture, partners, agents or employees. The insurance carriers used by the selected Pre-Qualified Vendor must be authorized to conduct business in the State of Illinois and have a BEST rating of not less than an "A." The insurance provided shall cover all operations under the awarded work, whether performed by the selected Pre-Qualified Vendor or by his, her or its subcontractors.

The premium costs associated with all insurance requirements shall not be development costs unless otherwise noted.

(i) **Required Insurance Coverage:**

(a) **Workers Compensation and Occupational Disease Insurance:** Workers Compensation and Occupational Disease Insurance in accordance with the laws of the State of Illinois along with Employer's Liability in an amount of not less than $500,000/$500,000/$500,000.

(b) **Commercial/General Liability Insurance** written on an occurrence form **(Primary)** and Umbrella Liability **(Excess):** Commercial/General Liability Insurance written on an occurrence form (Primary) and Umbrella Liability (Excess) is to have limits of not less than One Million Dollars ($1,000,000) per occurrence with an Aggregate of not less than Two Million Dollars ($2,000,000) (i.e. $1,000,000/$2,000,000). In addition to the stipulations outlined above, the insurance policy is to include coverage for Contractual Liability, Products-Completed Operations, Personal & Advertising Injury and will also cover injury to the selected Pre-Qualified Vendor's agents subcontractors, invitees and guests and their personal property. The XYZ Company is to be endorsed as an additional insured on the selected Pre-Qualified Vendor's policy and such insurance will be endorsed as primary and non-contributory with any other insurance available to the XYZ Company.

(c) **Comprehensive Automobile Liability Insurance:** When any motor vehicles (owned, non-owned and hired) are used in connection with the services to be performed, the selected Pre-Qualified Vendor shall provide Comprehensive Automobile Liability Insurance with limits of not less than One Million Dollars ($1,000,000) per occurrence CSL for bodily injury and property damage. The XYZ Company is to be endorsed as an additional insured on the selected Pre-Qualified Vendor's policy and such insurance will be endorsed as primary and non-contributory with any other insurance available to the XYZ Company.

(d) **Professional Liability Insurance:** Professional Liability Insurance covering acts, errors or omissions of the selected Pre-Qualified Vendor's product or work including representations/warranties to the Master Agreement, under this RFS and under the selected Pre-Qualified Vendor's proposal, shall be maintained with limits of not less than One Million Dollars ($1,000,000) per occurrence. Coverage extensions shall include Blanket Contractual Liability and Internet presented issues including but not limited to: Failure of Hotlinks to Work, Failure of Supply Chains, Loss of Data, Theft of Intellectual Property, Transmission of Computer Viruses, Disruption of Service attacks, etc. When policies are renewed or replaced, the policy retroactive date must coincide with, or precede, start of services under the Notice(s)-to-Proceed awarded under this RFS. A Claims-made policy, which is not renewed or replaced, must have an extended reporting period of two (2) years.

(e) **Umbrella Liability:** Umbrella Liability coverage, if applicable, is to follow form of the Primary Insurance requirements outlined in ARTICLE VII, Section D (i)(b) above.

(ii) Related Requirements:

The selected Pre-Qualified Vendor shall advise all insurers of these provisions regarding insurance. The failure of the selected Pre-Qualified Vendor to notify insurers of these provisions shall not relieve the selected Pre-Qualified Vendor from his, her or its insurance obligations under it. Non-fulfillment of the insurance provisions shall constitute a breach of the Master Agreement and the XYZ Company will retain the right to stop work until proper evidence of insurance is provided.

The selected Pre-Qualified Vendor must furnish the XYZ Company's Department of Procurements and Contracts, 626 West Jackson Blvd., 2nd Floor, Chicago, IL 60661, original Certificates of Insurance evidencing this required coverage to be in force on the effective date of the Notice-to-Proceed or such later date as said Notice-to-Proceed may specify, **but in any event no later than immediately prior to the commencement of any work under said Notice-to-Proceed.** In addition, copies of the endorsement(s) adding the XYZ Company to the selected Pre-Qualified Vendor's policy as an additional insured will be required to be submitted to the XYZ Company.

Renewal Certificates of Insurance, requested endorsements, or such similar evidence is to be received by the XYZ Company's Department of Procurements and Contracts prior to expiration of insurance coverage. At the XYZ Company's option, non-compliance may result in one or more of the following actions: (a) The XYZ Company will purchase insurance on behalf of the selected Pre-Qualified Vendor and will charge back all costs to the selected Pre-Qualified Vendor; (b) the selected Pre-Qualified Vendor will be immediately removed from XYZ Company property and the awarded contract evidenced by the Notice-to-Proceed will be revoked; (c) all payments due the selected Pre-Qualified Vendor will be held until the selected Pre-Qualified Vendor has complied with the Master Agreement, this RFS, and all other Project Documents; and/or (d) the selected Pre-Qualified Vendor will be assessed Five Hundred Dollars ($500) for every day of noncompliance. The receipt of any Certificate of Insurance does not constitute agreement by the XYZ Company that the insurance requirements herein have been fully met or that the insurance policies indicated on the certificate are in compliance with same. The insurance policies shall provide for thirty (30) days prior written notice to be given to the XYZ Company in the event coverage is substantially changed, canceled or non-renewed.

If the required insurance is underwritten on a claims made basis, the retroactive date shall be prior to or coincident with the effective date of the Notice-to-Proceed or such later date as said Notice-to-Proceed may specify, but in any event no later than the commencement of any work under said Notice-to-Proceed, and the Certificate of Insurance shall state the coverage is "claims made" and also the retroactive date. The selected Pre-Qualified Vendor shall maintain coverage for the duration specified in this RFS and/or the Notice-to-Proceed, whichever is longer. Any extended reporting period premium (tail coverage) shall be paid by the selected Pre-Qualified Vendor. The selected Pre-Qualified Vendor shall provide to the XYZ Company, annually, a certified copy of the insurance policies obtained pursuant hereto. It is further agreed that the selected Pre-Qualified Vendor shall provide the XYZ Company a thirty (30) days prior written notice in the event of the occurrence of any of the following conditions: aggregate erosion in advance of the retroactive date, cancellation and/or non renewal.

The selected Pre-Qualified Vendor shall require all subcontractors to carry the insurance required herein or the selected Pre-Qualified Vendor may provide the coverage for any or all of its subcontractors, and if so, the evidence of insurance submitted shall so stipulate and adhere to the same requirements and conditions as outlined above. Evidence of such coverage must be submitted to XYZ Company.

The selected Pre-Qualified Vendor expressly understands and agrees that any insurance programs maintained by the XYZ Company shall apply in excess of and will not contribute to insurance provided by the selected Pre-Qualified Vendor for the work awarded under this RFS.

E. Representations and Warranties

In addition to the representations and warranties provided in ARTICLE VIII, Section 8.1 of the Master Agreement, the selected Pre-Qualified Vendor represents and warrants to the XYZ Company that the selected Pre-Qualified Vendor rightfully and legally owns, holds a valid license in or otherwise controls and possesses all rights in all patents, trademarks, service marks, trade names, corporate names, copyrights and applications filed in connection with any of the foregoing, mask works, trade secrets and all other intellectual property rights used in, developed for use in or necessary to conduct the selected Pre-Qualified Vendor's obligations under a Notice-to-Proceed awarded to him/her/it under this RFS (such rights collectively, the "**Intellectual Property Rights**"); that the selected Pre-Qualified Vendor has taken such action to protect the Intellectual Property Rights as is necessary for the selected Pre-Qualified Vendor to perform its obligations under such awarded work as evidenced by such Notice-to-Proceed; that the selected Pre-Qualified Vendor has not received any notice of, nor are there any facts known to the selected Pre-Qualified Vendor which indicate a likelihood of, any infringement or misappropriation by, or conflict with, any third party with respect to the Intellectual Property Rights; that no claim by any third party contesting the validity of any Intellectual Property Rights has been made, is currently outstanding or is threatened; and that the selected Pre-Qualified Vendor has not (i) received any notice of any infringement, misappropriation or violation of any intellectual property rights of any third parties or (ii) infringed, misappropriated or otherwise violated any such third party intellectual property rights in any way that would adversely affect the Intellectual Property Rights.

F. Third Party Claims

The selected Pre-Qualified Vendor shall, at its expense, indemnify and hold the XYZ Company harmless from any third party claims involving the XYZ Company's use of any module, software product or technique provided by the selected Pre-Qualified Vendor.

General Instructions

The purpose of this component is to explain the basic protocols of response submission. Each Procurement Document contains the following:

- Acceptance of Proposals - Proposals for this RFS must be signed, sealed and received in completed form at the XYZ Company's Department of Procurement and Contracts located at 626 West Jackson Boulevard, 2nd Floor, Chicago, IL 60661, no later than the date and time set forth for it in the "CALENDAR OF EVENTS" above. Unsealed proposals will not be accepted. Proposals submitted after the designated date and time will not be accepted for any reason and will be returned, unopened, to the originator. ***Note***: *The XYZ Company reserves the right to accept or reject any or all proposals, issue addenda, or to waive any formalities. Pre-Qualified Vendor may be excluded from further consideration for failure to fully comply with the requirements of this RFS.*

- Time for Receiving Proposals - Proposals received prior to the due date and time will be kept unopened in a secure place. Proposals will not be publicly read or opened and once submitted will become the property of the XYZ Company.
- Withdrawals of Proposals - Proposals may be withdrawn by written or faxed request that is dispatched by the Pre-Qualified Vendor in time for delivery in the normal course of business prior to the time fixed for receipt. Faxed withdrawals must be accompanied by a signed confirmation of the faxed withdrawal, placed in the mail and postmarked by the Pre-Qualified Vendor, prior to the time set for receipt of proposals. The Pre-Qualified Vendor's negligence in preparing a proposal creates no right of withdrawal or modification after the date and time set for receipt opening of the proposals.
- Award of Contract - The XYZ Company may award one or more contracts according to the evaluation criteria contained in this RFS. The Pre-Qualified Vendors to whom awards are made will be notified at the earliest practical date. Each award may be subject to HUD approval. No award may be made to a contractor or firm who is on the list of contractors ineligible to receive awards from the XYZ Company or the United States, as furnished by HUD. **Note:** The XYZ Company reserves the right, at its option, to accept a proposal as submitted by a Pre-Qualified Vendor without negotiations or discussion, to negotiate a more satisfactory proposal, to reject all proposals and secure services by means of non-competitive negotiation in accordance with 24 CFR 85.36(d)(4), or to re-solicit competitive proposals.
- Preparatory Costs - All costs incurred in the preparation and presentation of Proposals shall be wholly borne by each Pre-Qualified Vendor. All supporting documentation and manuals submitted with each Proposal will become the property of the XYZ Company unless otherwise indicated by the Pre-Qualified Vendor at the time of submission. The XYZ Company is not liable for any costs incurred by any Pre-Qualified Vendor prior to issuance of a contract.
- Confidential Material - Any material submitted by a Pre-Qualified Vendor as part of a proposal that is to be considered confidential must be clearly marked as such, but may be subject to disclosure under applicable law.
- Subcontracting - All subcontractors to be used by the selected Pre-Qualified Vendor in its proposed work for the XYZ Company must be identified within the proposal. If the proposed services include the use of subcontractors, the XYZ Company will hold the selected Pre-Qualified Vendor responsible for the services provided by the subcontractors. All subcontracts awarded by the selected Pre-Qualified Vendor shall contain all of the clauses contained in the Master Agreement, this RFS, the Pre-Qualified Vendor's proposal (as applicable) and the awarded Notice-to-Proceed as flow down clauses to all subcontractors in any tier. No Pre-Qualified Vendor shall incorporate the entire agreement between the XYZ Company and the Pre-Qualified Vendor in its agreement with subcontractors. All subcontractors utilized by the selected Pre-Qualified Vendor, if not identified at the time of proposal submission, must receive approval in writing by the XYZ Company's Contracting Officer, prior to utilization of any subcontractors under the awarded work.

Addenda to This Request for Services

If the XYZ Company determines this RFS should be modified before the date set for receipt of proposals, it will inform all prospective Pre-Qualified Vendors by distributing addendum/addenda to this RFS using one or more of the methods described in, and subject to the terms of, Section 2.1 above.

Interpretation
Pursuant to ARTICLE I, Section 1.1 of the Master Agreement, in the event of any direct conflict between the Master Agreement and this RFS, this RFS shall control; and where no direct conflict exists, this RFS shall be deemed to supplement the Master Agreement.

Questions
Pre-Qualified Vendors may communicate only with the XYZ Company's Department of Procurement and Contracts regarding this RFS and the proposals to be submitted under it. All questions or requests for clarification must be made in writing and sent via regular or certified mail, courier delivery, fax or e-mail to John Doe, XYZ Company Buyer.

Attachments

- Attachment A -- Software Certification Verification
- Attachment B – Business and Technical Requirements
- Attachment C – Cost Schedule
- Attachment D – Software Training Questionnaire
- Attachment E -- Software Maintenance and Support Questionnaire
- Attachment F – Vendor Reference Information
- Attachment G – MBE/WBE/DBE Utilization Plan
- Attachment H – Section 3 Utilization Plan

PLEASE NOTE: Although an RFS is the most typical tool for procuring goods and services in The ITS PMO, you may have a need to develop a RFP, RFQ, or IFB at which time you will need to contact and work with your procurement liaison for an appropriate template.

Step 10 – Procurement and Legal Review

- Objective: Provide quality assurance in regards to compliance, to regulated and contractual standards on all formal procurement documents before they are released to the general market place or internal vendor pool.

- **Instructions:**
  - Hand off document to Procurement department.
  - Procurement will then forward Procurement document to legal for their review.

- **Estimated Time Duration**
  - Depends upon the complexity and scope of the product / solution sought.
    - 1 week for Procurement Department
    - 2 week for Legal Department

- **Resource Participation**
  - The Business Owner and The ITS PMO Owner is responsible for forwarding the Procurement document to Procurement Department.

Step 11 – Conduct Procurement Solicitation

Objective: The ITS PMO' role in the solicit response step is to support the procurement department in all communications with vendors responding to the procurement document.

- **Instructions**
  - Review all communications to vendors to ensure technical accuracy

- **Estimated Time Duration**
    - Depends upon the complexity and scope of the product / solution sought.

- **Resource Participation**
        - The ITS PMO PM is responsible for assisting the Procurement Department

Note: *Vendors have a specified time to review procurement document and formulate their response.*

Step 12 – Evaluate Responses

- **Objective:** To assist the Procurement in the evaluation of all vendor responses to the Procurement document

- **Instructions**
    - Review Submittals for responsiveness
    - Call meeting of evaluation committee
    - Distribute proposals to evaluation team
    - Conduct independent reviews follow prescribed guidelines
    - Provide individual score
    - Tally all responses for comparative range
    - Develop recommendations for competitive range/short list
    - Approve competitive range/short list
    - Review short list
    - Notify vendors for presentation
    - Develop demonstration scripts
    - Individually evaluate and rank demonstrations/presentations
    - Conduct site visits and reference checks
    - Tally individual rankings for phase 2; recommend best and final offer (BAFO) process
    - Review and approve request for BAFO
    - Develop and assemble negotiation team
    - Conduct competitive negotiations
    - Recommend awardees
    - Review/Approve recommended vendor
    - Execute Contract
    - Member of the Evaluation Committee – members of the evaluation committee are responsible for scoring the responses received from the vendors
    - Advisor to the Evaluation Committee -- evaluation advisors are called upon to provide specific guidelines to the Committee to facilitate their scoring, e.g., compliance with technology standards, ease of integration, alignment with business need

- **Estimated Time Duration**
    - Depends upon the complexity and scope of the product / solution sought and the volume of responses.
        - For a smaller project with limited duration and scope, e.g., an 8-week project within a specific area of the Authority, may take up to 8 hours to evaluate and score a vendor's approach
        - An enterprise-wide project may require up to one-week conducting research, draft and then validating the approach with the ACIO.

- **Resource Participation**
    - The ITS PMO PM and Business Owner is responsible for assisting the Procurement Department in the evaluations

Step 13 – Negotiate Best and Final Offer

- **Objective:** Obtain the best value for goods and services proposed by vendor.

- **Instructions**
    - Work with vendors to design statement of work
    - Work with vendors to design payment schedules

- **Estimated Time Duration**
    - Depends upon the complexity and scope of the product / solution sought and the volume of responses.

- **Resource Participation**
    - The Business Owner and The ITS PMO PM is responsible for assisting Procurement Department

    -  ***Tip(s) for Success:***
        - ***TIP 1**: Support Legal and Purchasing in defining the scope, timing and logistics for Best and Final Offer*
        - ***TIP 2:** Each project, regardless of size should have a negotiation team assigned, consisting of at least the Business Owner, The ITS PMO (PM), and the DPC.*

Step 14 – Prepare Contract Documents

- **Objective:** Ensure that all required paperwork is complete to allow vendor to start work..

- **Instructions**
    - Check with Procurement to be sure all needed contract and contract-related documents are prepared:
        - Notice to Proceed
        - Purchase Order
        - Contact Documents (Master Services Agreement and / or Amendment to the MSA)

- **Estimated Time Duration**
    - Depends upon the complexity and scope of the product / solution sought and the volume of responses.

- **Resource Participation**
    - The Business Owner and The ITS PMO Owner is responsible for assisting Procurement Department

Contract Types

If from the previous section your company has decided to procure services to complete all project deliverables there are many different ways in procuring contract work. Below are the most common:

- **Request for Proposal**
  The buyer will request one price and will submit a proposal describing in detail all the functional requirements of all deliverables to complete the project.

- **Invitation for Bid**
  The buyer will request one price. Usually these contracts are small in nature so not much detail in required.
- **Request for Quotation**
  Request a price quote for unit of measure: per foot, item unit, etc
- **Time and Material**
  Request a hourly fee to complete the work i.e. $150 per hr
- **Fixed Price**
  One price is agreed upon between the buy and seller to produce all the work. The cost risk is on the seller in that they must ensure that the price they are submitting to does include all of the scope required to do the job. In the public sector must contracts are issued out in the form of a RFP and are Fixed Price.
- **Cost Reimbursable**
  Seller will produce work and all cost are reimbursable to the seller. The buyer assumes the cost risk because normally under this type of contract the buyer doesn't have the experience to produce the product and as a result they are sometimes or can be at the mercy of the seller.
- **Cost plus fix fee**
  Seller cost is reimbursable and also have a fix fee assigned to the total project cost.
- **Cost plus incentive fee**
  Seller cost are reimbursable but the buyer will also give the seller a reward usually in the form of a bonus for completing the project early possible due to a time constraint or possible government mandate.

At the end of issuing out the selected contact type, the seller is award a Purchase Order which is a legal document allowing them to begin work. Once the purchase order is awarded to the seller, the project manager will then begin the logistics of project with his/her team to begin the Planning Process. All project cost, change orders, etc should be billed against the purchase order.

Procurement Process Tips & Tricks

From the buyers perspective:

- When deciding to make/buy or procure/lease ensure that the positive benefits and cash flow out weigh the negative benefits. During the business case perform in-depth quantitative when creating the net cumulative cash flow analysis. Quantitative analysis calculating shorter payback and high ROI projects are very attractive to senior management versus using a qualitative analysis approach.
- When creating the RFP ensure that the total scope of the project is included. Ensure that all functional requirements are detailed enough so that the seller can accurately make successful price bids. The lack of detail will lead to change orders on the seller's behalf which can impact total project time and total project cost. Many times hiring an external resource to review and verify the project requirements will mitigate the chances of the change orders, etc. and will also increase the buyer chances of receiving accurate bids.
- When possible, model the RFP as a fixed fee and model the schedule of payments based on the deliverables/milestones complete. This approach will make it easier for the buyer to manage change order or scope items that are not tied to the original RFP. Also, having the power to review the deliverables from a quality assurance perspective for payment will ensure that they seller is more likely to focus on the quality of the deliverable because it is tied to their payment schedule.

From the sellers perspective:

- Time and material contracts are the best for sellers because the cost risk is on the buyer. Having the ability to perform work for a specific time and cost ensures that the seller is not responsible for the project scope. This risk is on the buyer.
- Knowing when, what and how to bid on work, as a response to a RFP is key to a seller's success. Understanding the procurement process of the buyer is also key. Responding to a RFP may not be in the best interest of the seller when the buyer's scope of work is vague and is not concrete. This is something that the seller should consider because responding to a RFP just to increase a company's revenue may just act result in the opposite result. In this example, many vendors will low bid on the project in an effort quickly win the bid with the strategy of pushing through change-orders as a strategy to makeup for the low bid. Many times this strategy can work in reverse with the seller extending additional resources to the project than expected and the buyer forcing the seller to their fixed price. This approach usually will effect the entire project timeline and cost because additional processes to increase the vendor's scope, cost and then to send the request through the change control process and buyers/sellers internal procurement process can affect task dependencies and successors which can then affect the project's critical path. From the seller's perspective, knowing what projects to respond too is key.

Prepare for Execution

Planning Process, Stage 3

The last step in the Planning process is preparation for the execution phase. During this stage, The ITS PMO Management and the vendor prepare the statement of work. This collaborative step is the final chance for XYZ Company and the vendor to define or clarify the rules of engagement. In addition, The ITS PMO Management prepares to receive the vendor and engage them on the project. Everything from network access, ID badges, seating arrangements, hardware/software acquisitions, etc. are assessed and put in motion to enable the project team to begin their work. After the project logistics have been established a formal project kick-off meeting is held to welcome and identify all the project members from both the vendor and XYZ Company.

PROJECT PLANNING

Stage 1 – Update PID & Finalize Planning

Steps

1. Refine Project Schedule
2. Create and Execute Project Charter
3. Assign Planning & Execution Resources
4. Complete Market Research & Cost Estimate
5. Define Scope
6. Collect Requirements
7. Draft Project Approach
8. Develop Project Plan

Stage 2 – Develop and Implement Procurement Strategy

Steps

9. Development Procurement Document (Scope and Requirements)
10. Procurement and Legal review
11. Solicit Responses
12. Evaluate Responses
13. Conduct negotiations
14. Prepare Contract & Contract Support Documents

Stage 3 – Prepare for Execution

Steps

15. Conduct Project Organization Meeting
16. Develop Statement of Work
17. Develop Work Plan (MS Project Plan)
18. Finalize Engagement logistics

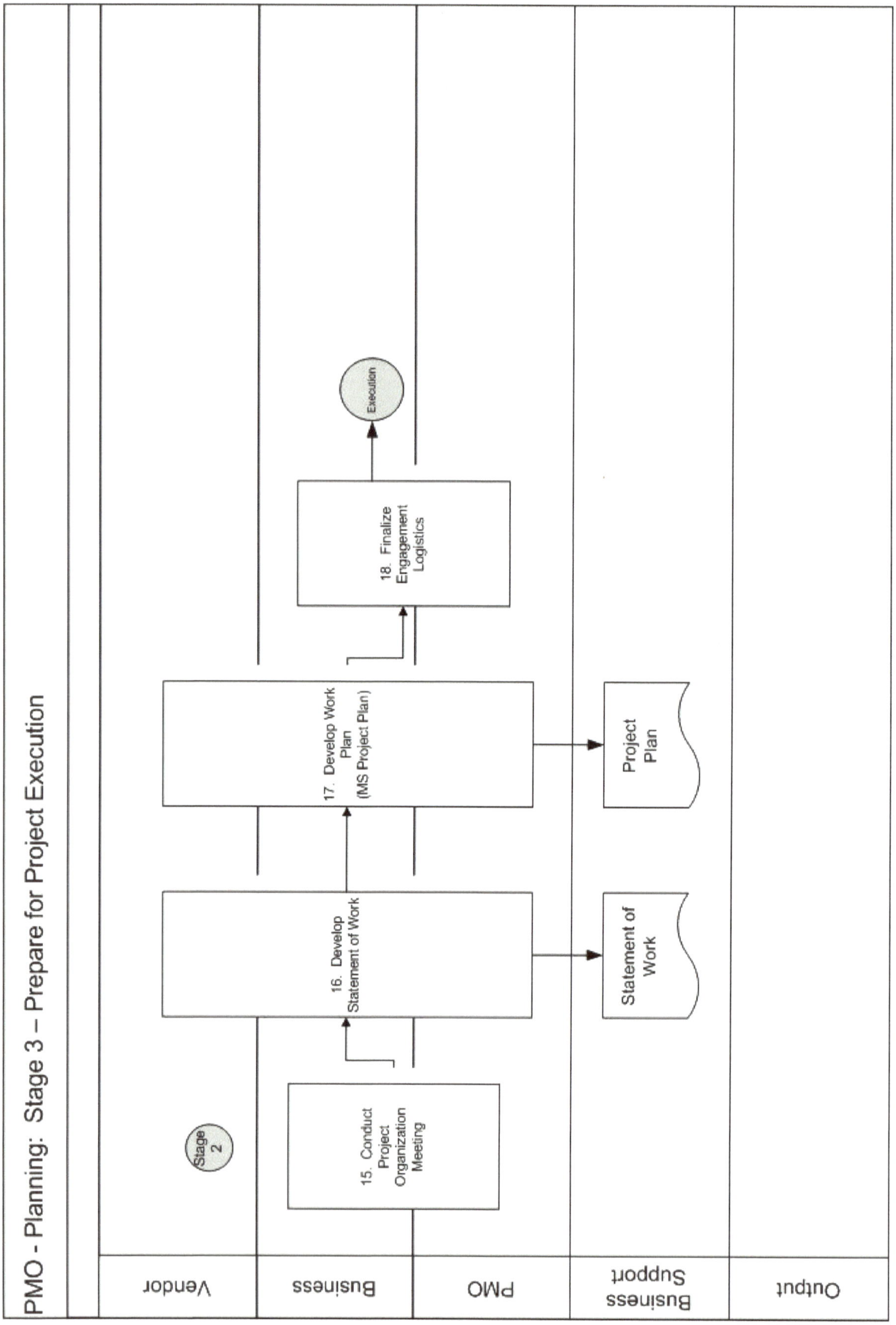
PMO - Planning: Stage 3 – Prepare for Project Execution
Vendor
Business
PMO
Business Support
Output
Stage 2
15. Conduct Project Organization Meeting
16. Develop Statement of Work
Statement of Work
17. Develop Work Plan (MS Project Plan)
Project Plan
18. Finalize Engagement Logistics
Execution

Inputs, Outputs and Tools

The Inputs and Outputs of the Planning Chapter will show what items, task or documents are to be considered in completing the three stages of the Planning framework. The inputs can be described as what work needs to be done which will lead to the actual output which can be described as the final deliverable, or series of deliverables for that particular stage.

The inputs and outputs for Stage 3 are:

- Inputs:
    - Project Plan
    - Vendor Proposal
    - Purchase Order
- Outputs:
    - Statement of Work

Timeframe/Total Duration (Ranges from 1 week to 3 weeks)

Resource Allocation

The following resources participate during the "Develop and Implement Procurement Strategy" Stage:

- Executive Sponsor
- Business Owner
- The ITS PMO Management – CIO or ACIO Application or Infrastructure depending on project scope and complexity
- Senior Portfolio Manager
- The ITS PMO Project Manager
- Project Team – includes business, technology, and vendor resources who work on the project on a day-to-day basis
- Other Key Stakeholders

Step	Executive Sponsor	Business Owner	The ITS PMO Mgmt	Sr. Portfolio Manager	The ITS PMO PM	Project Team	Other Key Stakeholders
15 – Conduct Organization Meeting	I	R	I	I	A/R	R	I
16 – Develop Statement of Work		A/R	A/R	C	R	R	C
17 – Develop Work Plan	I	A/R	I	C	A/R	R	I
18 – Finalize Engagement Logistics	I	R	C	C	A/R	C	I

Step 15 – Conduct Organization Meeting

- **Objective:** Introduce team members and client and make preparations to finalize overall project strategy.

- **Instructions**
    - Review vendor proposal and best and final offer materials and internal project plan
    - Setup meeting facility (reserve conference room, audio visual equipment, etc.)
    - Send invitations to vendor, business users and internal project team members

- **Estimated Time Duration**
    - Between 2-3 days

- **Resource Participation**
    - The Business Owner and The ITS PMO PM are responsible for assembling resources and attendees

Change Control Process

Change Control Process is the process in which a change is necessary due to the a change in project requirements and/or a change in the scope of the contract. This can consist of a the buyer wanting extended functionality that was not included in the original scope, additional equipment needed or from the seller's perspective discovering a missing requirements that wasn't accounted for in the original RFP. Whatever the situation there should be a concise system to account for any change in a project because often this can have a negative or positive impact on the project completion date. At a high-level the change control should be a simply flow of the following:

1. A scope change is discovered by buyer or seller
2. The Project Manager and Seller will review change to determine if scope is within or outside of the contract limits.
3. If outside of the contracts limit, the project manager will determine impact to project cost, time and the critical path.
4. Project manager would then discuss the change with the Executive Decision Team (EDT), which consist of the sponsor and procurement buyer at a minimum.
5. Change is approved or denied by EDT.
6. If approved, Procurement buyer would increase seller purchase order for extended amount. If denied, project would continue without scope with the buyer accepting the risk and impact to the quality of the deliverable.
7. Project manager determines impact to critical path and account for impacted project task and successors.

Depending on the size and complexity of the project, the change control process would be different for each case. A well systematic approach should be taken to account for change control within an organization. Not having a well developed system will negatively impact the project due to the lack of coordination required to get changes through in a timely manner as to not impact the quality and estimated cost and total project time of the solicited worked.

Change Control Process

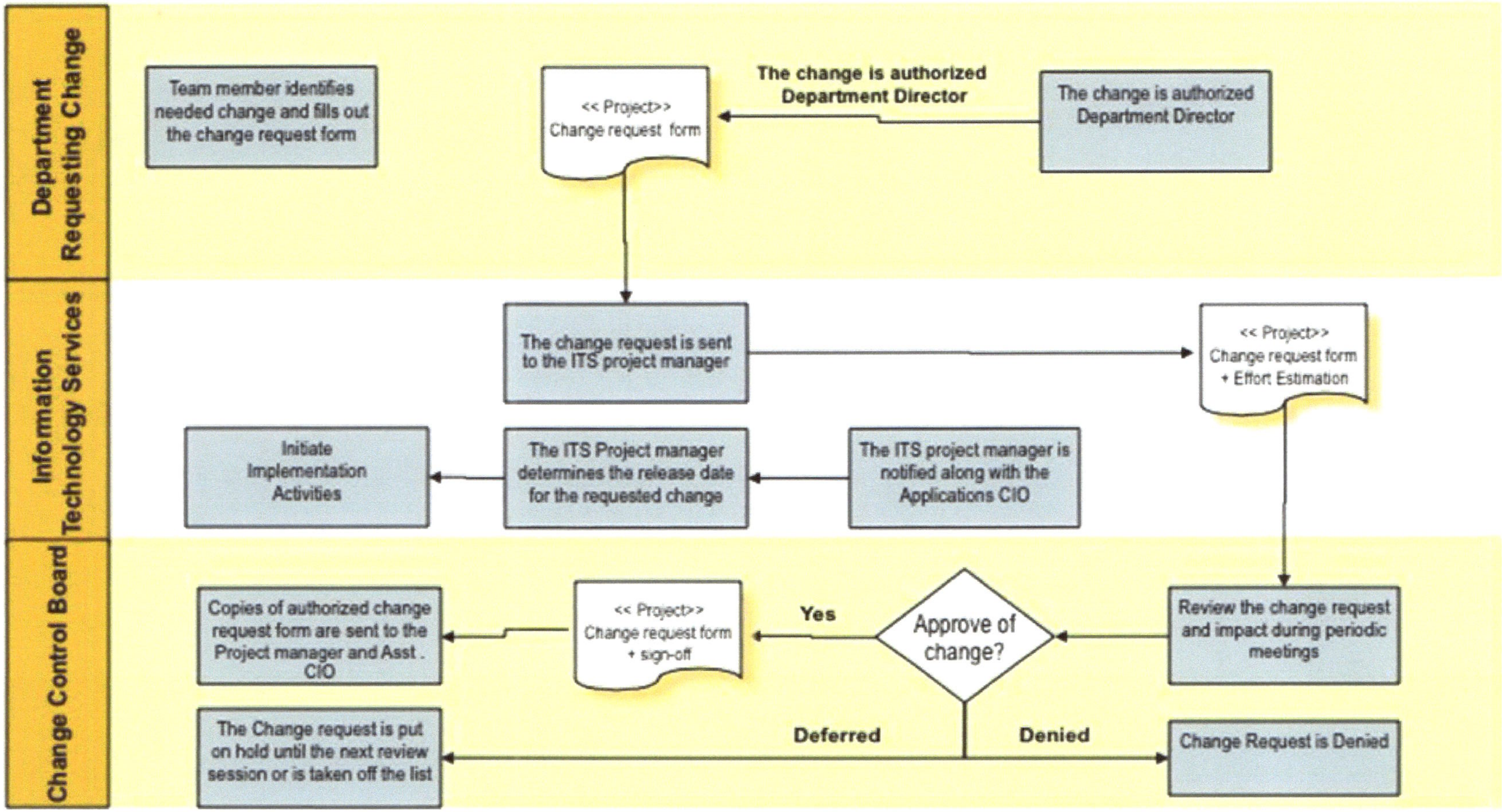

Quality Assurance Process

Quality Assurance is the process of ensuring the standards are being met within the project and that controls are in place to ensure that project processes exist. Within Quality auditing is the process of reviewing any milestone and/or deliverable before sign-off. During the quality assurance process any submitted milestone, scope of work or deliverable is presented to the project manager and/or team for review. Once the submitted work is reviewed and is agreed upon, the project manager can then sign it off. Below is a quality assurance checklist for any project milestone:

Quality Assurance Checklist

Intended use of this checklist	For a project team and/or a manager to use when planning or reviewing the quality assurance activities for a software implementation effort. The checklist helps ensure that the appropriate items have been included for effective software quality assurance (QA).

ID		Item to Consider
1		Is there a Quality Assurance Plan for the development effort? [This could be a separate document or part of the overall development plan.] Items to include: • Defined roles and responsibilities for QA • Minimum documentation requirements for the product • Standards, conventions, and processes for use in development of the product • QA role in preparing and reviewing the project's development plan, standards, and procedures • Measures for tracking project progress and product quality • Planned work product reviews, along with roles and responsibilities • Process reviews for examining the conformance of software engineering activities to the plan • Functional configuration audit, to ensure delivered product match requirements • Physical configuration audit, to ensure all deliverables are consistent and ready for delivery at the end of the project • In-process audits, to ensure consistency between work products of the different phases of the project life cycle • Timing and content of planned management reviews identified • Provision for post-project review of the project • Plan for testing of the product • Process described for handling defects discovered during product development • Is there a plan for quality records collection, maintenance, and retention?
2		Are adequate resources and funding provided for performing the activities?
3		Are members of the QA group trained to perform their QA activities?
4		Are members of the software project oriented to the roles, responsibility, authority, and value of the QA group?
5		Is the project performing QA activities according to the plan?
6		Are deviations from the project's plan being communicated to the project?
7		Are deviations from its plan being effectively addressed by the project?

ID		Item to Consider
8		Is management being notified of deviations that are not being addressed?
9		Are periodic reports of QA activities provided to the project?
10		Are measures of QA status gathered and reported?
11		Do project QA personnel review the supplier QA activities on a regular basis?
12		Is there some group who periodically reviews the activities and work products of the QA group?

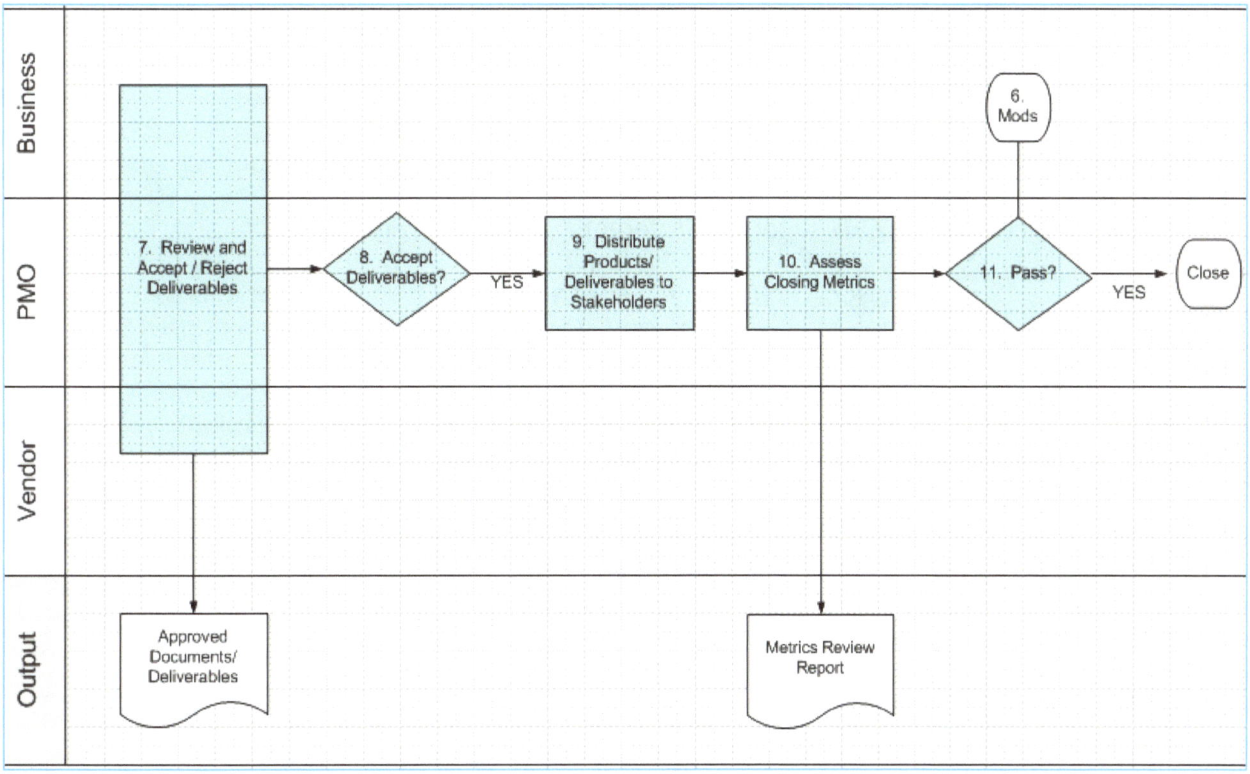

Step 16 – Develop Statement of Work

- **Objective:**
  - To clarify to a finalized state, the project scope, work activities and deliverables and approximate payments for the project
  - To document agreed upon actions needed by each project participant (XYZ Company & vendor) according to a specific timeframe
  - To provide "governance" over the project, or the specific "rules of engagement" for this project, for example, what constitutes a change order, how to review deliverables, etc.

- **Instructions**:
  - Use these templates:
    - Contract Document or Master Services Agreement (MSA); the MSA is generally available to all vendors who are pre-qualified in a particular The ITS PMO pool (e.g., management consulting, web development, etc. and is the governing document including language pertaining to how deliverables are to be reviewed, accepted, what rights the Authority has over the work delivered and the quality of the work delivered by the vendor, etc).

        - Project Plan as developed in Stage 1, Step 8
        - Request for Proposal (RFP), Request for Service (RFS) as developed in Stage 2, Step 9
    - Review the Master Services Agreement -- Contact the Legal Department to understand what clauses are particularly helpful and should be reiterated in the SOW, such as scope changes and deliverables review and acceptance. Using this document, you will not have to recreate language which is already in place and therefore, you will not risk developing language that competes with the MSA
    - Review the Project Plan – the Project Plan and its components are documented in Stage 1, Step 8 and generally consist of : Scope Document, Project Approach, Major Activities and High Level time frame for their completion, Project Resources: Project Assignment Document, Organizational Chart, Project Roles and Responsibilities, Project Management, Project constraints, Project Assumptions, Deliverables
    - Notify the Awarded Vendor that the XYZ Company and vendor will work together to develop the Statement of Work
    - Prepare an *Outline for the Statement of Work*. The following structure is suggested:

        - <u>Chapter 1: Introduction</u> – Mandatory - Overview, Scope, Expected Benefits
        - <u>Chapter 2: Vendor and XYZ Company Responsibilities</u> (by Service Area, Phase, etc.) – Mandatory - This is the second most important section of your Statement of Work, next to the definition of scope as documented in Chapter 1. The objective of the chapter is to detail the responsibilities, expectations, deliverables and assumptions that both parties (XYZ Company and vendor) make in order to deliver the solution within the time frame and budget identified. Identification of responsibilities and assumptions will remain iterative until all stated responsibilities and any assumptions, both the XYZ Company's and the vendors, become clear statements of fact. The Exhibit below depicts a sample matrix that will help you flush out XYZ Company and vendor's responsibilities and deliverables, by the various phases of a project:

Sample Statement of Work

1	PLANNING PHASE				
1.1	Project Initiation	Objective: Review the Lawson implementation methodology with all team members to establish a baseline understanding of all phases. Project goals and scope will be officially recognized. Team structures will be finalized and communication channels will be established.			
		Tasks	Deliverables/Outputs	OWNER	ASSIST
	See Appendix A	Complete Project Charter and Project Scope	Project Charter and Project Scope	BCS/Lawson	
		Finalize Statement of Work	Final Statement of Work	BCS/Lawson	
		Provide methodology overview to CHA	Lawson Methodology Template	BCS/Lawson	
	See Appendix A	Conduct Implementation Planning Workshop	Implementation Planning Workshop agenda and minutes	BCS/Lawson	
		Finalize Project Team Structure	Status report templates	BCS/Lawson	
			Project Team Organization Chart	BCS/Lawson	
	See Appendix A		Roles & Responsibilities Document	BCS/Lawson	
			Contact Information Sheet for Project Team members	BCS/Lawson	
		Develop Communication Plan	Project Communication Plan	BCS/Lawson	
			Team Status Meeting schedule	BCS/Lawson	
	See Appendix A		Issue Log and Worksheet Tracking System	BCS/Lawson	
	See Appendix A		Project Change Request Form and Procedures	BCS/Lawson	
	See Appendix A		Lawson Global Support Center (GSC) Support Manual	BCS/Lawson	
		Develop Education Plan	Education Plan	BCS/Lawson	
	See Appendix A	Provide Onsite Training Preparation Checklist	Checklist provided to CHA	BCS/Lawson	
		Develop Change Management Plan	Change Management Plan completed	BCS/Lawson	
	See Appendix A	Kick off Planning Meeting	Kick off Meeting Agenda	BCS/Lawson	
		Prepare project work space	Work space prepared		
		Conduct Project Kick off Meeting	Project Kickoff Meeting completed	BCS/Lawson	

The matrix as presented above can be completed by referring to your Project Plan, which should have a similar "inventory" of tasks by major phases of the project. It is important that the matrix be finalized in collaboration with the awarded vendor. The matrix will easily identify who is responsible for specific tasks and what the deliverables of the task are.

- Chapter 3: Project Governance – Mandatory - ("Rules of Engagement" – Risk and Issue Management, Communication Management, Scope/Change Management, Deliverable Review Process); refer to your Master Services Agreement and Project Plan for what has already been documented regarding these important governance principles.
- Chapter 4: Vendor's Detail of the Solution - Mandatory – this chapter is the responsibility of the vendor, and should mostly mimic what had been proposed as the solution in the winning proposal. Changes to this section should only be betterments to the vendor's proposed solution. This is not an opportunity to scale back unless explicitly directed to do so by the XYZ Company
- Chapter 5: Vendor's Implementation Methodology with Timeline / Milestones – Mandatory - this chapter, also is the responsibility of the vendor and again, should mostly mimic what had been proposed as the implementation approach in the winning proposal. Changes to this section should only be betterments to the vendor's proposed implementation approach. The milestones should be drawn from your already developed Project Plan, and those proposed in the vendor's solution. The XYZ Company and vendor will need to collaborate and agree upon what constitutes a milestone and the "value" of the identified milestone.
- Chapter 6: Training Approach - if needed – typically the infusion of technology will require training for either a core team and/or end users. This chapter, if needed, should specifically define when training will be conducted, by whom (the vendor or the XYZ Company), what materials will be developed and by whom.
- Chapter 7: Payment Schedule and Deliverables – Mandatory - XYZ Company is only entertaining a deliverables-based payment plan. The Vendor and the XYZ Company, in this Chapter will lay out their agreed upon payment schedule.
- Appendices: Functional and Technical Requirements – include your functional and technical requirements as developed for the Procurement solicitation document. These requirements will serve as the basis for the user's acceptance of the proposed solution.

- **Estimated Time Duration:**
  - One – five business days, depending on the size, complexity of the project, as well as the quality and completeness of the documents prepared in Stages One and Two: Project Plan, Request for Proposal

- **Resource Participation:**
  - The Business Owner, The ITS PMO PM, vendor project lead, and other key stakeholders participate together in the development and acceptance of the Statement of Work.
  - **Prior to final acceptance, the SOW must be reviewed and approved by the project's The ITS PMO sponsor (CIO or ACIO's depending on project scope and complexity) as well as by the Senior Portfolio Manager.**
  - Other key stakeholders that must be consulted include the XYZ Company's Legal Department.

- **Tip(s) for Success**
    - Development of the Statement of Work must be a collaborative process between the vendor and the XYZ Company, and not driven by the Vendor alone.
    - SOW development is the final chance for the Authority and vendor to agree upon what the XYZ Company wants and how it will be delivered, who is responsible for what specific tasks, and how payment for services is to be made.

Step 17 –Develop Work Plan (MS Project Plan)

- **Objective:** Defines the detailed tasks, which when completed, will achieve the results stated in the SOW; provides a means to track project progress.

- **Instructions**
    - Use available templates: Project Plan (Work Break Down Structure – High Level) and the Statement of Work
    - Further delineates the tasks within the broad categories of work
    - Defines the sequence of tasks
    - Assigns timelines and durations to each task (begin and end dates)
    - Identifies dependencies and constraints between / among tasks
    - Assigns resources to each task
    - Tasks are rolled up into "milestones"

- **Estimated Time Duration**
    - Between 2-3 days

- **Resource Participation**
    - The Business Owner, vendor PM (if applicable), and The ITS PMO PM are responsible for putting together the project work plan (also referred to as project schedule.) While the business PM or vendor PM may update the project work plan throughout the project, ultimately the ITS PMO PM is accountable for ensuring that it is of acceptable quality.
    - **The ITS PMO PM should review the project work plan with the Senior Portfolio Manager prior to final approval to ensure that it meets The ITS PMO project management standards**

The Baseline Project Schedule

Base lining the project schedule is probably the most important part of the planning process. At this point, there is no turning back in terms of allocating task, time and resources to the project schedule. Once baseline all milestones or task that are on the critical path will be used in the earned value calculation. Before base lining the schedule approval from the sponsor is required for guy-in purposes. It is important that the sponsor or all key stakeholders are in agreement with the project schedule. Once the process is baseline, the project manager will measure variances against the baseline schedule as a method of project performance. Looking at planned vs. actual start/finish task variance is key for managing the project schedule and also to provide corrective action for task that become late. In this case, two methods can be perform on the task to bring it back aligned with the baseline scheduled. Fast Tracking is the process of performing task in parallel in an effort to bring the project schedule back aligned with the baseline schedule due to late start/finish variance. Crashing is the process of adding additional resources to a task parallel in an effort to bring the project schedule back aligned with the baseline schedule due to late start/finish variance

The Project Plan

The Project Plan is the final team document that should be presented and distributed to the team at the kick off meeting and consist of the following:

- Project Initiation Document
- Business Case or Project justification
- Project Charter
- The Project Schedule with task, time & resource assignments
- The Communication Plan
- Stakeholder analysis
- The Procurement Plan
- Change Control Plan
- The Critical Path and Task
- Project financials: cost, resources
- Team Roles and Responsibilities
- Risk management Plan
- Quality Assurance Process

Step 18 – Finalize Engagement Logistics

- **Objective:** Make preparations for onsite deployment of vendors.

- **Instructions**
    - Locate and prepare office space for vendors
    - Setup network access
    - Setup email and voicemail
    - Provide security access (id badges, pass codes to The ITS PMO floor)
    - Prepare phone tree
    - Alert other The ITS PMO PM and Management that new vendors will be on premises

- **Estimated Time Duration**
    - 1 week

- **Resource Participation**
    - The ITS PMO PM is responsible for ensuring that engagement logistics are completed in a timely way. Issues encountered in procuring physical working space, accessibility to systems, etc. should be managed through the Issues

Management process (described in Chapter 4 of the Handbook) in order to minimize impact to the project's timeline and costs.

The Kickoff Meeting

The kickoff meeting is the last step in the Planning Process. This is the team meeting where the Project Plan is presented to the team, sponsor and other key stakeholders and the project is moved into the Execution Phase. Approval from the sponsor is required in order to move the project into the Execution stage.

Technical Case Scenario – The Planning Phase

- Review of Lifecycle Approach
- Make or Buy Decision
- WBS Overview
- Earned Value Approach
- Review of Networking Infrastructure
- OSI model
- Routing Protocols
- VoIP Infrastructure Review and Configuration
- IP Subnetting
- Microsoft Project & Publishing to Project Server
- Project Server overview and configuration

3 Project Execution

Topics Covered:

- ❖ Process Initiation Document (PID) and Processes
- ❖ InfoPath Web Forms
- ❖ SharePoint List, Libraries and Workflows for PIDS
- ❖ Understanding of Strategies: 23-27

How To Videos & Templates on CD :

- ❖ Walk Through of the Execution Process
- ❖ Producing status report
- ❖ Action Item & Issue Logs
- ❖ VOIP Infrastructure overview
- ❖ Project Server
- ❖ Extracting data from SharePoint
- ❖ Excel VBA & SharePoint data
- ❖ Excel Pivot Tables & SharePoint data
- ❖ MS Project VBA → Pert Table Example

STRATEGY for Execution:

- ✓ **Executing the Work plan**
- ✓ **Evaluating team performance**
- ✓ **Holding Status Meetings**
- ✓ **Producing Status Reports**
- ✓ **Action Item and Issue Logs**

Project Execution Overview:

Inputs	Processes	Outputs
• Project Governing Documents (RFP, SOW) • Project Planning Documents (Project Plan, Project Schedule, Payment Schedule)	Process 1 – Execute Work plan Process 2 –Manage Resources/Team Process 3 -Manage Communication Process 4 -Manage Procurement/Contract	• Updated Project Governing Documents (SOW, Changes) • Updated Project Documents (Project Plan, Project Schedule, Payment Schedule) • Project Deliverables • System/Solution

Project Execution represents the activities of the XYZ Company Project Manager and the Vendor team in delivery of the project. It involves most of the contractual obligations of the PM including Vendor payments, as well as the review and acceptance of project deliverables. .

Key Definitions:

There are several key terms that must be understood to fully comprehend the aspects of this section. These terms are defines to provide a common framework from which XYZ Company Project Managers can effectively communicate between one another.

Project Manager (PM): Although there are many persons involved in the project who may have the title "Project Manager", for the purposes of this section, references to a Project Manager solely involve the person on XYZ Company's The ITS PMO staff assigned to oversee and deliver the project. There can be only one Project Manager assigned to a project. Other individuals within XYZ Company may be assigned to assist the PM in oversight and control of the project; however their role is always secondary to the designated PM. The Project Charter established as part of the Project Initiation section of this handbook, defines the steps involves in assigning a Project Manager to the team.

Vendor Project Manager (VPM): This is the corresponding project leader assigned by the Vendor's management. The VPM is referenced in the Vendor's proposal, and is a key member of the project team and an element of the Vendor's contract with XYZ Company.

Key Stakeholder(s): In short, Stakeholders are The ITS PMO' customer. Stakeholders may be an individual or a group of individuals and they usually are representatives from the requesting department or departments. Key Stakeholders are the individuals who have completed the PID and have expressed a need for a product, system, or solution to solve their needs. Stakeholders are critical to properly defining the scope of a project and are the arbiters of whether or not a project or deliverable meets their needs, goals and objectives. While the PM is involved in evaluation of whether or not a Vendor is fulfilling their contractual obligations, Stakeholders evaluate whether or not the items being delivered meet their requests from The ITS PMO.

Executive Business Sponsor: – Highest-level representative of business unit (usually Managing Director) for which the project is being delivered. The Executive Sponsor retains overall responsibility for project's success

Engagement Manager: The Engagement Manager is a senior member of the vendor's staff and a superior of the Vendor Project Manager. Their title may vary widely from vendor to vendor; it can range from a company president or vice president, to a senior sales representative, accounts manager or regional manager. Whatever the title, the role is the same: this person is responsible for the vendor's work. He or she is the company representative, which has authorized the project and signed their name to the project proposal. It is critical that the PM to know whom the Engagement Manager is for their project. If a PM experiences a problem related to vendor performance that the Vendor's Project Manager is unable to correct, Project Managers can escalate the problem to the Engagement Manager.

The ITS PMO Senior Portfolio Manager – Senior The ITS PMO manager who provides guidance and oversight to all projects in the ITS PMO portfolio. She/he is responsible for providing overall status reporting to EDT/PDT for all The ITS PMO projects as well as compliance with The ITS PMO project management standards

Project Decision Team (PDT) – Managing Directors, Directors, The ITS PMO management and others with a significant stake in the project. Executive Business Sponsor is typically the chairperson. The PDT is collectively responsible for removing obstacles and enabling any type of change required for the project to be successful

Executive Decision Team (EDT): A group of organizational executives who are the high-level stakeholders and are responsible for providing guidance on overall strategic direction (The Plan for Transformation) and decisions for guiding the portfolio of The ITS PMO-related projects to support the direction and goals of the Authority. The current composition of the EDT includes the CIO, ACIO's, The ITS PMO Senior Portfolio Manager, the Managing Directors, and the Chief of Staff.

Project Team: References to the project team involves only members of the project responsible for delivery and acceptance of the project. That is to say: the Project Manager, the Vendor Project Manager, The Business Owner and the Key Stakeholders. The Project Team is the group solely responsible for project execution. Note that other parties, including The ITS PMO management, the Senior Portfolio Manager and Executive sponsors are parties involved in controlling processes.

Processes:

Project Execution involves four primary processes: Execution of the Work plan (or Project Schedule), Managing Resources, Managing Communication and Managing Procurement. These correspond directly to processes as defined in PMBOK. Processes of Project Execution are continuous and repetitive activities, which occur throughout project delivery.
In addition to these four main processes, Project Execution involves three sub processes: Change Orders, Deliverable Review and Stop Work. Unlike the primary processes, sub processes are not done continuously during project delivery; they are done on an "as-needed" or "ad hoc" basis.

3.1 Execution of the Work plan

Objective:

- To methodically design, build and test the intended solution in accordance to an accepted plan of action.
- To iteratively review, assess and make corrective action relating to solution development.
- To fairly compensate vendors for solution development progress in accordance to mutually agreed upon terms.

Instructions: Project Execution is a continuous and repetitive activity. Work plan execution not only involves the actual building of the system itself, it also involves the continuous processing of contract paperwork as well as the continuous review and amendment of project documents.

The Project Manager is responsible for managing all resources of a project. This involves the oversight of development/installation of the system being acquired, as well as managing any changes that may be necessary to the project's Statement of Work. The Project Manager is also responsible for building the repository of project documentation, which captures all official correspondence relating to activities, payments, deliverables, and adherence to contract requirements.

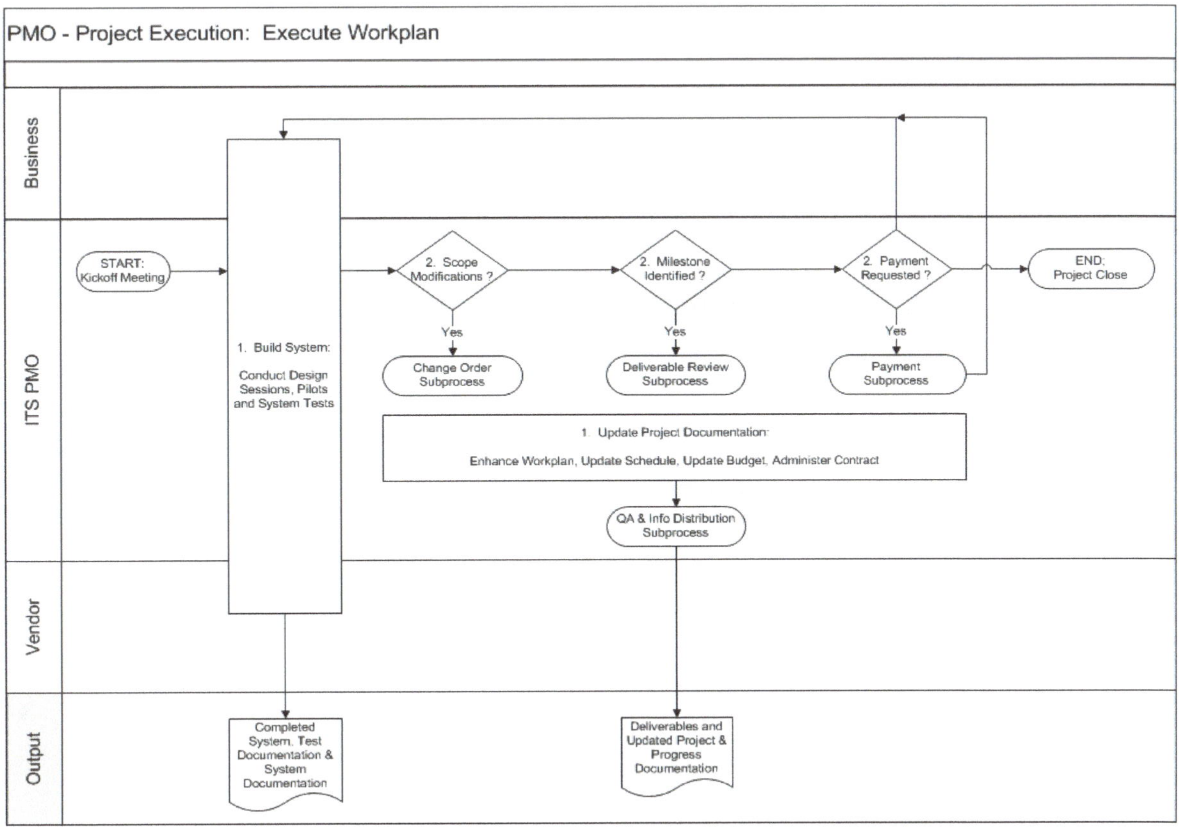

Following the Kickoff Meeting, the project manager holds weekly or bi-weekly status meetings and coordinates the review of project deliverables. This is accomplished through the use of four templates produced at the end of the Planning Process:

- Statement of Work
- Project Work plan/Schedule
- Payment Schedule
- Project Plan

Inputs, Outputs and Tools

Outputs from the Planning Stages serve as inputs to Project Execution:

Inputs	Processes	Outputs
• Project Governing Documents (RFP, SOW) • Project Planning Documents (Project Plan, Project Schedule, Payment Schedule)	Process 1 – Execute Work plan Process 2 –Manage Resources/Team Process 3 -Manage Communication Process 4 -Manage Procurement/Contract	• Updated Project Governing Documents (SOW, Changes) • Updated Project Documents (Project Plan, Project Schedule, Payment Schedule) • Project Deliverables • System/Solution

Step 1 – Manage Statement of Work:

Instructions: The Statement of Work contains details of how the vendor intends to deliver the system and what fundamental features it will contain. Throughout work plan execution, the Project Manager must make adjustments to the Statement of Work to reflect the current goals and objectives of the project Team.

While some changes are necessary and acceptable during project execution, Project Managers should insure that revisions to the Statement of Work do not constitute a "Cardinal Change" to the project.

Estimated Time Duration:

Management of the Statement of Work occurs throughout the project lifecycle. The duration will vary based on the scope of the project. Project Managers should strive to obtain updates to Statements of Work within 1-week to allow for updated status to be reviewed prior to the following Status Meeting.

Resource Participation:

The key parties involved in the administration of the Statement of Work are the Project Manager, Business Owner and the Vendor Project Manager. While the Project Manager and Business Owners are contributors to the document, the Vendor Project Manager is responsible for updating the Statement of Work and obtaining final approval from the Project Manager and Business Owner for any amendments.

Step	Executive Decision Team	Project Decision Team	Business Owner	Key Stakeholders	ITS Management	ITS PMO	Project Manager	Vendor Project Manager	Engagement Manager	Accounts Payable
1 - Statement of Work		C	A/C	A/C	I	C	R	A/R	C	

Executing the Work plan

During this phase of the project the project manager is managing each task to ensure that all work packages are complete on time. At this stage, the project manager should look for start/finish variances and provide correction action to keep the project schedule on track with the knowledge of float and impact to delays that will affect the overall project schedule. The distribution of work packages and WBS dictionaries should also be distributed to each team member to ensure that all resources have all the necessary information to complete their task. Executing the work plan and noting delays may affect the critical path so the project manager using either earned value approach must be aware of all task that have zero float and formulate contingency plans and funding to assist with keeping the project aligned with its baseline schedule.

Step 2 – Manage Project Schedule

Instructions: Throughout the execution of a project, the project schedule should be updated on a regular basis. Depending on the nature of the project, Vendors should be asked to provide updates at least on a weekly basis.

Although the baseline schedule is established prior to the Kickoff Meeting, project schedules should always reflect the most current projections of milestones and completion percentages. Vendors should be made aware that until they obtain approval of a milestone by XYZ Company, that the milestone is not to be marked as complete.

During the course of the project, vendors may face difficulties in completing their tasks due to any number of reasons. Project Managers should note that whatever obstacles the Vendor encounters along the way, that it is the responsibility of the Vendor's Project Manager to propose recommendations to put the project back on track.

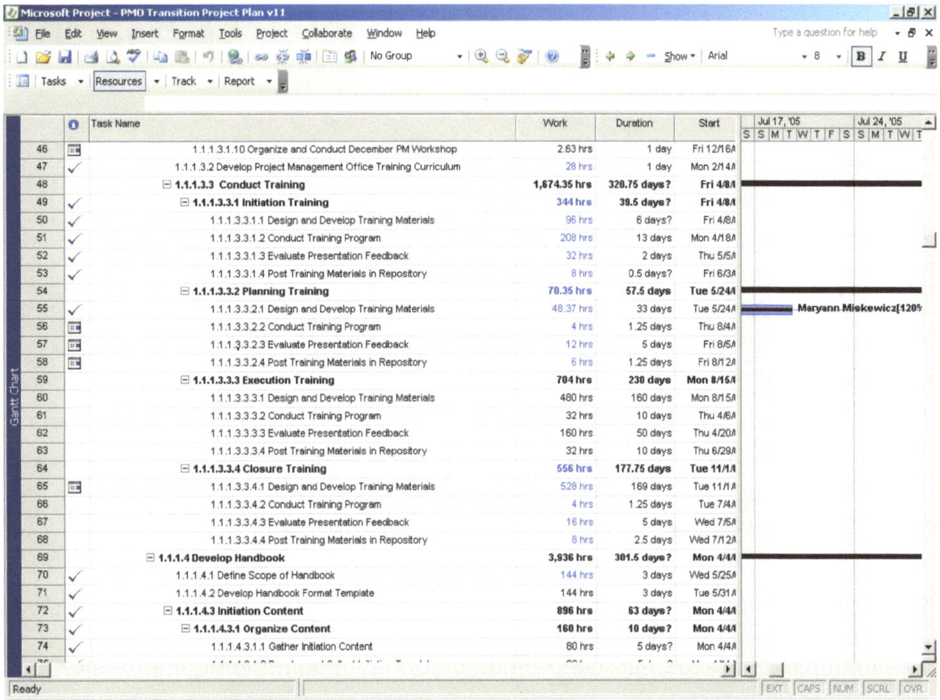

Microsoft Project - PMO Transition Project Plan v11

	Task Name	Work	Duration	Start
46	1.1.1.3.1.10 Organize and Conduct December PM Workshop	2.63 hrs	1 day	Fri 12/16/
47	1.1.1.3.2 Develop Project Management Office Training Curriculum	28 hrs	1 day	Mon 2/14/
48	**1.1.1.3.3 Conduct Training**	**1,674.35 hrs**	**320.75 days?**	**Fri 4/8/**
49	**1.1.1.3.3.1 Initiation Training**	**344 hrs**	**39.5 days?**	**Fri 4/8/**
50	1.1.1.3.3.1.1 Design and Develop Training Materials	96 hrs	6 days?	Fri 4/8/
51	1.1.1.3.3.1.2 Conduct Training Program	208 hrs	13 days	Mon 4/18/
52	1.1.1.3.3.1.3 Evaluate Presentation Feedback	32 hrs	2 days	Thu 5/5/
53	1.1.1.3.3.1.4 Post Training Materials in Repository	8 hrs	0.5 days?	Fri 6/3/
54	**1.1.1.3.3.2 Planning Training**	**70.35 hrs**	**57.5 days**	**Tue 5/24/**
55	1.1.1.3.3.2.1 Design and Develop Training Materials	48.37 hrs	33 days	Tue 5/24/
56	1.1.1.3.3.2.2 Conduct Training Program	4 hrs	1.25 days	Thu 8/4/
57	1.1.1.3.3.2.3 Evaluate Presentation Feedback	12 hrs	5 days	Fri 8/5/
58	1.1.1.3.3.2.4 Post Training Materials in Repository	6 hrs	1.25 days	Fri 8/12/
59	**1.1.1.3.3.3 Execution Training**	**704 hrs**	**230 days**	**Mon 8/15/**
60	1.1.1.3.3.3.1 Design and Develop Training Materials	480 hrs	160 days	Mon 8/15/
61	1.1.1.3.3.3.2 Conduct Training Program	32 hrs	10 days	Thu 4/6/
62	1.1.1.3.3.3.3 Evaluate Presentation Feedback	160 hrs	50 days	Thu 4/20/
63	1.1.1.3.3.3.4 Post Training Materials in Repository	32 hrs	10 days	Thu 6/29/
64	**1.1.1.3.3.4 Closure Training**	**556 hrs**	**177.75 days**	**Tue 11/1/**
65	1.1.1.3.3.4.1 Design and Develop Training Materials	528 hrs	169 days	Tue 11/1/
66	1.1.1.3.3.4.2 Conduct Training Program	4 hrs	1.25 days	Tue 7/4/
67	1.1.1.3.3.4.3 Evaluate Presentation Feedback	16 hrs	5 days	Wed 7/5/
68	1.1.1.3.3.4.4 Post Training Materials in Repository	8 hrs	2.5 days	Wed 7/12/
69	**1.1.1.4 Develop Handbook**	**3,936 hrs**	**301.5 days?**	**Mon 4/4/**
70	1.1.1.4.1 Define Scope of Handbook	144 hrs	3 days	Wed 5/25/
71	1.1.1.4.2 Develop Handbook Format Template	144 hrs	3 days	Tue 5/31/
72	**1.1.1.4.3 Initiation Content**	**896 hrs**	**63 days?**	**Mon 4/4/**
73	**1.1.1.4.3.1 Organize Content**	**160 hrs**	**10 days?**	**Mon 4/4/**
74	1.1.1.4.3.1.1 Gather Initiation Content	80 hrs	5 days?	Mon 4/4/

Project Managers should also note that in project schedules, there will be review and assessment requirements and timetables for the XYZ Company. It is the Project Manager's responsibility to insure that the XYZ Company lives up to its expectations with respect to deliverable review timelines and to insure that vendors fulfill those expectations. Vendors often attempt to use XYZ Company delays as justification for time extensions or additional monies; success of the effort depends on the vendor's ability to prove their case.

A vendor is free to make whatever changes are necessary to reflect the tasks and durations required to complete the project. They may add, change and remove tasks as necessary. However, a vendor's updates to timelines of milestones and deliverables do not constitute changes to the baseline schedule. Changes to a schedule's baseline are only achieved through Change Orders or recommendation of the PDT. The process for re-base lining project schedules is covered in the Project Control: Schedule Management section of this manual.

Estimated Time Duration:

Management of the Project Schedule occurs throughout the project lifecycle. The duration will vary based on the scope of the project. Project Manages should strive to obtain updates to Project Schedules within 1-week to allow for updated status to be reviewed prior to the following Status Meeting.

Resource Participation:

The key parties involved in the administration of the Project Schedule are the Project Manager, Business Owner and the Vendor Project Manager. While the Project Manager and Business Owners provide input to the schedule, the Vendor Project Manager is responsible for updating the Project Schedule and obtaining final approval from the Project Manager and Business Owner for all updates.

Step	Executive Decision Team	Project Decision Team	Business Owner	Key Stakeholders	ITS Management	ITS PMO	Project Manager	Vendor Project Manager	Engagement Manager	Accounts Payable
3 - Payment Schedule		I	I	I	I	I	A/R	A/R	C	

Step 3 – Manage Payment Schedule

Whenever there is a Change of Scope, the Payment Schedules must be updated.

Instructions: For change orders involving additional products, services or tasks, new line items are added to the project schedule, which summarize the requested activity and identify its amount. Once added to the Payment Schedule, the new items are to be treated as if they are additional project milestones.

Project Payment Schedule				
Number	Milestone / Deliverable	Project Phase	Scheduled Completion	Value
4.1	Software License Upgrade Payment (1 of 2)	Initiation	Contract Award	$10,223.00
6.8	Software Installed	Planning	Dec-04	$4,860.00
9.2	As-Is Assessment Report	Design	Feb-05	$9,580.00
9.7	System Setup Complete / Software License Payment (2 of 2)	Design	Mar-05	$10,233.00
12.1	Conference Room Pilot	Design	Apr-05	$25,640.00
12.8	Custom Reports Completed	Implementation	Jul-05	$29,520.00
12.8.1	Additional Custom Reports	Implementation	Jul-05	11,200.00
15.4	End User Training Materials Completed	Implementation	Jul-05	$12,950.00
16.9	Culover Checklist Completed	Implementation	Jul-05	$5,960.00
18.1	Conference Room Pilot Issues Log and Action Plan Completed	Design	Aug-05	$34,980.00
19.2	End User Training Completed	Training	Sep-05	$71,270.00
20.3	System Test Plan Completed	Implementation	Sep-05	10,983.00
20.4	System Load Testing Complete	Implementation	Oct-05	$20,150.00
22.5	Administration Training Completed	Training	Nov-05	$19,020.00
30.11	Go Live / Initiate Post Implementation Support	Operation	Oct-05	$6,260.00
			Project Total	$281,849.00

For change orders involving changes to the scope of current milestones, line-item amount(s) should be adjusted to reflect the new totals. Summaries of the line items should also be adjusted to reflect the nature of the revised milestone.

Estimated Time Duration:

Adjustment of the Payment Schedule occurs throughout the project lifecycle. The duration will vary based on the scope of the project. Note that in many instances, projects will not require any amendments to the Payment Schedule.

Project Managers should strive to obtain updates to Payment Schedules within 1-week to allow for updated status to be reviewed prior to the following Status Meeting.

Resource Participation:

The key parties involved in the administration of the Project Schedule are the Project Manager, the Vendor Project Manager and the Engagement Manager. As project finances are critical to the success of a project, the Vendor's Engagement Manager is also consulted. As with most administrative matters, however, the Vendor Project Manager is responsible for performing any updates to the Payment Schedule and obtaining final approval from the Project Manager..

Step	Executive Decision Team	Project Decision Team	Business Owner	Key Stakeholders	ITS Management	ITS PMO	Project Manager	Vendor Project Manager	Engagement Manager	Accounts Payable
2 - Project Schedule		C	I	I	I	C	A	A/R	I	

Step 4 – Manage Project Plan

While the Statement of Work defines the objectives of the project, the Project Plan defines the manner by which these objectives will be achieved. The Project Plan can be seen as being analogous to a team's "Playbook", while the Statement of Work is analogous to the "Rules" of the game.

The Project Plan takes the baseline goals of the Project Schedule and Statement of Work such as key milestones and delivery dates and adds to them internal and external constraints, processes and objectives. These additions include (but are not limited to) deliverable and invoice review procedures, interfaces with other projects, team membership, organizational charts and physical resource information (i.e.: offices).

Project Plan Templates can be found in the PMO Templates Library.

The initial Project Plan will have been developed as part of the Planning Process. As with other Project documentation, the Project Plan should be updated throughout the Execution process when circumstances surrounding project execution change.

Project Plans will likely be updated on a fairly frequent basis as the team manages its approach to Project Delivery. Although a Project Schedule changes frequently, Project Managers should note that changes in the plan do not affect project baselines of schedule and budget. Changes to baseline schedules and project budgets are managed under separate Controlling processes, which can be found in Chapter 4.

Project Plans also are to be used by the Senior Portfolio Manager to evaluate project execution relative to stated goals, Project Managers must submit copies of Project Plan to the Senior Portfolio Manager at the start of the Project Execution. If a Project Plan is changed, Project Managers must also provide the Senior Portfolio Manager with a copy of the updated plan.

Estimated Time Duration:

Adjustment of the Project Plan occurs throughout the project lifecycle. The duration will vary based on the scope of the project and the nature of any updates being performed. Project Managers should strive to obtain updates to Project Plans within 1-week to allow for updated status to be reviewed prior to the following Status Meeting.

Resource Participation:

While the entire Project Team is involved in the development of the Project Plan, the ITS PMO Project Manager and Vendor Project Manager are responsible for all updates to the Project Plan.

Step	Executive Decision Team	Project Decision Team	Business Owner	Key Stakeholders	ITS Management	ITS PMO	Project Manager	Vendor Project Manager	Engagement Manager	Accounts Payable
4 - Project Plan	I	C	C	I	C	C	A/R	A	I	

Tips for Success

Be Wary of Cardinal Changes:

Cardinal changes are changes to the contract so significant that the intent or objective of the project is substantially different from the original agreement made between the XYZ Company and a Vendor.

Cardinal Changes are not as difficult to achieve as one might think. This is because Cardinal changes often do not happen in one instance; they most likely will occur over time due to the collective and well-meaning efforts of the project team. Project Managers must review the nature of all project changes to insure that the end result has not altered the Statement of Work so severely that it constitutes a breach of contract.

The point at which a change becomes Cardinal is subjective in nature, however examples of this include:

- A change of the primary product or solution proposed.
- Change order(s) doubling or halving the project budget.
- Changes to the majority of items requested in an RFP.
- Changes to requested services such that they are beyond the Vendor's area of expertise.

Project Managers should note that Cardinal changes are inherently breaches of XYZ Company's contract with the vendor –be they initiated by the Vendor or by the XYZ Company. In some events, Cardinal Changes may require a new competitive process. In the event a change might be believed to rise to the level of a Cardinal change, the Project Manager must consult with the Procurement office and the Senior Portfolio Manager to determine if the contract can and should continue.

Evaluating Team Performance

Completing task on time and with quality is the most important task of each team member because re-work will add both time and money to the project. Team members should be awarded if possible for great accomplishments. Giving out dinner vouchers, awards and /or certificates can add positive value to the team moral spirit, which intangibly adds positive to the project. People are more likely to work harder when they enjoy what they do or believe in the end result of what's being delivered. Providing quarterly reviews will assist in personal and career team building for the team members and allow them the opportunity to voice their possible negative and/or positive concerns about the project. Providing this opportunity will bring cohesiveness to the team because each team member will feel as though their work is not going unnoticed and that they are part of a larger vision. For poor performing team members it is important to provide additional training to those who need it. If team performance doesn't improve then by working with the resource manager for a replacement can sometimes be a project manager's only option if improvements are not happening. By charting team performances, the project manager will mitigate his/her risk of task delay and budget overruns due to poor team performance and will give the project manager the opportunity to decide where task can be fast-tracked or crashed.

3.2 Management of Team Resources

Objectives: Throughout the course of a project, it is sometimes necessary to replace members of the Project Team. This can be for many reasons ranging from promotion or reassignment by managers to resignations or transfers. The need to replace members of a team however should not be taken lightly, particularly when that team member has a major role in the execution of the project.

Team members to be replaced may be part of the Vendors team or may be one of the Key Stakeholders. The procedures for managing a team member's replacement are similar in either case.

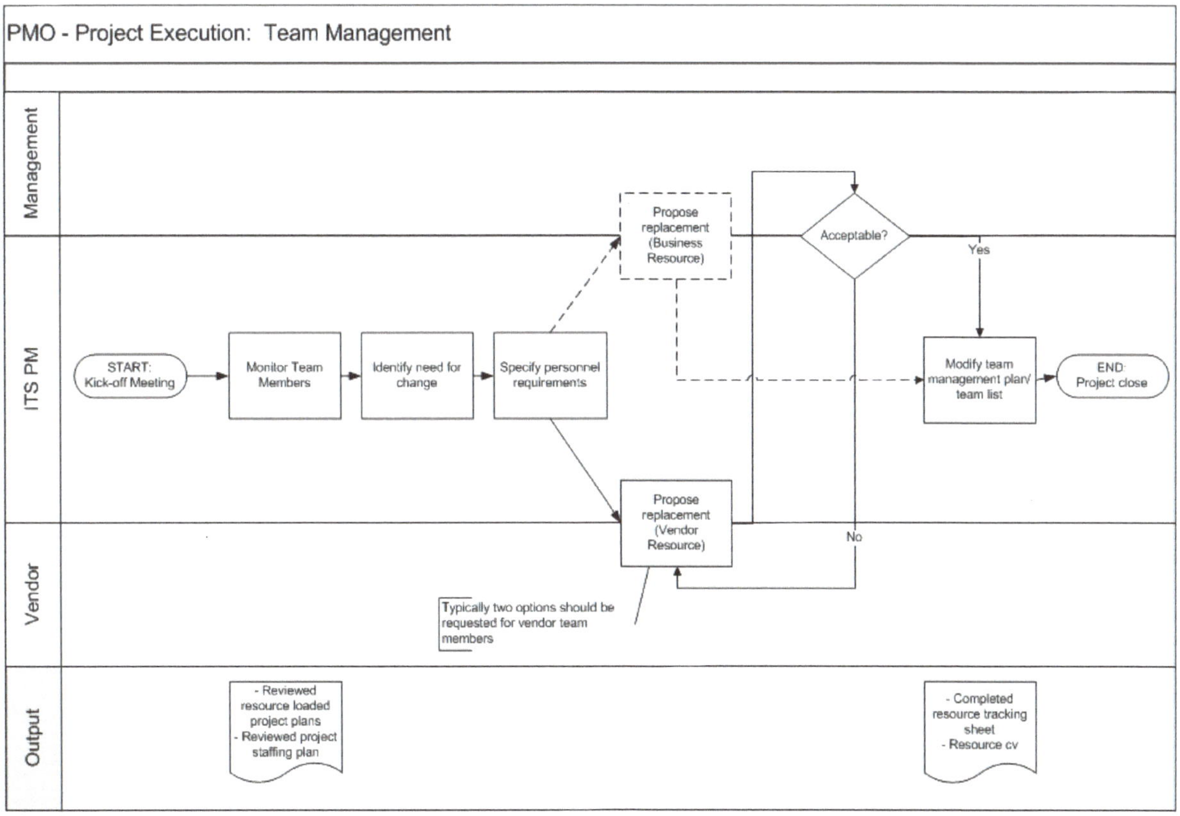

Instructions: Once the need to replace a team member has been identified, that party should be asked to recommend a replacement. If the Vendor is replacing a key team member, they should be asked to submit the resumes of two (2) individuals, which the XYZ Company can select from.

The names or qualifications of the recommended replacement(s) should be brought before the PDT for review and approval. The Project Manager should provide a recommendation to the PDT and the PDT should vote to accept or reject the recommendations and/or the proposed replacement. Where multiple individuals are submitted for selection, the PDT should select the most suitable candidate.

For replacement of Key Stakeholders, the PDT meeting minutes will serve as the official record of the approved change in staff. As the Key Stakeholders are members of the PDT, no further notification is required.

For replacement of Vendor staff, Project managers should notify procurement of their intent and prepare a letter on XYZ Company letterhead which communicates to the vendor the acceptance or rejection of the proposed team member. A copy of this letter should be sent to the Procurement department for their files.

If the Project Manager has rejected all candidates, they should provide a short explanation and a reasonable deadline for receiving new candidates from the Vendor.

If the PDT happens to rejects a Key Stakeholder candidate, the Project Manager should work with the respective department to select a suitable individual. In some instances, the rejection of a department's candidate may be met with resistance. In this event, Project

Managers are advised to escalate the issue to senior members of the PDT (such as the Executive Sponsor) so that they can work with the department head directly.

For approved changes in staffing, Project Managers should update the Project Plan and insure that the Project Team List is revised to include contact information of the new team member. If internal XYZ Company resources are used (i.e. email, id badges or network access) the new resources contact information should be forwarded to the XYZ Company help desk and/or HR department for processing.

Project Managers should also use the next Status Meeting to communicate all approved staffing changes to the entire project team.

Inputs, Outputs and Tools

The PDT is used to evaluate the vendor's resource selection and transition plan.

Inputs	Tools & Techniques	Outputs
• Resource Resumes	• PDT Meetings • Vendor Transition Plan	• PDT Meeting Minutes

Step 1 – Manage Transition

Once a replacement team member has been approved, the Vendor or Key Stakeholder must provide a resource replacement plan, which includes a timeline for transitioning team members. At a minimum, this plan should have both the incoming and outgoing resources actively involved in the project simultaneously for at least two weeks to allow them to become acclimated to the project environment and history. For key members of the project team, this transition period may be substantially longer and may include additional activities such as a graduated increase in the member responsibilities.

The goal of any transition period is that by the time an existing team member departs, the new team member should be able to assume all roles and responsibilities of the former team member. Project Managers may need to request additional transition time from Stakeholders or Vendors if it appears that a suitable progress is not being made towards transitioning the new team member.

For all Vendor initiated changes, Vendors are responsible for all costs associated w/ the exchange of resources, including any transition or ramp-up time. Likewise, vendors are also responsible for fulfilling their schedule commitments for the project in spite of the need to transition their staff.

Estimated Time Duration:

Transition periods for project team members vary for each project. Project Managers should, however insure that there is at least a two-week overlap of transitioning staff for all key team members. For senior members of the project team, the transition period may be as long as one month.

Resource Participation:

The key parties involved in the administration of the Project Team are the Project Manager, Business Owner and the Vendor Project Manager. For Vendor Initiated changes, the Vendor Project Manager is responsible for managing the transition period as well providing the qualifications of the proposed resources to the PDT.

For transitions initiated by the Business Owner, the Business Owner is responsible for providing the necessary qualifications and resources to the PDT. However, in most instances, the Project Manager will assume responsibility for management of the transition period with the support of the Business Owner.

Managing Team

Step	Executive Decision Team	Project Decision Team	Business Owner	Key Stakeholders	ITS Management	ITS PMO	Project Manager	Vendor Project Manager	Engagement Manager	Accounts Payable
1 - Managing Team							A/R	A/R		
2a - Replace Vendor Team Member		A/C	I	I	I	I	A	A/R	C	
2b - Replace Key Stakeholder		A/C	A	A/R	I	I	A	I		

Key: R – Responsible A – Accountable C – Consulted I - Informed

Tips for Success

XYZ Company's Master Services agreement gives Project Managers a great deal of leverage in controlling Vendor Resources. All XYZ Company contracts contain language, which prohibits substitution of any member of the vendor's team unless they obtain acceptance from the Procurement Department. Vendors can be held in default of their contract if they do not obtain approval from XYZ Company for replacing a member of their team.

Holding Status Meetings

Team status meetings should occur once a week via face-to-face, by phone conference or via other web medium like Web-X. The project manager should present the agenda at least 3 days prior to the meeting and keep the meeting at a defined length (1hr at minimum). At this meeting the following at a minimum should be discuss in detail:
1. Over Project Performance
2. Review of Issue logs and action items
3. Status of change orders
4. High risk items
5. Review of project assumptions and constraints
6. Next steps
7. Open up discussion for concerns, etc

During the meeting, notes should be taken for distribution to the team and prior to the start of the meeting an attendance log should be created. All project documentation should be stored in a repository such as SharePoint for all team members to view at a later time or at their convenience. Executive Decision Team (EDT) meeting which consist of the Steering committee should take place once a quarter and provide a high level view of
1. Project Performance (Red, Green, Yellow)
2. Review of Project Financials at a high Level
3. Review of high impacting risk items
4. Provide High Level of Next Steps
5. Open discussion up for concerns, etc

Date:
Version No.

Project Meeting

Date: Friday, February 28, 2003
Time: 10:00 am to 12:00 pm

Meeting called by:	Amy Joe	Type of meeting:	IP/Naming Convention Project Closure and Presentation of Deliverables
Attendees:	Project Team		
Please bring:	Questions to be answered		
Location:	1st Floor Conference Room		

----- Agenda Topics -----

Item	Person Responsible	Alloted Time
1. Over Project Performance	John Doe	10 minutes
2. Review of Issue logs and action items	John Doe	10 minutes
3. Status of change orders	John Doe	45 minutes
4. High risk items	Idris Parks	10 minutes
5. Review of Project Assumptions/Constraints	John Doe	20 minutes

Other information

Special notes:			

XYZ Company Master Services Agreement (excerpt)

3.9 *Key Personnel*

(b) No Substitutions. The Contractor will not reassign or replace Key Personnel without the written consent of the CIO which consent will not be unreasonably withheld. The Director of Procurement and Contracts may at any time in writing notify the Contractor that the XYZ Company will no longer accept performance of Services under this Agreement by one or more Key Personnel. Upon such notice the Contractor will immediately cease to assign that person or those persons to perform the Services and will replace him or them with personnel qualified to perform the function and acceptable to the CIO. If any Key Personnel furnished by the Contractor to perform Services under this Agreement are unable to continue in the performance of assigned duties for reasons beyond the Contractor's control, the Contractor shall promptly notify the XYZ Company, explaining the circumstances. Within 10 days of notification by either party of the need to replace Key Personnel, the Contractor must furnish to the XYZ Company the name of the substitute person and any other information the XYZ Company may require. If the XYZ Company does not approve such substitute person, the Contractor must propose another substitute person within 5 days. Such 5-day cycle shall be repeated no more than twice. In the event the Contractor is unable to tender a replacement, satisfactory to the XYZ Company, the Contractor shall maintain the personnel then assigned to the performance of professional services to the XYZ Company or be in Default.

Project Managers can use this leverage to insure that vendors replace a team member with another person of at least equal qualifications and/or experience. Project Managers do not have to accept a proposed team member if they believe the proposed replacement would increase the risk of the project. The inclusion of this language in XYZ Company contracts was established to protect the Authority from Vendors who propose senior or experienced staff but provide less qualified staff after the project is awarded.

3.3 Manage Communication

Objectives: Managing Communication involves the flow of information between the Project Team. It consists primarily of meeting minutes. These can be minutes of regular status meetings, issue resolution meetings, or milestone review meetings. Processes of PDT, EDT and Key Stakeholder meetings involve Project Control, and are discussed in the following chapter.

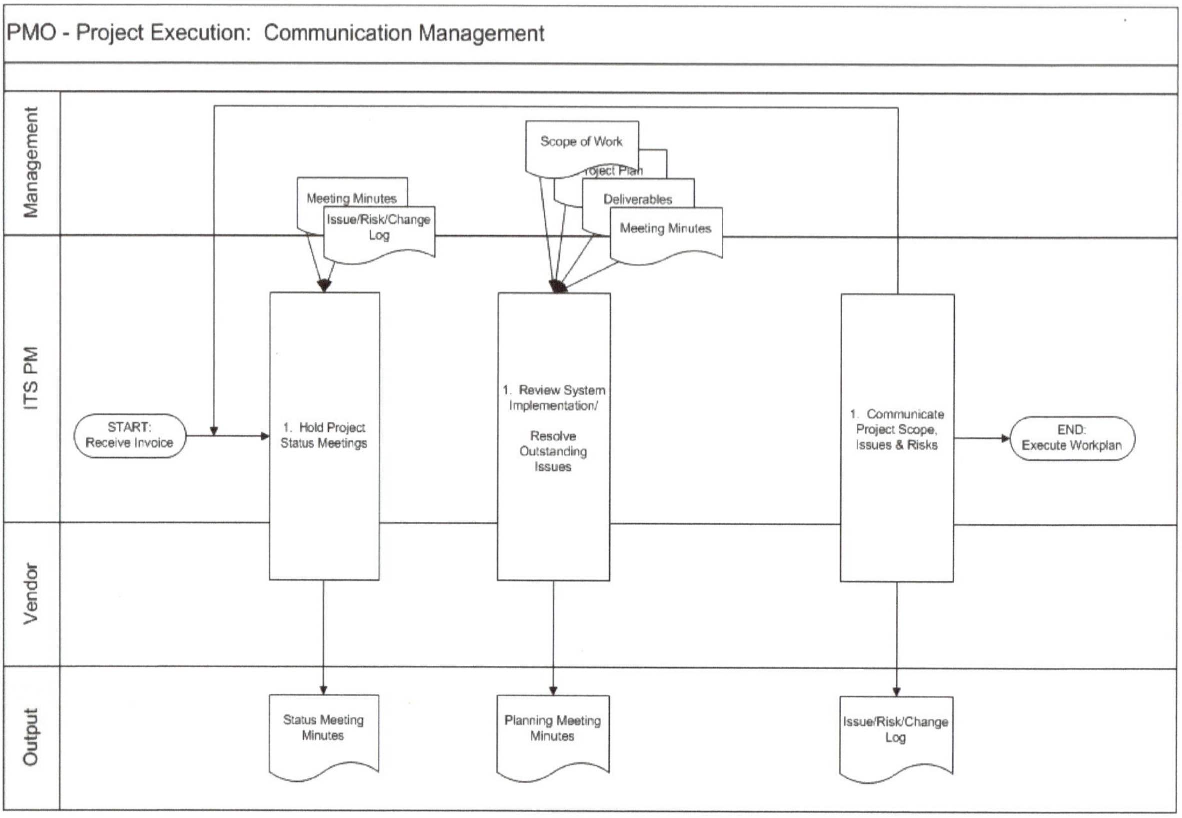

Inputs, Outputs and Tools

Inputs	Tools & Techniques	Outputs
• Previous Status Meeting Minutes • Statement of Work • Project Schedule • Milestone/Deliverable Approval Notices • Project Plan • Issue/Risk/Change Log	• Status Meetings • Project Meetings	• Status Meeting Minutes • Project Meeting Minutes • Updated Issue/Risk/Change Log

Step 1 – Hold Status Meetings:

Instructions: The primary means by which a Project Manager communicates the status of a project to the entire team is by regular status meetings. Depending on the length and complexity of the project, these meetings will be held either weekly or bi-weekly and should include all members of the Project Decision Team (PDT). During these meetings, project managers should review:

- Project Schedule
- Near-term Deliverables
- Key Issues
- Team Resources
- Next Steps

Meetings should be targeted for 30-minutes whenever possible; for very large projects, an hour should suffice to communicate project status to the team. In order for this to occur, the Project Manager must keep the team focused on identification of issues and the assignment of parties responsible for problem resolution. In other words, avoid using the status meeting as an opportunity to solve issues. Merely use the meeting as a period where issue owners can communicate the status of an issue that they have or will resolve in another forum. By keeping status meetings short, Project Managers are far more likely to receive regular attendance by senior members of the EDT; the short duration allows them to attend without adversely affecting an Executive's busy schedule.

Upon completion of the status meeting, the Project Manager should create meeting minutes of the session and should also update the issues, deliverable and risk logs based on the information discussed in the meeting. Note that the procedures for updating these logs will be addressed in the Control portion of this Chapter.

Status Meeting Templates can be found in the PMO Templates Library.

Project Schedule Review:

Review of the Project Schedule is an essential step in every status meeting. Vendors must be advised that they will be required to provide and present any updates to the schedule as part of the Status Meeting. This includes any changes to milestone or deliverable dates, as well as noteworthy progress within project tasks. Project Managers may even wish to include a version of the Vendor's GANTT in Status Meeting minutes.

Regularly reviewing project schedules helps keep the project team advised of where the project currently stands, what has been completed and what its next steps are.

Near Term Deliverables:

In order to allow the team to note the status of upcoming or recently completed milestones, Project Managers should note near-term Deliverables in the meeting minutes. This should include the status of deliverables or milestones recently delivered to the XYZ Company for review, as well as the status of the next milestone(s) and its due date.

While the overall review of Project Schedule provides a large-scale roadmap of the project, the near-term deliverables section provides a magnified view of progress immediately surrounding the current environment.

By referencing milestones recently submitted for review, Project Managers are able to communicate progress to the team. For deliverable reviews, which have concluded, PM's can communicate the disposition of the review to the entire team. Although many individuals may have been responsible for review or approval of a deliverable, in most cases the entire project team will not be involved. The inclusion of the state of deliverable review in the meeting minutes allows all team members to be apprised of the state of a deliverable. In those cases where deliverables were not approved (in whole or in part), the team can use the Status Meeting to determine a resubmission deadline if one has not been established already.

1. Milestones & Deliverables

Number	Milestone / Deliverable	Status
12.2a	Install & Configure Test Environment	Completed 1/19/04
14.6	Conference Room Pilot #3	Due 1/14/04

In addition to deliverables, which have already been submitted, Status Meetings are an opportunity for the team to look forward and identify the next milestones to be reviewed. This helps insures that the Vendor is prepared to deliver the milestone on schedule and/or communicate any necessary changes to upcoming dates. In the case of milestones involving presentations or meetings, the team can use the status meeting to coordinate dates and/or times for the presentation.

Notifying the team of upcoming deliverable doesn't just help the Vendor; it also advises XYZ Company staff of upcoming demands of their time so that reviewers can prepare their calendars and/or adjust their workload so that they can review the Vendor's submission in a timely manner. Upcoming milestones should include the scheduled delivery date, as well as either the due date or duration of XYZ Company review.

Project Managers should use the Deliverable Acceptance Reports or project schedule to obtain the information concerning deliverable status (for submitted deliverables) and identify the next deliverable. (Information on Deliverables Acceptance Reports can be found in Chapter 0)

In order for the team to adequately review the status of near term deliverables, the Project Manager should reference these items in the Status Meeting Agenda. Agenda's should be distributed to the project team at least one-day prior to the meeting to allow the team to prepare reports on near-term milestone status.

Meeting Agenda Templates can be found in the PMO Templates Library.

Issue Review:

Status Meetings are the periods during which most issues are officially opened and closed. The meeting minutes themselves will serve as the official record of issue closing by the Project Manager. The "closed date" of an issue is typically the date of the Status Meeting where it was formally closed; however Project Managers can also make reference to the date a task was completed or the date of an issue-resolution meeting if some other reference more clearly identifies the date an issue was closed.

Likewise, status meetings are the vehicles under which new issues are identified and brought to the attention of the team. Anyone in the meeting can bring up an item for the team to consider as an issue. But it is the Project Manager's responsibility to assess whether the item is of sufficient severity to warrant placement on the project's Issue or Risk log. In order to do this, the team must discuss the nature of what led to the issue. Project Managers must take care so as not to let the "discovery" portion of an issue lead to an extended discussion or become an attempt to resolve the issue. Not all items brought up for consideration will be treated as a formal Issue or Risk. Items of minor effort (such as scheduling a conference room for training) or of little impact (such as obtaining a shipping date for material delivery) need not be tracked as Project Issues.

If an item is deemed significant enough to warrant placement on the Issue log, then the Project Manager assigns a party responsible for monitoring the issue during the meeting. It is critical that there be a responsible party identified immediately, as many issues have time constraints associated with them. In addition, some issues tend to be lost or forgotten if they are not assigned to someone to manage and/or resolve.

Additional information regarding Issue management can be found in Chapter 4 – Project Control.

In addition to an assigned party, project managers must obtain a date for issue resolution immediately. Often, this may be relative to a milestone. Use of the project schedule may be required to determine when resolution is required so as to minimize impact to project delivery. However, in some instances the team cannot immediately assess when an issue can be resolved or when it must be resolved. In those instances, Project Managers must obtain a "date for a date" during the status meeting. There should never be a reason why a team member cannot provide a date to the team by which they will provide the issue resolution date.

A critical element towards project success is obtaining both an issue date and an issue owner for each and every issue and to do so at the time the issue is opened. After meetings, teams go off into different directions; unassigned and undated issued can be left orphaned and outstanding for months on end. By immediately assigning a responsible party, Project Managers will find that very few issues will get lost. Furthermore, when questions regarding issues come up, team members all know whom to contact for the most current status.

Following each Status meeting, Project Managers are responsible for adding the issue to the Project's Issue Log and assigning a number to it. During this time, the Project Manager assigns a severity to the issue based on the feedback of the project team during the status meeting. The issue number, assigned party, due date (or date for a date) and severity identified in this log should all be included in the published meeting minutes so that the entire team can note the addition of the item. Details of the Issue Log are detailed in Chapter 4 – Project Control.

Similarly to issue closure, the "open date" of an issue is typically the date of the Status Meeting where it was first brought before the team. However, Project Managers can also make reference to an earlier meeting or event during which the problem was occurred or was identified if this more accurately references the date an issue should be "opened".

1. Major Issues

#	Title	Description	Status	Owner	Status
12	Security groups in team management screens.	Users cannot be placed in security groups. XY Systems to investigate alternatives	no change. XY Systems still researching alternatives.	XYS	Open
21	Server hardware	Server hardware needed for final implementation.	1st order: PO issued on 1/20. No date on delivery. 2nd order: no change. In procurement.		Open
22	Testing software	Load testing software to be supplied	Software delivered to XY Systems on 1/18/04		Closed 1/22/04
26	SQL Server	Software License Required	New issue		Open 1/22/04

In addition to opening and closing issues, Status Meetings are periods during which the status of "key" open issues is reviewed. "Key Issues" refers to issues, which are either 1) ranking highest in impact and/or severity or, 2) are either past due or are next due. Details of issue ranking criteria can be found in Chapter 4 – Project Control.

Prior to the Status Meeting, Project Managers should identify all open issues to be discussed during the meeting. Unless the issues list is short, the list of "Key Issues" should be only a subset of the entire issues list. Ideally, there should be no more than 10 issues to earmark for assessment during the status meeting, however project circumstances may dictate that more issues be identified for status assessment. These "Key Issues" should be identified in the Status Meeting Agenda. Agenda's should be distributed to the project team at least one-day prior to the meeting to allow the team to prepare to report on issue status.

During a status meeting, Project Managers should review the status of all Key Issues with the project team and ask the issue "owner" to report on the status of their issue. If the issue remains open, the issue owner should report any progress being made since the last status meeting. If no progress has been made, then the Project Manager should simply note "no change" in the meeting minutes. Reports on issue progress should be noted in the "notes" section of the issue log.

During the course of a status meeting, issue owners may sometimes bring forward reports on current issues, which had not been earmarked, for discussion. PM's should welcome and encourage this input and should simply treat reports on other open issues in the same manner as Key Issues.

Project Managers will find that issue owners become reluctant to repeatedly show little or no progress from week to week on issues assigned to them. By regularly identifying issues and obtaining status, Project Managers will find that issues are often resolved much quicker than they would be if their status is not published to the team. Furthermore, in those instances where sufficient progress is not being been made by an issue owner, Project Managers will have sufficient evidence in meeting minutes to escalate the issue's resolution to the next level.

Resources

The Resource Section is where Project Managers note periods where key resources will be unavailable. They should be included at least 2-3 weeks prior to the event/activity to allow the team time to make suitable adjustments. Absences may be due to vacations or company obligations; however this section is not intended for unplanned absences (i.e.: illness or other meetings). As many vendors may not celebrate some of the holidays given to XYZ Company staff, all holidays should be noted as well as other XYZ Company events or activities during (i.e.: Annual Filing Day or Departmental Retreats). As with other absences, these should be noted a several weeks prior to allow the team to plan accordingly.

In addition to temporary absences of team members, Project Managers should include any requests by Stakeholders and Vendors to replace team members. Most likely Vendors and Stakeholders will notify the PM and the team of their intent to replace a team members during the status meeting. Note that the notification of the team by a stakeholder/vendor does not necessarily mean that the replacement will be allowed. Project Managers should follow the procedures outlined in the Managing Team section of this chapter.

Project Managers should also include any approved changes to team members in the meeting agenda and list the information in this area of the Status Report. If proposed team members have recently been rejected however, Project Managers need not communicate details surrounding the decision it may be sensitive in nature. They need only communicate that the Vendor or Stakeholder is submitting additional candidates for review and include the deadline for this information.

When critical resources are being replaced, Project Managers should use this section to also include the status of the approval process as well as the progress of the transition. This will help insure that the team is not caught off guard during the replacement period.

Next Steps

The Next Steps section is a summary of the key actions discussed in the meeting are necessary to keep the project on track or to get the project back on track. While the other sections discuss the activities and problems, which need to be overcome, this final section describes what needs to take place to accomplish them.

Examples include:

- The date, time and place of an upcoming Milestone presentation and review.
- The due date for the Business Owner's Deliverable Review comments.
- The date of a Project Meeting, which is needed to address an open Issue.
- The date of the next PDT Meeting to review a Change Order proposal.
- The date by which the Vendor Project Manager has promised updates to the Project Schedule

Next Steps are generally items, which can be accomplished within the next few weeks. As such, each of the steps should have a target date associated with it. In the event the team proposes a task that evolves over several weeks or several months, Project Managers should work with the team to break the task down further and define what needs to be accomplished within the next few weeks.

Estimated Time Duration: For most project Status meetings should be scheduled for 30-minutes. For large or complex projects, Status Meetings should not exceed 1-hour.

The preparation of Status Meeting Minutes will likewise vary based on the complexity of the project. However in most instances, Status Meeting Minutes can be completed in 30 to 90 minutes.

Resource Participation: Although the entire Project Team is involved in status meetings, the Project Manager is responsible for running the status meetings and is also responsible for managing the content of the Project Status Meeting Minutes.

Step	Executive Decision Team	Project Decision Team	Business Owner	Key Stakeholders	ITS Management	ITS PMO	Project Manager	Vendor Project Manager	Engagement Manager	Accounts Payable
1 - Status Meetings		C	C	C	C	I	A/R	A		

Status Meetings and the PMO

There are many items to cover during a status meeting. In order to adequately cover the items within a 30-minute timeframe, the team must be focused on identification and reporting. The team must be counseled to refrain from using the period as a time to resolve issues and problems. Status meetings are a time when the team can huddle together and make sure they are all on the same page in terms of project activity. And it is the responsibility of the Project Manager to communicate critical reference points to the entire team.

Project Managers should note that it is the responsibility of the Vendor's Project Manager to coordinate nearly all activities outside of the Project Status meeting. These activities not only include a Vendor's own work on deliverable progress, but also meetings to resolve most project issues. While the Project Manager or Business Owner will be responsible for those few issues fully within the domain of the XYZ Company, most issues will in some way be linked to Vendor commitments in terms of deliverables and due dates. Vendors must be advised that even for issues that XYZ Company is responsible for, at a minimum, scheduling, logistics and coordination of nearly all issue-resolution activities are their responsibility. The role of XYZ Company's project manager is one of oversight and management. The Vendor's role is one of project execution and coordination.

Project Managers may elect to enlist the assistance of Vendor Project Managers in the preparation and completion of Status Report Minutes. Project Managers may also require Vendors to submit their own status reports or take minutes of the Status meeting. A Project Manager is free to use their own judgment as to how best to complete Project Status reports; however the end result must reflect their own assessment of the state of the project and the items discussed.

Status meeting minutes are the primary means of communicating project status to the Senior Portfolio Manager. The elements identified in the status report will be used by the Senior Portfolio Manager in the completion of the monthly Project Dashboard and therefore must allow one to create an accurate and independent assessment of the state of the project.

Details of the Project Dashboard can be found in Chapter 4 – Project Control.

Step 2 – Project Meeting Minutes:

While Status Meeting minutes represent the assessment of the project as a whole, Project Meeting Minutes represent a detailed assessment of individual aspects of a project. While Status Meetings provide a sort of "30,000-foot view" of the project, Project Meeting minutes are on the ground level and often get into minute details related to project execution.

Project meetings are ad-hoc or special topic meetings where issues are resolved or where deliverables are presented. Unlike status Meetings, Project meetings do not have the inherent structure as is represented in their templates. Project meetings are simply records of discussions surrounding and issue or a presentation.

Project Meetings Minutes are sometimes entirely developed by the Vendor or a XYZ Company Subject Matter Expert (SME) –particularly when they involve highly technical issues, which may be beyond the expertise of the Project Manager. In addition, the Project Manager may not be present at many issue resolution meetings, deferring the meeting to other parties. Project Managers must use good judgment in determining when and whom to delegate Project Meeting responsibilities to.

For deliverable review presentations, however, Project Managers should always be in attendance and should take responsibility for the presentation minutes. Although both issue meetings and deliverable meetings will become part of the official record, the record of deliverable presentations has far more weight in terms of contract liability. As such, Deliverable review minutes should always be completed by the Project Manager and should not, under any circumstances, be delegated to the Vendor.

Estimated Time Duration: The duration of Project meetings will vary widely depending on the topics discussed or being presented. For short discussions or conferences, meetings may not exceed 30-minutes, however in some involved presentations or reviews (particularly involving off-site work), meetings may consume an entire day.

Although the duration of the meeting itself varies most instances, Project Meeting Minutes can be completed in 30 to 90 minutes.

Resource Participation: The resources involved in Project meetings vary based on the topics being discussed or presented. However, for all meetings EXCEPT deliverable presentations, the Vendor Project Manager is responsible for preparing and distributing the meeting minutes. In the case of deliverable presentations, the Project Manager is the responsible party.

Step	Executive Decision Team	Project Decision Team	Business Owner	Key Stakeholders	ITS Management	ITS PMO	Project Manager	Vendor Project Manager	Engagement Manager	Accounts Payable
2 - Project Meetings			I	C			C	A/R		

Tips for Success:

Although Vendors are required to constantly update their schedule to reflect changes in milestone delivery dates, Project Managers should note that these dates do not constitute changes in delivery terms or changes to the baseline schedule. In other words, because a Vendor encounters difficulties delivering a milestone by an agreed upon date, Vendors cannot extend the delivery schedule by simply submitting a new date.

Changes to baseline schedules are not regular events and should only occur due to certain unforeseen circumstances or external events. In any event, all changes to schedule baselines must go through an approval process and must be authorized by a Change Control Board (this process will be outlined later in the Control sections). To allow Vendors to extend delivery schedules whenever they encounter problems would prevent the XYZ Company from measuring their progress towards stated goals. As such, Vendors will always be required to meet their baseline target dates. Project Managers should note, however that the communication of any foreseen missed dates is critical to the team, so that realistic expectations can be met. Although this information cannot change a project's baseline, the communication of any missed targets is vital towards the team's ability to take corrective action in current and future activities to get the project to get back on its baseline targets.

3.4 Process 4 – Manage Procurement & Contracts

Objectives: Management of procurement consists of processing payments to the Vendor. This is one of the most critical elements of Project Execution as it involves balancing the financial needs of the Vendor with the goals and objectives of the Business Owner.

Payment for goods and services in a retail environment is easy. As soon as a product is received the Vendor is paid for the product. However, this formula must be adapted for Projects since they are 1) more complex than a simple exchange of goods, and 2) take place over an extended period.

Inputs, Outputs and Tools

Inputs	Tools & Techniques	Outputs
• Payment Schedule • Milestone/Deliverable Approval Notices • Vendor Invoice • Vendor Expenses	• Project Budget	• Invoice Approval Notice

Instructions: To manage procurement of projects, PM's will use 4 main components: Invoices, Payment Schedules, Deliverable Acceptance Reports and Project Budgets.

Each component is used in conjunction with the others to form a comprehensive picture of project finances and contract execution. Used properly, these components insure that XYZ Company fairly compensates Vendors for their work while at the same time protecting the interests of the Authority and the XYZ Company.

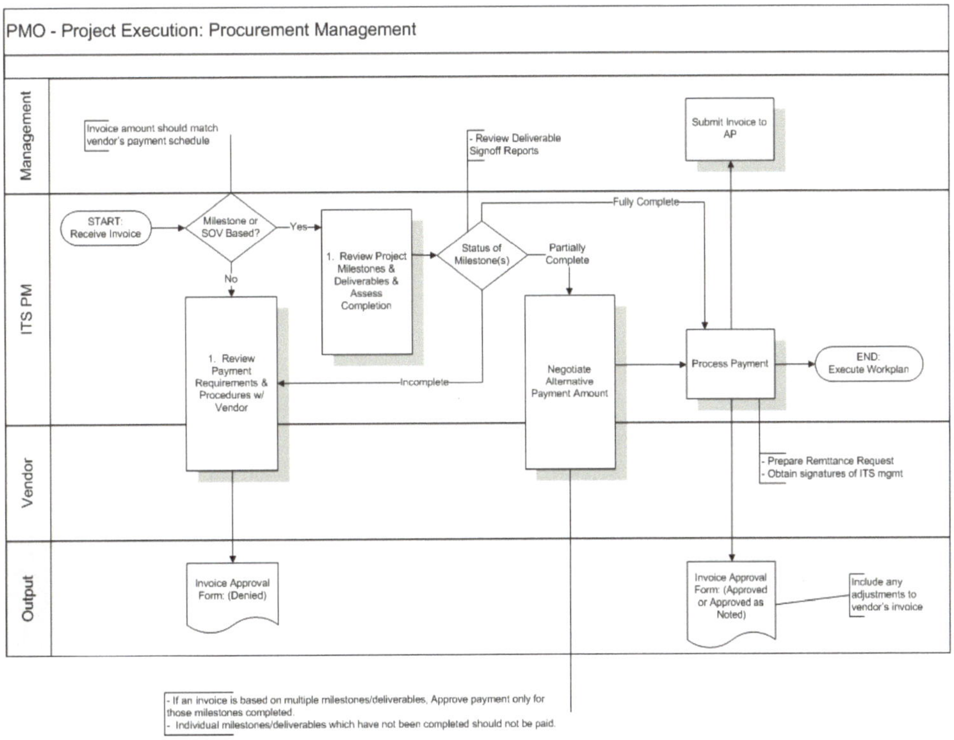

Step 1 – Process Invoices:

Most The ITS PMO contracts should be structured around fixed project deliverables. As such, project managers can expect to receive invoices for accepted deliverables at least once a month. To simplify their own workload, Project Managers should ask Vendors to submit only one invoice per project per month. Project Managers may also wish to request a regular date for submission of invoices where possible. If you are responsible for managing a large number of active projects spreading/consolidating invoice reviews across/on particular days may help you manage your own workload. Managing projects has enough unexpected activities, so providing structure to elements you are able to control helps free you to deal with the day-to-day fires and crises that inevitably emerge. Please note however, that some Vendors have their own billing procedures and policies and they may have no flexibility on which day invoices are submitted. But it never hurts to ask.

Step	Executive Decision Team	Project Decision Team	Business Owner	Key Stakeholders	ITS Management	ITS PMO	Project Manager	Vendor Project Manager	Engagement Manager	Accounts Payable
1 - Invoices							A/R	C		I

Step 2 – Review Payment Schedules, Line Items, and Deliverable Acceptance Reports:

There are three necessary elements for approval of a Vendor's invoice. Only when these elements are in alignment can a Project Manager approve all or part of a Vendor's invoice.

Payment Schedules

At the end of the Planning Stage, the Project Team should have completed a Payment Schedule. This payment schedule lists all project milestones and the value of those milestones. The total of all milestones should equal the project budget or contract amount. When reviewing any invoice, the payment schedule will be referenced to insure that the invoice line item matches the payment schedule. As the Payment Schedule is submitted and approved by the Vendor, there should be no valid reason why any line item within an invoice should not match the amount identified in the current Payment Schedule.

Payment Schedule Templates can be found in the PMO Templates Library.

Split Deliverables:

On some large projects, completion of milestones might take several months to complete and may involve expensive external resources. Some Vendors simply cannot absorb the cost of these expenditures and must receive some compensation during the execution of the milestone.

In these rare exceptions, deliverables can be split into multiple components to allow Vendors to be compensated for part of a milestone. Split deliverables should not be used on a regular basis and must never be used as a surrogate for progress payments. Note that each split deliverables must be included as separate line items in the payment schedule. Each of these line items must have some demonstrable deliverable (a test or installation report, a pilot review, an inspection, etc.) which the XYZ Company can review and evaluate.

Note that Project Managers must complete Deliverable Acceptance Forms for each component of a split deliverable.

Deliverable Acceptance Form:

Details of deliverables acceptance will be discussed later on in this chapter; however the use of the Deliverables Acceptance Form is critical for approval of invoices.

Upon review and approval of the any deliverable, PM's will complete and deliver an Acceptance Form to the Vendor corresponding to that deliverable. This form is the official notification to the project team that XYZ Company has approved that deliverable. When a PM reviews a Vendor's invoice, they must compare the invoice line-item to a corresponding deliverable approval notice. Only approve payments for deliverables, which have been approved.

Approved as Noted References:

For deliverables that have been "Approved as Noted", invoices require an additional step in the approval process. Project Managers must first insure that an additional deliverable has been submitted by the Vendor, and that the exceptions noted in the Deliverable Acceptance Form have been corrected.

Invoice approval represents a "last chance" for Project Managers to catch previously noted deficiencies. However this authority should not be used to add *additional* requirements or conditions for invoice approval. Once a deliverable has been approved, vendors are permitted to invoice for the full amount of that milestone.

Line Items

Vendors must be required to submit invoices, which include line items, which correspond to a deliverable or change-order. Project Managers should not accept any invoice without line-items that cannot be clearly and unambiguously tied to a project deliverable. Invoices can contain single line items or multiple-line items. However, Vendors should not be allowed to submit invoices for services or activities not referenced in their Payment Schedule. The sole exception to this being project expenses (discussed in the next section).

INVOICE:

Invoice No: 0006
Date: October 28, 2005
Project No: 1305-05
Project Name: New Computer Room

CHA-ID	Description	Part No	Unit Price	#	Total
4	HP-Server	MSA-1000.3	13,275.00	2	$26,550.00
5	Network Switch	C-12442	$4,988.50	4	$19,954.00
7	Rack Installation	-	$15,600.00	1	$15,600.00
12	Software Installation	-	$3,500	1	$3,500.00
44	12-months support	-	$24,000	1	$24,000.00
	Grand Total				**$89,604.00**

Many Vendors are used to submitting labor reports to their clients, which identify their expenditures for a given period. Project Managers should reject these invoices in their entirety unless labor-reports serve as backup documentation associated with invoice line-items.

Likewise, some Vendors are also used to submitting invoices based on the project's schedule. These types of invoices include line-items for partially completed deliverables. These types of invoices are generally termed "progress payments". Although these invoices contain line-items for services, and these line items may match the payment schedule, Project Managers must take care to only approve payment for line-items that have been completed. Project Managers should reject all invoice line-items unless which do not have a corresponding deliverable acceptance form.

Step	Executive Decision Team	Project Decision Team	Business Owner	Key Stakeholders	ITS Management	ITS PMO	Project Manager	Vendor Project Manager	Engagement Manager	Accounts Payable
1 - Invoices							A/R	C		I

It is the responsibility of the Vendor to manage their staff's resources; submission of Labor Reports. Progress Payments shift much or all of the responsibility of a projects finances to the XYZ Company.

Invoices must be rejected in whole or in part whenever:

- There are no line items.
- Line items do not match the payment schedule.
- Line items do not have a corresponding deliverables acceptance form.

Invoices can be partially paid whenever:

- At least one of the invoice's line items meets the conditions for approval.
    - A reduced payment can be issued which corresponds only to line items meeting approval conditions.
- Line items have a deliverables acceptance form but the invoice line-item does not match the amount listed in the payment schedule.
    - Payments can be issued for the amount resulting from substitution of the amount identified in the payment schedule.

Step	Executive Decision Team	Project Decision Team	Business Owner	Key Stakeholders	ITS Management	ITS PMO	Project Manager	Vendor Project Manager	Engagement Manager	Accounts Payable
2 - Payment Review							A/R			

Step 3 – Review Expenses

Some projects are structured to allow for reimbursement of certain expenses. These expenses would typically be things like travel expenses or materials and supplies. However, some statutes prohibit reimbursement of certain types of expenses (such as parking tickets or fines). Project Managers should consult with the Procurement office to be sure they are up-to-date on what current statutes and policies allow in terms of expenses.

Not all projects are structured to reimburse a Vendor's expenses; provisions for expenses should be clearly outlined within the Vendor's proposal and/or the project contract. If you find that a project proposal or contract does not expressly reference expenses, PM's should assume that expenses are not reimbursable. Be certain to discuss the inclusion or exclusion of expenses in the Planning Stages so neither you or your Vendor is surprised down the road.

If your project allows for reimbursement of expenses related to the project, be sure to have the Vendor include expenses as line-items in their invoices with supporting documentation.

Step 4 – Update Project Budget

The project budget can be seen as the "checkbook" for an individual project. The Budget is generally a spreadsheet, which is used to record three items:

- Payments made to the Vendor.
- Changes in the contract financials (including all Change Orders)
- The balance of funds remaining under the contract.

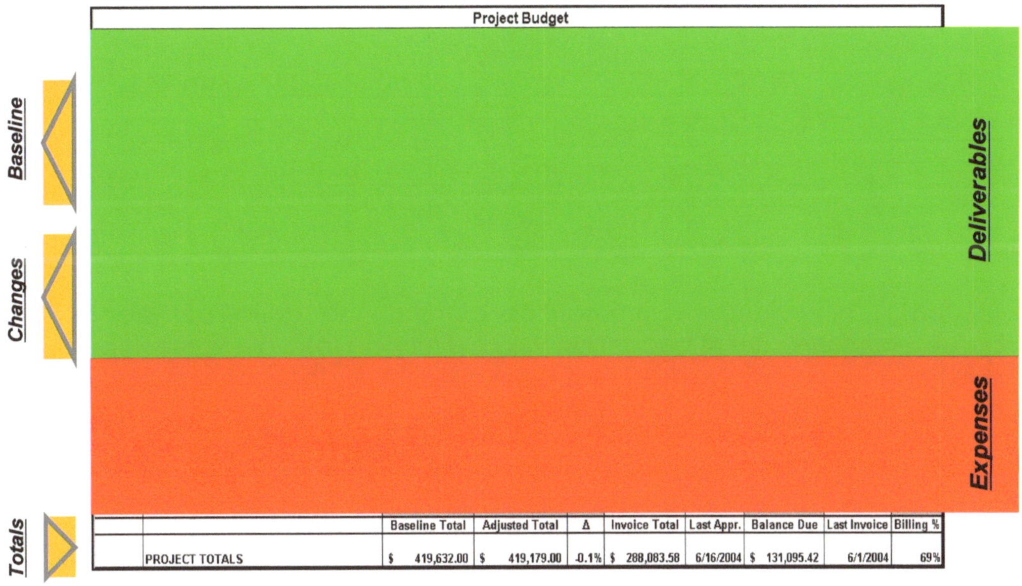

One of the most important elements of the Budget is the baseline. This contains all line items and values of the initial contract. These line items and values must never be altered once the Execution Phase of the project is initiated. All elements of the budget have some relationship to the baseline elements. By maintaining these elements separate from the baseline, PM's can communicate all financial activities relating to the project as well as any adjustments to the contract.

Project Budget Templates can be found in the PMO Templates Library.

The Project Budget is divided into two primary sections: Deliverables and Expenses

Expenses

The expenses section is the most straightforward element of the budget, and may be omitted for projects where a vendor's expenses are not reimbursed. The section contains a column for the baseline expense total, and the adjusted total. As mentioned earlier, <u>once a project's baseline is established, baseline values never change</u>. However should a PM increase the vendor's expense budget, the adjusted total column should be used to store the updated expense ceiling.

Unlike the baseline column, the adjusted expense total can be changed as needed throughout the project.

Every time an invoice's expenses are paid, PM's should record expenses separately from milestones. As mentioned earlier, expenses should be submitted only monthly to avoid overloading the PM with unnecessary paperwork. The expense period should be the main reference point in the Expense portion of the budget. Note that the expense period is generally the month preceding the vendor's invoice.

Whenever Invoices are submitted for payment, Project Managers should add the expenses paid and the approval date to the project budget along w/ a reference to the date of the invoice being processed.

Project Expenses	$ 15,000.00	$ 15,000.00	0.0%	$ 8,644.58		$ 6,355.42	
March 2004				$ 2,500.00	4/4/2004		4/1/2004
April 2004				$ 3,931.50	5/24/2004		5/1/2004
May 2004				$ 2,213.08	6/16/2004		6/1/2004
June 2004							
July 2004							
August 2004							

The template provided will automatically compute the "delta" between the expense baseline and the current budget as well as a running total of expenses paid to date. In addition it will automatically compute an expense budget balance as a dollar figure and as a percentage of the current budget.

These last two items can be used to assess the rate at which the Vendor is consuming their expense budget. They should be used in conjunction with the project schedule to determine the likelihood that the Vendor will exceed their expense budget before the end of the project.

Deliverables

The deliverables section is where Project Managers record all payments made to a vendor as they relate to a deliverable, milestone or change order.

The Deliverables section is divided into two subsections: Baseline and Changes. The baselines section is a direct copy of the milestones and deliverables referenced in the <u>first</u>

approved payment schedule. While the payment schedule itself changes over time to reflect the current milestones and deliverables, the milestones referenced in the baseline portion of the Budget never change.

All changes to the project are executed through change orders; as such, each and every change-order is included as its own line-item in the Change Order section of the Budget. Changes to the budget follow standard "ledger" principles for finances, which prohibit any changes to recorded line-items.

New tasks or deliverables items are referenced on their own line. However, changes to any milestone are referenced on two lines in the budget. The first line deducts the original line-item, from the budget and the second line adds the revised line to the budget.

	Change Orders	CO Subtotal	$ (453.00)					
999.1	Testing Software		$ 3,550.00		$ 3,550.00		$ -	5/1/2004
6.1	Legacy System Data Mapping (Original)		$ (9,500.00)		n/a	n/a	n/a	n/a
6.1	Legacy System Data Mapping (Revised)		$ 12,000.00		$ 12,000.00	2/14/2004	$ -	3/1/2004
12.1	Test Servers (supplied by CHA)		$ (33,883.00)		n/a	n/a	n/a	n/a
999.2	Additional Reports		$ 8,000.00		$ 8,000.00	3/15/2004	$ -	6/1/2004
999.3	Additional User Licenses		$ 19,380.00		$ 19,380.00	4/28/2004	$ -	5/1/2004

It is critical to follow these standard accounting principles in using the project budget to allow one to easily understand the financial state of a project. By including all changes as line-items in a budget, anyone referencing the project's finances can understand all payments and changes to a contract without reviewing the entire file of project correspondence.

Payments will be approved for all milestones and deliverables for which there are Deliverable Approval forms. Whenever such payments are made, Project Managers should record the activity in the Project Budget in the appropriate area.

Baseline

For approved milestones/deliverables, which have not been changed, Project Managers should record the amount paid, the date of approval, and the date of the invoice.

		Baseline Value	Adjusted Value	Δ	Invoice Amt.	Appr. Date	Balance Due	Invoice Date
Number	**Milestones / Deliverables**	$ 404,632.00	$ 404,179.00	-0.1%	$ 279,439.00		$ 124,740.00	
3.2	System Design Document	$ 43,966.00			$ 43,966.00	1/10/2004	$ -	3/1/2004
6.1	Legacy System Data Mapping	$ 9,500.00			n/a	n/a	n/a	n/a
10.3	System Pilot	$ 184,133.00			$ 184,133.00	4/28/2004	$ -	5/1/2004
12.1	Test Servers	$ 23,883.00			n/a	n/a	n/a	n/a
15.3	System Documentation	$ 46,400.00					$ 46,400.00	
15.5	Reports	$ 8,410.00			$ 8,410.00	5/15/2004	$ -	6/1/2004
19.1	System Testing	$ 13,340.00					$ 13,340.00	
22.8	User Training	$ 75,000.00					$ 75,000.00	

If a milestone or deliverable has been revised by a Change Order, the same information should be recorded in the Change Order section, however. The baseline section should never be used.

Changes

For any new or changed milestone / deliverable, Project Managers should record the amount paid, the date of approval, and the date of the invoice. Note that for changed milestones, the original (deducted) line-item should not be used for recording payment information.

Totals

As with expenses, the Budget Template will compute the "delta" between the milestone/deliverable baseline and the current budget. It will also provide a running total of milestone totals paid to date. It will also automatically compute a deliverable/milestone budget balance as a dollar figure and as a percentage of the current budget.

In addition to the totals for milestones and expenses, the template also computes the same totals for the entire project at the bottom of the worksheet. These totals can also be used to assess the rate at which the Vendor is consuming their budget (burn rate), but they are also used in reports to the Senior Portfolio Manager, which outline the project budget and delta from the baseline.

	Baseline Total	Adjusted Total	Δ	Invoice Total	Last Appr.	Balance Due	Last Invoice	Billing %
PROJECT TOTALS	$ 419,632.00	$ 419,179.00	-0.1%	$ 288,083.58	6/16/2004	$ 131,095.42	6/1/2004	69%

Step	Executive Decision Team	Project Decision Team	Business Owner	Key Stakeholders	ITS Management	ITS PMO	Project Manager	Vendor Project Manager	Engagement Manager	Accounts Payable
3 - Project Budget							A/R			

Step 5 – Review Monthly Finance Reports

Particularly for large projects, it is recommended to obtain a project finance report from the Finance office each month. These reports are like bank-statements and show all charges which have been assigned to your Project's PO. As one reconciles their personal checkbook with their bank statement each month, so should Project Managers reconcile their project budget with the finance report each month.

Project Managers should check to see if:

- Each invoice approved has been paid to the vendor.
- The amount paid matches the approved amounts.
- There are any payments made which are not referenced in the project budget.

Project Managers should note that often finance reports are not always in synch with the project budget, and that this does not *necessarily* mean that payments have not been processed. As mentioned earlier, the approval of an invoice by The ITS PMO may not mean that a payment will be issued to the vendor. There are rules and procedures within the Finance office which further govern when a vendor can be paid and how much they can be paid. If a vendor, for example, is not in compliance with Section 8 or MBE requirements of their contract, payment may not be released until those conditions are resolved to the satisfaction of the Procurement Department.

However, the Project Manager should contact the Procurement Department whenever there are differences between the approved and posted amounts or there is a payment which has been missing for more than one month. In most instances, terms for vendor payments are "net-30" meaning that payment must be made to a vendor within 30-calendar days of invoice receipt.

By checking with the Finance office regarding "missing" payments, Project Managers can help XYZ Company avoid any interest associated w/ late payments. Furthermore, Project Managers obtain information about any outstanding compliance issues should the vendor ask them about an invoice or reduced payment amount.

Occasionally, Finance offices mix up purchase orders for projects and sometimes credit payments to the wrong project; sometimes other departments inadvertently mistype a PO number. By checking for both missing payments as well payments not referenced in your budget, Project Managers can identify any non-assigned payment associated w/ their project or another project.

Step 6 – Complete Invoice Approval Notice

Once Project Managers have completed their review a Vendor's invoice, they must prepare a formal notification letter to the Vendor and direct the approved invoice to XYZ Company's Accounts Payable Department

The invoice approval notice serves two purposes: first, it documents amount of the invoice approved and second, it documents the date on which the invoice was submitted to accounts payable for processing.

Invoice Approval notices apply only to one invoice. If a vendor has submitted multiple invoices for review and approval, Project Managers must complete Approval Notices for each invoice.

Invoice Approval Notice Templates can be found in the PMO Templates Library.

Project Managers should note that the Accounts Payable Department requires several days to process payments. For this reason, the ITS PMO Project Managers must complete the approval of vendor invoices **within 5 business days of receipt**. For contracts that have terms less than 30-days, Project Managers must review a vendor's invoice immediately upon receipt. As the approval process rarely involves more than comparing invoices against existing documentation (payment schedules and deliverable acceptance forms), Project Managers should have little difficulty completing the Invoice Approval form within this timeframe.

One critical thing for Project Managers to communicate to Vendors early on is that invoice approval notices are not guarantees of payment, they represent the acceptance of a vendor's invoice by the ITS PMO Department. As noted earlier, the Procurement Department may sometimes delay payment or it may withhold additional funds based on their own contract requirements.

The Invoice Approval Notice has two sections. In the upper right corner, Project Managers should fill out information relating to the contract, including the official title, solicitation number, Purchase Order number and The ITS PMO project number. Also included are the payment terms of the contract. All of this information (with the exception of the ITS PMO project number), will be used by the Accounts Payable department in processing each invoice. This information will also be consistent in every Invoice Approval Notice prepared for this project.

The second, and main section of the Invoice Approval Notice is the approval section itself. There are checkboxes for the disposition of the invoice, as well as reference information identifying the invoice being reviewed. This section also contains a place to list the amount authorized for payment as well as a place to list individual line items. Lastly, this form contains an area for including notes related to invoice review.

July 14, 2004

RFS No.	03-00018-06
Upgrade Café Infrastructure	
PO Number	CHA12-23345
Contract Terms	Net 30
ITS Project No.	04-01234-01

Mr. Louis Mitchell
Lou Mitchell's and Assoc.
550 West Jackson St.
Chicago, IL 60606

Dear Mr. Mitchell,

The ITS Department has received your request for payment dated 6/30/04 for the referenced project. The disposition of your request is as follows:

☐ APPROVED:	Invoice Number:	23348-Q
☒ APPROVED AS NOTED	Invoice Date:	6/30/04
☐ NOT APPROVED:	Authorized Payment	$9,500

Deliverable / Milestone	Value	Approval Date
Deliverable 23.1a – As-Is Assessment	$9,500	5/15/04

Comments:

The invoice for the referenced deliverable is greater than the amount specified in your payment schedule. ITS has authorized payment for the amount listed in your payment schedule.

Invoice Disposition

Invoices are either: Approved, Approved as Noted or Not Approved.

"Approved" invoices are accepted in total. The entire amount, including all line items and expenses, are approved in full. The amount listed in the "Authorized Payment" section of the notice should equal the total amount of the invoice. In the Deliverable/Milestone area, Project Managers should include all milestones associated with the invoice as well as the value identified in the Payment Schedule and the approval date listed in the corresponding Deliverable Acceptance Form.

"Not Approved" invoices are rejected in total, and no monies are to be paid to the Vendor. For Invoices that are Not Approved, the "Authorized Payment" section of the invoice should always be "0". Invoices can be rejected for any number of reasons, ranging from missing line-items to failure to adhere to contract requirements. Project Managers should summarize the reasons why they have rejected the invoice in the Comments area. A summary of the invoice line items (if any) should be listed in the "Deliverables/Milestones area" along with the values listed in the invoice; however, the approval date area should be left blank or listed as "not approved".

"Approved as Noted" invoices are often the most involved as they result in a partial payment to the vendor; the form must therefore summarize the payment which is being made. All approved, rejected and/or adjusted invoice line items and expenses should be listed. As with approved invoices, Project Managers should include all line items values identified in the Payment Schedule along with and the approval date listed in the corresponding Deliverable Acceptance Form. Project Managers should note that these values may not match the corresponding value listed on the invoice. For milestones invoiced but not approved, or for line-items, which do not have a corresponding milestone, Project Managers should summarize the invoice line item and list the Approval date as "not approved". In the Comments area, Project Managers should explain the reasons why they have rejected or took exceptions to portions of the vendors invoice as well as what adjustments were performed.

Once completed, Project Managers should sign and date the Invoice Approval form and immediately mail and/or email the form to the vendor. Copies of the vendors invoice and the invoice approval form must both be retained in the official contract file.

Invoices, which are either Approved or Approved as Noted, should also be forwarded to the Accounts Payable office with the Invoice Approval Form. Invoices, which are Not Approved, need not be submitted to Accounts Payable.

Step	Executive Decision Team	Project Decision Team	Business Owner	Key Stakeholders	ITS Management	ITS PMO	Project Manager	Vendor Project Manager	Engagement Manager	Accounts Payable
5 - Invoice Approval Notice			I		I		A/R	C		A/C

Tips for Success

Many vendors new to XYZ Company are not familiar with the Accounts Payable Processes and the requirements of that department to receive prompt payment. Project Managers can avoid many of the inevitable monthly inquiries into invoice processing by helping them understand the procedures, requirements and timelines established by Accounts Payable.

Why should Project Managers process partial payments?

Processing partial payments simplifies the negotiation of any problems or disputes between XYZ Company and Vendors. By making payment for items not in dispute, discussions are limited to only items or amounts to which the XYZ Company and the Vendor have not agreed upon. Partial payments are not progress payments. Payments are to be made for deliverables XYZ Company has already accepted; the completion or quality of the work is not in question.

There is no reason to withhold payment for activities XYZ Company has approved and taken delivery of. Where there is a dispute in terms of the value of a completed deliverable, making payments equal to the minimum allows both parties to concentrate solely on the differential. Lastly, it also shows "good-faith" on behalf of the XYZ Company in compensating Vendors fairly for work performed in accordance with their contract.

Why Project Managers should NOT make progress payments towards deliverables?

While making payments for approved deliverables does not increase XYZ Company's risk, making a progress payment substantially increases XYZ Company's risk. Unlike a partial payment, progress payment constitutes payment for a deliverable or milestone which is incomplete. By making progress payments, Vendors have little incentive to complete milestones in a timely manner or at a level of quality, which meets the expectations of the XYZ Company.

Although most Vendors are forthright and will make a genuine effort to complete the milestone in accordance with contract requirements, problems arise in those instances where there is a dispute with the Vendor over a milestone. When this occurs, monies are XYZ Company's most effective tools for insuring Vendors fulfill the terms of their contract.

3.5 Execution Sub-Processes

Objectives: In addition to four main processes, Project Execution involves three sub processes: Change Orders, Deliverable Review and Stop Work. These processes correspond to individual tasks, which, although related to the major processes of Project Execution, are inherently self-contained. Sub processes are also distinguished from Execution Processes in that they are done on an "as-needed" or "ad hoc" basis. Major processes of Project Execution are continuous and repetitive activities.

3.5.1 Sub-Process 1 – Deliverable Review

Instructions: Deliverable review is the cornerstone of vendor payments and represents one of the key metrics by which vendor performance can be measured. With the exception of expenses, invoices should never be paid unless Project Managers have a deliverable review form, which corresponds to the invoice.

Project Managers should note that the term "Deliverable" and "Milestone" can are used in this section interchangeably as it relates to reviewing progress. However, at the end of this section, we will outline one subtle difference between a Deliverable and a Milestone as it relates to the Deliverable Review form.

Deliverable Review Templates can be found in the PMO Templates Library.

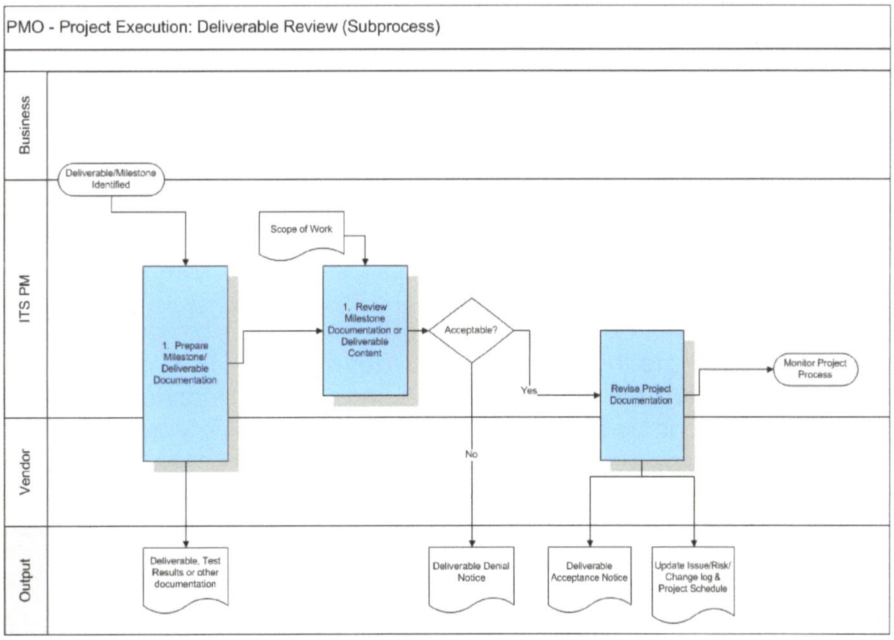

Deliverable Review Form

Instructions: The Deliverable Review Form contains four sections. The top of the form contains the information about the review event while the second part of the form contains information about the disposition of the review. The third section of the form contains an optional reference to the project schedule, and the fourth and final section contains signatures of the review team.

Inputs, Outputs and Tools

Inputs	Tools & Techniques	Outputs
• Statement of Work • Change Proposal • Vendor Deliverable/Presentati on	• Issue/Risk/Change Log	• Milestone Approval Notice • Project Meeting Minutes

Step 1 – Review Events

Project:	ProjectCenter Upgrade	Vendor:	Honest Abe Software, Inc.
ITS Project No:	05-0014-01	ITS Project Manager:	J. Doherty
RFS Number:	04-00018-01	Review Date:	6/11/05
Notes: Additional reports (deliverable 12.8.1) were not submitted for review at this time.			

The review event is defined as the activity, which prompted the review of a milestone or a deliverable. This could be a review of a Vendor's deliverable or a presentation involving a milestone. Project Managers should note the basic information of the project in the top of the form and include a short description of what the review event consisted of.

In the event a vendor is required to resubmit a deliverable or redo a presentation, Project Managers must note that the event is a reevaluation. They must also note which element(s) are being reevaluated. To minimize the amount of paperwork to be maintained, Project Managers should include ALL elements of previous review events in the disposition section (see below) including those previously approved. While the approved events need not be reevaluated, they must be referenced in any reevaluation of part of a deliverable. This allows project managers to use avoid having to reference multiple Deliverable Review forms during the Invoicing Procedures.

Project Managers should be able to see how difficult management of Project Deliverables can become should they elect to use a Deliverable Review form for more than one event. This is particularly evident should any portion of an event require resubmission or reevaluation. For these reasons, it is imperative that multiple review forms be used for multiple review events.

Step 2 – Review Disposition

The disposition area of the review form contains areas for both the reference number and a short description of the milestone or deliverable and the associated dollar value. Reference numbers and dollar values must match items contained in either the payment schedule or an approved scope change. Project Managers will always have one or both of these references in a milestone or deliverable review. The Project Execution process does not allow for a deliverable or milestone to be reviewed without a value assigned to it.

As the review process is a precursor to the invoicing and payment process, it is critical that the references to deliverables and milestones match the payment schedule. If there are inconsistencies or discrepancies between the two elements, it will become more difficult to process payments and resolve budgetary problems later on in the project.

Project Deliverable / Milestone Review

Number	Completed	Milestone / Deliverable	Approved	Approved as Noted	Not Approved	Value
6.8		Software Installed	X			$4,660.00
9.2		Assessment Report	X			$9,590.00
15.4		End User Traning Materials	X			$12,550.00
16.9		Cutover Checklist	X			$5,560.00
Comments:						

The format of the disposition section is similar to that of the invoice approval section. There are areas where a milestone or deliverable can be marked as "Approved", "Not Approved" and "Approved as Noted". The rules for approval are identical to those mentioned in the Invoice Approval section except that they apply to individual line items and not to the entire event:

> "Approved" deliverables are accepted in total. The Project Team has determined that the reviewed item fully meets the requirements and obligations of the contract. No further work on the deliverable is required by the vendor and Project Managers need not provide any comments on these deliverables.
>
> "Not Approved" deliverables have been rejected and resubmission and reevaluation is required. The Project Team has determined the reviewed item has substantial deficiencies w/ respect to contract requirements. Project Managers must note the line-item number in the "Comments" section and summarize deficiencies of the deliverable.
>
> "Approved as Noted" deliverables have minor problems in quality, which the Project Team believes can be corrected without *formal* reevaluation. Vendors are, however, required to correct the referenced deficiencies and resubmit the deliverable. Project Manager may elect to withhold payment for that like item until a resubmission is received. Project Managers must note the line-item number in the "Comments" section and summarize the exceptions taken.

As with Invoice processing, deliverables designated "Approved as Noted" are the most complex. While this disposition is often the most effective in moving a project along, Project

Managers should take great care to insure that the XYZ Company's interests are always being protected to the best extent practicable.

In theory, Vendors should always be required to resubmit a deliverable with this disposition; however in practice it is often more practical to review a correction in a subsequent review that is already on the project schedule. For example, if there are grammatical errors in an early presentation of a new Web Portal, it is generally impractical to assemble the Project Team for an additional presentation of the Portal's corrected grammar. In this example, it would be more prudent for a Project Team to review the corrected grammar in a subsequent presentation that was already planned.

In the event any or all deliverables have not been designated "Approved", Project Managers should also use the comments section to identify what corrective action is required and the date by which it is to be delivered.

Issues and Deliverables

To insure that critical issues related to a milestone are addressed, Project Managers should be certain to associate those items with a particular milestone line-item and insure that the deliverable is at least marked "Approved as Noted".

Vendors are allowed to invoice XYZ Company for the entirety of milestones, which have been designated Approved or Approved as Noted. However the Approved as Noted disposition offers Project Managers additional leeway so that they can insure that "noted" issues are addressed prior to payment.

Timeliness

Project Managers may note that there has been no mention of the timeliness of deliverables as a part of the review process in Project Execution. While the timeliness of deliverables and XYZ Company review of deliverables is critical to meeting project scheduling goals, the timeliness of deliverables and evaluations are simply part of the control process. These elements will be outlined in the following chapter of the PMO Handbook.

Step 3 – Project Schedule (optional)

The Project Schedule is the only optional section of the Deliverable Review form. Project Managers are often required to communicate to the project team where deliverables stand in relation to other activities in the project schedule. In addition, for large projects it is often difficult to remember where deliverables and milestones stand in relation to other activities. In those cases, Project managers may wish to include a screen-capture of a portion of the schedule, which relates to the milestones and deliverables being reviewed in this form.

In addition, by including the timeline in the approval form itself, one can also create a permanent record of the timeliness of the milestone and of XYZ Company's approval. Often this sort of information becomes critical in evaluating a vendor's performance.

Project Managers should also annotate the image where necessary to highlight the relevant sections as well as any key dates involved in the review process.

Step 4 – Authorizations

The final section of the form involves signatures of the team. In the event that all deliverables/milestones reviewed have been rejected, only the Project Manager needs to sign the authorizations section. However, if any of the items reviewed have been approved or approved as noted, the Project Manager is responsible for obtaining signatures of all required parties.

At a minimum, signoffs by the Project Manager and the Business Owner are required for any project deliverable. This helps insure a fundamental level of control and oversight w/ respect to deliverables acceptance.

Deliverables vs. Milestones

Up until this point, Project Managers will note no difference between Milestones and Deliverables; in fact, the term is frequently interchanged throughout this Chapter. However, there is one subtle difference between the two items.

Deliverables are tangible items, which are transferred from Vendor to Owner. Milestones are specific metric points in the project lifecycle, which may or may not involve deliverables.

The difference between Deliverables and Milestones however, is not academic. While the deliverable review process defined above works equally well for milestones and deliverables, Milestones offer an additional option for review.

Segmented Milestones

Instructions: As seen in above, milestones can be composed of multiple tasks. Likewise, the Deliverable Review form can be used to note the completion of tasks, which in turn make up the milestone.

Project Deliverable / Milestone Review

Number	Completed	Milestone / Deliverable	Approved	Approved as Noted	Not Approved	Value
6.8		Software Installed	X			$4,660.00
9.2		As-Is Assessment Report		X		$9,590.00
9.7		System Setup Complete / Software License Payment (2 of 2)			X	$10,233.00
	X	Software setup: 622 West Jackson				
		Software setup: 600 West Jackson				
	X	Software setup: 4859 S. Wabash				

Comments:

9.2: The as-is assessment report is acceptable; however there are several typos and grammatical errors which should be corrected.

9.7: The system setup was not completed. During the installation review on 6/15/04, we noted that workstations in the Operations department (600 w/ Jackson St.) did not have software installed. Please complete the installation for this department and schedule a subsequent review of the outstanding installations.

In some instances it may be preferable for the Project Team to note the completion (or omission) of individual tasks involving a milestone. This is particularly useful when the milestone involves elements, which cannot be easily documented. It can also be useful to streamline the amount of paperwork required to review a milestone, as each task may involve relatively small activities performed at different times. In either event, a segmented milestone can be viewed as a sort of "checklist" or "punch list" of individual tasks.

Segmented milestones are also useful for milestones of high-dollar values as a means of insuring that all steps have been taken to protect XYZ Company interest before making a large payment to a Vendor. Likewise, segmented milestones should also be used for milestones particularly critical to a project's success or which may involve a high degree of risk to the Project Team. By breaking the milestone into components, the Project Team can often mitigate many project risks or failures.

Although a milestone is separated into individual components, Project Managers should take care to insure that these components are not "trivial" in nature. Milestone components should involve only the most important items, which are critical to the successful completion of the milestone. For this reason, the components of a segmented milestone may sometimes differ from the tasks listed in the project schedule. However, as with all elements of the Deliverable Review form, must also be identified in the Payment Schedule.

One important thing to note is that the milestone is ONLY composed of subtasks. In other words, the milestone line item itself must not involve any activities or deliverables. Milestones, which have been segmented, are "summary tasks" which rely solely on several "subtasks" to define them.

A second thing to note is that subtasks of segmented milestones do not have values associated with them. Only the milestone itself has a value, which will be represented in the Payment Schedule. Milestone subtasks are simply checkpoints to determine whether or not the milestone has or has not been completed.

Lastly, only the milestone itself marked as approved or not approved when segmented milestones are used. The components of the milestone are marked simply checked off as "completed". If all of the tasks are completed, then the milestone should me marked as both "Completed" as well as "Approved". Likewise, if any of the subtasks are NOT completed, the milestone should not be marked as complete and the milestone should be marked as "NOT approved".

A key difference between discrete milestones and segmented ones is that segmented milestones can NEVER be given the designation "Approved as Noted". If any of the subtasks have not been completed, then the milestone itself must be listed as incomplete.

The reason for this is that unlike deliverables and discrete milestones, which may involve complex tasks, or large deliverables which a Project Team can take some exceptions to, segmented milestones are always composed of small discrete tasks. In essence, the milestone itself is broken up into simple and easily managed components. Because of this simplification, there should be little reason for Vendors to fail the completion of any individual subtask, which by its nature is deemed critical to milestone completion.

In addition, segmented milestones often involve tasks of high-dollar values and/or critical risk areas. To protect the interests of XYZ Company, these milestones should be treated with particular consideration as they represent some of the most vital success factors of the project. So if any one of a segmented milestone's tasks does not meet the requirements of the contract, Project Managers are obligated to reject the milestone in its entirety and require the completion of the subtask(s) as a condition of milestone approval.

Estimated Time Duration:

Review of Vendor deliverables varies widely depending on the nature of what was submitted for review. However the preparation of the Milestone Review form itself should take less than 30-minutes

Resource Participation:

Members of the Project Team have contributed to the process via the CCB and the Change Request Form. The Project Manager is solely responsible for preparation of the Change Approval Notice. There is minimal additional input from other members of the Project Team.

Procedures involving the Change Control Board are discussed in Chapter 4 – Project Control.

3.5.2 Sub-Process 2 – Change Approval Notification

Objectives: Throughout the course of a project there are many circumstances, which require changes to the Vendor's Statement of Work. The vehicle for administering these changes is the Change Approval sub process.

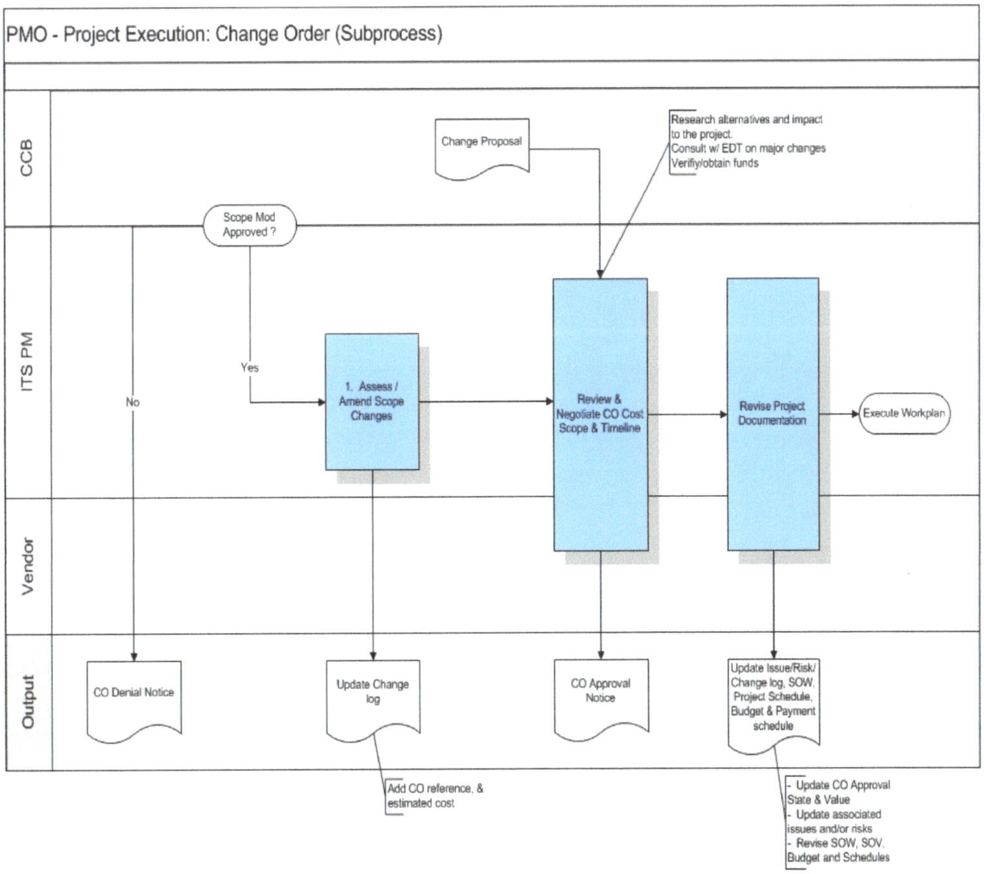

Instructions: There are two keys to Scope Change control: The first and most important aspect is proper Scope Definition. This not only refers to the scope of the Change Proposal, but in the scope of the project itself (the Statement of Work). The second is that Project Managers must be actively involved managing scope changes. See the section on Change Control in Chapter 4 for a more robust discussion of this topic.

Examples of this include:

- Working with the Key Stakeholders on alternatives to costly requests.
- Negotiating credits with vendors for omissions and scope reductions.
- Working with the Project Team to define efficiencies, which can offset or mitigate costs.
- Researching market prices to insure XYZ Company is receiving a fair deal.
- Obtaining goods and services from competitively priced sources.

Changes to contracts are not, in and of themselves, a bad thing or a sign that a project is in trouble. In reality, most projects have and require Scope Changes throughout the project's lifecycle. However, Scope Changes become problematic when no one but the vendor or key stakeholder is managing them. Many Project Managers know of projects they or their colleagues were involved in which may have contained a seemingly endless stream of changes to the contract and spiraling costs. In these instances, it is the lack of containment of scope change, which signifies that a project is in trouble:

	Date	Project A	Project B
Change A	1/05	-	$1,900
Change B	1/05	-	$1,000
Change C	1/05	$3,500	($2,500)
Change D	2/05	-	$10,000
Change E	3/05	-	$12,000
Change F	3/05	-	$6,500
Change G	4/05	$11,000	$20,000
Change H	4/05	-	($9,500)
Change I	4/05	-	$6,000
Change J	4/05	-	$3,800
Change K	5/05	$1,500	$9,400

If one assumes that each of the projects is valued at $200,000 one can clearly see which project is likely headed for trouble. Irrespective of the dollar amounts referenced, one can see that Project B has little or no control over the scale and quantity of Scope Changes.

Inputs, Outputs and Tools

Inputs	Tools & Techniques	Outputs
• Vendor Change Proposal • Scope Change Request Form	• Project Budget • Change Control Board (CCB)	• Updated Payment Schedule • Updated Statement of Work • Updated Project Schedule • Updated Project Plan • Change Approval Notice

Step 1 – Request Scope Change Proposal

Once a need for a Scope Change has been identified, the Project Manager generally requests a change from the vendor. Although most commonly done in an informal manner, such as an email, it is more practical to include the request on XYZ Company Letterhead. Vendors will respond to the request with a Scope Change Proposal.

Request for Scope Changes and Proposals, are akin to small-scale RFS' and Vendor Proposals. Requests should be clear and unambiguous, and Proposals must address the requests stated in the proposal and provide a firm fixed price (or credit) for the additional (or omitted) services. They must have clearly defined scope and must also define any impacts to the project schedule.

Project Managers should note that Scope Change is fundamentally a negotiation, and negotiation is required to get the best value for the XYZ Company. As with the RFS Process, the best value may, or may not be the lowest price. However, unlike the RFS process, XYZ Company Project Managers are working with a single source for those services, which often puts them at a competitive disadvantage. Most reputable vendors will not attempt to exploit this position; however Project Managers must be wary of those vendors who are looking for Scope Changes as a means of correcting deficiencies in their proposal, or enhancing their profit margins.

Project Managers can and should request new versions of the proposal as part of the negotiation process when elements of the Change Proposal's scope or budget is not in line with the needs and goals of the Business Owner or the goals of the project. This can be done through subsequent requests for Scope Change, but Change Proposal Negotiation is most commonly done via face-to-face or teleconferences.

One of the most common omissions in Change Control is to require vendors to assess impacts to the Project Schedule. While cost containment is most often the most actively investigated Project Managers should not forget that the addition or removal of work usually has some impact on the project schedule. Even if a Vendor is procuring those goods and services from a third party, the timely delivery of that product is likely to impact the project's Critical Path.

Critical Path analysis and the means and methods of Change Proposal evaluation will be discussed in the next Chapter of this handbook.

Step 2 – Receive Scope Change Proposals

Vendors Change Proposals will vary widely from vendor to vendor. However, Project Managers must inure that vendors include seven items in each and every change proposal:

1. Proposal Numbering
2. Proposal Versioning
3. Statement of Work
4. Delivery Schedule
5. Impact Analysis
6. Cost Breakdown
7. Vendor's Signature

Often vendors will obtain goods and services from other sources and will include a proposal prepared by one of their subcontractors or suppliers. However, the vendor is responsible for adding any of the necessary components that their partner may be unable to prepare on their own. While a supplier can complete the statement of work, delivery schedule and cost, the vendor is likely the only one who can assess impacts to the project's schedule.

Project Managers should also insure that the proposal is authorized by the vendor and not only their partner. Just as the vendor is responsible for all work defined in their proposal, the vendor is likewise responsible for any and all change proposals. Although any number of drafts can be negotiated w/ the vendor's partner(s), the final Change Proposal must be submitted by the vendor.

Once the Project Team has agreed to the terms of the Scope Change Proposal, the proposal is then brought before the Change Control Board for assessment. Details of the Change Control Board process will be discussed in the next chapter of this handbook.

Step 4 – Change Control Board

The Change Control Board will issue its approval (or rejection) of the Vendor's Change Proposal to the Project Manager. However, the Change Control Board process is an internal process, which is not known to the Vendor. It is the Project Manager's responsibility to assemble the Change Control Board's comments in an approval (or rejection) letter forwarded to the Vendor.

The Change Control Board completes a Change Request Form, which contains signatures and comments from each of the CCB's member groups. If any one of the CCB's groups recommends that the proposal be rejected, the Project Manager must reject the vendor's proposal. The vendor's proposal can only be approved (or approved as noted) if all members of the Change Control Board approve the proposal

Step 5 – Prepare Change Approval Notice

As the approval of a vendor's proposal constitutes an Official notice, the Change Approval Notice is authored on XYZ Company letterhead and must be signed by the Project Manager.

Change Approval Templates can be found in the PMO Templates Library.

The Change Approval Notice consists of four sections: Project Information, Disposition, Impact and Authorization.

The Project Information section is contained in the upper right corner, and contains basic information about the contract being amended. As a Project Manager (or vendor) may be working on multiple projects with similar change descriptions, the inclusion of basic project data allows the Project Team to keep track of what project a request is associated with.

Change Proposal Name / Description:		**Six Custom Reports**	
Change Proposal No:	004	☐ APPROVED:	
Change Proposal Date:	6/30/04	☒ APPROVED AS NOTED: *(see below)*	
Approved Value:	**$93,500**	☐ NOT APPROVED: *(see below)*	
Milestone Delay:	0 days	Net Project Impact:	0 days
Comments: Scope Change proposal is approved for the additional custom reports. However, the due date for all reports will not be extended. All 14 reports must be completed by 11/3/04.			

Just as the Project Information section contains information about the project, the Disposition Section begins with information about the Change Proposal including its number (and version), submission date and title.

The form also contains a general summary of any delays to the next major milestone as well as to the project as a whole. This information is garnered from the Vendor's change Proposal.

The section also contains the disposition of the Change Proposal. As with all other forms, if the proposal is either not approved or approved as noted, the Project Manager must summarize the exceptions in the comments area.

Step 6 – Migrating Change Control Board Comments

If none of the Change Control Board members has taken exceptions to the Vendor's Proposal, then the Change Approval Notice should be "Approved" by the Project Manager. No additional comments are required.

However, if the Change Control Board has approved the Proposal but has noted exceptions, the Project Manager must assess the nature of those comments and make a determination as to whether they are appropriate to communicate to the Vendor. In many instances, the CCB will issue exceptions to the proposal; however, in some instances they may direct the Project Manager, and not the vendor, as to how to proceed with implementing the current Change Proposal or with future change proposals.

The Project Manager must assess the comments of the CCB and only include exceptions to the change proposal in the Change Approval Notice. If there are any exceptions included, the Project Manager must designate the Change Proposal "Approved as Noted". However if none of the CCB's comments can be associated with the vendor's current proposal, the Project Manager can elect to designate the Change Proposal "Approved".

Step 7 – Impact and Authorizations

The third section of the Change Approval Notice is the Schedule Impact. For all change proposals, vendors should be required to submit a revised Project Schedule, which includes the proposed changes to the Statement of Work. Project Managers should include an excerpt from the revised schedule in the Change Approval Notice to communicate to the project team the new or omitted services and deliverables stand in relation to other activities in the project schedule. The excerpt should clearly show what items are new and highlight any impacts to current milestones.

The last section of the Change Approval Notice involves authorizations. Although the CCB has authorized (or rejected) the Vendor's Change Proposal, the final Change Approval Notice must also be authorized by key members of the Project Team to insure that they are in concurrence with what is being communicated to the Vendor. This provides a degree of checks and balances to insure that CCB's exceptions are being communicated to the vendor.

2. Authorizations

*Project Sponsor (CHA)	Date	Project Sponsor (CHA)	Date
*Project Manager (CHA ITS)	Date	PDT Member (CHA)	Date
*Assistant CIO (CHA ITS)	Date	PDT Member (CHA)	Date
CIO (CHA ITS)	Date	Executive Sponsor (CHA)	Date

*Required Signatures

At a minimum, signoffs by the Business Owner are required for any scope change.

Estimated Time Duration:

The request and preparation of a Change proposal varies depending on the nature of the change and the scope of the project. Completion of a Change Approval notice should take between 1 and 2 hours

Procedures involving the Change Control Board are discussed in Chapter 4 – Project Control.

Resource Participation:

Members of the Project Team have contributed to the process via the CCB and the Change Request Form. The Project Manager is solely responsible for preparation of the Change Approval Notice. There is minimal additional input from other members of the Project Team.

Procedures involving the Change Control Board are discussed in Chapter 4 – Project Control.

3.5.3 Sub-Process 3 – Work Stoppage

Objectives: Occasionally, projects do run into difficulties –even under the best of constraints and oversight. However, once significant problems are observed, it is up to the Project Manager to exercise their authority to demand a correction to the problem.

Instructions: Problems however, may or may not be the fault of any one party. They can, of course, be due to failings of the vendor, but they may also be due to failures of the XYZ Company as well. Lastly, they may be due to lack of support or need for the project entirely.

> Lack of Need: A Project Manager may find that their project is cancelled or no longer needed at some point during the project lifecycle. The reason for the change of heart could be due to a larger scale project taking on key roles that their project undertakes. Or it could be due to a loss of funding for the project. Through no fault of the project team, the Project Manager may find themselves in a situation where all or some of the project must be stopped. The vehicle for this activity is the Stop Work Order.
>
> Change in Scope: In some instances, the Business Owner may have a change of heart with respect to a key portion of a project. The organizations needs may change, or there may be a change in technology, which they feel, is more suitable to their goals. While this may, or may not necessitate the termination of the contract (depending on the scale of the change needed), the one thing that often does become clear immediately is that the current system or module being implemented is not needed. To prevent the Vendor from expending additional funds in pursuit of an unwanted goal, Project Managers can issue a Stop Work Order.
>
> Critical Deficiencies: In the event that a Vendor is not fulfilling their contractual obligations as it relates to deliverables and performance, it may become necessary to formally notify the Vendor that they are to refrain from performing work on subsequent aspects of the project until the current deficiencies are corrected. This is particularly useful when those deficiencies are tied to deliverables in the design or early implementation stages. By issuing a Stop Work Order, Vendors are placed on notice that they will be unable to submit invoices for any work or milestones beyond the current date until the deficiency is corrected.

Work Stoppage can be structured for all project activities, as well as for specific products, technologies or deliverables.

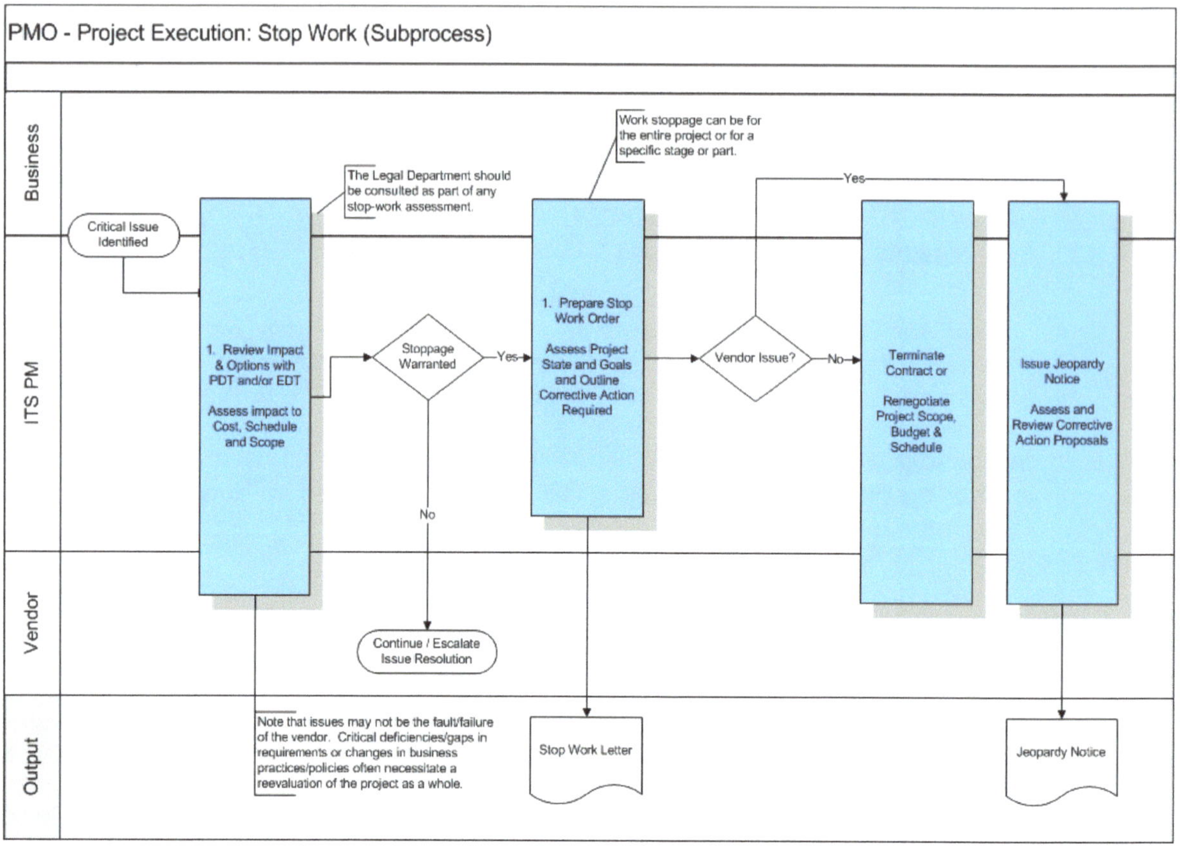

Stop Work Orders and Contract Termination

Project Managers should note that a Stop Work Order does not constitute a termination of the Vendor's contract –either for Default or for Convenience. Contract termination is solely within the domain of XYZ Company's Procurement Department, and they are the only persons who have the authority to terminate a vendor's contract.

Stop Work Orders are strictly "stop loss" measures, designed to protect the project budget during a crisis within the project.

The vast majority of projects will never experience a Stop Work Order as it is strictly an emergency procedure. If implemented inappropriately or incorrectly, <u>Stop Work Orders can have an adverse affect on a project that is not in crisis.</u>

When is a Project "In Crisis?"

There is no hard and fast rule for when a project is in crisis or not. Project Managers will generally find themselves in a situation where there is "no way out" under the current plan.

They may:

- Find themselves with insufficient monies to pay upcoming milestones and invoices.
- Find the system called for is now obsolete or redundant.
- Find the vendor is implementing a system using specifications the Project Team rejected.

- Find the vendor unilaterally switched core products, which were referenced in their proposal.
- Find that a dependent project or system has been cancelled.
- Find that a manufacturer has declared Bankruptcy or is discontinuing the product.

In all of the above examples, there is no practical way to continue a project along its present course. The team must make a significant change to the project in terms of scope, schedule, budget or deliverables to either get the project on track or define and shift resources to a completely new track.

However, a project is most likely not in crisis when:

- There are insufficient monies to pay for a Scope Change Request.
- The project is several months behind schedule.
- A dependent project or system is several months late.
- A new product or version has just been released.
- A product's manufacturer is being bought out by its competitor.

When a project is not in Crisis, Project Managers must not use Stop Work orders as a problem resolution vehicle. Project Managers should use other alternatives, such as escalation to resolve issues.

Inputs, Outputs and Tools

Inputs	Tools & Techniques	Outputs
• Issue/Risk/Change Log • Meeting Minutes • Statement of Work • Scope Changes	• Project Budget • Consultation (Legal, Procurement, Senior & Executive Mgmt)	• Stop Work Notice

Step 1 – Consultation w/ Procurement & Legal Departments

Prior to any Stop Work order, Project Managers should always consult with both the Legal and Procurement Departments to at least make the Buyer aware of the actions about to take place and the reasons for them. In the event the project does need to be cancelled – either for termination or default—Project Managers need to be certain that their actions will not hinder the activities planned by the Procurement Department. Ideally, the Legal and/or Procurement Departments can provide Project Managers additional guidance w/ respect to the steps needed to best protect the Authority.

Step 2 – Issuing Work Stoppage

Work Stoppage consists of a letter on XYZ Company letterhead, which outlines the crisis and clearly lists tasks identified in the Payment Schedule which vendor is prohibited from performing additional work on.

Stop Work Templates can be found in the PMO Templates Library.

The Stop Work Order Template is similar in structure to a Change Approval notice and has the same project information section at the upper right. However, instead of a disposition section, there is a place for Project Managers to list the affected milestones and deliverables, which are to be affected.

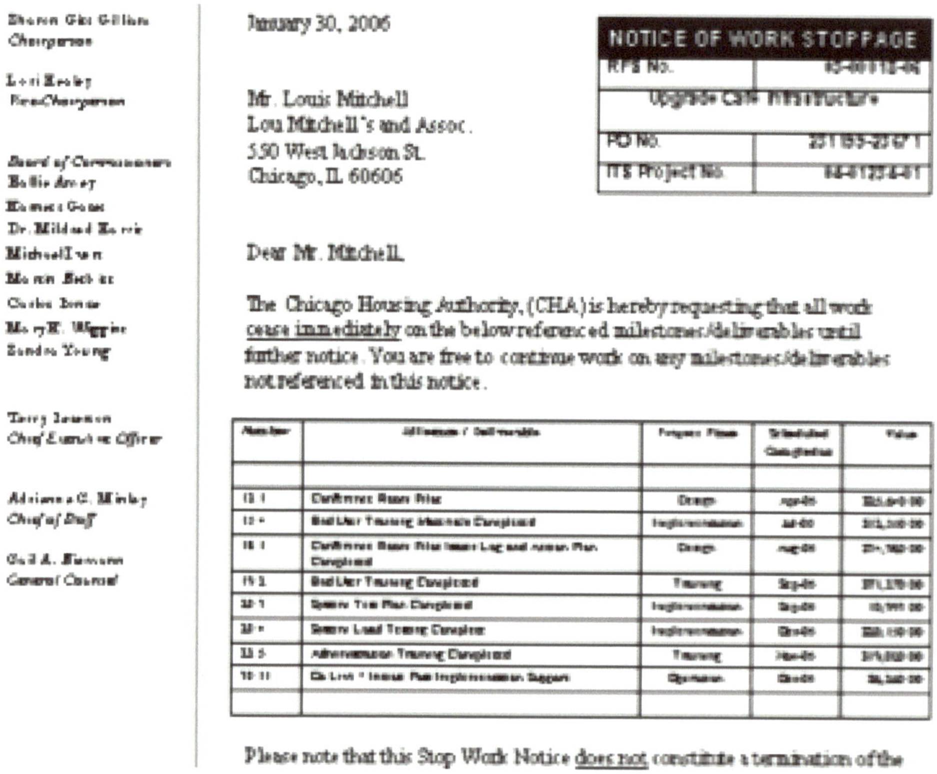

Sharon Gist Gilliam
Chairperson

Lori Healey
Vice Chairperson

Board of Commissioners
Hallie Amey
Earnest Gates
Dr. Mildred Harris
Michael Ivers
Martin Nesbitt
Carlos Ponce
Mary K. Wiggins
Sandra Young

Terry Peterson
Chief Executive Officer

Adrienne C. Minley
Chief of Staff

Gail A. Niemann
General Counsel

January 30, 2006

NOTICE OF WORK STOPPAGE	
RFS No.	[illegible]
Upgrade CHA Infrastructure	
PO No.	[illegible]
ITS Project No.	[illegible]

Mr. Louis Mitchell
Lou Mitchell's and Assoc.
550 West Jackson St.
Chicago, IL 60606

Dear Mr. Mitchell,

The Chicago Housing Authority, (CHA) is hereby requesting that all work cease immediately on the below referenced milestones/deliverables until further notice. You are free to continue work on any milestones/deliverables not referenced in this notice.

Number	Milestone / Deliverable	Project Phase	Scheduled Completion	Value
[illegible]	Conference Room Pilot	Design	[illegible]	[illegible]
[illegible]	End User Training Materials Completed	Implementation	[illegible]	[illegible]
[illegible]	Conference Room Pilot Issues Log and Action Plan Completed	Design	[illegible]	[illegible]
[illegible]	End User Training Completed	Training	[illegible]	[illegible]
[illegible]	System Test Plan Completed	Implementation	[illegible]	[illegible]
[illegible]	System Load Testing Complete	Implementation	[illegible]	[illegible]
[illegible]	Administration Training Completed	Training	[illegible]	[illegible]
[illegible]	[illegible] Implementation Support	Operation	[illegible]	[illegible]

Please note that this Stop Work Notice does not constitute a termination of the

Project managers should copy the milestones, reference numbers and dollar amounts from the payment schedule.

The vendor's most current Project Schedule should be included in the third section to represent a "snapshot" of work performed as of the date of the Stop Work Order. The inclusion of the Schedule helps both parties assess what work had and had not been performed as of a particular point in time; this is critical when negotiating what monies are due to the vendor for work milestones which were already underway.

It is likely that Vendors will enquire immediately about the nature of the Stop Work order and whether its issuance amounts to contract termination. Project Managers <u>must assure the Vendor that the contract has not been terminated</u>, even though work must cease –at least temporarily—on the referenced items while the Project Team assesses the best course of action to address the crisis at hand.

In the event a Stop Work Order must be issued to resolve a problem related to vendor performance, Project Managers must issue a Jeopardy Notice prior to or in conjunction with a Stop Work order.

Step 3 – Authorizations

The last page of the Stop Work Order involves authorizations. Due to the significance of this action, a high degree of authorizations are required.

2. Authorizations

*Assistant CIO	Date	Project Sponsor	Date
*CIO	Date	Executive Sponsor	Date

*Required Signatures

At a minimum, signoffs by the ACIO and CIO are required for any Stop Work Order. However for larger projects, concurrence is also required by the Executive Sponsor to insure that Executive Management has acknowledged the impact of a work stoppage.

Costs of Work Stoppage

Project Managers should note that the issuance of Stop Work Orders **will result in the expenditure of additional funds.** While Vendors cannot claim monies for work performed on Milestones and Deliverables after the date of the Stop Work order, <u>they may be entitled to monies related to overhead and project management during this period</u>. The noted exception to this is the issuance of Stop Work Orders related to performance.

In addition, Vendors are entitled to receive payment for work performed on a milestone up until the Stop Work Order <u>even if those tasks are later cancelled</u>. The purpose of the Stop Work Order is to limit and contain the amount of work done by the Vendor on tasks, which are scheduled for omission or major changes.

For goods and services, orders may have already been shipped or have been received by either XYZ Company or the vendor for which restocking or cancellation fees may apply. In most instances, XYZ Company is obligated to pay for those goods received or for any expenses (shipping, restocking, etc) related to their return to the supplier.

<u>Stop Work Orders will not completely eliminate expenditures on forthcoming milestones</u>. The evaluation process which determines when –or even if—a Stop Work Order is to be issued must take into account the added expenses related to both work in progress as well as and additional Vendor efforts during the resolution of a crisis they did not cause.

Stop Work Orders are solely "Stop Loss" measures. In some instances, it may be more cost effective to complete a milestone or even an entire project rather than to cease work.

Step 4 – Restoring Work

The most effective means of restoring work that was not stopped due to vendor deficiencies is by means of a Scope Change. As the reason for the work stoppage was the anticipation of a significant scope change, the issuance of the scope changes effectively places the project onto the new track.

For work stoppages related to performance, Project Managers need only send a letter rescinding the Stop Work Order issued on a certain date. Most likely, this will be done after the deficient milestones have received at least an "approved as noted" rating, which will allow for work to continue.

In the event the project requires termination (for either Default or Convenience), work of course will not continue. Project Managers will need to work with the Procurement Department in the event a project appears headed towards this result. XYZ Company's Procurement Department will assume the lead role in all termination proceedings.

Estimated Time Duration:

Once the need for Stop Work order has been identified, the process for issuance should take between 2 days and 2-weeks due to the time it will takes to consult with the Procurement Department and Senior Management.

Resource Participation:

The Project Manager is solely responsible for issuing Stop Work Orders. However, early consultation with Legal, Procurement and Senior Management is required.

Producing Status Report

Team status reports should be presented at the weekly team meeting. EDT status reports should be presented on quarterly basis. The formats for both reports are as follow:

1. High Level Project Status (Red, Green, Yellow)

ITS HQ RELOCATION PROGRAM MANAGEMENT STATUS REPORT

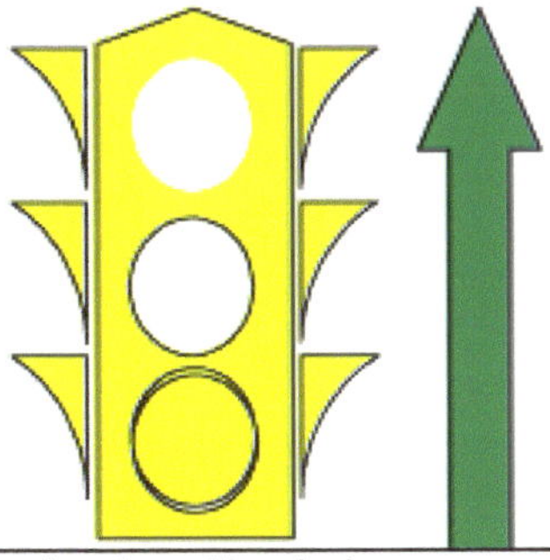

Period Ending: November 24, 2006
Project Number: 06-0027-001
Remaining Weeks until December 15, 2006: 2 weeks

Status & Priority		Project Name
Sub project:	1	Infrastructure and Data Center Services – 06-0027-002
Sub project:	2	SONET (OC48) Migration and Implementation @ CNA
Sub project:	3	IPT Voice System Design and Implementation-06-0027-003
Sub project:	4	IPT IVR Development and Implementation
Sub project:	5	LAN Migration @ CNA
Sub project:	6	CHAC Network Migration: Exchange 2003 and Active Directory **(On Hold)**

2. Work plan Update

WORKPLAN UPDATE

Major Accomplishments since Last Update

1. Infrastructure and Data Center Services Status: "Green"
   - ☐ Project Dependency: **No Project Dependencies**
   - ☐ As of 09/06/06 via a status update give by Bryan Land, the construction work at 333 S. Wabash location is on schedule for the 11th and 12th floors and is due to be completed by 10/30/06. No further information has been reported to the team regarding construction progress as of 09/15/06.
   - ☐ Project is "Green" because it is on schedule and within budget

3. Issues and Action Items

ACTION ITEMS

- As of date, below are the past due action items

47	R	T	40	83 528 835 418 81	8/8/2006	Lead time to order CPE equipment (Non-IPT) necessary for LAN and WAN Migration requirements (40 Days) may impact desired lead time necessary to implement equipment at 333 S. Wabash. At the present there is no procurement plan in place to secure this equipment thru CHA Procurement. Need procurement plan/strategy	A. Owens	M	8/22/2006		(22)	
40	A	T		414	8/3/2006	AT&T Contract Amendment signoff	V. Wilkes	H	8/10/2006		(34)	Have CHA Senior Management issues Letter of Intent (LOI) so that AT&T can begin order submission for SONET

4. Detail Project Performance

PAST PROJECT PERFORMANCE

As of 11/08/2006 we are executing at 80% of our Critical Path Schedule due to the slippage of the Critical Path Items. From the below figure you can graphically see the variance of the planned vs. actual schedule as a result of the delay in completing the current and past Critical Path tasks (See Figure below). As of 11/08/06 all past due task have been complete.

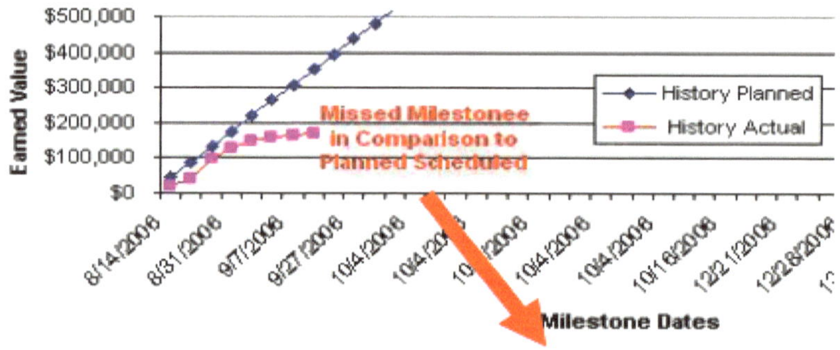

Wbs	Critical Path Task	Finish Date	Days Late (-) Slack Avail (+)	Weight	Proj Com.	Act% Com.
445	LAN/WAN Assessment and Analysis Complete	8/14/2006	-29	2.17	2%	70%
406	AT&T Contract amendment and signed off by CHA	8/18/2006	-25	2.17	4%	86%
455	Selection of IPT Vendor	8/21/2006	Complete -21	2.17	7%	100%
60	Approval of CHAC Network Migration	8/31/2006	-12	2.17	9%	65%
394	Document findings and Report for LAN BOM	9/1/2006	-11	2.17	11%	50%
497	Procure Moving Company for Data Center Move	9/2/2006	-10	2.17	13%	50%
83	Procure Migration Tools for CHAC Migration	9/7/2006	-5	2.17	15%	10%
61	Procure TM Resources for CHAC Migration	9/8/2006	-4	2.17	17%	10%

From the above analysis the following task are impacting the total project completion date and the Legal Department 12/15/06 move-in date::

1. WBS 445: 29 Days Late
2. WBS 406: 25 Days Late
3. WBS 60: 12 Days Late
4. WBS 394: 11 Days Late
5. WBS 497: 10 Days Late
6. WBS 83: 5 Days Late
7. WBS 61: 4 Days Late

5. Risk Management

RISK MANAGEMENT

Due to the delay in the Critical Path items being completed our estimated "GO LIVE" date of 12/15/06 has a 90% probability of being met. There is a 90% probability that the CHAC move in GO LIVE date will take place between 1/29/07 and 2/8/07, most likely 2/4/2006 will be the "GO-LIVE" date if the project continue to execute at a Schedule Performance Index (SPI) of 70%. From the regression analysis simulation of all coefficients (*inputs and outputs*) shows that the AT&T Order submission has the most impact in the delay of the targeted move-in date of 12/15/06 for the Legal Department.

Simulation Results for Relocation GO LIVE/Finish

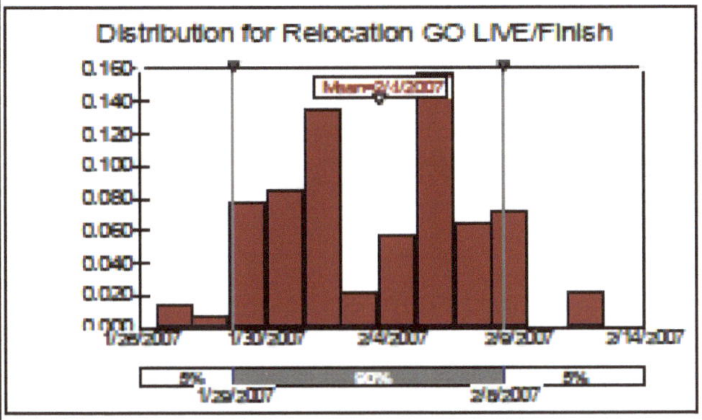

Summary Information	
Project Name	RiskModel.mpp
Number of Simulations	1
Number of Iterations	100
Number of Inputs	133
Number of Outputs	6
Sampling Type	Latin Hypercube
Simulation Start Time	8/22/2006 9:19
Simulation Stop Time	8/22/2006 9:21
Simulation Duration	00:01:40
Random Seed	1758307203

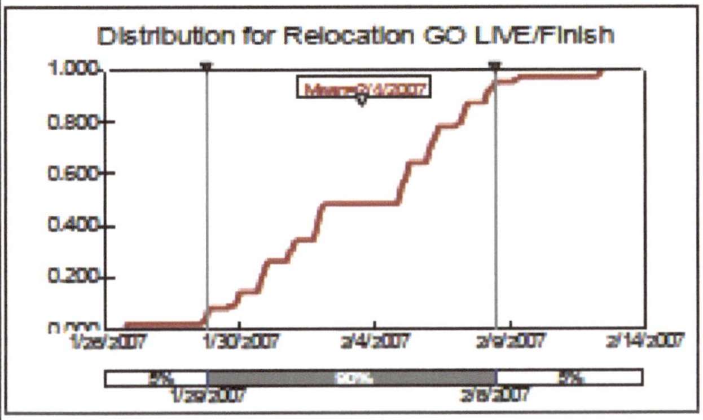

Statistic	Value	%tile	Value
Minimum	1/26/07	5%	1/29/07
Maximum	2/12/07	10%	1/30/07
Mean	2/4/07	15%	1/31/07
Std Dev	3.670391382	20%	1/31/07
Variance	13.4717729	25%	1/31/07
Skewness	-0.002484777	30%	2/1/07
Kurtosis	2.382036283	35%	2/2/07
Median	2/5/07	40%	2/2/07
Mode	2/2/07	45%	2/2/07
Left X	1/29/07	50%	2/5/07
Left P	5%	55%	2/5/07
Right X	2/8/07	60%	2/5/07
Right P	95%	65%	2/6/07
Diff X	10.13671875	70%	2/6/07
Diff P	90%	75%	2/6/07
#Errors	0	80%	2/7/07
Filter Min		85%	2/7/07
Filter Max		90%	2/8/07
#Filtered	0	95%	2/8/07

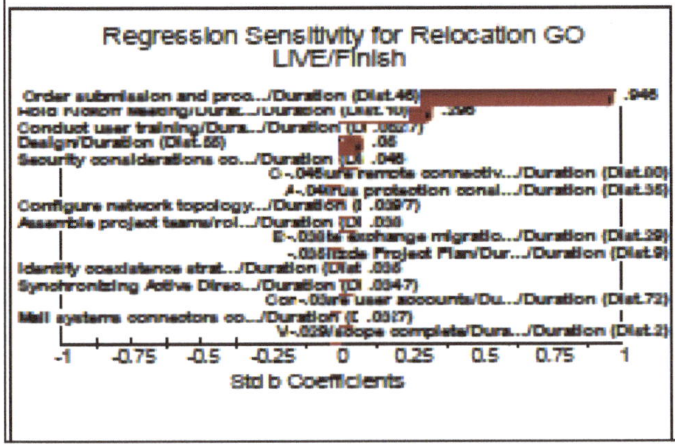

Rank	Name	Regr	Corr
#1	Order submission and proce	0.946	0.962
#2	Hold Kickoff Meeting/Duratio	0.296	0.258
#3	Conduct user training/Durati	0.052	0.141
#4	Design/Duration (Dist.55) / T	0.050	-0.032
#5	Security considerations comp	0.046	-0.061
#6	Configure remote connectivity	-0.046	-0.009
#7	Antivirus protection consider	-0.040	0.091
#8	Configure network topology a	0.039	0.107
#9	Assemble project teams/roles	0.038	-0.044
#10	Evaluate exchange migration	-0.038	0.038
#11	Finalize Project Plan/Durati	-0.035	-0.027
#12	Identify coexistence strategie	0.035	-0.060
#13	Synchronizing Active Directo	0.034	-0.043
#14	Configure user accounts/Dur	-0.030	-0.001
#15	Mail systems connectors con	0.030	-0.039
#16	Vision/scope complete/Durati	-0.029	-0.024

Action Item and Issue Logs

Action items and Issue logs are great tools to use for managing the work plan during the team weekly meetings. Grouping the issues/actions by person/group(s) is best to allot for meeting time constraints if they exist. Only open items should be reviewed but all closed items should be listed in the report for contingency against assumptions/constraints that are directly affected by a once opened action item. Step through each open issue/action item and update the "Last Update" status field with the latest team member information regarding that item.

ITS Relocation Project
Project Number:06-0027-001

Last Item assigned: 82

Status as of : Friday, January 05, 2007
Weeks Remaining Until 2/15/07: 16.00

Type:
(A - Action Item
(I - Issue Item
(R - Risk Item
(AS - Assumption

Department:
T-Telecom Team — C- CHAC
P - Project Management — A - Application Dev
N - Network Team — M - Maron
PDT - Project Decision Team — B - Berebee

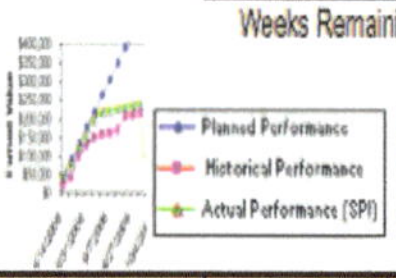

IMPACT: Low / Medium / High

STATUS: Task Slack / Task Late

November 06

M	T	W	T	F	S	S
		1	2	3	4	5
6	7	8	9	10	11	12
13	14	15	16	17	18	19
20	21	22	23	24	25	26
27	28	29	30			

Schedule Move In Dates:
Floor(s): 11 (IT), 12 (Legal) - 12/15/06
Floor(s): 1,8, 9 (CHAC) - 2/16/07
Floor: 10 - 3/02/07
Floor: 13 - 3/30/07

Item #	Type	Dpt	Item Depd	WBS Depd	Post Date	Description	OWNER	IMPACT (H, M, L)	Due Date	Closed	Days Late vs Slack Time	Resolution Strategy	Last Update	% Cmple	Status
58	A	N			9/20/06	Label and document phyiscal cabling plan (Ethernet/Fiber) for all servers and hardware in MDF. Store data in Excel in order to reconnect all MDF devices @ 333. Wabash i.e. SAN/SUN Equipment	A. Owens	L	11/30/06		16		10/02/06: Need documentation of cabling for Unix and BackUP Equipment	10%	OPEN
66	A	P			10/10/06	Signoff of Berbee Financing Contract	B. Land	L	10/31/06	12/15/06	16		10/19/2006: Waiting for signature. Training credits will not be released until financing contract is signed.	30%	OPEN
73	A	N	74		10/26/06	Receive Sup Tradein for 4506 for Legal Department	S. Hondras	H	11/6/06	12/15/06			11/30/06: Equipment not due to ship until 12/05/06 due to back order in Sup Component.	10%	CLOSE

Technical Case Scenario – The Execution Phase

- ❖ Producing status report
- ❖ Action Item & Issue Logs
- ❖ VOIP Infrastructure overview
- ❖ Project Server
- ❖ Extracting data from SharePoint
- ❖ Excel VBA

4 Project Monitoring and Control

Topics Covered:

- Risk Management
- Quality Control Tools
- Project Reporting
- Managing the Project Schedule
- Executive Decision Team Reporting
- Understanding of Strategies: 28-31

How To Videos & Templates on CD :

- Walkthrough of Monitor/Control Process
- Monte Carlo Simulation
- Quality Tools
- Producing EDT Material
- SharePoint Designer Workflows
- Nintex Workflow

STRATEGY for Monitoring and Control:

- ✓ Risk Management
- ✓ Determine variances & providing corrective action
- ✓ Reporting on Project Performance
- ✓ Hosting EDT Meetings

Project Monitor and Control Overview

Like Project Execution, Project Control encompasses activities that are carried out continuously by the project team from the Planning through the Closure phases. The processes, tools, and outputs involved in Project Control are the primary means by which the Project Manager and Senior Portfolio Manager can identify threats or opportunities to completing the project within time, staffing, cost, and quality constraints. While every project member is responsible for participating in the control process, the project manager is accountable for making sure that the processes are set up and carried out.

Project Control consists of six (6) primary processes:

1. Scope Management;
2. Risk Management;
3. Issue Management;
4. Schedule Management;
5. Performance Management;
6. Budget Management

Each process is described in greater detail in this chapter.

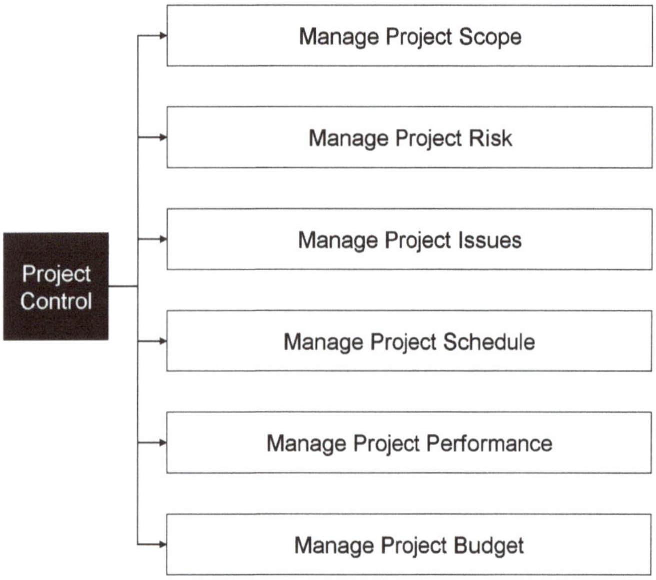

Objectives and Benefits

The purpose of the Control Processes is to manage change in a structured way over the life of the project. Changes over the life of the project from the baseline are inevitable; the key to a successful project is management of the changes so that original objectives are met, the "proper" trade-offs among key project dimensions (i.e. scope, time, quality, and cost) are made, and that stakeholders are kept informed about decisions along the way.

The following 3 main objectives are identified for control processes in "IT Project Management:"

1. Influence factors that create changes to ensure that changes are beneficial;

2. Understand that change has occurred;
3. Manage changes as they occur.

The subsequent sections describe the primary processes and a tool used by the XYZ Company's The ITS PMO Project Managers (PM's) over the course of a project.

Tools

The *primary tools* used to support the Project Control Processes include:

- Process flow diagrams for each of the 6 processes - visual representation of the steps in each process
- Project Plan – a document fully describing the work to be undertaken, time frame for completion, and high level approach to governing the project:
  - Project Management
  - Issue, Risk and Change Management
  - Scope Management

(The Project Plan is a separate document from the Project *Work Plan* which is jointly developed by the awarded vendor and the XYZ Company.)

- Requirements Document – a formal document identifying the functional and technical requirements for the project. This document is prepared to support the procurement process.
- Statement of Work
- Project Work Plan (also referred to as Project Schedule)
- Project Budget
- The ITS PMO Change Control Board (CCB) Charter
- Project Scope Change Request
- The ITS PMO Risk Scoring Worksheet
- The ITS PMO PM Issue Risk Change Log
- Project Status Reports
- The ITS PMO Executive Dashboard
- EDT Presentations

Secondary tools to conduct Project Control include:

- XYZ Company Master Services Agreement

Sections 4.2 through 4.7 describe when and how to use each tool and provide examples.

Inputs and Outputs

The primary inputs to Project Control processes are the outputs developed during the Planning and Execution phases. The primary outputs from Control processes are documentation on the scope, benefits, costs, resources, and timeline for an approved technology project. The outputs are used throughout project execution to ensure that the project is on track and during project closure to assess the overall performance of the project. The primary inputs and outputs are listed below, with further detail on how they are used, how they are created, and/or any interim work products described in Sections 4.2 through 4.7.

Inputs	Processes	Outputs
• Project Governing Documents (RFP, SOW) • Project Planning Documents (Project Plan, Work Plan, CCB Charter) • Project Execution Updates	Process 1 -Manage Scope Process 2 -Manage Risks Process 3 -Manage Issues Process 4 -Manage Schedule Process 5 -Manage Performance Process 6 -Manage Budget	• Corrective Actions/ Workarounds • Modified Project Governing Documents • Project Auditing/ Tracking Tools • Project Reporting Tools

Timeframe/Total Duration

- Project Control processes are carried out concurrent to the Project Planning, Execution, and Closure phases.

Resource Participation

The following resources participate in the Project Control Process:

- Executive Business Sponsor – Highest level representative of business unit (usually Managing Director) for which the project is being delivered. The Executive Sponsor retains overall responsibility for project's success
- Business Owner – Business department manager (usually Director or Manager level) who reports to the Executive Business Sponsor and ensures that the project definition and execution meet the business objectives
- The ITS PMO Mgmt – Chief Information Officer and/or Assistant Chief Information Officers
- The ITS PMO Senior Portfolio Manager – Senior The ITS PMO manager who provides guidance and oversight to all projects in the ITS PMO portfolio. She/he is responsible for providing overall status reporting to EDT/PDT for all The ITS PMO projects as well as compliance with The ITS PMO project management standards
- The ITS PMO Project Manager – XYZ Company person (usually from The ITS PMO) responsible for delivering the project as defined in project scope and overall project plan, leading and managing the overall project team (incl. any vendor project managers and other XYZ Company staff in The ITS PMO or business departments) on a day-to-day basis. Depending on the size, scope, nature, and complexity of the project there may be an The ITS PMO Project Manager and a Business Project Manager.
- Other Key Stakeholders - departments in addition to the primary Business Department that will be significantly impacted by the initiative
- Project Decision Team (PDT) – Managing Directors, Directors, The ITS PMO management and others with a significant stake in the project. Executive Business Sponsor is typically the chairperson. The PDT is collectively responsible for removing obstacles and enabling any type of change required for the project to be successful
- Executive Decision Team – Managing Directors with large stake in technology investments
- Budget Department – primarily the Budget Director

Sections 4.2 through 4.7 go into further detail as to when and in what capacity each resource participates.

4.1 Manage Scope

Overview

Scope control is not the prevention of changes, but the identification and management of changes. The purpose of implementing a scope control process is to manage all elements (e.g. business requirements) both inside and outside a project that either increase or decrease the originally defined project scope. Since changes are inevitable, they need to be managed carefully to ensure that the project is completed on time and on budget.

Some common terms often heard in the scope management process are **scope expansion** and **scope creep**. Performance of work that is outside or beyond the originally stated project scope is considered an expansion of scope. Scope creep, as defined by Max Wideman's Glossary of Project Management Terms, is:

A progressive increase in scope. As some projects progress, especially through development, requirements continuously change incrementally, causing the user or developer to add to the project mission or objectives, i.e. with more work involved, and consequent increases in time and budget required.

Per the Project Management Body of Knowledge (PMBOK) 2000 Edition, scope management is defined as, "processes required to ensure that the project includes all the work required, to complete the project successfully".

A change control method should be agreed upon early in the project during the Project Planning phase. Scope control includes:

- Reviewing and determining if a new request is in or out of scope
- Facilitating agreement on project changes and ensuring the changes are beneficial
- Managing changes when and if they occur –scope changes affect resources, costs, and schedule

Scope changes often impact resources, costs, and schedule. These changes need to be reflected in the project plan.

It is important to set up a governing body to approve changes. This group is called the Scope/Change Control Board (CCB) and consists of management personnel and key stakeholders. They review all scope change requests, authorize impact analyses, and determine if changes should be implemented, denied, or deferred. Scope Change Board members vary for each project and it is the responsibility of the Project Manager and Business Owner to determine the board members. (The ITS PMO PM should also consult the Senior Portfolio Manager for advice.) Any changes that are agreed upon should be documented and signed by the CCB. *(More information on the CCB is found in Section 4.2.4.)*

Below are some typical reasons for scope change:

- An external event (e.g. new legislation)
- An error or omission in the original scope of the product (e.g. functionality that was left out)
- An error or omission in the original scope of the project (e.g. interface that was not included)
- A value adding change (e.g. upgrading hardware components to the latest available in the marketplace)

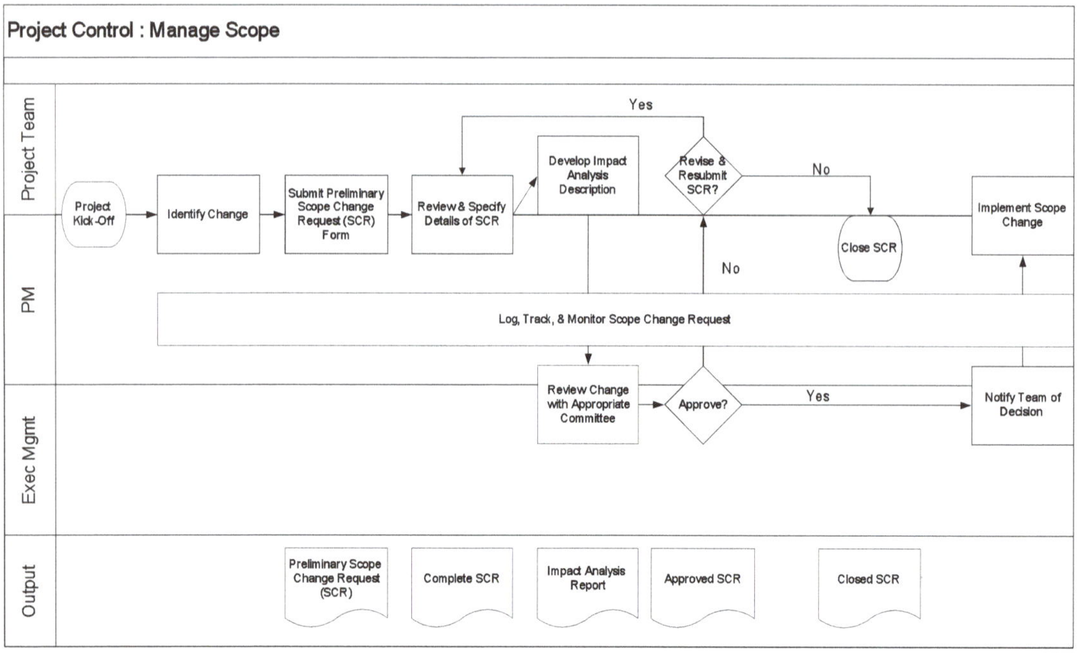

Inputs, Outputs, and Tools

Outputs created during the Planning Phase and developed during the Execution Phase serve as the inputs to the Scope Management Process.

Inputs	Tools & Techniques	Outputs
• Project Plan • Statement of Work • Requirements Document • XYZ HOUSING AUTHORITY RFP • Approved Scope Change Requests (SCR's)	• Impact Analysis • Change Control Board • Scope Change Request • Change Control Log	• Approved/Rejected/ Deferred change request • Modified Project Documents

As a result of the Scope Change Control process, the ITS PMO PM and project team should know:

- Reason for proposed change;
- Person requesting change;
- Cost of change;
- Appropriate resources allocated to make the change;
- Definition of how the change will be made;
- Risk and potential impact of change failure;
- Conflicts between multiple proposed changes;
- Parties whom change will impact (and who must be informed of change);
- Historical audit trail of changes.

Timeframe/Total Duration

- The Scope Management process is carried out concurrent to the Project Planning, Execution, and Closure phases.

Resource Participation

While any team member may propose a change, the ITS PMO project manager is accountable for managing the review and approval process so that it operates efficiently and effectively. The Change Control Board (CCB) ensures that only the most critical changes are accepted and that adequate resources will be provided or trade-offs made so that the project can succeed under defined time, cost, resource, and quality constraints.

Change Control Board

The exact composition of the Change Control Board will vary by size and complexity of project, but every Board should include:

- Business Sponsor – depending on scope of project, either the Dept. Director the overall project impact is limited to the department alone or the Division MD if the project impacts multiple departments
- Customer/End-user Representative – party being impacted
- Technology Representative – usually the ACIO for Applications or Infrastructure
- The ITS PMO Project Manager

For larger projects, the following individuals might participate in a non-voting capacity:

- The ITS PMO CIO
- The ITS PMO Senior Portfolio Manager

PM's should keep in mind that the larger the CCB, the more difficult to schedule from a coordination standpoint. The frequency of CCB meetings should be set during the Planning phase; the CCB should expect to meet more frequently (e.g. bi-monthly after an application goes live for 2 months, and then less frequently thereafter.)

The composition, scope of responsibilities, frequency of meeting, and decision process should be captured by the ITS PMO PM in the CCB Charter during the Planning phase. A CCB template can be found in SharePoint for the PM's use.

The matrix below shows in what capacity each resource participates throughout the stage. The Project Team participation from steps 1-5 refers to the individual that proposed the change, while steps 3 and 8 refer to the project team as a whole.

Step	**Project Team**	**The ITS PMO PM**	**Control Board (CCB)**	**Other Key Stakeholders**
1 – Identify Change	R	A		
2 – Submit Preliminary SCR form	A/R	R		
3 – Review & Specify Details of SCR	R/C	A		
4 – Develop Impact Analysis Description	A	R	C	
5 – Review Change Request	C	R	A/R	
6 – Approve/Reject/Defer Request		R	A	
7 – Notify Team of SCR Decision		A		I
8 – Implement Scope Change	R	A	I	I

9 – Log, Track, & Monitor SCR	I	A		

Process Description

The Scope Management consists of nine primary steps. The ninth step (Log, Track, & Monitor SCR via the Change Log is carried out by the ITS PMO PM in parallel to steps 2 through 8.) This section provides detailed instructions for each of those steps.

Step 1 – Identify Change

- **Instructions**
  - Recognize need for change. Scope change requests may be initiated from 2 primary sources:
    1. Via the Issues Management process as a potential resolution to an issue; or
    2. Independently by the project team
  - Complete Scope Change Request form. In order to be considered, all scope change requests must be documented in writing. Scope Change Request (SCR) forms can be found in the templates section of SharePoint.
    - Every Scope Change Request requires the following information:
      - Name of requestor
      - Date change required
      - Change description
      - Business justification
      - Deliverable description
      - Reason(s) why outside of original SOW
  - Before committing too much time to conducting an Impact Analysis, the change initiator and the ITS PMO PM should meet to determine whether the change is critical and crucial to the success of items on the critical path.
- **Estimated Time Duration**
  - Variable depending on extent of change
- **Tips for Success**
  - Effective scope control assumes good scope definition and scope verification has occurred.
    - Scope Definition
      - Include user input as much as possible up front to avoid scope creep later in the project. These should be incorporated into project governing documents such as the RFP, SOW, and Requirements document.
    - Scope Verification
      - Project information such as the Project Plan, Statement of Work, Project Work Plan, and the Scope Change log must be posted in the appropriate project folder in SharePoint in order to avoid confusion and duplication and assist in shared understanding.
      - Regular meetings with full participation will ensure that expectations do not deviate substantially among the project members (including end users.)
      - To verify whether something is truly a change, the PM should encourage frequent communication among the team (e.g. Co-locate users with developers when possible.)

Step 2 – Submit Preliminary SCR Form

- **Instructions**
  - After completing the first section (section entitled *XYZ Company Change Request Details*) of the SCR, the change initiator should submit the form to the ITS PMO PM to be recorded in the Change Log. While available to all project members, the Change Log is owned solely by the ITS PMO PM.
- **Estimated Time Duration**
  - 2 hours.

Step 3 – Review and Specify Details of SCR

- **Instructions**
  - The ITS PMO PM should review the details of the preliminary SCR with the change initiator to ensure that the proposed change meets the following criteria:
    - It is critical to the goals and objectives of the project (*Business Justification*)
    - It is crucial to the success of items on the critical path

- **Estimated Time Duration**
  - 1-3 hours.

- **Tips for Success**
  - Ensure all required fields are completed and the majority of the effort in completing the change request rests with the change initiator in order to avoid unnecessary changes and impacts to time and budget resources.

Step 4 – Develop Impact Analysis Description

- **Instructions**
  - If deemed critical to the objectives of the project, the ITS PMO PM should work with the change initiator and the functional and technical subject matter experts (including the vendor) to determine the schedule, cost, staff, and quality impacts of the implementing the change.
  - Just as important to detail is the impact to project and ongoing cost, staff, and quality if the change is NOT approved. This should include workarounds, if they exist.

- **Estimated Time Duration**
  - Variable.

- **Tips for Success**
  - All impacts should be quantified whenever possible (e.g. failure to implement change will increase overall effort of completing business process by 4 days/month.)
  - The ITS PMO PM should conduct reality check to verify that subject matter experts have been consulted and understand clearly the high level activities associated with the change.
  - To prevent unnecessary changes, The ITS PMO PM should also work with project team to creatively identify alternative solutions to a given problem.
  - By doing all of the above, the ITS PMO PM will be well prepared to present the proposed change to the CCB.

Step 5 – Review Change Request

- **Instructions**
  - All SCR's must be reviewed by the Change Control Board. The frequency with which the Change Control Board meets will vary by project and will be described in the Change Control Board Charter developed during the Planning Phase of the project
  - Prior to presenting the SCR's to the CCB, the ITS PMO PM should work with the project team to prioritize them according to the following criteria:
    - Critical
    - Important
    - Desirable
  - The ITS PMO PM should review each SCR with the CCB.

- **Estimated Time Duration**
  - Variable.

- **Tips for Success**
  - The ITS PMO PM should understand the reasons for, the impacts of, and alternatives to the proposed change PRIOR to the Change Control Board meeting.
  - The ITS PMO PM should also understand the impact to the overall project timeline and budget. Impacts must be communicated by the PM to the CCB prior to their decision.

Step 6 – Approve/Reject/Defer Change Request

- **Instructions**
  - Based upon the merits of each request and the resource constraints faced by the project, the CCB will decide to:
    - Approve,
    - Reject, or
    - Defer until a later time the proposed Scope Change Request.
  - The ITS PMO PM should document the final decision, obtain the signatures from the designated CCB members, and ensure a record is kept of the discussion for historical review.

- **Estimated Time Duration**
  - Variable

- **Tips for Success**
  - An important responsibility of the PM in the Change Process is facilitation of the decision process in a timely manner. Impacts to the project from a schedule, budget, and quality standpoint will likely increase the longer a change request is pending, should it be approved.

Step 7 – Notify Team of SCR Decision

- **Instructions**
  - Once a decision is made, the ITS PMO PM is responsible for ensuring that the decision is communicated to both the change initiator as well as the project team as a whole. Communication of the decisions should at minimum be made via the following:
    - Directly to the change initiator
    - At regular project status meeting (and reflected in status meeting minutes)

        - Change Log
    - If the decision requires vendor action, the ITS PMO PM should initiate the Change Notification process described in the Execution Chapter (*Sec 3.3.2.*)

- **Estimated Time Duration**
    - 1-2 hours

- **Tips for Success**
    - A useful technique for ensuring that the team is up to date with proposed changes and their impacts is to publish a month end (or bi-weekly) summary of changes approved for that period.

Step 8 – Implement Scope Change

- **Instructions**
    - If approved, relevant project documentation should be modified to formally record acceptance of the change decision. Relevant documentation includes:
        - Statement of Work
        - Requirements Document
        - Technical Design Document
        - Project Work Plan
        - Change Log
        - Project Budget (if necessary)

To ensure traceability, the first 3 documents should employ a version control system that clearly calls out the date and description of the change, and name of the document modifier.

- **Estimated Time Duration**
    - Variable

Step 9 – Log, Track, & Monitor Scope Change Request

- **Instructions**
    - Throughout the scope change management process, the ITS PMO PM is accountable for logging, tracking, and monitoring the status of the SCR in an orderly way.
    - As described above, he/she is also responsible for communicating the status of the SCR to the change initiator and any interested parties.

- **Tips for Success**
    - Availability of current, accurate information is critical to keeping expectations consistent and stakeholders happy. The ITS PMO PM's should keep a READ ONLY copy of the Change Log (and other governing project documents) on SharePoint for project team reference.
    - The ITS PMO PM's should frequently review the status of open SCR's. Because the Impact Analysis will often take some time to conduct and because the perception of the need for change might itself change as users learn more about various options, open change orders that can be closed may easily be overlooked. During the Planning phase, The ITS PMO PM's may set a target that all open SCR's will be closed within a certain time period (i.e. accepted, rejected, or deferred within 2 weeks after identification.)

Risk Management

Risk management is the process of mitigating, decreasing and/or eliminating the possibility of any negative impact effecting the project time, cost, quality and scope in an effort to provide positive impacts to project time, cost, quality and scope. Knowing how to identify risk and measure it's probability impact from a qualitative and quantitative perspective is key.

Identifying Risk

	Risk Item Description
Project Name:	
Risk ID:	
Last Update:	
Current Rank in Top N	
Risk Statement Condition:	
Risk Statement Consequence:	
Probability:	
Impact:	
Exposure:	
Rank:	
Current Mitigation Plan:	
Plan Owner:	
Date Mitigation Started:	
Date to Complete Mitigation:	
Mitigation Plan Status:	
Trigger and Value for Contingency Plan:	
Contingency Plan:	
Revision History:	
Point of Contact:	
Date Closed:	

Risk Management Initiation Checklist

Intended use of this checklist	For a risk management team and/or Risk Manager to use when initiating risk management, or updating the risks at project phase transitions. The checklist contains items to consider when verifying that a project team has been assembled and has begun its project with appropriate risk management.

ID		Items to be considered
		Consider these when initiating the overall process

ID		Items to be considered
1		Has funding been allocated to support a risk management?
2		Have resources been assigned for risk identification?
3		Are the following organizations represented on the risk identification team?
		• Project Team
		• Support Groups (SQA, CM, test, documentation, training, etc.)
		• Representatives from other elements of the program, if the project is part of a larger program
		• Partner or supplier representative
		• User representative
4		Has time been made available for the risk identification team to perform their tasks?
5		Have risk factors been selected for use by the identification team? Have they included the following?
		• General risk table (or one tailored to the organization)
		• Specific risk factor table for this type of project
		• Lessons learned on previous projects
		Use these items when reviewing the results of risk identification
6		Has relevant risk factor been rated?
7		For each factor rated high, has a specific risk statement been written?
8		For each specific risk statement, have the conditions and consequences to the project been stated?
9		Have the specific risks been organized into sets that support the analysis of impact and the development of mitigation actions?
10		Have the risks been reviewed to determine which require further analysis?
		Use these items when reviewing the results of analysis of specific risks.
11		Has each risk statement been assigned a probability of occurrence?
12		Has each risk statement been assigned a loss if risk occurs?
13		Has the risk exposure (= probability x loss) been calculated for each risk statement?
14		Have the risks been ranked in order of exposure and agreed to by the team?
15		Have other project members and stakeholders reviewed and commented on the list?
16		Has the risk identification team reviewed and incorporated comments from other project members and stakeholders?

ID		Items to be considered
17		With the risks as identified, should the project proceed as planned?
		Use these items when reviewing the results of planning risk handling actions
18		Is there a mitigation action plan for each risk that is to be mitigated?
19		For each risk to be mitigated, has an effort and/or cost been estimated for the mitigation action plan?
20		Has a contingency plan been identified for the appropriate risks?
21		Does the work breakdown structure for the project include risk management and mitigation actions?
22		Have all the contingency plans been documented and do they include anticipated cost and effort?
23		Has an agreement with management been made on when and if to authorize the use of a contingency plan?

Measuring Risk: Qualitative Assessment
Consist of measuring the Probability and Impact using High, Medium and Low Values

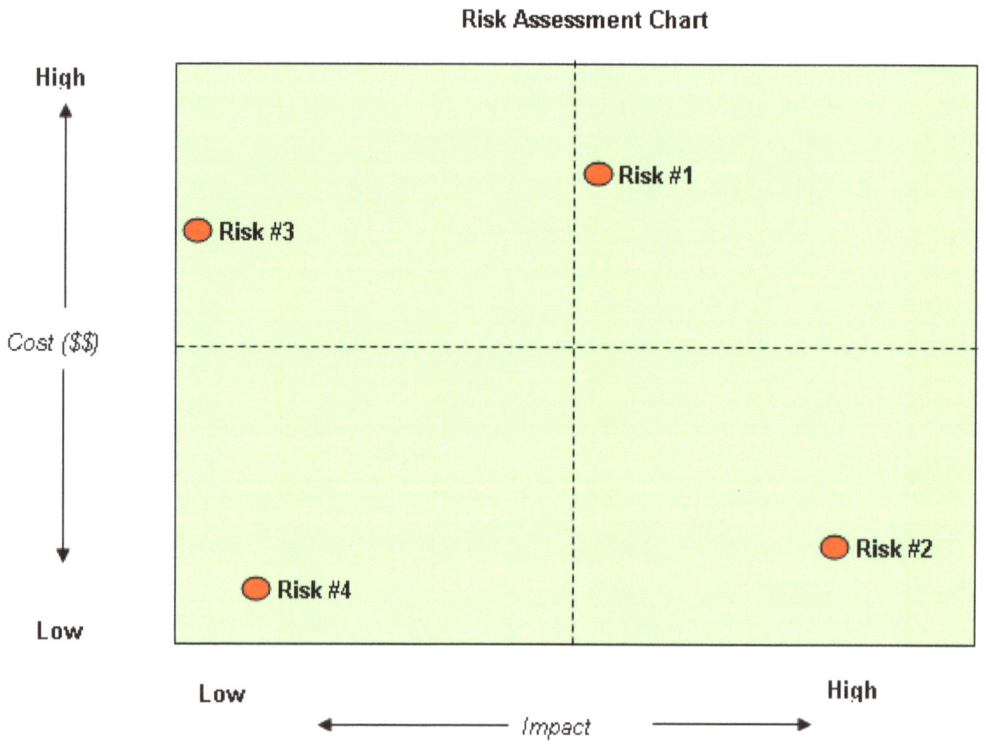

Information Resources Management Division

DEPARTMENT OF ADMINISTRATIVE SERVICES

Project Management Office

Risk Summary and Priority List

This document provides a tracking tool for risk management.

Project Name/ID:	

Document	Information
Date:	
Contact:	
Project Manager:	

Potential	Description of Risk	Project Impact	Response	Responsibility

Potential Level		Project Impact	
1 =	High	1 =	High
2 =	Medium	2 =	Medium
3 =	Low	3 =	Low

Measuring Risk: Quantitative Assessment

Consist of measuring the Probability and Impact using numerical values:

Date:	Monday, April 02, 2012
Project Name:	ITS HQ Relocation
Project Number:	06-0027-001
Report Name:	Risk Summary and Priority List
IT Owner:	
Business Owner:	
Project Sponsor:	
Portfolio Manager:	Idris Parks

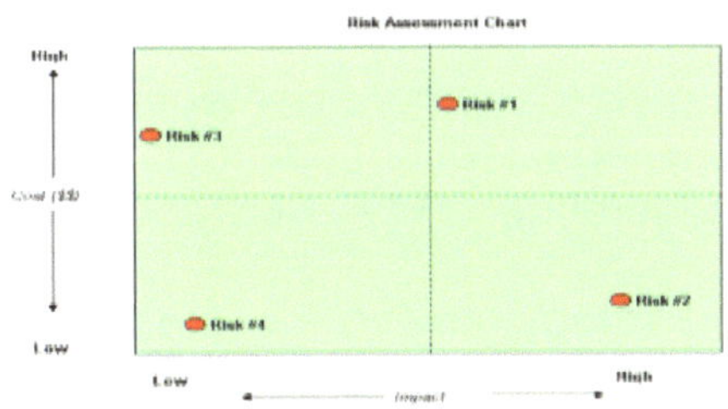

Total Project Risk Position ($$) = $85,500.00

RISK IDENTIFICATION		RISK ASSESSMENT								RISK MITIGATION				
		PROBABILITY of OCCUR (%)			ITS Qual $ AT STAKE	ITS Quan Project Impact	Expected Value (EV)	Enterprise Wide Impact	ITS Triple Constraint Impact					
		Low	Medium	High										
RISK #	DESCRIPTION OF RISK EVENT	0-.35	.35-.65	.65-1.0						CONSEQUENCES	SOLUTION	OWNER	Posted	Closed
1	Due to the complete Procurement of Services behind planned schedule by 2 months, our planned date of 04/1/06 will be impact by the scope of work necessary to complete the Data and Voice Implementation planned date of 10/06. This will as a result effect the overall move-in date for the Legal department (11/06) and possibly XYZC (01/07) to the new CNA building			0.75	Med Risk Two Additional Consultants for two months at $125 per hour.	$60,000.00	$45,000.00	High	Cost: High Time: Med Quality: CS:	XYZ will have to spend additional consulting services dollars that will be used to "crash" and "fast track" the ITS relocation project in order to make the planned Data and Telecom implementation date of 10/06 and 01/07. The additional	**(1) Have XYZ resources begin some of the planning task now in an effort to fast track the project to make the 10/06 Data and Telecom implementation date (2) Hired additional consultants to "Crash" the project in order to make up for the loss of time due to the late completion of the Procurement of Services to mitigate risk involved in Legal Department move-in of 11/06 and XYZC move-in of 01/07.**	PDT	03/17/06	

4.2 Manage Risk

Overview

Formal risk management is a new discipline for XYZ Company The ITS PMO projects but has been identified by The ITS PMO management as a critical process to be conducted diligently for each project. Given the high priority placed on risk management, and the potential savings to schedule, budget, and quality, The ITS PMO Project Managers are required to follow risk management practices and will be closely supervised by The ITS PMO' Senior Portfolio Manager.

A risk is defined as "an uncertain future event or condition that, if it occurs, has a positive or negative effect on a project's objectives." *(Project Management Body of Knowledge)*

Most risks are identified and tracked because of the potentially negative effects on project performance; however, uncertain future events with potentially positive consequences should also be tracked if the magnitude of the potential effect is significant.

Many types of risks are possible; common types are technology, legal, regulatory, resource, schedule, or cost. They are most often described in terms of their possible impact on project scope, cost and schedule.

Risk management is defined as (a) the process of identifying and analyzing risks, (b) monitoring actions intended to mitigate the potential effects of these risks, and (c) planning actions to be taken if the risk occurs. Key elements include the following:

- Capturing risk information in a central repository
- Communicating and addressing significant risks as early as possible
- Providing visibility to project managers, stakeholders, vendors, executives, and others
- Establishing a record of decisions made and the rationale for each

The primary activities related to risk management fall into two categories: Mitigation and Contingency. (These are related to, but distinct from, other risk management responses which include Avoidance, Transference, and Acceptance. Refer to the PMBOK for more information.)

Mitigation: A mitigation strategy answers the question: "What should we do now that we are aware of the risk?" It is a series of preventative actions taken (a) to reduce the probability of a risk occurring or (b) to reduce the projected impact of a risk.

Contingency: A contingency plan answers the question "What should we you do if the risk (event) occurs?" It is a series of actions that are planned to be taken in the event that a risk (event) occurs.

Both types of risk responses can be developed in a variety of ways; Project Managers should always refer to Lessons Learned from previous projects as a reference when developing risk responses.

Risk management, which deals with uncertain events, should be distinguished from issue management, which deals with certain events, although both share the common goal of insuring positive project outcomes. An issue is a certain event that is hindering project progress; a risk is an uncertain event that may or may not affect the project.

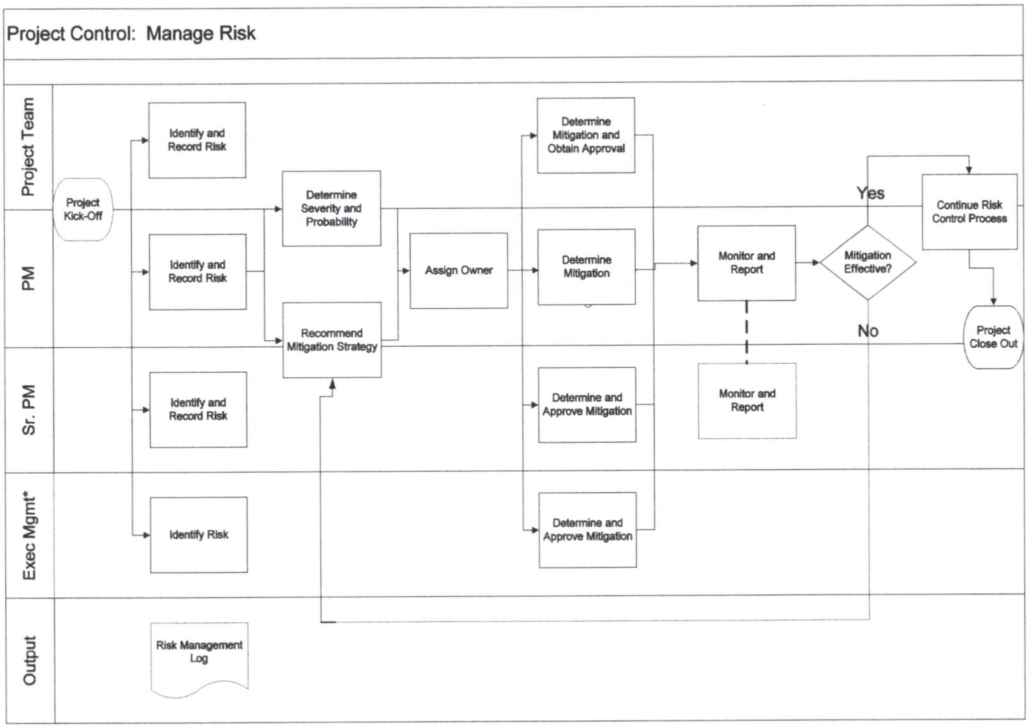

* EDT or PDT depending on the circumstances

Inputs, Outputs, and Tools

Outputs created during the Planning Phase and developed during the Execution Phase serve as the inputs to the Risk Management Process.

Inputs	Tools & Techniques	Outputs
• Project Plan (*incl. assumptions & constraints*) • Historical Information • Scope Changes	• Documentation Reviews • Assumptions Analysis • Risk Scoring Worksheet • Project Risk Tracking Log • Expert Judgment • Qualitative Analysis/Quantitative Ranking	• Project Risk Log • Mitigation Plans • Contingency Plans

Timeframe/Total Duration

- The Risk Management process is carried out concurrent to the Project Planning, Execution, and Closure phases.

Resource Participation

The following resources participate in the Risk Management process:

- The ITS PMO Project Manager
- Project Team
- The ITS PMO Senior Portfolio Manager
- PDT/EDT
- Other Key Stakeholders

The matrix below shows which steps within the stage and in what capacity each resource participates.

Step	The ITS PMO Project Mgr	Project Team	Senior Portfolio Mgr	PDT/EDT	Other Key Stakeholders
1 – Identify & Record Risk	A	R	C	R	R
2 – Determine Severity & Probability	A	R	C		C
3 – Recommend Mitigation Strategy	R	A	C		C
4 – Assign Owner	A/R	R	I		
5 – Determine & Approve Mitigation Strategy	R	R	I	A	C
6 – Monitor & Report Risk Status	A/R	R	I		
7 – Close Risk (if possible)	A/R	R	I		

Process Description

The Risk Management process consists of seven primary steps.

Step 1 – Identify & Record Risk

- **Instructions**
  - Risks can be identified by any member of the project team, including key stakeholders, at any time during the project. Teams should employ various techniques to adequately capture all significant risks. The individual who identifies the risk (risk identifier) will provide a description of the risk and classify the risk (see below for risk categories). He/she will communicate this information to the ITS PMO PM, who will record the information in the Project Risk Tracking Log.
  - An initial inventory of project risks should be developed during the Planning Phase. The ITS PMO PM's should use the Risk Scoring Worksheet to facilitate discussions with the project team. (*The Risk Scoring Worksheet is located in the Templates and Tools folder in SharePoint.*)
  - The ITS PMO requires that all projects track risks; the minimum requirements for risk tracking are shown in the following section of this document.
    - The Senior Portfolio Manager will periodically conduct audits of each project to ensure that risk management is occurring as required.
  - The following information is tracked in the Risk Log:

Field	Description
Risk #	Unique identifier for each risk
Priority	Priority for risk mitigation effort
Severity	Impact on project if risk occurs
Probability	Likelihood of realization

Type	Classification of risk (*see table below*)
Title	Brief description of risk
Mitigation Strategy	Brief description of mitigation strategy/contingency plan
Date Identified	Date risk identified
Identified By	Name of risk identifier
Status	Open or Closed
Assigned To	Person responsible for monitoring & prompting action
Date Last Reviewed	Date risk last reviewed
Date Closed	Date risk closed
Comments	May include notes regarding progress made towards resolution as well as names of parties to be notified of status

The following risk categories may be used to classify the risk:

Type of Risk	**Criteria**
Technical	Related to technology being used or specific technical processes (e.g. reliance on unproven or complex technology, changes in the technology used)
Quality	Related to the quality of project performance or project production (e.g. changes to industry standards during the project)
Performance	Related to the performance/behavior of the project team, subcontractors, or stakeholders
Schedule	Related to the timeliness of work plan task completion
External	Related to project dependencies with other projects, legal risks, or other

The following definitions can be used to determine risk status:

Status	**Definition**
Open	Risk remains a threat to project performance Actions are being taken to mitigate risk impact and/or prepare contingency
Closed	Risk is no longer a threat to project performance No actions are being taken to mitigate risk impact and/or prepare contingency

- **Estimated Time Duration**
    - Variable

- **Tips for Success**
    - Full participation of project subject matter experts is critical to the success of this step.

Step 2 – Determine Severity & Probability

- **Instructions**
  - The risk identifier will make an initial assessment of the probability of occurrence (low, medium, or high) and severity of impact (low, medium, or high), based on their best judgment and consultation with key stakeholders.
    - Because risk probability assignment is a relatively new practice at the XYZ Company, a qualitative assessment should be assigned. Over time, more quantitative methods may be employed.

The following guidelines should be used to assign risk severity:

Severity	Description	Details
High	Impact on project from schedule, cost, scope, or quality standpoint is sufficient to warrant RED criteria on dashboard	• >4 wks or 25% of baseline schedule • >40% of baseline cost • Scope insufficiently detailed to determine baseline • Quality well below XYZ Company expectations
Medium	Impact on project from schedule, cost, scope, or quality standpoint is sufficient to warrant YELLOW criteria on dashboard	• 2-4 wks or 10-25% of baseline schedule • 21-40% of baseline cost • Scope disagreement in >2 critical areas • Quality below XYZ Company expectations but meets contractual obligations
Low	No impact on project schedule, cost, or deliverables	• <2 wks or 10% of baseline schedule • <20% of baseline cost • Scope disagreement in <2 critical areas • Quality below XYZ Company expectations but meets contractual obligations

- **Estimated Time Duration**
  - Variable.

- **Tips for Success**
  - As with Step 1 above, full participation of project subject matter experts is critical to the success of this step.

Determining variances & providing corrective action

Understanding project slippage is key to knowing how to construct contingency plans when project slippage occurs. Using the earned value method based critical path items, milestones or project deliverables is a great tool for measuring project performance and variances within the project. Once slippage is identified you can then come up with corrective action. Some of the key indicators when using earned value to determine slippage is as follow:

- Schedule Performance Index – We are only executing at x% of our original planned schedule.
    - SPI Between 90 and 100% should show "Green" as a reporting status
    - SPI Between 80 and 90% should show "Green" with a "Yellow" down arrow as a reporting status which indicates that the project maybe turning "Yellow"
    - SPI Between 75 and 80% should show "Yellow" as a reporting status
    - SPI Between 70 and 74% should show "Yellow" as a reporting status with a "Red" down arrow as a reporting status which indicates that the project maybe turning "Red"
    - Less than 70 should show project status as "RED"
- Cost Performance Index – For every $1 of work effort we are only getting X value worth.
    - Same reporting criteria as SPI
- Estimate at Completion – How much will total project cost as of today
- Estimate to Complete – How much more will the project cost
- Variance at Completion – How much over/under budget will the project be

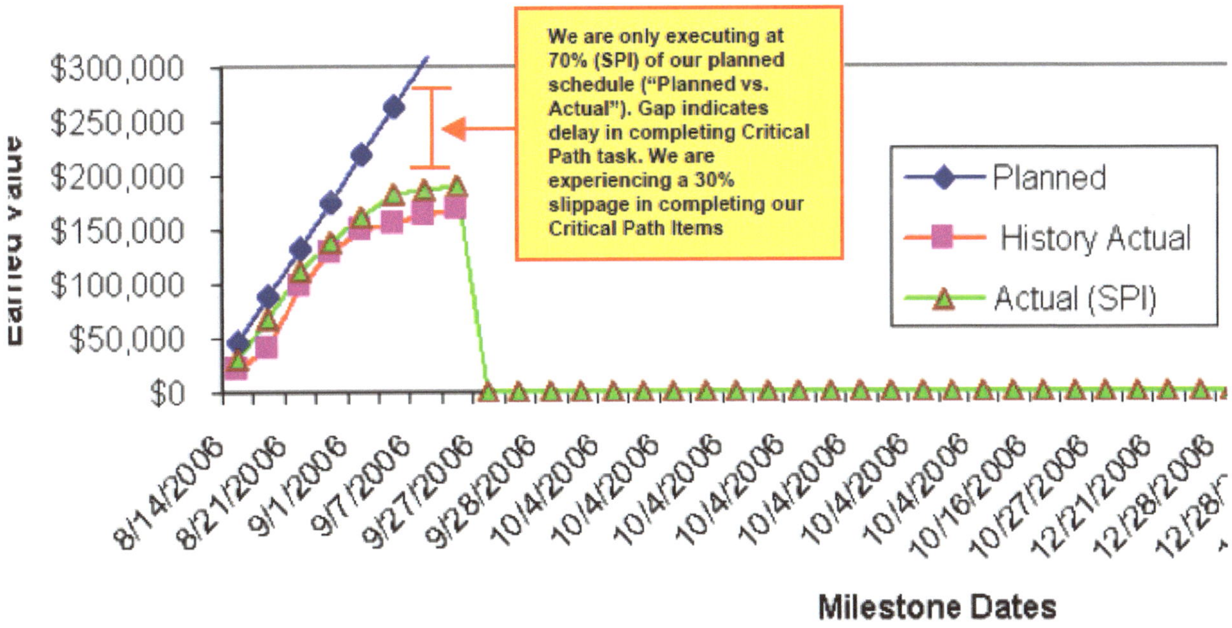

Other Tools to consider:

- Pareto Charts – Focuses on the frequency of the problems to show opportunities for improvement

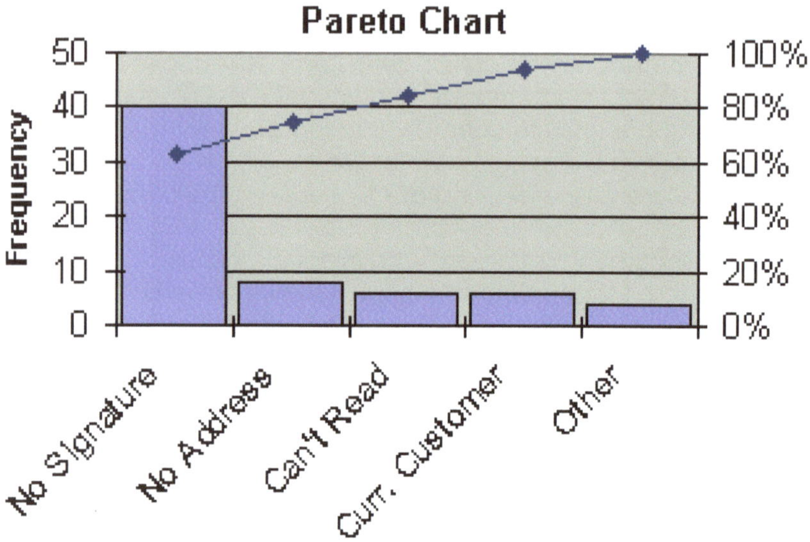

- Fishbone Diagram – Shows the root causes to problems

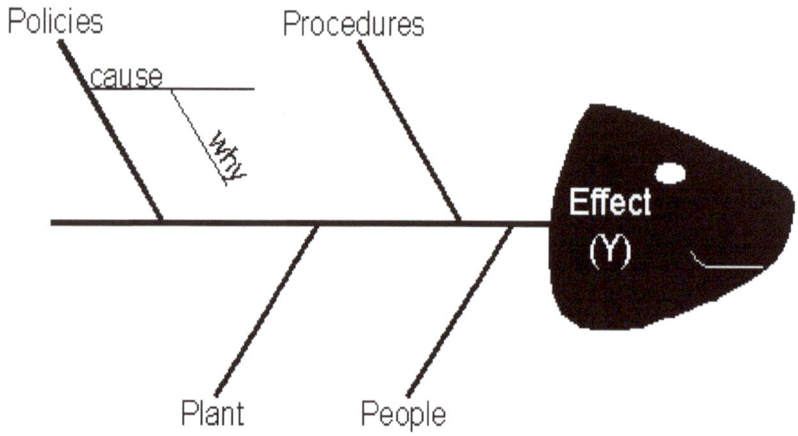

- Run charts – Will allow a team to study data in an effort to analyze trends and variances

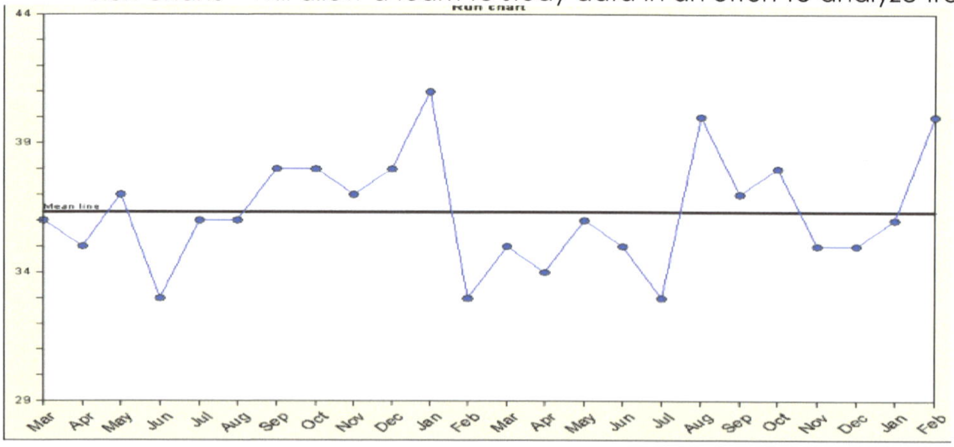

- Regression Line Analysis – Will show the correlation between a special circumstances. The closer the inputs are too the line, the greater possibility of the correlation existing.

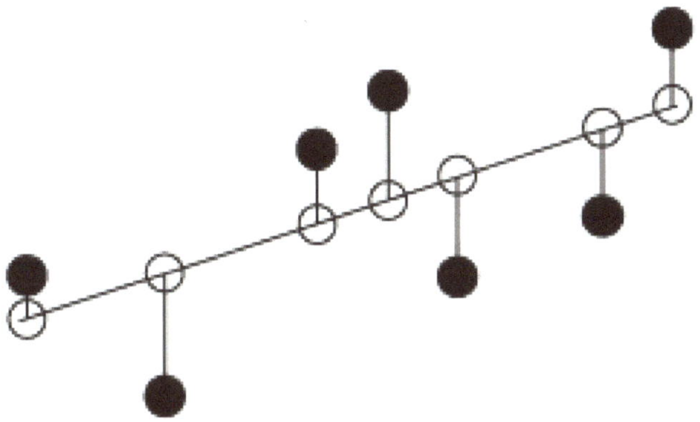

- Scatter Diagrams – A study and investigation of two variables changes over a time period

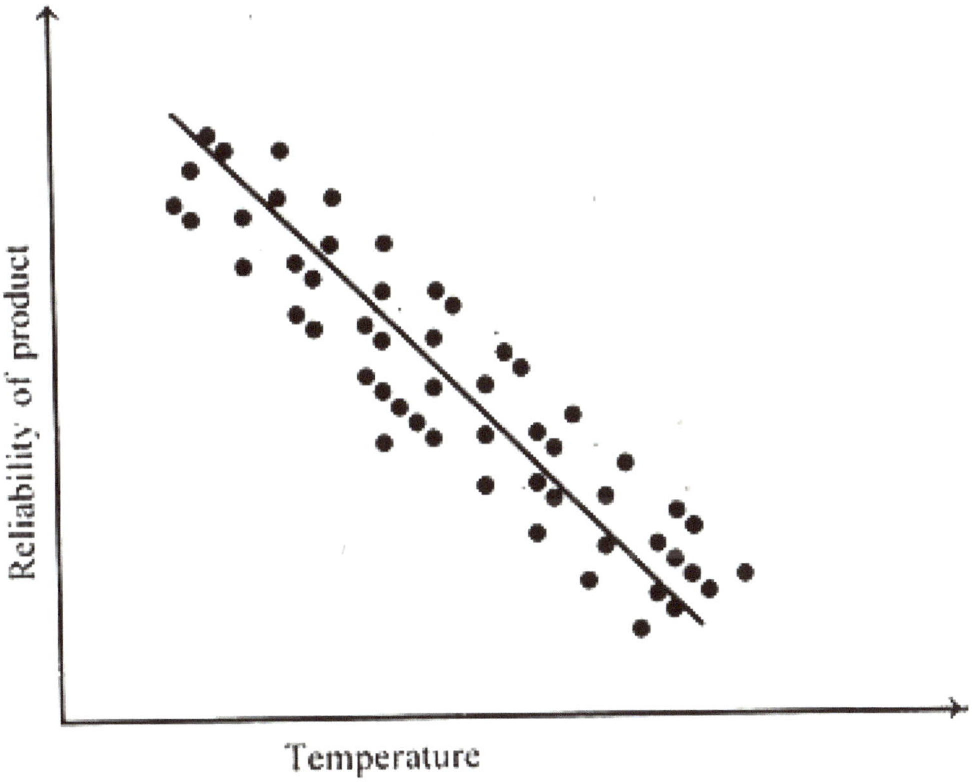

- Control Charts – To study and monitor control sources over a period of time to increase quality

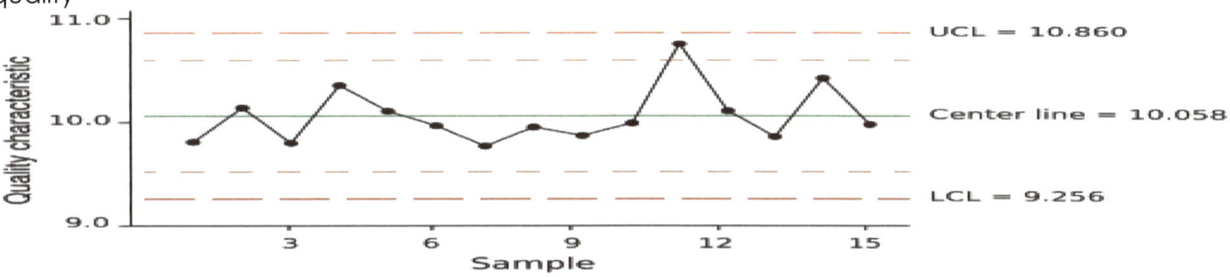

- Distribution- Use to Investigate the probability of an event by sampling the events given certain inputs in an effort to predict a future outcome (output) in respect to it's standard mean.

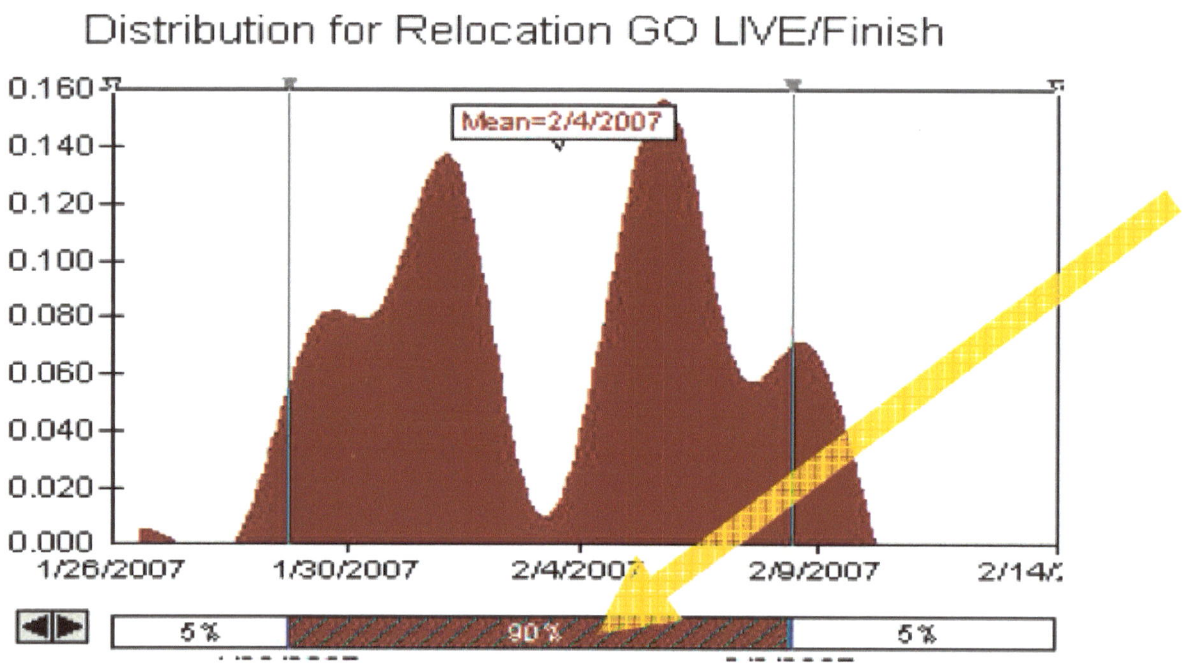

Step 3 – Recommend Mitigation Strategy (and Contingency Plan)

- **Instructions**
    - The risk identifier, in collaboration with the project team subject matter experts and The ITS PMO PM, should recommend a mitigation strategy to address the risk. For high probability or high impact risks, the risk owner (*described below*) will develop a contingency plan to preserve project performance in the event that the risk occurs.
        - Judgment must be used to ensure that the costs of risk management do not outweigh the benefits. The project team should focus therefore on developing contingency plans for only those risks deemed high probability and high impact.
    - The Project Manager must review all High and Medium risks with the Senior Portfolio Manager after the initial risk planning session, as new risks are identified, and on an ongoing basis.
        - Additionally, for large projects, a formal risk review should take place at the end of each major system development phase prior to starting the next phase:
            - Analyze phase (identification of business and technical requirements);
            - Build phase (development of solution);
            - Test phase (Conference Room Pilot testing, user acceptance testing, etc.);
            - Implementation phase (launching of solution).
- **Estimated Time Duration**

- Variable

- **Tips for Success**
    - Significant impacts to schedule, budget, and quality may be lessened or avoided entirely if the entire project team remains involved in the risk management process, particularly in the definition of a mitigation strategy. At all costs, the Project Manager should ensure that all key stakeholders are up to date with the project's top risks.
    - *Risk triggers* should be identified as part of the risk mitigation strategy development. An example of a risk trigger might be a missed intermediate milestone.

Step 4 – Assign Owner

- **Instructions**
    - The risk identifier should assign ownership of the risk to the appropriate team member or stakeholder. Ownership implies overall responsibility for the risk; it does not imply that the owner will act alone in addressing the risk. The risk owner must confirm acceptance, and in most cases the Project Manager should approve ownership assignments.

- **Estimated Time Duration**
    - Immediate (whenever a risk is identified.)

- **Tips for Success**
    - If no one voluntarily assumes ownership for a given risk, the ITS PMO PM should not hesitate to assign ownership.
    - Choose/assign owners based on their familiarity with the functional/technical area as well as the potential impact to their position/department/division. This will tend to ensure that these risks are tracked more carefully.

Step 5 – Determine Mitigation (& Obtain Approval)

- **Instructions**
    - After review of the risk by the owner and Project Manager, the recommended activities (mitigation and / or contingency) should be presented to the appropriate parties for approval. All mitigation and contingency actions must be approved by the Project Manager; actions that have a significant effect on budget, resources, or schedule should be addressed with the Senior Portfolio Manager, the business owner, and possibly the PDT or EDT.

- **Tips for Success**
    - This may require collaboration between multiple parties.

Step 6 – Monitor & Report

- **Instructions**
    - Updates to probability, impact, or status of mitigation efforts should be recorded in the Risk Tracker. The ITS PMO Project Managers should include progress updates for significant risks in Project Status reports.
    - The Project Manager and Senior Portfolio Manager should have regularly scheduled risk review meetings, which will be specific milestones in the project work plan. Frequency will vary by project and be determined during the Project Planning phase.
        - The risk review should address the following:
            - Summary of status of top 10 sources of risk on the project. For each risk item, the following should be analyzed:

- Risk item's current ranking;
- Risk item's previous ranking;
- Number of times item appears on list over time;
- Summary of progress made in resolving the risk item since last review.

▪

- As stated above, the Senior Portfolio Manager will periodically conduct risk response audits in order to ensure that the risk management process is operating as intended.

- **Tips for Success**
  - This is a critical area of focus and thus tracked on a regular and frequent basis by the Project Manager. Project team reviews of risks can occur less frequently but should be taken very seriously.

Step 6 – Modify Course of Action or Escalate (as necessary)

- **Instructions**
  - If the severity and / or probability of a risk increases, or the actions to mitigate the risk are not effective, a change in course may be necessary. This change in course could include a modification of the mitigation plan or an escalation of the risk to a higher decision-making level.
  - The ITS PMO PM should use the following criteria in his/her decision to escalate the risk:

Level	Owner	Criteria
1	Team Lead	• Actions required to mitigate risk can be effected by the project sub-team
2	Project Manager	• Risk mitigation cannot be effected by project sub-team alone • Ownership of risk is not decided • Risk mitigation not completed on schedule • Risk may threaten overall project timeline • Risk may have cross-functional impacts

3	PMO (CIO, ACIO's, Senior Portfolio Manager)	• Risk probability is high and cannot be mitigated by project team alone • Risk may impact other projects or departments • Risk may impact overall project timeline and budget • PM lacks resources or support needed to effect risk mitigation
4	EDT or PDT (as applicable)	• Risk probability is high and cannot be mitigated by The ITS PMO Senior Mgmt alone • Risk may impact overall project timeline and budget • Risk severity level is High • Significant additional resources are required to resolve the issue

- **Tips for Success**
  - Project Managers should use best judgment in deciding which risks must be escalated. As a general rule of thumb, risks are more easily addressed if done proactively than if done reactively when they are issues.

Step 7 – Close Risk (if possible)

- **Instructions**
  - Risks will rarely be closed; more often the probability or severity ratings will be reduced as the risk is successfully mitigated. In the event that a risk does occur, it can be closed and converted to an issue to be addressed.

- **Tips for Success**
  - Project Managers should document in detail the reasons/actions taken that enable the risk to be closed. If the risk should be reopened, this will provide useful information for the project team in assessing risk severity and impact as well as developing a mitigation strategy.

4.3 Manage Issues

Overview

The purpose of issue management is to minimize the impact of issues on project performance by providing a structured approach to managing, escalating, and resolving issues.

For definition purposes, **an issue is an obstacle that inhibits the completion of a project task and requires action by parties other than those responsible for the task.**

Many types of issues are possible; common types are technology, legal, regulatory, resource, schedule, or cost issues. They are often described in terms of their impact on project scope, cost and schedule.

Key elements of issue management include (a) providing visibility to project managers, stakeholders, vendors, executives, and other related parties, (b) encouraging timely action by these parties to address open issues, and (c) recording issues and actions taken to resolve them.

Issues must be clearly distinguished from risks. Issues and risks are tracked in a similar fashion, but they are very different in practice. An issue is a certain event that is hindering project progress; a risk is an uncertain event that may or may not affect the project. If left unresolved, an issue can:

- Change the direction or scope of the project
- Impair the solution
- Dampen the quality of the final product

Issue management can be defined as the management, prioritization, and resolution of issues which are inhibiting project progress. Key elements include the following:

- Capturing issue information in a central repository
- Communicating and resolving major issues as early as possible
- Establishing a record of decisions made and the rationale for each

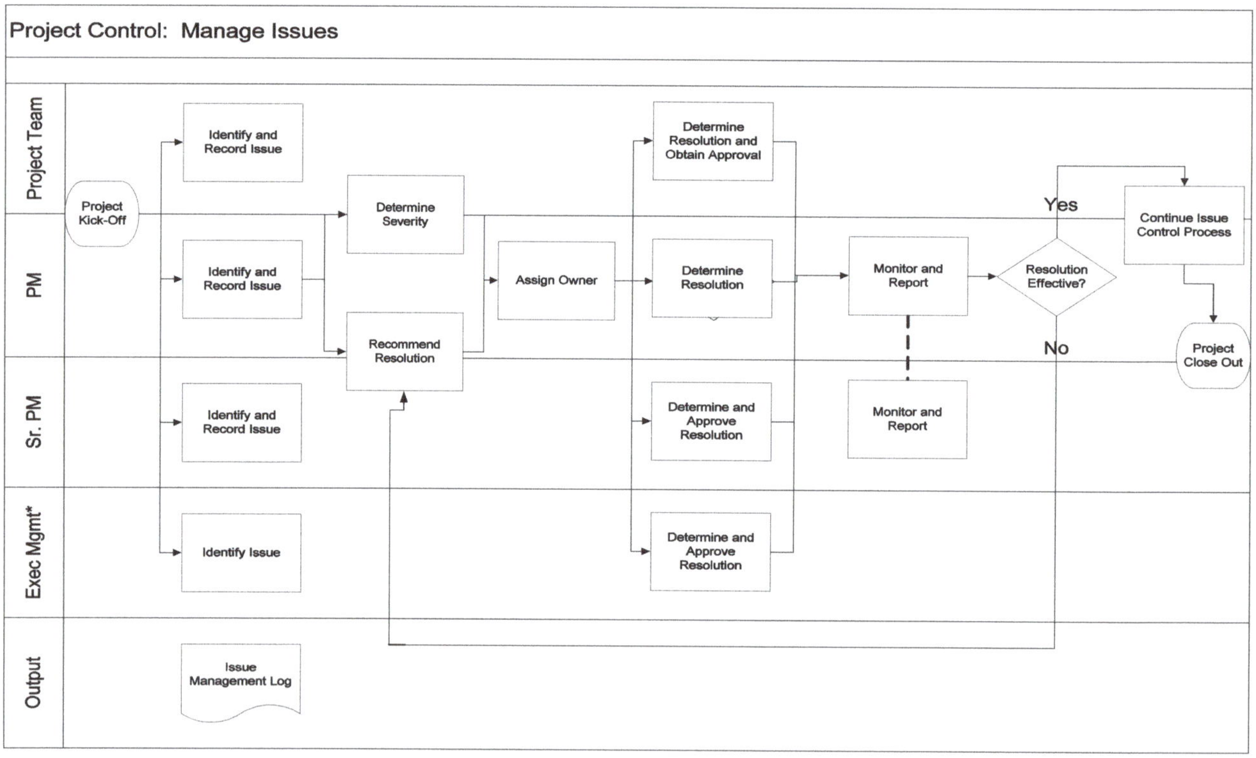

* EDT or PDT depending on the circumstances

Inputs, Outputs, and Tools

Outputs created during the Planning Phase and developed during the Execution Phase serve as the inputs to the Issue Management Process.

Inputs

- Project Plan (*incl. assumptions & constraints*)
- Project Status Reports
- Issue Meeting Minutes
- SOW/Project Requirements
- Project Work Plan
- Project Budget
- Deliverable Reviews

Tools & Techniques

- Documentation Reviews
- Assumptions Analysis
- Project Issue/Risk Tracking Log
- Expert Judgment
- Severity Qualification Matrix

Outputs

- Project Issue Log
- Action Plans
- Contingency Plans

Timeframe/Total Duration

- The Issue Management process is carried out concurrent to the Project Planning, Execution, and Closure phases.

Resource Participation

The following resources participate in the Issue Management process:

- The ITS PMO Project Manager
- Project Team
- The ITS PMO Senior Portfolio Manager
- PDT/EDT
- Other Key Stakeholders

The matrix below shows which steps within the stage and in what capacity each resource participates*.

Step	The ITS PMO Project Mgr	Project Team	Senior Portfolio Mgr	PDT/EDT	Other Key Stakeholders
1 – Identify & Record Issue	A/R	R	C	R	R
2 – Determine Severity	A	R	I		C
3 – Recommend Resolution	R	A	C		C
4 – Assign Owner	A	R	I		
5 – Determine & Approve Resolution	R	R	I	A	C
6 – Monitor & Report Issue Status	A	R	C		
7 – Evaluate Issue	A	R	I	R	R
8 – Resolve/Close Issue	A	R	I	I	I

* Note that the actual responsibility for certain steps in the Issues Management process will vary according to escalation level. Guidelines for the escalation level are described in Section 4.4.5, Step 4.

Process Description

The Issue Management process consists of seven (7) primary steps, which closely mirror those of the Risk Management process. This section provides detailed instructions for each of those steps.

Step 1 – Identify & Record Issue

- **Instructions**
  - Issues can be identified by project managers, stakeholders, vendors, executives, or related parties. The identifying party should give the issue a title, provide a description, provide a description of the impact, and recommend a series of actions to resolve the issue.
  - The Project Manager is accountable for set-up and management of the Issues Log.
  - The following information is tracked in the Issue Log:

Field	Description
Issue #	Unique identifier for each issue
Severity	Impact on project
Workstream	Project activity/critical path impacted
Description	Brief description of risk
Date Identified	Date risk identified
Identified By	Name of risk identifier
Status	Open or Closed
Assigned To	Person responsible for monitoring & prompting action
Issue Level	Level to which issue must be escalated for resolution approval (*see Step 4 below*)
Date to Resolve	Target resolution date
Resolution	Action plan to resolve issue
Action Required	Immediate action needed to resolve and owner of action
Date Closed	Date issue closed
Approved By	Person who approves the ownership assignment, the action required, and the target resolution date. Also who officially approved closure of issue when actions taken to resolve the issue.
Comments	May include notes regarding progress made towards resolution (or lack thereof) as well as names of parties to be notified of status

- **Tips for Success**
  - Framing the issue description so that all project stakeholders can easily understand the issue (and not the symptom) takes some work. To ensure that the project team is not spending its energy on addressing the root cause of the symptom (e.g. headache) versus the issue (e.g. too much stress from doing too many things), the Project Manager should spend some time analyzing and framing the issue prior to recording it in the Issue Log.
  - Identification of the "Approver' is critical to keeping the issue resolution process operating properly. The Approver is often the original issue identifier, but not always.

- While the Project Manager owns the Issue Log, it should always be available for review by all project stakeholders

Step 2 – Determine Severity Level

- **Instructions**
  - All issues will be assigned a severity level (low, medium, or high) based on the projected impact of the issue on the performance of the project. Refer to the Severity Qualification Matrix below.
  - The Project Manager is accountable for ensuring that each risk is assigned a severity level.

Severity	Description	Details
Critical	Possible show-stopper with cross project impacts	**Resolution required immediately**
High	Impact on project from schedule, cost, scope, or quality standpoint is sufficient to warrant RED criteria on dashboard	**Resolution required in short term (within 2 weeks)**
Medium	Impact on project from schedule, cost, scope, or quality standpoint is sufficient to warrant YELLOW criteria on dashboard	**Resolution required before next milestone can be achieved (more than 2 weeks in future)**
Low	No impact on project schedule, cost, or deliverables	**Resolution can occur subsequent to next milestone/project's completion**

- **Tips for Success**
  - The Project Manager may find that issue identifiers tend to assign a severity of *Critical* or *High* for those issues that impact them directly, leading to a majority of *Critical* and *High* issues. While all issues should be considered and addressed, not all issues will need to be addressed right away. The Project Manager will find that assignment of ownership of that issue to the original identifier will assist in normalizing the severity ratings. Familiarization of the entire project team with the Severity Qualification Matrix will also help to keep ratings objective.

Step 3 – Develop Recommendation for Resolution

- **Instructions**
  - As part of the initial analysis of the issue, a recommendation for the resolution of the issue should be developed. The recommendation should include a breakdown of the actions necessary, the resources necessary, and a time frame that takes the

Project Work Plan into account. Issue identifiers should be encouraged to do this analysis before raising the issue to be logged on the Issue Log.

- **Tips for Success**
  - As described in the Communication Management section of the Execution Chapter, the Project Manager will find that project members have a tendency to raise, analyze, and brainstorm fixes for issues during Project Status Meetings. The Project Manager should encourage project team members to use the separate Project Working Sessions to do this (i.e. "taking it off-line".)
  - A critical ingredient to conducting efficient, effective Project Working Sessions is to ensure that the meeting contains only those participants who are *informed* and *authorized* to diagnose the problem and take action.

Step 4 – Assign Ownership (& Escalation Level)

- **Instructions**
  - An owner who will take primary responsibility for resolution should be assigned to each issue. The level of escalation should also be recorded, and this will often have a bearing on the ownership assignment. Issue ownership should be confirmed by the owner if the identifying party is different from the owner, and the Project Manager should approve all assignments to all high severity issues. (Note: Level 4 issues requiring attention at the executive level must be identified and recorded as early as possible to allow sufficient time to address it appropriately.)
  - Use the Issue Ownership and Escalation guidelines below. Owner refers to level of escalation, not individual responsible for resolving the issue:

Level	Owner	Criteria
1	Team Lead	• Issue can be resolved by the project sub-team
2	Project Manager	• Issue cannot be resolved by project sub-team alone • Ownership of issue is not decided • Issue resolution not completed on schedule • Issue threatens overall project timeline • Issue has cross-functional impacts
3	PMO (CIO, ACIO's, Senior Portfolio Manager)	• Issue cannot be resolved by project team alone • Issue impacts other projects or departments • Issue impacts overall project timeline and

		budget • PM lacks resources or support needed to resolve issue
4	EDT or PDT (as applicable)	• Issue cannot be resolved by The ITS PMO Senior Mgmt alone • Issue impacts overall project timeline and budget • Issue severity level is Critical or High • Significant additional resources are required to resolve the issue

- Recording and tracking of level 1 issues will be conducted at the discretion of the Project Manager.

- **Tips for Success**
  - ALWAYS assign ownership. Project Managers should avoid assuming ownership for too many issues (although this may happen by default). Instead, he/she should stress the fact that common ownership of issues accompanies ownership of the project's success at completion.

Step 5 – Determine Resolution

- **Instructions**
  - Once steps 1 through 4 have been completed, the issue and the proposed resolution can be escalated to the appropriate level for review and approval.

- **Tips for Success**
  - As with the Mitigation Strategy for the Risk Management process, this may be a collaborative exercise that requires multiple parties.

Step 6 – Monitor & Report Issue Status

- **Instructions**
  - The Project Manager is responsible for insuring that all project-related issues are addressed. The issue owner is responsible for insuring that their issues are resolved. The ITS PMO PM standards require that all projects monitor issues, and maintain an Issues Log to be kept up-to-date on SharePoint for project use. In addition, the Senior Portfolio Manager will support all projects to insure timely resolution of issues that are escalated to The ITS PMO Senior Management or the EDT/PDT.
  - The ITS PMO PM standards require that issue status be reported as a component of Project Status reports. A summary of issue-related activity should be provided, as well as a complete record of open and recently closed issues. Issues should be addressed in meetings as needed, and special meetings may be called to address high severity issues.

    - The Senior Portfolio Manager will periodically audit Issues Logs to ensure that the Issues Management process is operating effectively.

- **Tips for Success**
    - The Project Manager should regularly review the status of all Critical and High issues at project status meetings to ensure progress on issue resolution.
    - The Project Manager and Senior Portfolio Manager should also periodically review Issues Management metrics (e.g. % of issues older than 3 weeks) to ensure that the process is operating effectively and take corrective action if not.

Step 7 – Evaluate Issue (Resolution Effective?)

- **Instructions**
    - If the actions taken to address the problem do not yield a satisfactory resolution, then the issue should be re-evaluated. An escalation to a higher level may be necessary, or simply a different course of action.

- **Tips for Success**
    - The issue owner and originator should participate in the evaluation and confirmation that an issue has been resolved.

Step 8 – Resolve/Close Issue

- **Instructions**
    - If the actions taken to resolve the issue are effective, then the resolution should be recorded in the Issue Log and included in the next status report.
    - The ITS PMO PM should communicate to the project team that the issue has been closed with the owner's approval at the subsequent project status meeting.

- **Tips for Success**
    - Issues cannot be closed until the issue's assigned owner and approver have formally been notified of the issue's status and agree that it can be closed.
    - All impacted stakeholders should likewise be notified when and how relevant issues have been closed.
    - The ITS PMO PM's should keep track of all closed issues for archive/Lessons Learned purposes.

4.4 Manage Schedule

Overview

Schedule management (analogous for the purposes of this PMO Handbook with PMBOK's process of Schedule Control) is one of the most critical tools in the Project Manager's toolkit to master due to 3 primary reasons:

1. Schedule problems are relatively easy to spot and measure (versus scope and cost);
2. Project schedule is historically the factor over which XYZ Company The ITS PMO Project Managers have most control;
3. Project schedule is the most common metric of project success at the XYZ Company.

The goal of schedule control is to know the status of the project's schedule, influence the factors that cause schedule changes, confirm that whether the schedule has changed, and most importantly managing the changes as they occur. Since project schedule is such an important factor in overall success at the XYZ Company, The ITS PMO PM Standards require that any significant changes to the schedule (i.e. "re-baselining") are approved by the Senior Portfolio Manager and in most cases, the project's PDT.

For reference purposes, project schedule and project work plan are used interchangeably throughout this section.

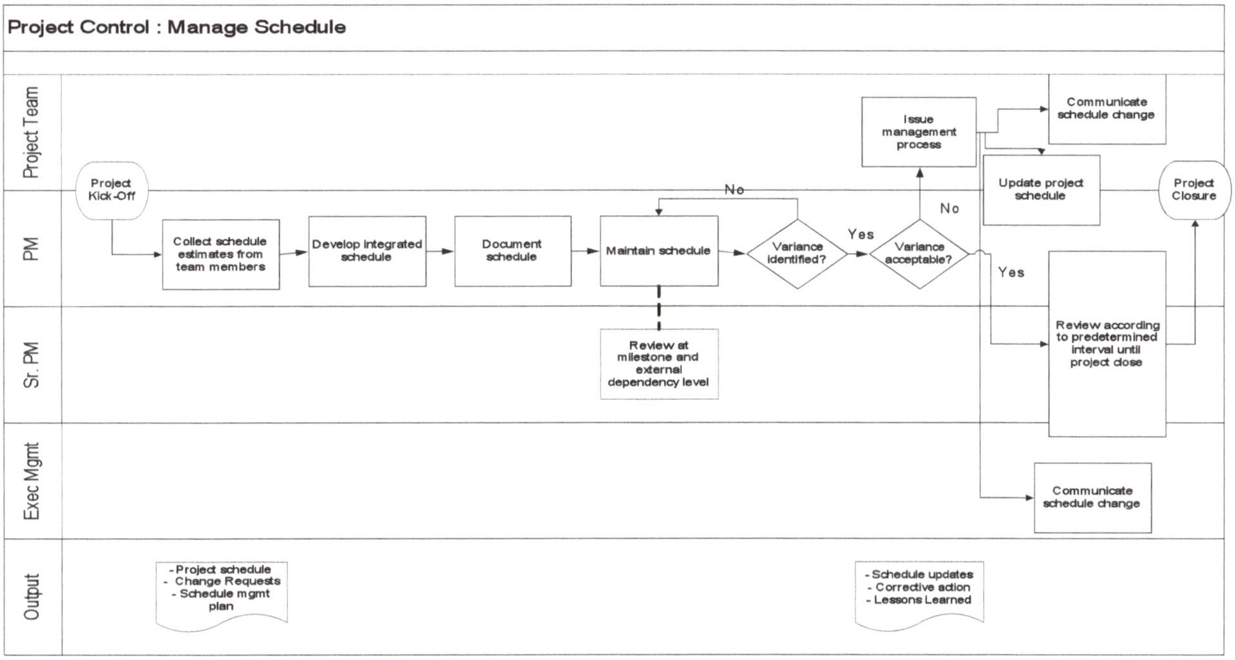

Inputs, Outputs, and Tools

Outputs created during the Planning Phase and developed during the Execution Phase serve as the inputs to the Schedule Management Process.

Inputs	Tools & Techniques	Outputs
• Project Plan • Project Work Plan • Approved SCR's	• Critical Path Analysis • MS Project Work Plan • Additional Planning	• Schedule/Work Plan Update • Corrective Action

Timeframe/Total Duration

- The Schedule Management process is carried out concurrent to the Project Planning, Execution, and Closure phases.

Resource Participation

The following resources participate in the Schedule Management process:

- The ITS PMO Project Manager
- Project Team
- The ITS PMO Senior Portfolio Manager
- PDT/EDT
- Other Key Stakeholders

The matrix below shows which steps within the stage and in what capacity each resource participates.

Step	The ITS PMO Project Mgr	Project Team	Senior Portfolio Mgr	PDT/EDT	Other Key Stakeholders
1 – Collect schedule updates from team members	A	R			
2 – Develop/update integrated schedule	A	R	I		
3 – Document schedule	A	R	C		C
4 – Maintain schedule	A	R	C		
5 – Monitor and review for variance	A	R	C		R
6 – Initiate Issue Management process (if needed)	A	R	C	I	
7 – Update schedule	A	R	I	I	I
8 – Communicate schedule change	A/R	R	I	I	I

Stage Description

The "Validate Need" stage consists of eight (8) primary steps. This section provides detailed instructions for each of those steps.

<u>Step 1 – Collect Schedule Estimates From Team Members</u>

- **Instructions**
    - Once the integrated schedule/work plan baseline is developed during the Planning phase, the Project Manager should obtain updates from each of the team members for their respective workstreams prior to the regular project status meetings. Once status is known for each workstream, their status should be presented to the entire project team by the respective task/activity owners.
    - Submission deadline prior to the project status meeting shall be defined during the Planning phase and documented in the Project Plan.
    - The Project Manager is the owner of the work plan.
        - For projects where a vendor project manager is used to maintain the project work plan/schedule (i.e. he/she is "responsible" as the "doer," the ITS PMO PM is still accountable (i.e. he/she has yes/no authority over the deliverable) for the work plan's accuracy. Thus, the PM **must** know the schedule/work plan intimately.

- **Estimated Time Duration**
    - 1-2 hours

- **Tips for Success**
    - Realistic project schedules are essential to a successful project. One of the first reality checks that the Project Manager must perform is to review the draft schedule included in the PID/Project Charter. Although the draft schedule is a high-level estimate, it does set initial expectations for the project. The Project Manager is accountable for leading the project team in the preparation of a more detailed schedule and getting the stakeholders' approval (during the Planning phase.) It is critical to get involvement and commitment from all project team members (including vendors), top management, and other key stakeholders.
    - It is VERY important for the Project Manager to verify schedule progress periodically. ("Trust and verify.") Project Managers MUST review the actual work and develop good relationships with team members to ensure that work is completed as planned or changes are reported as needed.

<u>Step 2 – Develop/Update Integrated Schedule</u>

- **Instructions**
    - Based upon the inputs from the various team members, the Project Manager is accountable for developing and updating the project's integrated schedule with actual data.
        - Analysis of the integrated schedule must include identification of the project's critical path ("critical path analysis");
        - The Project Manager should consult with the Senior Portfolio Manager should assistance be needed in identifying the critical path.
    - Project Managers should also maintain a baseline version (original) of the schedule to be compared to actual when evaluating project performance.
    - A current version of the work plan should be kept updated and readily available to all project team members on SharePoint.

- **Tips for Success**
    - Project Managers should keep in mind that a project's critical path may change over the course of the project. Schedule analysis, critical path identification, and critical path monitoring are therefore ongoing activities led by the Project Manager.
    - Likewise, the Project Manager should remember that the completion of critical path activities are drivers of the project's end date but not sufficient to complete the project. A common approach taken by project teams with schedule problems is to focus all resources on completing the critical path tasks. While the original tasks lying on the critical path may be complete, this simply shifts the critical path to other tasks/deliverables.
    - For activity and task identification and duration estimation, use historical information whenever possible as an input. Past project work plans will be available on SharePoint for PM use.

<u>Step 3 – Document Schedule</u>

- **Instructions**
    - **The ITS PMO Project Managers are required to document the project's schedule as a MS Project work plan and review it with the Senior Portfolio Manager for acceptance**. Written work plans enable the Project Manager to:
        - Communicate progress relative to milestones;

        - Understand dependencies;
        - Identify project "slippage" early through project milestone (dependency) delays;
        - Provide clarity of focus, priorities, and responsibilities across teams;
        - Improve communication across project teams (through publication of milestones.)
    - Once reviewed by the Senior Portfolio Manager, the work plan must be posted in SharePoint for project use.

- **Tips for Success**
    - Remember to document all major assumptions that underlie the project schedule. A change in assumption should trigger a review of the project work plan.
    - Tracking Gantt charts are an effective way to illustrate progress to users unfamiliar with MS Project.

Step 4 – Maintain Schedule

- **Instructions**
    - At minimum, the Project Manager should do a formal weekly review of the schedule with the project team. However, as the primary tool for managing project effort and understanding project status, the Project Manager should review the actual progress against schedule daily (at a minimum progress against the critical path, if not all work streams.)

Step 5 – Monitor & Review For Variance

- **Instructions**
    - Frequent updates and vigilant monitoring of milestones enable the Project Manager to sooner identify variance from the baseline schedule and take corrective actions if needed. When variance occurs from the baseline schedule (which is normal), the Project Manager should frankly discuss the status of the work and determine if/how the approach, resources, or working time can be altered to bring the work back on schedule. This is obviously most important for critical path tasks.
    - As described in the Performance Management section, the Project Manager should frequently (at least once a week) consult with the Senior Portfolio Manager to ensure schedule status for the project is known at a milestone and dependency level. The following table describes the status levels (i.e. RED, YELLOW, or GREEN) that should be used to communicate status:

Schedule Status	Details
RED	• >4 wks or >25% of baseline schedule
YELLOW	• 2-4 wks or 10-25% of baseline schedule
GREEN	• <2 wks or <10% of baseline schedule

- **Tips for Success**
  - The Project Manager must be clear and honest in communicating project status. To avoid surprising top management, the Project Manager must avoid at all costs creating the illusion that the project is on track when in fact it is not. A tough part of the Project Manager's job is his/her responsibility to alert top management that a schedule problem exists and then to work with them to identify alternatives to resolve the problem.

Step 6 – Initiate Issue Management Process (if needed)

- **Instructions**
  - If critical path/schedule variance analysis suggests that the project is experiencing (or will experience) serious schedule problems, the Project Manager should identify the root causes behind the problem and initiate the Issues Management process. Proper management of the issue using the Issues Management process should lead to resolution and a change of schedule, budget, staff, or scope if necessary.

- **Tips for Success**
  - MS Project is a useful tool for developing "what if" scenarios when identifying a resolution to a given problem. The Project Manager should make full use of this functionality to negotiate alternative solutions.

Step 7 – Update Schedule

- **Instructions**
  - If the result of the Issue Management process is to take a corrective action that will modify the schedule, the Project Manager should ensure that the proper change process is employed in order to understand and communicate the schedule impact of the corrective action.
  - Once the change associated with a corrective action is approved, the Project Manager must review the entire project schedule and document revised estimates for activities in progress or yet to be started. This will often result in a new critical path and project end date.
  - Re-baselining of schedules should occur very rarely, if at all. If re-baselining is deemed necessary (e.g. because the original schedule is meaningless from a management and communication standpoint), the following approvals should be obtained PRIOR to re-baselining:

    - The ITS PMO Senior Portfolio Manager (if no PDT exists);
    - PDT or EDT.

The original baseline should be retained for project archive and project performance review purposes.

Step 8– Communicate Schedule Change

- **Instructions**
  - Whether the schedule change impacts a activity not on the critical path or affects the overall project end date, the Project Manager is accountable for communicating the revised information to the project team, the project PDT, and other key stakeholders. The revised schedule should be communicated via the following means:

- Revised work plan on SharePoint;
- Regular project status meetings;
- PDT meeting.

- **Tips for Success**
  - An important lesson learned regarding changes of any kind during the project is that it is very difficult to over communicate the message. Given the fast pace of many projects and many details that the project team and other key stakeholders must manage, the Project Manager should make all reasonable efforts to communicate the schedule change, reasons for the change, and who approved the change.

4.5 Manage Performance

Overview

The Performance Management, or Executive Reporting, process formalizes the link between the individual project and the entire The ITS PMO project portfolio. The primary objectives of the Performance Management process are to:

- Ensure senior level oversight for individual projects;
- Enable management to identify portfolio level impacts of project level activity;
- Coordinate ongoing IT and other XYZ Company departmental workstreams within departments and across the overall Authority;
- Provide a path for escalation of issues to the proper decision making level.

The key benefit of the Performance Management process is better alignment of technology initiatives with departmental and Authority goals and objectives in order to accomplish the Plan for Transformation.

While the Project Manager and project team participate in the Performance Management process, accountability for the associated activities lies with the Senior Portfolio Manager.

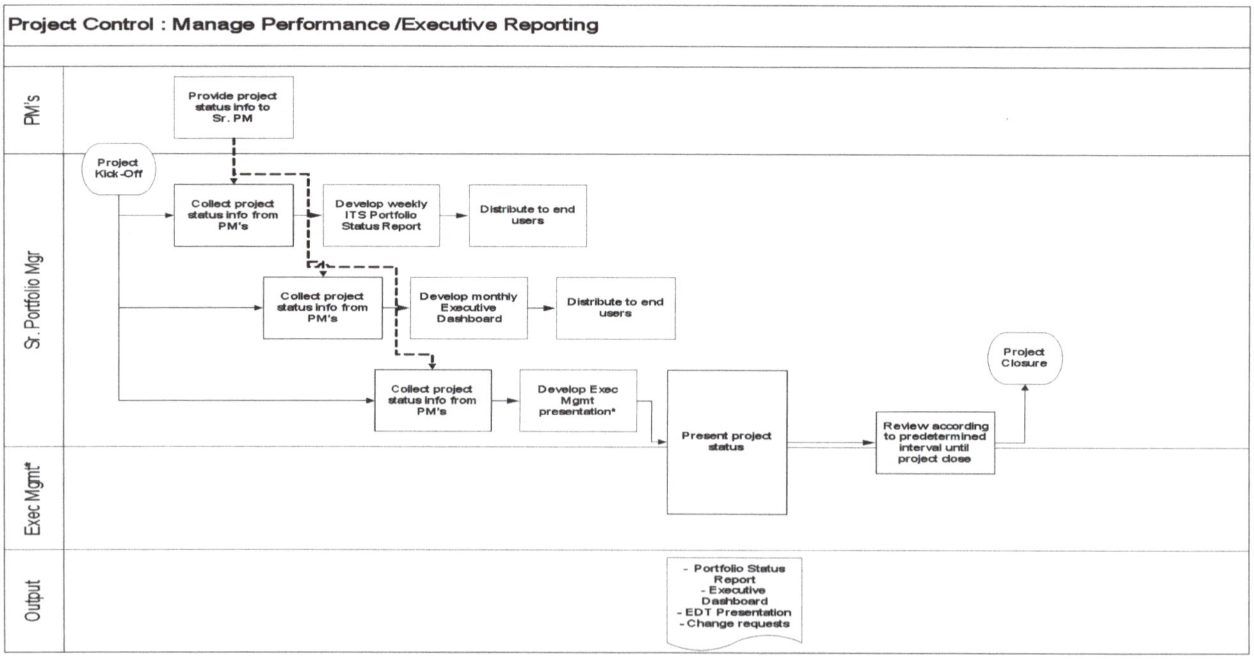

* EDT or PDT depending on the circumstances

Inputs, Outputs, and Tools

Outputs created during the Planning Phase and developed during the Execution Phase serve as the inputs to the Performance Management Process.

Inputs	Tools & Techniques	Outputs
• Project PID/Charters • Project Plans • Project Status Reports • Approved Change Requests • Historical Project Documents from The ITS PMO Portfolio	• Variance Analysis • Project Manager/Key Stakeholder Reviews • The ITS PMO Resource Capacity Model • Weekly Portfolio Status Meetings • Monthly Executive Dashboards • EDT Meetings & Presentations	• Weekly Portfolio Status Reports • Monthly The ITS PMO Portfolio Executive Dashboard • Bi-monthly EDT Meetings & Presentations • Bi-monthly EDT Minutes

Timeframe/Total Duration

- The Performance Management process is carried out concurrent to the Project Planning, Execution, and Closure phases.

Resource Participation

The following resources participate in the Performance Management process:

- The ITS PMO Project Manager
- The ITS PMO Senior Portfolio Manager
- PDT/EDT
- Other Key Stakeholders

The matrix below shows which steps within the stage and in what capacity each resource participates.

Step	The ITS PMO Project Mgr	Senior Portfolio Mgr	CIO/ACIO's	PDT/EDT	Other Key Stakeholders
1 – Collect project updates from Project Managers	C	A/R			
2 – Develop periodic status report	C	A/R			
3 – Present portfolio/project information to end-users	A/R	A/R	C	C	C
4 – Record decisions and action items and communicate results	I	A	C	C	
5 - Archive documents for portfolio/project history		A			

Process Description

The Performance Management/Executive Reporting process consists of five (5) primary steps. Reporting tools and frequency vary by communication vehicle but the overall process is the same for each. This section provides detailed instructions for each of those steps.

Executive reporting formally occurs through 3 different vehicles: weekly Portfolio Status reports and meetings, monthly The ITS PMO Portfolio Executive Dashboard, and bi-monthly EDT presentations and meetings.

Weekly Portfolio Status Meetings

Step 1 – Collect Project Updates from Project Managers

- **Instructions**
    - By close of business each Friday, Senior Portfolio Manager receives a written project status report from each of the Project Managers with active projects in the ITS PMO portfolio
    - By close of business each Monday, Senior Portfolio Manager consolidates all project status reports into weekly The ITS PMO Portfolio project status report
        - Senior Portfolio Manager should understand the following about each project:
            - Progress since last week towards milestones;
            - Pending/recently accepted deliverables;
            - Critical/High issues and risks;
            - Activities for upcoming week.
- **Estimated Time Duration**
    - Approximately 1 hour per project
- **Tips for Success**
    - The Senior Portfolio Manager should set a firm schedule by which updates are received so that he/she can ask clarifying questions and consolidate the information for Senior The ITS PMO Management use.

Step 2 – Deliver Periodic Status Report

- **Instructions**
    - A copy of the Weekly The ITS PMO Portfolio status report and any related discussion documents should be sent via email by the Senior Portfolio Manager to meeting attendees in advance of the meeting for their review.
- **Estimated Time Duration**
    - Less than 1 hour weekly
- **Resource Participation**
    - CIO
    - ACIO's
    - Senior Portfolio Manager

Step 3 – Present Portfolio/Project Information to End-users

- **Instructions**

- The Senior Portfolio Manager is accountable for scheduling and facilitating the regular weekly The ITS PMO Portfolio Status meetings with the CIO, the ACIO for applications, and the ACIO for infrastructure.
  - Presentation content should focus progress since last weekly review and top issues and risks, as well as required action items for senior The ITS PMO management.
    - Level 3 issues (issues that cannot be resolved by the project team alone. See *Issues Management* section for details) should be escalated to and resolved at this level.

- **Estimated Time Duration**
  - 1 hour weekly

- **Resource Participation**
  - CIO
  - ACIO's
  - Senior Portfolio Manager

<u>Step 4 – Record Decisions and Action Items and Communicate Results</u>

- **Instructions**
  - The Senior Portfolio Manager is accountable for recording all decisions and action items discussed by The ITS PMO Senior Management. These should be summarized in an email and sent to the meeting attendees, as well as the Managing Director for Internal Support by COB the next day.
  - The Senior Portfolio Manager should also communicate all project specific decisions and action items to the respective Project Managers.

- **Estimated Time Duration**
  - 2 hours weekly

- **Resource Participation**
  - CIO
  - ACIO's
  - Senior Portfolio Manager
  - MD Internal Support
  - The ITS PMO Project Managers

- **Tips for Success**
  - The Senior Portfolio Manager should publish notes, decisions, and action items as soon as possible after the project status meeting.

<u>Step 5 – Archive Documents for Project History</u>

- **Instructions**
  - The Senior Portfolio Manager is accountable for archiving the Weekly Portfolio status reports in the ITS PMO project archive, SharePoint.

- **Estimated Time Duration**
  - Less than 1 hour weekly

- **Resource Participation**
  - Senior Portfolio Manager

Monthly Executive Dashboard

Responsibility and accountability for the Monthly Executive Dashboard lies with the Senior Portfolio Manager. He/she is accountable for adding, updating status, and removing projects from the Dashboard so that it provides a complete, accurate, and timely snapshot of the health of the ITS PMO portfolio at any given point in time.

This following section describes separately:

1. Dashboard structure related tasks (adding, changing status, removing projects);
2. Active project status related tasks (updating project detail.)

Adding, Changing Status, and Removing Projects from the Executive Dashboard

Step 1 – Adding Projects

- **Instructions**
    - New projects are added to the Executive Dashboard after the ITS PMO portfolio is approved as part of the annual PID process as well as throughout the year at The ITS PMO Senior Management's discretion.
    - The decision to add a project to the Executive Dashboard is typically made during the weekly The ITS PMO Portfolio Status Meeting and should be captured in the status meeting minutes.
    - Once approved, projects should be assigned a formal project status number according to the following numbering system:
        - "Last 2 digits of year project initiated" – "Project number" – "If applicable, subproject number"

[example: 04-006-01 for the Housing Mgmt Software project (Yardi)]

- An example of a project (program) with a subproject number is the Sensible Home initiative
    - 04-0037-01: Sensible Homes
    - 04-0037-02: Wireless Infrastructure
    - 04-0037-03: OC Implementation

- **Estimated Time Duration**
    - 1-2 hours weekly

- **Resource Participation**
    - Senior Portfolio Manager
    - The ITS PMO Senior Management (CIO, ACIO's)

- **Tips for Success**
    - The Senior Portfolio Manager should carefully manage the process by which projects are added, status changed, and removed from the Dashboard given its wide and senior level distribution.
    - Key decisions regarding project status in the portfolio should be documented by the Senior Portfolio Manager. These decisions are usually made during The ITS PMO Portfolio Status meetings.

Step 2 – Updating Project Status in Dashboard

- **Instructions**
    - The ITS PMO projects are categorized as being in "Planning" or "Execution" status. The Planning Summary page tracks projects in the initiation stages, from the

documentation of the basic idea/need (PID), to the issuance of award, to the establishment of the Project Plan. The Execution Summary tracks active projects, typically indicating that a contract has been awarded and work is in progress.

- Planning
  - Project progress is tracked via the "key task" (columns) and "status" cell. Note that not all tasks will apply to a project (e.g. an RFS may not be employed.)
  - Projects in Planning may be assigned the following status:
    - On Track
    - Slippage from initial timeline, low risk to objectives
    - Slippage from initial timeline, high risk to objectives
    - Not Started
    - On Hold
  - Reasons for assigning a given status should be documented in the individual detail tab for the project
  - Once the applicable key tasks have been completed, project can be moved by the Senior Portfolio Manager to the Execution summary/detail sections, subject to The ITS PMO Senior Management approval.
- Execution
  - Project progress is tracked via performance metrics (columns) and the "current phase" cell.
    - Performance metrics reflect the key project dimensions of schedule, cost, scope, and quality as well as risk. Based on defined quantitative/qualitative criteria, metrics are assigned a color of RED, YELLOW, or GREEN.
  - As described in section below "Updating Individual Project Status," Project Managers are responsible for updating the detail and summary sections for their individual projects and submitting the updates to the Senior Portfolio Manager.

- **Estimated Time Duration**
  - 1 hour per project

- **Resource Participation**
  - Senior Portfolio Manager
  - The ITS PMO Project Managers
  - The ITS PMO Senior Management (CIO, ACIO's)

- **Tips for Success**
  - The Senior Portfolio Manager should remind all Project Managers of the objectives and users of the Dashboard and coach them to be as objective and rigorous as possible when reporting project status.

Step 3 – Removing (Closing) Projects From the Executive Dashboard

- **Instructions**
  - Projects may be removed from the Executive Dashboard due to cancellation, completion, deferral, or recommendation of senior The ITS PMO management.
    - Individual Project Managers will notify the Senior Portfolio Manager when a specific project is in the Closure phase.
  - The Senior Portfolio Manager should document decisions, including reasons, for removal.

    - Project detail worksheets for removed projects should be moved to back of Executive Dashboard workbook for archiving purposes.

- **Estimated Time Duration**
    - Less than 1 hour weekly

- **Resource Participation**
    - Senior Portfolio Manager
    - The ITS PMO Project Managers
    - The ITS PMO Senior Management (CIO, ACIO's)

- **Tips for Success**
    - Careful documentation of decisions is important to keeping a decision trail for archiving purposes.
    - The Senior Portfolio Manager should communicate removal of projects and reasons why to stakeholders of project (executive sponsor, business owner) and users of the Executive Dashboard.

Updating Individual Project Status on the Executive Dashboard

Step 1 – Collect Project Updates from Project Managers

- **Instructions**
    - One week before Executive Dashboard publication, the Senior Portfolio Manager sends an email reminder to each Project Manager with last period's dashboard and a Dashboard template for their use
        - Typical time required for each Project Manager to update the dashboard for each project should not exceed 1 hour
    - Four days before Executive Dashboard publication, the Senior Portfolio Manager collects updates and reviews the following with each Project Manager:
        - Overall project health (RED, YELLOW, or GREEN status)
        - Project status (RED, YELLOW, or GREEN) for schedule, cost, scope and quality
        - Progress since last period (% project completed)
        - Milestone status (completed on time, missed, likely late)
        - Major accomplishments for period
        - Key next steps for upcoming period
        - Key issues and risks, as well as recommended mitigating actions from the Senior Portfolio Manager
- **Estimated Time Duration**
    - *Update Preparation* = 1 hour/project
    - *Review* = 1 hour/project
    - *Consolidation* = 1-2 hours/project

- **Tips for Success**
    - The Senior Portfolio Manager will spend more time preparing and reviewing project status at the beginning of each project, but should see a reduction in cycle time over the course of the project due to greater familiarity with each project.
    - The Senior Portfolio Manager plays a critical check and balance role to the Project Manager. While good Project Managers should always understand the big picture related to their project, the Senior Portfolio Manager is more likely to see overall The ITS PMO portfolio impacts and thus present a normalizing perspective when assessing project health criteria (i.e. ensuring that RED for one project is equivalent to RED for

another.) The Senior Portfolio Manager must also enforce application of the quantitative criteria when assigning health indicators.

Step 2 – Deliver Periodic Status Report

- **Instructions**
    - After consolidation, the Senior Portfolio Manager is accountable for publishing the Executive Dashboard via email to the following recipients:
        - CIO
        - ACIO Application and ACIO Infrastructure
        - MD of Internal Support
    - Prior to sending the Dashboard out via email, the Senior Portfolio Manager should first review the Dashboard and major items with the CIO

- **Estimated Time Duration**
    - Less than 1 hour weekly

- **Resource Participation**
    - CIO
    - ACIO's
    - Senior Portfolio Manager
    - MD Internal Support

Step 3 – Present Portfolio/Project Information to End-users

- **Instructions**
    - No formal presentation of the monthly Executive Dashboard is necessary.

Step 4 – Record Decisions and Action Items and Communicate Results

- **Instructions**
    - No decisions or action items typically result from the monthly Executive Dashboard.

Step 5 – Archive Documents for Project History

- **Instructions**
    - The Senior Portfolio Manager is accountable for archiving the monthly Executive Dashboards in the ITS PMO project archive, SharePoint.

- **Estimated Time Duration**
    - Less than 1 hour weekly

- **Resource Participation**
    - Senior Portfolio Manager

Executive Decision Team (EDT) Meetings

The Executive Decision Team is the highest level of oversight for technology initiatives in the Authority. Active participation by XYZ Company business and technology leadership ensures that overall initiatives are aligned with XYZ Company organizational mission and that critical resource trade-offs are made if issues arise.

The primary responsibilities of the EDT are:

- Provide leadership, direction, and oversight for The ITS PMO portfolio of projects. Focus on:
  - Alignment of technology with Authority/department strategy and objectives;
  - Fulfillment of IT strategic plan;
  - Soundness of technology investments;
  - Progress of projects through periodic reviews.
- Ensure that XYZ Company obtains business case level justifications for projects and applies consistent process and rigor to all projects under management;
- Helps develop strategic vision for the XYZ Company's The ITS PMO organization;
- Resolve Level 4 "showstopper" risks and issues.

Step 1 – Prepare for EDT

- **Instructions**
  - EDT meetings occur on a bi-monthly basis. Preparation should begin at least 2 weeks in advance and includes the following tasks:
    - Develop and communicate preparation and delivery schedule;
    - Reserve room and projector;
    - Brainstorm agenda;
    - Assign EDT presentation sections;
    - Develop EDT presentation 1st draft;
    - Conduct preliminary walkthrough;
    - Develop EDT presentation 2nd draft;
    - Conduct final walkthrough with MD of Internal Support;
    - Develop EDT presentation final draft;
    - Send presentation to production center for final copies.

- **Estimated Time Duration**
  - 40 hours over 2 week period

- **Resource Participation**
  - CIO
  - ACIO's
  - Senior Portfolio Manager
  - The ITS PMO Project Managers, as necessary

- **Tips for Success**
  - Adequate preparation, including formal walkthroughs of the presentation, is important to successful EDT meetings.
  - When preparing the room for the EDT meeting, plan to arrive 45 minutes to 1 hour ahead of time in order to ensure sufficient time to address logistical issues.

Reporting on Project Performance

Project performance should be presented at every team meeting as well at every Executive Decision Team meeting. Using quantitative vs. qualitative method for metrics will make project performance numbers more credible due to the required research, calculations and factual research that go into producing quantitative numbers. Using indicators such as Green, Yellow or Red help to paint a easy picture of project status to team members and EDT members. A project manager should strategize of what tool he/she will use for project performance. The tools used will be dependent upon the size and complexity of the project which will vary.

Step 2 – Present Portfolio/Project Information to End-users

- **Instructions**
  - The chairperson, and sponsor, of the EDT is the CIO. He/she is accountable for kicking off the meeting and ensuring its smooth operation.
  - Agendas will vary, however, the historical format has been:
    - Meeting Kick-off;
    - Review of Decisions/Action items from last EDT;
    - The ITS PMO Dashboard Update;
    - Project Focus;
    - Closing & PMO Next Steps.

- **Estimated Time Duration**
  - 2 hours

- **Resource Participation**
  - CIO;
  - ACIO's;
  - Senior Portfolio Manager;
  - Chief of Staff;
  - MD Internal Support;
  - MD Resident Services;
  - MD Operations;
  - CFO;
  - MD Int/Ext Communications;
  - Senior Portfolio Manager;
  - Rotating slot determined by EDT per topic and decision focus areas (e.g. Legal, Audit, ODM);
  - The ITS PMO PM's (as needed.)

- **Tips for Success**
  - When developing the content and delivering the presentation, always keep in mind the audience. Information should be presented at the appropriate senior executive level. Also every effort should be made to avoid technical jargon and instead focus on the Authority/departmental impacts/benefits of IT.

Step 4 – Record Decisions and Action Items and Communicate Results

- **Instructions**
  - The Senior Portfolio Manager is accountable for documenting decisions and action items resulting from EDT.
  - Draft version of EDT minutes should be reviewed by CIO and ACIO's prior to final distribution to EDT participants.
    - Target turnaround time for minutes is 1 week after EDT.

- A modified version of the Executive Dashboard (with vendor name and project budget number hidden) should also be sent out to all business owners of active projects (Director level)
  - Distribution list prepared by the Senior Portfolio Manager from period to period should be reviewed and approved by CIO;
  - Copies of the dashboard are distributed by CIO's administrative assistant with standard letter from the CIO.

- **Estimated Time Duration**
  - 2-4 hours

- **Resource Participation**
  - Senior Portfolio Manager

Step 5 – Archive Documents for Project History

- **Instructions**
  - The Senior Portfolio Manager is accountable for archiving the EDT presentation and minutes in the ITS PMO project archive, SharePoint.

- **Estimated Time Duration**
  - Less than 1 hour

- **Resource Participation**
  - Senior Portfolio Manager

4.6 Manage Budget

Overview

The role of the ITS PMO PM in the Budget Management process is primarily to identify variances from planned budget and initiate the Issues Management process if variance beyond determined thresholds occur (analogous to the Cost Control process of PMBOK.) Above all, the Project Manager should be proactive and ensure that signs of trouble are recognized early and that preventative actions are taken in an organized and timely way.

The ITS PMO PM's should be alert to the most common causes of budget problems and use the risk and issue management control processes described earlier to manage threats to the project's budget objectives. Most common causes for budget variance include:

- Technical difficulties requiring more resources;
- Increases in scope of work;
- Unrealistic initial bids or estimates;
- Poor or untimely reporting;
- Initial budget inadequate (e.g. missing important items or using out of date assumptions);
- Change in resource prices over the course of the project.

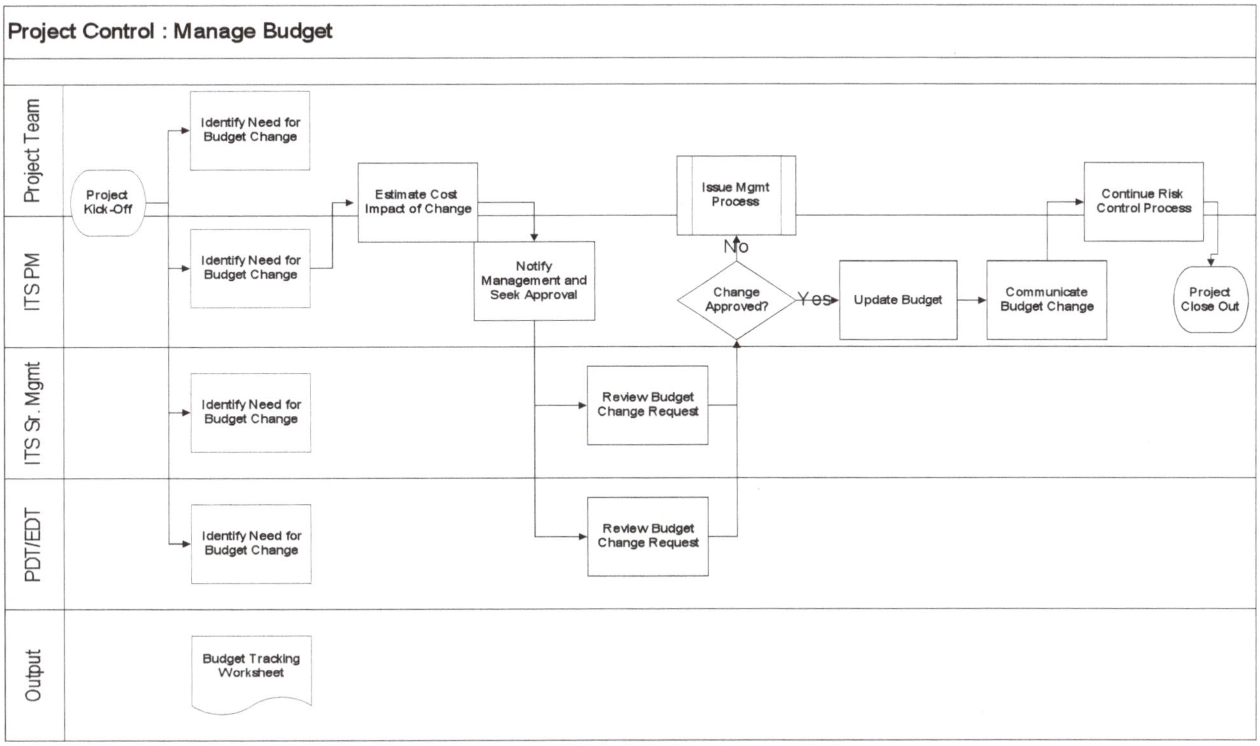

Inputs, Outputs, and Tools

Outputs created during the Planning Phase and developed during the Execution Phase serve as the inputs to the Performance Management Process.

Inputs	Tools & Techniques	Outputs
• SOW • Baseline cost/budget • Vendor payment schedule • Change requests • Vendor invoice	• Budget tracking tool • Variance analysis	• Identified cost/budget variances • Revised cost estimates • Lessons Learned

Timeframe/Total Duration

- The Budget Management process is carried out concurrent to the Project Planning, Execution, and Closure phases.

Resource Participation

The following resources participate in the Budget Management process:

- The ITS PMO Project Manager
- Project Team
- Senior Portfolio Manager
- The ITS PMO Management
- Executive Management (PDT/EDT)

The matrix below shows in what capacity each resource participates throughout the stage.

Step	The ITS PMO Project Mgr	Project Team	Sr. Portfolio Manager	The ITS PMO Mgmt	PDT/EDT
1 – Identify need for budget change	A/R	R	I		
2 – Estimate cost impact of change	A/R	R	I		
3 – Notify management and seek approval	A/R		I	C	C
4 – If unacceptable, begin Issue Management process	A/R	I	C		I
5 - If change to cost/budget baseline is approved, update budget	A/R		I	I	I
6 – Communicate budget change	A/R	I	I	I	I

Process Description

The Budget Management process consists of six (6) primary steps. This section provides detailed instructions for each of those steps.

Step 1 – Identify Need for Budget Change

- **Instructions**
  - The PM must remain vigilant for the occurrence (potential or actual) of events that would cause the project to fail to meet its objectives with respect to cost. The PM may become aware of events that result in a need for a budget change through the scope change, risk, or issue management process. The reasons for cost variance are many but some of the most common are:
    - Technical difficulties requiring more resources;
    - Increases in scope of work;
    - Unrealistic initial bids or estimates;
    - Poor or untimely reporting;
    - Initial budget inadequate (e.g. missing important items or using out of date assumptions);
    - Change in resource prices over the course of the project.

- **Estimated Time Duration**
  - 1-2 hours

- **Resource Participation**
  - The ITS PMO Project Manager

- **Tips for Success**
  - The most effective way to identify problems early and resolve them at minimal cost is for the Project Manager to be proactive in his/her identification of variances (cost, schedule, scope) from the planned baseline.

Step 2 – Estimate cost impact of change

- **Instructions**
  - Once the PM has determined that a change may be needed, he/she should work with the project subject matter experts to estimate the costs of the change. This activity may overlap with the change management process described earlier in the chapter.

- **Estimated Time Duration**
  - Variable

- **Resource Participation**
  - The ITS PMO Project Manager
  - Project Team

- **Tips for Success**
  - Estimates are meaningful if they involve the proper subject matter experts.
  - If the estimate requires vendor input, the ITS PMO PM should obtain a specific commitment for when that estimate will be produced (e.g. within 3 days after request.)

Step 3 – Notify management and seek approval

- **Instructions**
  - Project Managers should use their expert judgment when deciding whether a variance in the cost is acceptable. If he/she determines that the variance is part of a possible trend that could lead to greater issues down the line, then he/she should take appropriate action. If the variance is likely to be offset elsewhere in the project budget, then the Project Manager may refrain from escalating the issue. Variances that result in an overall YELLOW or RED rating for project budget are deemed unacceptable variances. Quantitative thresholds that the Project Manager should use as a guide are listed below:

Budget Status	Variance Details
RED	• >40% of baseline cost
YELLOW	• 21-40% of baseline cost

GREEN	• <20% of baseline cost

- Any variances should be discussed with the Senior Portfolio Manager and The ITS PMO Senior Management. Variances that result in a YELLOW or RED cost impact should be discussed with the PDT.

- **Estimated Time Duration**
    - Variable

- **Resource Participation**
    - The ITS PMO Project Manager
    - Senior Portfolio Manager
    - The ITS PMO Management
    - PDT

Step 4 – If Variance Unacceptable, Initiate Issue Management Process

- **Instructions**
    - As stated above, if the variance appears to be part of a larger trend or if the variance falls within the criteria that constitute a YELLOW or RED status above, then the Project Manager should immediately initiate the Issue Management process described earlier in the Handbook.

- **Resource Participation**
    - The ITS PMO Project Manager

Step 5 – If Change to Budget Approved, Update Budget Information

- **Instructions**
    - If the Issue Management process results in an approved change to the budget, the Project Manager should document the description of the change and the reasons for the change. He/she should likewise update all relevant governing documents such as the Project Plan, SOW, and baseline budget.

- **Resource Participation**
    - The ITS PMO Project Manager

- **Tips for Success**
    - Detailed documentation of reasons for change are critical for future Lessons Learned and better budget estimates for future XYZ Company The ITS PMO projects.

Step 6 – Communicate Budget Change

- **Instructions**
    - Once approved, changes must be communicated by the Project Manager to the PDT (in the event that the Change Control Board is a subset of the PDT), the project team, and other key stakeholders. Communication vehicles include:
        - Regular project status reports
        - Regular PDT status meetings
        - Executive Dashboard (budget section)
- **Resource Participation**

- The ITS PMO Project Manager
- Senior Portfolio Manager

Hosting Executive Decision Team Meetings

EDT meeting should take place on a quarterly basis and should consist of Senior Management and other key stakeholders. The objective of the EDT meetings is to provide senior management at high level overview of the Project Portfolio that consist on all approved Project Initiation Documents (PIDs). The presentation should be presented in Microsoft PowerPoint and the presentation should be printed out and distributed to the EDT members for note taking opportunities. The agenda at a minimum should be as follow:

1. Review of EDT previous action – Discussion of last meeting actions as review

Review of Previous EDT Actions

8/11/2005 EDT Decisions Taken

Recommendations	Pros	Cons	Approved?
No Decisions Taken			

- **Meeting Take-Aways**
  - Re-prioritize 2006 Initiatives given MD guidance (ITS)
    - Conduct further research on selected initiatives (*detail follows*)
  - Meet with Budget director to determine funding available for prioritized initiatives (ITS)
  - Explore contingency plans with Procurement for Sensible Homes – OC project (ITS)
  - Finalize details of Yardi post-implementation activities, ensure business teams prepared for 11/28 XYZ Go Live, and send list of financial data to be converted to M. Krug (J. Porter)

2. Portfolio Dashboard Update – Provide Green, Yellow and Red status of all projects

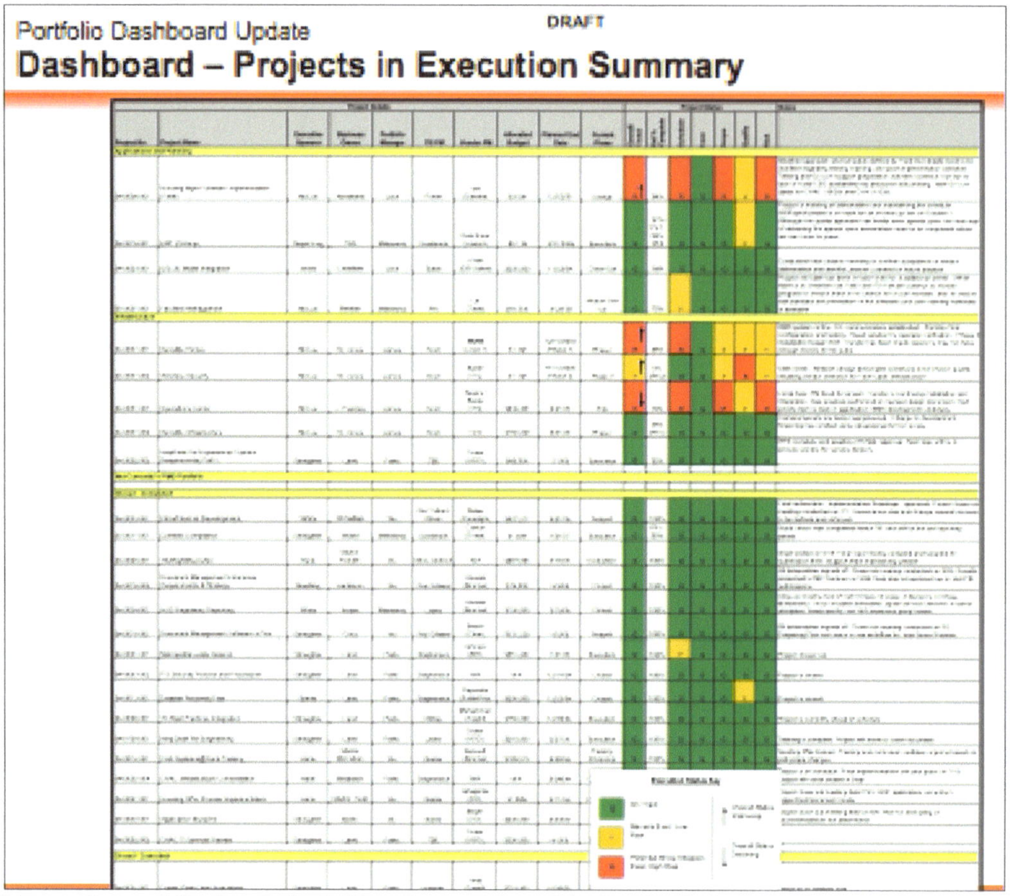

3. Discussion of Projects in RED – Target trouble high dollar projects only for discussion

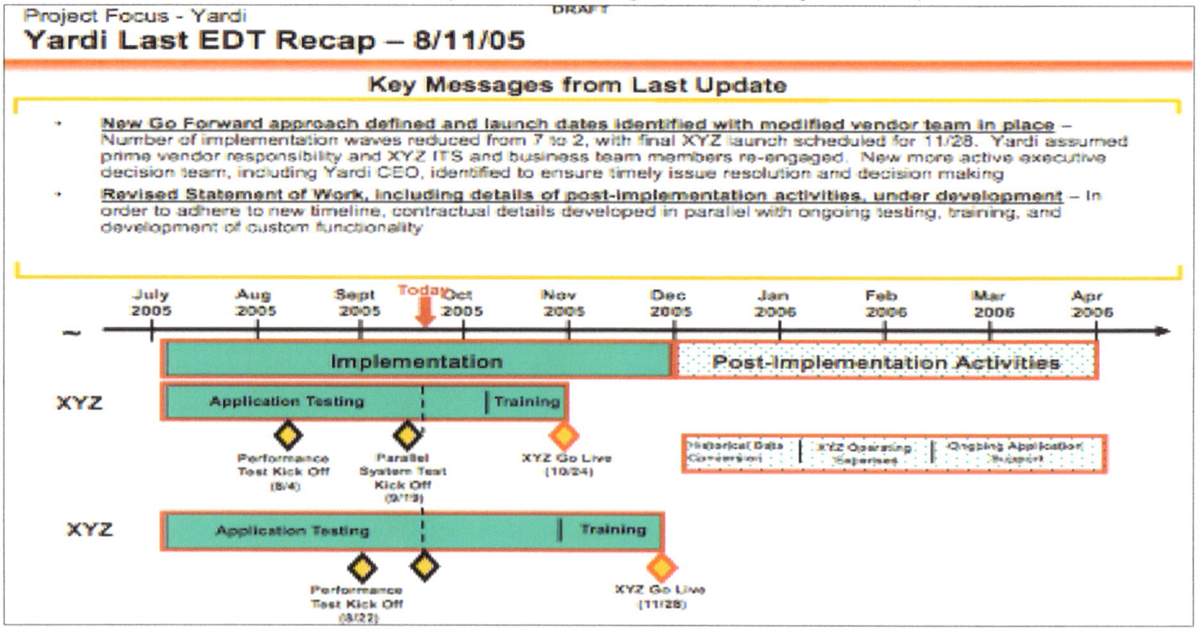

4. Recommendations of the PMO – Discuss PMO recommendation for corrective actions for project in Red status

PID	Recommended Action	Status
Senior Designated Housing Plan Database	• Confirm details & timing of HUD mandate	• Mandate confirmed. MAP defining procedures to comply with policy. Functionality to be built into Yardi in 2006
Home Site Visit Survey Application	• Continue planning process to identify other less costly technologies	• Research in progress • Per Budget Director, alternate funding source must be sought
eRecruiting	• Continue planning process to identify other less costly implementation approach	• Confirmed initial estimate. Project team anticipates that actual costs will decrease once project submitted to competitive bid process
• XYZ Document Mgmt • Fixed Asset Document Mgmt • CCB Document Mgmt	• Determine if possible to consolidate Document Mgmt PID's and consider XYZ-wide implementation of historical document scanning to obtain volume discount from vendor	• Consolidated all PIDs for economies of scale and to employ single enterprise-wide approach; identified Nov as target date for release of RFS with services to begin Q1 2006 • Determining sequence of department implementation given move and specific department initiatives
Workforce Development Application	• Determine if pilot approach could be used to ensure viability of solution, esp. given anticipated tight funding for 2006	• Alternate approach identified whereby existing infrastructure can be used to provide functionality at a lower overall cost; new cost estimate roughly 40% lower

Planning will continue for projects depending on guidance from today's EDT.

5. Closing and PMO next steps – Discuss PMO next steps toward progress and open meeting up for discussion

Closing and PMO Next Steps

DRAFT

Next Steps - PMO

- **Confirm ITS resource capacity for EDT approved 2006 ITS projects**
- **PMO reporting activities (EDT, Dashboard) continue**
- **Continued maintenance of PMO project oversight and participation**
  - –Yardi and Sensible
  - –ERP as Phase I nears implementation in October
- **PMO to continue knowledge transfer and transition of key responsibilities to XYZ ITS personnel**
  - –Develop 2nd half of ITS PM Handbook
  - –Continue PM training sessions
  - –Complete development of ITS knowledge repository

2005 ITS Portfolio

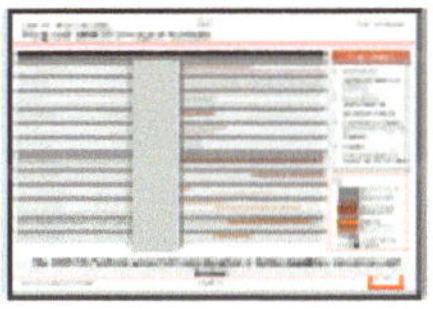

2005 PMO Plan

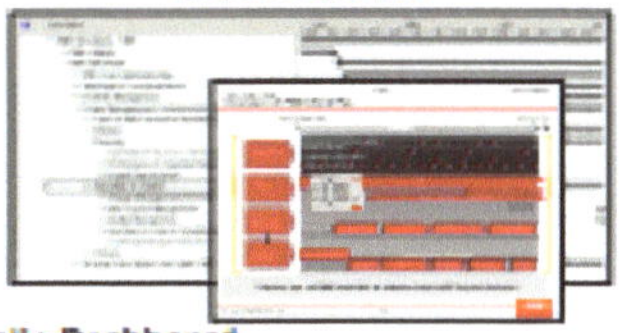

Portfolio Dashboard

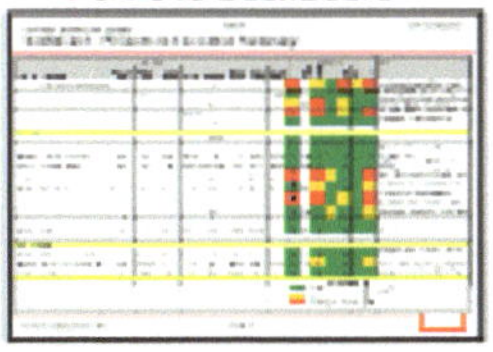

The focus of the PMO over the next period will be finalization of the 2006 ITS Portfolio, provision of critical assistance to ITS projects in crisis, and transition of key PMO activities to internal XYZ personnel.

Technical Case Scenario – Monitor/Control

- Monte Carlo Simulation
- Producing EDT Material
- SharePoint Designer Workflows
- Nintex Workflow

5 Project Closure

Topics Covered:

- ❖ Process Initiation Document (PID) and Processes
- ❖ InfoPath Web Forms
- ❖ SharePoint List, Libraries and Workflows for PIDS
- ❖ Understanding of Strategies: 32-33

How To Videos & Templates on CD :

- ❖ Walkthrough of Closing Process
- ❖ Conducting Lessons Learned

STRATEGY for Closure:

- ✓ Confirm all deliverables
- ✓ Conduct Lessons Learned

Project Monitor and Control Overview

Projects by their very definition are temporary and unique work efforts -- temporary in that they have a defined timeframe, and unique in that they have not previously been undertaken. In the project closure phase of the project life cycle, it is the Project Manager's (PM) primary responsibility to close the project at hand, and equally important, prepare the organization to transition into maintenance and operations. Project Closure actually starts at the beginning of the project's lifecycle, during the Project Initiation Process, when the project's goals, objectives and performance measures are first documented and approved. It is against these goals, objectives and performance measures that the Project Manager can gauge the overall success of the project.

The Closure Phase is greatly impacted by the Execution and Monitoring Phases (Chapters Three and Four, respectively). If the PM has effectively and rigorously managed the project's scope, cost, schedule and risk, Project Closure will be fairly routine and administrative. A simplified, successful Closure relies on careful project planning and sound management throughout the entire project.

Closure is the final phase of a project's lifecycle. A project cannot be closed out unless the following major tasks are completed:

1. The final product / solution meets the requirements, goals and objectives as stated by the Authority
2. XYZ Company(the customer or user) has formally accepted the final product / solution, and,
3. The transition of the product / solution into operation has been completed.

Using approaches and concepts for Project Closure from the Project Manager's Book of Knowledge (PMBOK), the Authority can complete the project closure phase and complete the three tasks called out above, by employing two discrete stages. They are as follows:

Stage 1: Complete Administrative Tasks, Prepare for Transition to Maintenance
Stage 2: Conduct Procurement Audit

Each stage is described in greater detail in the next three sections of this chapter.

Information Technology Services: Two Stages of Project Closure

PROJECT CLOSURE

Stage 1: Complete Administrative Tasks and Prepare for Maintenance

1. Review SOW & Deliverable Documentation
2. Review Contract
3. Formally Accept Project Deliverables
4. Conduct Lessons Learned Exercise (AAR)

5a. Update Records and Archive Project Documents

5b. Update and Archive Contract Files

6. Release Project Team to the Organization
7. Celebrate

Stage 2: Perform Procurement Audit

1. Review Scope and Requirements Development Process
2. Review Procurement and Legal Process
3. Review Solicitation Process
4. Review Evaluation Process
5. Review Negotiation Process
6. Review Contract Documentation Development Process

Objectives and Benefits

The primary objectives of project closure are:

- To determine that the solution delivered meets its specifications / requirements and that transfer of the consultant(s) specialized knowledge to the customer has occurred.
- To formally identify and communicate gap(s) between the solution as delivered and solution specified, if needed.
- To formalize customer acceptance.
- To transition maintenance / operation activities to the customer and designated support group.

User acceptance of the product / solution is a critical prerequisite to Project Closure. Acceptance should be based upon the project objectives and performance measures defined during Project Initiation and finalized during the development of a Statement of Work (SOW) in the early stages of Project Execution.

Some benefits to be realized through using this process are as follows:

- Quantification of project outcomes and relative success through analysis and assessment of the project performance measures.
- Quantification, documentation of the vendor's performance for use when contemplating future business with the same vendor.
- Assurance that the Authority receives and accepts that which has been delivered.
- Initiation of maintenance and operations activities in a timely manner.
- Documentation of lessons learned and reference materials for initiating a future, similar project.

- Assurance of the success of projects with a start date dependent upon the completion of this project.

Tools

The following lists the primary tools used to support the Project Closure Process:

- Closure Process flow diagrams -- for each of the three main stages – visual representation of the steps in each stage are documented; use this flow diagram to guide you through the initiation and completion of discrete activities needed to formally close a project at the XYZ Company.
- PMO Monthly Dashboard - a "scorecard" for each project, assessing status and likelihood of completion, compiled by the Senior Portfolio Manager on a monthly basis; the dashboard is a compilation of all projects within the PMO portfolio.
- Project Closure / Transition Checklist - a tool used to organize and support the Closure Process.
- After Action Review Template (AAR) – AAR's document the outcomes of a project and then, via a group session with the project team, documents "lessons learned" as a result of implementing a project. The document can be used as a reference when embarking upon a project of a similar scope and nature.
- SharePoint Project Folders - the electronic "library" used by The ITS PMO to document project materials.
- Milestone/Deliverable Acceptance Documents – compiled during Phase 3 – Phase Execution.

Inputs and Outputs

The Inputs and Outputs of the Planning Chapter will show what items, tasks or documents are to be considered in completing the three stages of the Closure framework. The inputs can be described as what work, when completed, will lead to the actual output or the final deliverable or series of deliverables for a particular stage of Closure. For project closure the inputs frequently mirror the "tools" available when closing a project. The main inputs into closing project are primarily:

1. Identifying the Performance Measures (found in the Project Plan developed in Phase 2 – Project Planning)
2. Reviewing the Schedule of Values or List of Milestones and Deliverables for the Project
3. Reviewing all Project Deliverable Acceptance Documents (including Knowledge Transfer activities)
4. Reviewing the Statement of Work and the Contract Document

Closure Process, Inputs and Outputs

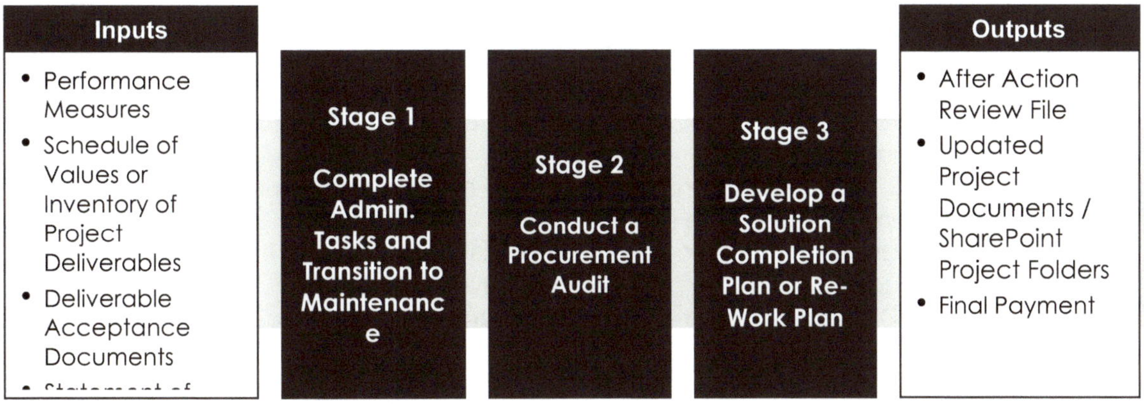

Timeframe/Total Duration

The Project Closure process begins once the Project Manager has been notified by the vendor that they are about to submit or have submitted their final deliverable for review and approval. Depending upon the size and scope of the project, and upon the determination that no further work is needed, project closure may take from 2 to 10 business days.

Project Closure begins, then:

1. When the vendor presents the "final" deliverable for the project, and,
2. The Business Manager and Project Manager review and approve final deliverable.

Resource Participation

The recommended The ITS PMO and business resource participation required during the three (3) stages of Project Closure are identified in the sections that follow. Resource participation requirements are presented using a "RACI" matrix which identifies, by suggested participant, each participant's specific role, according to the following possible choices:

- **R**esponsible – person(s) who is working on the activity ("the doer(s)");
- **A**ccountable – person(s) with ultimate yes/no authority. This should be pushed down to the lowest level possible;
- **C**onsulted – person(s) involved prior to decision or action;
- **I**nformed – person(s) who need to know of decision or action.

The following resources participate throughout the three (3) stages of the Project Closure Process:

- Executive Business Sponsor – Highest level representative of business unit (usually Managing Director) for which the project is being delivered. The Executive Sponsor retains overall responsibility for project's success
- Business Owner – Business department manager (usually Director or Manager level) who reports to the Executive Business Sponsor and ensures that the project definition and execution meet the business objectives
- The ITS PMO Mgmt – Chief Information Officer and/or Assistant Chief Information Officers

- The ITS PMO Senior Portfolio Manager – Senior The ITS PMO manager who provides guidance and oversight to all projects in the ITS PMO portfolio. She/he is responsible for providing overall status reporting to EDT/PDT for all The ITS PMO projects as well as compliance with The ITS PMO project management standards
- Project Manager – XYZ Company person (usually from The ITS PMO) responsible for delivering the project as defined in project scope and overall project plan, leading and managing the overall project team (incl. any vendor project managers and other XYZ Company staff in The ITS PMO or business departments) on a day-to-day basis. Depending on the size, scope, nature, and complexity of the project there may be an The ITS PMO Project Manager and a Business Project Manager.
- Other Key Stakeholders - departments in addition to the primary Business Department that will be significantly impacted by the initiative
- Project Decision Team (PDT) – Managing Directors, Directors, The ITS PMO management and others with a significant stake in the project. Executive Business Sponsor is typically the chairperson. The PDT is collectively responsible for removing obstacles and enabling any type of change required for the project to be successful

5.1 Complete Administrative Tasks

Overview

The first stage of the Planning Phase is initiated by the vendor's notification that they are about to or have completed their final deliverable as defined in the Statement of Work (SOW). This section of the chapter focuses on all the discrete steps that are to be completed in Stage One – Complete Administrative Tasks. A process map depicting Stage One follows:

Stage One Process Flow: Complete Administrative Tasks

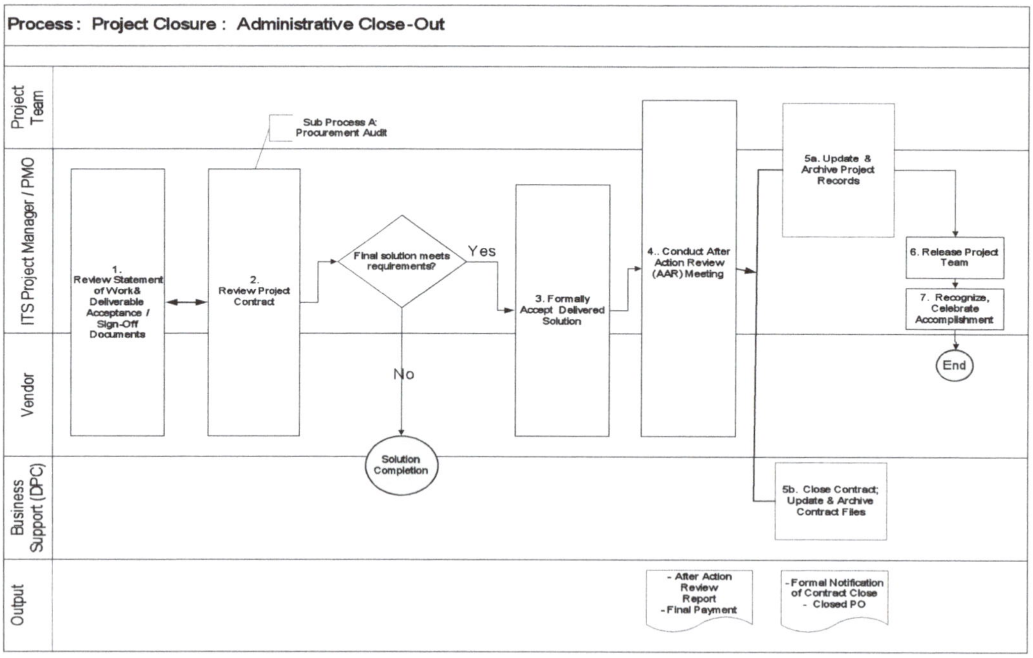

There are a total of seven (7) unique steps, which when completed by the Project Manager, will lead to the official close of the project. After receiving notification from the vendor that a final deliverable is ready for submittal, it is the responsibility of the Project Manager and Business Owner to review and either accept or reject the work product as delivered. By referring to and working through the steps depicted above, the PM can successfully close out a project.

The Exhibit below lists all necessary action items, which need to be completed in Stage One.

Planning Closure, Stage 1: Complete Administrative Tasks

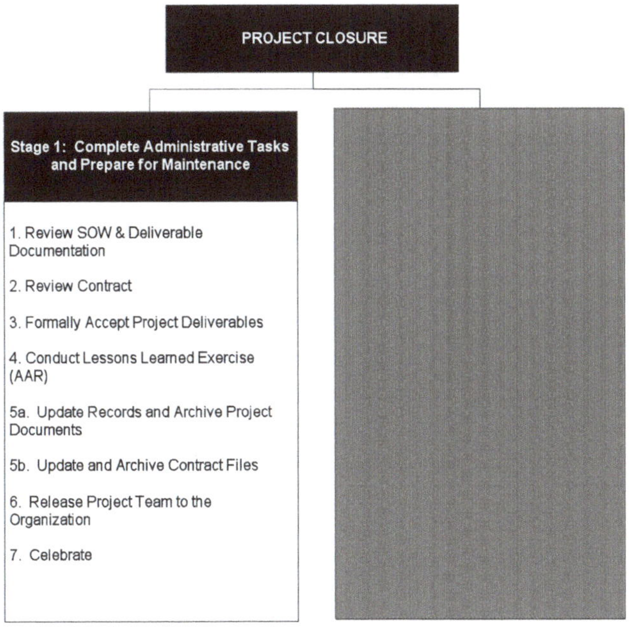

Of the seven steps in "Complete Administrative Tasks" Stage, the most important steps will be that of conducting a review of what work has been committed to, by reviewing the statement of Work and the contract document and determining whether it meets the specifications / requirements of the Authority. The outcome of this assessment will support the PM's decision and recommendation about whether to close the project or if more work is required.

Stage One: Inputs, Outputs, and Tools

Determining whether or not a project is ready to close is primarily accomplished through the review and assessment of project documents. The major inputs into the "Complete Administrative Tasks" Stage are as follows:

- Review of the Statement of Work – herein should be a determination of the milestones / deliverables of the project.
- Review of the Contract Document – the contract document will contain specific terms and conditions impacting the project, such as intellectual property rights, specific considerations when closing a project.

STAGE ONE: Inputs, Tools and Outputs

Inputs	Tools	Outputs
• Statement of Work • Contract Document • Schedule of Values or Inventory of Project Deliverables • Deliverable	• Process flow diagram - Stage 1 • PMO Dashboard • After Action Review Template	• Final Payment •After Action Review Report • Formal Notification of Project Close • Closed PO

Tools used to support the Stage One Project Closure Process:

- Process Flow Diagram, Stage One - provides a ready reference for understanding the discrete steps, which when accomplished in total, will formally close the project.
- The PMO Dashboard - provides the PM with information about the status of all projects in the PMO portfolio. It is important to review project status because your project may be dependent upon the completion of another project, and there may have been issues identified in the more recent Dash Board Reports.
- After Action Review Template – as projects are completed, an "After Action Review" session is conducted to discuss lessons learned and determine what may be applied, re-used in future projects. Check the PMO Library for an After Action Review document if undertaking a project similar to one which has been completed, for example, software development, for relevant information.

The anticipated deliverable or outcome for Stage One is Formal Notification of Closure of the Project, Final Payment and an AAR Report.

Stage One: Timeframe/Total Duration (2 – 10 business days)

The total time it will take to complete all the activities in Stage One is dependant upon both the size and complexity of the project.

Stage One: Resource Participation

The following resources participate during the "Complete Administrative Tasks" Stage:

- Business Owner
- Executive Sponsor
- The ITS PMO Management – Chief Information Officer and/or Assistant Chief Information Officer(s)
- Senior Portfolio Manager
- The ITS PMO Project Manager
- Project Decision Team

Step	Executive Sponsor	Dept Director	Business Owner	The ITS PMO Mgmt	Senior Portfolio Manager	The ITS PMO PM	Purchasing	Other Key Stakeholders	Dept BIS Resource
1 - Review Statement of Work		I	R	A	I	R			
2 - Review Contract Document		I	R	A	I	R		I	
3 – Formally Accept Project Deliverables	I	I/A	R/A	I/A	C	R			
4 – Conduct Lessons Learned Exercise (AAR)	C	C	R	A	C	R		I/C	
5a – Update Records and Archive Project Documents			R	A	C	R		I	
5b – Update and Archive Contract Files	I	I	I	A	I	I	R	I	
6 - Release Project Team to the Organization	I	I	R	A	C	R			
7 – Celebrate	P	P	P	P	P	P	P	P	P

Key: R – Responsible A – Accountable C – Consulted I – Informed P - Participate

Stage One: Step Description / Instructions

Stage One consists of seven (7) primary steps. This section provides detailed instructions for the authorized Project Manager (PM) to conduct the review needed to determine if the project's final product / deliverables can be accepted and closed.

Step 1 – Review Statement of Work and Deliverable Acceptance Documents

- **Objective:**
  - To ensure that all deliverables/milestones/products have been submitted, reviewed, approved and ultimately recorded in SharePoint Project Folders.
- **Instructions:**
  - Use these templates:
    - Statement of Work (finalized in the Execution Phase)
    - Deliverable Acceptance Documents (used in the Execution Phase)
    - Most recent Monthly Dash Board
    - Performance measures (identified initially in the PID document – Phase 1 -- and finalized in the SOW – Phase 3)
    - Project Close Out/Transition Checklist (developed to manage administrative tasks)
  - Review and verify delivery and acceptance of all deliverables; review the project files (SharePoint Project folders) for Deliverable Acceptance Documents indicating the approval and payment of unique deliverables.
  - Review performance measures identified for the project; for those that are quantifiable, assess and document these statistics; for example, if the new financial system's objective was to reduce the number of hours/days to process payroll, document the results.
  - Review the more recent, monthly Dashboards; these status reports prepared for the Executive Decision Team (EDT) provide clues about the overall health of the project during its life, by specific risk categories: time, resources, budget, quality, etc.

- Identify all areas and timing for "knowledge transfer"; look for evidence of knowledge transfer events such as, user sign – in sheets, training sessions, user acceptance of "knowledge transfer.
- Complete the first section of the Project Close Out / Transition Checklist – SOW Review – by indicating "Complete" in the status column.
- Document identified gaps (if any).
- Call a meeting of the Project Team, to communicate found gaps.

- **Estimated Time Duration:**
  - Four (4) – ten (10) hours, depending on project size and scope

- **Resource Participation:**

The Business Owner and The ITS PMO PM are jointly responsible for reviewing the Statement of Work, assembling and reviewing the Deliverable Acceptance Documents previously completed throughout the life of the Project.

- **Tip(s) for Success:**
  - Project Closure is largely administrative if the Project Execution Process and its Sub Processes for Deliverable Review have been rigorously followed.
  - Be sure your final review of deliverables includes the delivery of Knowledge Transfer events, materials, sessions so that the customer is really ready to assume operational responsibility.
  - The Project Close-Out / Transition Checklist is used throughout all steps of Stage One – Complete Administrative Tasks.

Step 2 – Review Procurement Contract

- **Objective**: to ensure that the contract terms and conditions, which may not be in the Statement of Work have been adhered to.

- **Instructions:**
  - Use these templates:
    - Master Services Agreement (MSA) – typically The ITS PMO requests various services from a pre-qualified pool of vendors who have already signed a MSA
    - Amendments to the Master Services Agreement, if executed
    - Software License and Maintenance Agreements (if software was included in the solution)
    - The unique contract document for this project, if a MSA is not in effect; periodically, The ITS PMO might request services that cannot be provided by the pre-qualified pool of vendors; a Request for Proposal would be released, and a unique contract drawn up to govern the project.
  - Review key terms, which may not be in the SOW. Examples include:
    - Intellectual property – review to ensure compliance with who "owns" products, software developed specifically for the Authority
    - Contract termination language - review for specifics about how the contract should be closed and determine if there are steps in addition to those included in Stage One – Complete administrative Tasks, Steps 1 through 7.
  - Review Software License And Maintenance Agreement(s), if for software to:

- Determine support and maintenance coverage details
- Understand applicable Service Level Agreements (SLA's)
- Identify and communicate XYZ Company's responsibilities regarding support and maintenance (e.g., patch, upgrade installation, infrastructure upgrades, etc.)
- Determine and communicate on-going annual costs for budgeting purposes

- **Estimated Time Duration**
  - Four (4) hours – eight (8) hours

- **Resource Participation**
  - The Business Owner and The ITS PMO PM are jointly responsible for reviewing the Contract documents.
  - At a minimum, the Chief Information Officer and ACIO for Applications and Infrastructure should be consulted regarding the software maintenance agreements and specific XYZ Company responsibilities.
  - Legal (Business Support) may be required to interpret specific language.

- **Tip(s) for Success:**
  - Be sure to review the Master Services Agreement prior to project closure to gain an understanding of project governance concepts that may not be in the SOW.
  - Ask Legal (business support) to explain various terms and conditions contained in your contract.

DECISION: The Solution as Delivered is Acceptable? -- NO

A. If the SOW and Contract Review Reveal Specifications Are NOT Met
Proceed to Solution Completion (Stage 3)

- **Decision Objective**: To assess whether the product, final solution is, in fact, ready to close, or if additional work, re-work is required for the solution to meet XYZ Company's specifications.
- **Instructions**
  - Use these templates:
    - Project Close-Out/Transition Checklist
  - Communicate "findings" to the Senior Portfolio Manager, the Project Decision Team and vendor.
  - In collaboration with the vendor, develop a plan to complete specific work, or the rework of areas that may not be acceptable.
  - Initiate the appropriate sub process of the Execution Process: Change Request, Scope Change.
  - Amend / Revise Project Documents, if needed, e.g., the SOW, Project Plan, Issues and Risk Log.
  - Refer to Stage Three instructions for complete detail.

-  **Tip(s) for Success:**
    - The Statement of Work and contract document may contain specific, vendor responsibility for knowledge transfer. Be sure to include its delivery in your review of submitted deliverables.
    - Notify the vendor immediately if you suspect the project may not be able to be closed.

- **Estimated Time Duration**
    - Four (4) – eight (8) hours

- **Resource Participation**

  The Business Owner and The ITS PMO PM are jointly responsible for determining the solution / product does not meet the requirements or specifications of the Authority.

DECISION: The Solution as Delivered is Acceptable? Yes

B. If the SOW and Contract Review Reveal Specifications ARE Met, Proceed as follows:

- **Objective**: to assess whether the project / solution is, in fact, ready to close, or if addition work, re-work and /or 'knowledge transfer' is required for the solution to meet XYZ Company specifications.

- **Instructions**

    - Use these available templates:
        - Project close Out/Transition Checklist
        - Final Deliverable Acceptance Form
    - Complete the Project Close Out/Transition Checklist with:
        - Status of "complete" in the Review of SOW and Contract Document rows
        - Status of "complete" in the "knowledge transfer" row; document how "knowledge transfer was completed, attach evidence of customer sign-in sheets, notifications of training sessions, training calendar, etc. to Checklist
    - Clearly reference where and how Maintenance / Support Services will be obtained
        - Document the web address for the vendor's help desk
        - Document the 1-800 number, if available
        - Reference availability of end user documentation, frequently asked questions, etc. in the SharePoint Project Folders
    - Meet with The ITS PMO ACIO for Infrastructure to review.
    - Update the (MS) Project Plan as "Complete".
    - Prepare Final Deliverable Acceptance Form for Senior Portfolio Manager, ACIO, CIO and Project Decision Team.
    - Have business owners (Managing Director and Department Head(s) of impacted departments) sign Page 2, Part 1: **Acceptance of Transition From Project Status to Operations**

- **Estimated Time Duration**

    - Four (4) - Eight (8) hours

- **Resource Participation**

  The Business Owner and The ITS PMO PM are jointly responsible for determining that the solution / product is acceptable as delivered.

  The Executive Sponsor and Department Head(s) of affected business areas must sign off that they accept the daily operation of the product / solution delivered.

  The ITS PMO Owner (relevant ACIO) will sign off if there are The ITS PMO support / maintenance responsibilities involved.

- **Tip for Success**:

Throughout the life of the project, reinforce (customer's) business owner and The ITS PMO Support Staffs understanding of the temporary nature of a project and that at project end, they will own and maintain the solution according to guidelines specified by the vendor.

Step 3 – Formally Accept the Project Deliverable(s) / Solution

- **Objective**: To provide the documentation and a forum for the Project Team and customers to formally accept the deliverables / solution.

- **Instructions:**
  - Use these templates:
    - Final Deliverable Acceptance Form
  - Complete the Final Deliverable Acceptance Form; Major Components are as follows:
    - Project Detail: name, PO number, Contract Number etc.
    - Inventory of Project deliverables and their status: Approved, Approved as Noted, Not Approved
    - Recommendation: when the deliverable is found to be acceptable, the recommendation to the Senior Portfolio Manager and PDT is "close Project"
    - Acceptance of Transition from Project Status to Operations
      - Signature of Managing Director
      - Signature of Department Head(s)
    - Authorizations (signatures) for Project Close-Out: all PDT members, the CIO, ACIO, and Senior Portfolio Manager
  - Sponsor Customer Acceptance Meeting with key stakeholders, Senior Portfolio Manager, ACIO, PDT and Project Sponsor.

- **Estimated Time Duration**

  8 – 16 hours

- **Resource Participation**

  The Business Owner and The ITS PMO PM are jointly responsible for completing the Final Acceptance Document.

- **Tip(s) for Success:**

The Customer Acceptance Form includes a transfer of ownership section, which reinforces the operations / maintenance role the customer (business) now assumes.

Step 4 – Conduct "After Action Review"

- **Objective:**
  - To openly discuss the project and record all major events, both positive and negative, that has transpired during the project lifecycle. The end result should be to identify best practices that could benefit the Authority for application future projects.
- **Instructions**:
  - Use these templates:
    - Project Closeout Checklist
    - After Action Review Document
  - Invite attendees for After Action Review (AAR) discussion. Attendees should include project team, stakeholder representation, Senior Portfolio Manager, Project Decision Team, and future maintenance and operations staff.
  - Distribute AAR form and instructions for completion prior to session. The project manager should collect all completed forms and aggregate and organize information in a logical format to aid in facilitating discussion in the upcoming AAR meeting.
  - Provide project documentation for discussion: (Statement of Work, Milestone Completion forms, Status Reports, etc.).
  - Prepare for and facilitate AAR sessions
    - State the rules for discussion: informal and non-antagonistic
    - Review events leading to the activity (what was supposed to happen).
    - Give a brief statement of the specific activity.
    - Summarize the key events. Encourage participation.
    - Have team members restate portions of their part of the activity.
    - Do not turn it into a critique or lecture. The following will help:
      - Ask why certain actions were taken.
      - Ask how they reacted to certain situations.
      - Ask when actions were initiated.
      - Ask leading and thought provoking questions.
      - Exchange "war stories" (lessons learned).
      - Ask project team what happened from their own point of view.
      - Relate events to subsequent results.
      - Explore alternative courses of actions that might have been more effective.
      - Complaints are handled positively.
      - When the discussion turns to errors made, emphasize the positive and point out the difficulties of making tough decisions.
      - Summarize.
      - Allow project managers to discuss the events with their people in private.
      - **Follow-up** on needed actions.
  - Document / consolidate additional ideas, responses that are generated from discussions.
  - Project Manager compiles AAR "findings" and presents to ACIO, CIO, Senior Portfolio Manager, and Project Team.

Note: The AAR facilitator needs to:

1. Remain unbiased throughout the review.
2. Try to speak to draw out comments from all.
3. Do NOT allow personal attacks.

4. The focus should be on learning and continuous improvement.
5. Strive to allow others to offer solutions, rather than you offering them.

Meeting Agenda:

- **Statement of Problem** – Describe the problem that occurred. Provide sufficient detail about factors contributing to what happened.
- **Discussion** – Discuss in detail the root cause and impact of the problem.
- **Citations** – Provide any references used or other sources of project information that may be helpful in understanding the problem or corrective actions needed.
- **Corrective Actions** – Identify what corrective actions where taken and discuss the results. If a corrective action was not taken, but became apparent later, identify this action for future reference.

- **Estimated Time Duration:**
  - Three (3) – Five (5) business days, depending on project size and scope

- **Resource Participation:**

  The Business Owner and The ITS PMO PM are jointly responsible for ensuring full participation of all project resources in the AAR. It is also beneficial to include the vendor and maintenance/operations staff in these sessions.

-  **Tip(s) for Success:**
  - For a successful lessons learned session, provide an open forum for frank discussions of the problems encountered by the project.
  - The meeting agenda outline is used to identify not only project problems, but also successes and best practices emanating from the project. A properly conducted AAR can have a powerful influence on the climate of your organization. It is part of the communication process that educates and motivates people on to greatness by sensitizing them to do the right thing. It can prevent future confusion on organizational priorities and philosophies and drive home the point that we learn from our mistakes.

After Action Review (AAR) Document

- **Overview:**
  - This document is used to capture project related information from project team members for the purposes of discussion in the AAR meeting.
- **Components**:
  - Part 1- Introduction:
    - Description
    - Objectives
    - Instructions
  - Part 2- Assessment of:
    - Project Scope
    - Project Schedule
    - Project Team
    - Project Approach

        - Project Deliverables
    - Part 3 – Conclusion / Comments

    When completing the form identify specific goals and outcomes for each item in Part 2.

- **Estimated Time for Document Completion:**
    - One (1) – Two (2) business days, depending on project size and scope

-  **Tip(s) for Success:**
    - For a successful lesson learned session, provide an open forum for frank discussions of the problems encountered by the project.

<Project Name> Project Close-out After Action Review

Individual Participant Pre-meeting Form

1. What is an After Action Review?

Developed by the military, the term After Action Review (AAR) refers to a professional discussion of an event, focused on performance standards, that enables soldiers to discover for themselves what happened, why it happened, and how to sustain strengths and improve on weaknesses.

As part of the ITS project close-out process, an After Action Review (a.k.a. Lessons Learned) will be conducted for each completed technology project with the intent of examining the following:

1. What was the scope of the project?
   - Specific goals and outcomes
2. What worked during the project?
   - Specific examples of what was achieved successfully
3. What did not work on the project?
   - List of reasonably specific items but also generic enough to be applicable to future projects. The items should also be actionable in that there should be something that can be done to mitigate the problem. For example, "Lack of backup personnel (single point of failure) caused disruption and delays" is actionable.
4. What could be done differently next time?
   a. Again, specific suggestions that target item #3 above. For example, for our single point of failure example one might suggest: "Define back up roles early in case of unforeseen sickness or absence".

2. What do you have to do?

Each AAR participant is asked to complete **Sections 3 through <last section>** of this form. The forms will then be collected, "anonymous", and combined to create the Project After Action Review document. When completed, the participants will gather for an hour-long debriefing to review the key items discovered.

Please be frank but constructive. When completing this form, feel free to offer constructive criticism that could assist other projects besides this one. Remember, the AAR is not a time to blame or point fingers but a chance to learn from mistakes and to offer suggestions on what can be improved.

Step 5a – Update Records and Archive Project Documents

- **Objective:**
  - Update records of all tools and documents used to plan, deliver, monitor and close the project. Then proceed to archive those documents to project repository.
- **Instructions:**
  - Use these templates:
    - Project Closeout Checklist
    - SharePoint Project Folders
  - Gather all project information.
  - Update project documentation to reflect current project status (closed) and accurately account for milestones.
  - Archive information in SharePoint Project Folders.
  - Store all hard copy documentation in the appropriate areas.

- **Estimated Time Duration:**
  - One (1) – two (2) business days, depending on project size and scope

- **Resource Participation:**

  The Project manager takes the lead in insuring that all vital project documents and deliverables are archived. The PM must obtain the cooperation of all members of the project team (to consistently utilize SharePoint Project Folders throughout the project lifecycle.

- **Tip(s) for Success:**
  Use the SharePoint Project Folders throughout the project lifecycle; this will ensure easy access to all project materials to review and update.

Step 5b – Close Contract: Update and Archive Contract Files

- **Objective**: to ensure that the Contract and all supporting documentation is officially closed.

- **Instructions**:

  Contract Closure is completed by the Department of Procurement and Contracts. Working with your buyer, be sure that all needed contract documents are updated and formally issued a "closed" status, once the project deliverables / solution are formally accepted:

  - Use available templates: Final Deliverable Acceptance Form.
  - Complete all 4 major sections of the "Final" Deliverable Acceptance" Form:
    - Part 1 – Project Information (name, RFS number, PO number, The ITS PMO Project number, etc.
    - Part 2 – Inventory of deliverables / milestones and the status of their review; all status should be complete at this time
    - Part 3 – Businesses' Acceptance of the transition from project status to operations (must be signed by the Managing Director, Department Head(s)

        - of affected business areas, and The ITS PMO CIO, if they are to play a support and maintenance roll.
        - Part 4 – Project Close Authorizations – signatures of all PDT members, as well as the Project Sponsor, Project Manager and involved ACIO.
    - Present Form to Procurement as evidence of project completion.
    - Review the contract Document to identify language and activities that formalize the contract closure process.
    - Ensure that the Purchase Order is closed so that:
        - remaining funds are prohibited from being inadvertently spent
        - remaining funds can be re-allocated to maintenance and operations, if necessary.
    - Ensure that the contract is closed in the Purchasing System.
    - Notify the vendor that all deliverables are acceptable, no further work is required and the contract is closed.

- **Estimated Time Duration**

    4 (four) - 8 (eight) hours

- **Resource Participation**
    - It is the responsibility of the Department of Procurement and Contracts (DPC) to close the contract, update and archive contract files. The PM, however, is responsible for providing evidence of "closure" by submitting a copy of the Final Deliverable Acceptance Form to the Department.
    - The ITS PMO Management is responsible for closing out the Purchase Order in the financial system.

- **Tip for Success:**
  Be sure to understand the terms and conditions for contract closure particularly if you need to terminate a contract for cause.

<u>Step 6 – Release Project Team to Organizational "Homes"</u>

- **Objective:** To free up resources to be redeployed where needed.

- **Instructions**:
    - Use available templates: Employee Evaluation Form (check with Human Resources Department)
    - Evaluate resource(s) prior to release.
    - Notify Assistant CIO's and Senior Portfolio Manager that project resources are available for redeployment.
    - Encourage team to update skills matrix.
    - Update Resource Capacity Planning Model (Senior Portfolio Manager and ACIO's).

- **Estimated Time Duration:**
    Three (3) – Five (5) days, depending on project size and scope

- **Resource Participation:**
  The Procurement Department resources are the lead on this task. PM must initiate process via communication to Procurement Department informing them that the project has come to a conclusion and all open Purchase Order(s) must be closed.

-  **Tip(s) for Success:**
  Be sure to notify business owners that original project resources have been released and the business now consults with the project support team (maintenance/operations group) for future assistance.

Step 7 – Recognize, Celebrate Project Close

- **Objective:** to acknowledge key contribution of project team members and announce to organization the availability of the new product/service.

- **Instructions**:
  - Reserve meeting location and order refreshments.
  - Prepare tokens of appreciation: (awards/certificates of achievements).
  - Alert organization of Recognition Meeting and invite contributors, stakeholders, and executive management.
  - Prepare demonstration of project deliverable (if not already demonstrated).
  - Conduct meeting.
  - Prepare resolution/notification to the XYZ Company Board indicating project completion and organizational benefit.

- **Estimated Time Duration:**
  Three (3) – Five (5) days

- **Resource Participation:**
  The Procurement Department resources are the lead on this task. PM must initiate process via communication to Procurement Department informing them that the project has come to a conclusion and all open Purchase Order(s) must be closed.

-  **Tip(s) for Success:**
  Be sure to acknowledge all contributors to the project's success.

Confirm all Deliverables

At the end of the work plan all deliverables should be complete. Ensure the following:

- All deliverables have proper signoff
- All deliverables have met all contract and quality requirements
- All deliverable documentation have been received by the project manager
- The document repository system (SharePoint) has all documents in the team's library for lessons learned.
- All scheduled seller payments have been resolved

5.2 Conduct Procurement Audit

Overview

The procurement process is integral to the acquisition of products and services for the Authority. It becomes increasingly important as the demand for products and services increase as well as the impact of those purchases expands the entire enterprise, that the procurement process be monitored to ensure overall quality and consistency. The Procurement audit therefore becomes essential to instituting best practices throughout the procurement lifecycle. PMBOK suggests that as a component of project closure, the PM should conduct a procurement audit at the end of the project.

The exhibit below depicts the activities, which when followed, will complete a Procurement Audit.

Closure Process, Stage 2

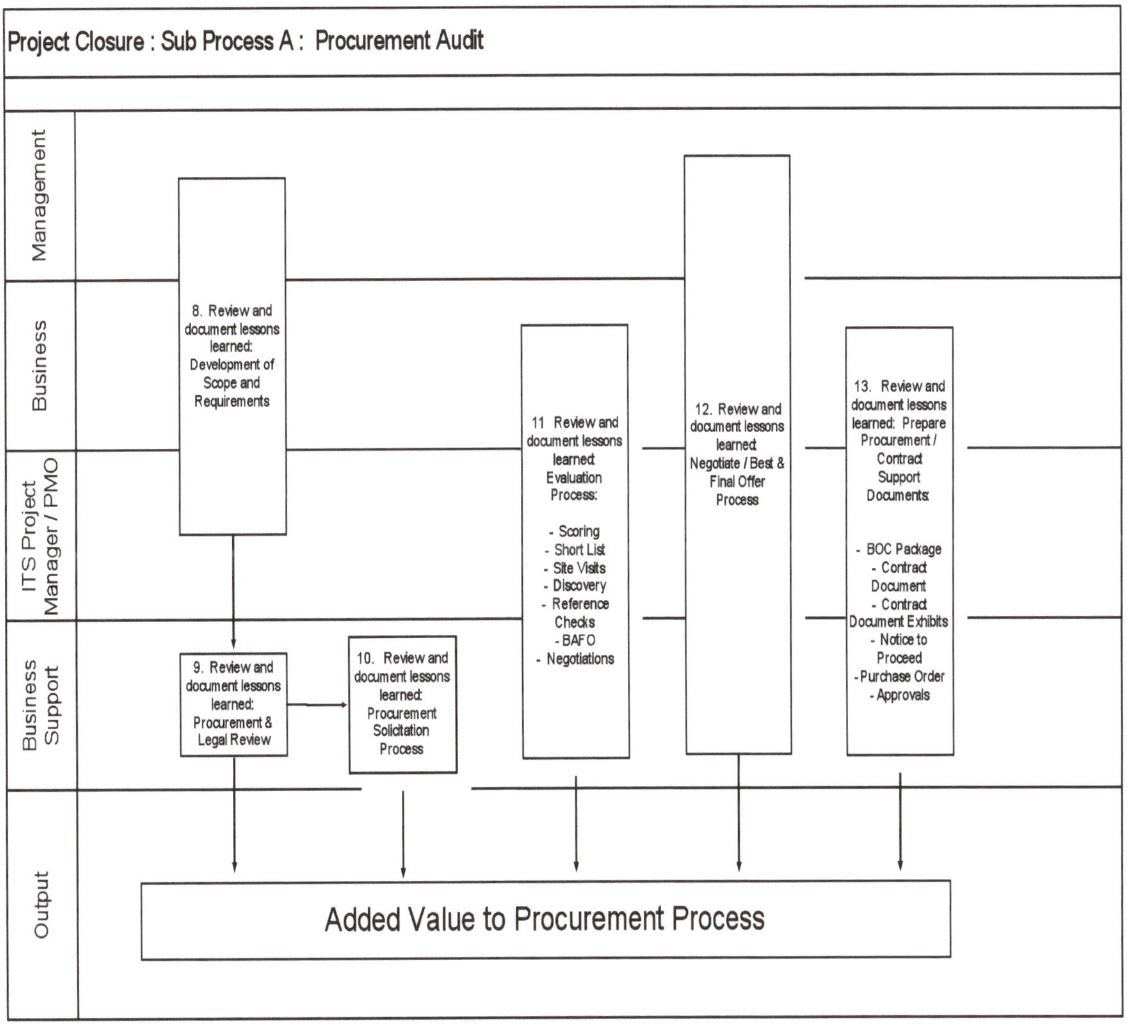

Stage 2 – Conduct Procurement Audit Activities

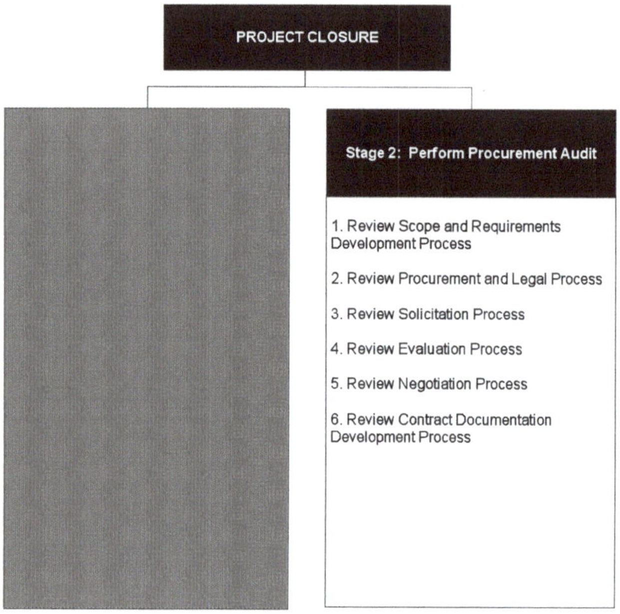

The second stage of the Planning Phase is initiated by the development of the Procurement Document otherwise known as Request for Proposal (RFP), Request for Information (RFI), Request for Services (RFS), and Invitation for Bid (IFB). As can be seen in the diagram above, there are six steps in "Perform Procurement Audit". Each step in this stage is very important to undergo; as a result each step will leverage the protocols established in Step 4 – After Action Review. The PM will conduct a careful and thorough analysis of key milestones/tasks performed during those subsequent procurement phases.

Stage Two: Inputs, Outputs and Tools

The Inputs and Outputs for Stage Two – Perform Procurement Audit, identifies items, task or documents to be used at the completion of the procurement process audit. The inputs can be described as what work has been done which prompts the need to use the second process flow and complete all steps in the flow to reach the desired outcome, that being an audit of all steps undertaken in the procurement of products or services. The inputs and outputs for Stage 2 are depicted below.

Closure Process, Stage 3 – Develop Work-Out, Re-Work Plan: Inputs, Tools, Outputs

Inputs	Tools	Outputs
• Completion of: - Requirements Defined - Business Review - Solicitation - Evaluation - Negotiation - Contract	• Process Flow • Project Plan • Statement of Work • After Action Review	• After Action Review Form

Stage Two: Timeframe/Total Duration

Depends upon the nature of the work to be completed or what type of procurement process was undertaken.

Stage Two: Resource Participation

The following resources participate during the "Develop and Implement a Solution Completion, Re-work Plan" Stage:

- Department Director
- Business Owner
- The ITS PMO Management – Chief Information Officer and/or Assistant Chief Information Officer(s)
- Senior Portfolio Manager
- The ITS PMO Project Manager
- Evaluation Team
- Procurement Department
- Legal Department

Step	Executive Sponsor	Dept Director	Business Owner	The ITS PMO Mgmt	Senior Portfolio Manager	The ITS PMO PM	Other Key Stakeholders	Procurement & Legal
8 - Development of Scope and Requirements	I	I	R	A	C	R	I	C
9 - Procurement and Legal Review Process	I	I	R	A	C	R	I	C
10 – Solicitation Process Review	I	I	R	A	C	R	I	C
11 – Evaluation Process Review	I	I	R	A	C	R	I	C
12 – Negotiation Process	I	I	R	A	C	R	I	C
13 – Development of Contract Documents	I	I	R	A	C	R	I	C

Stage Two consists of six (6) tasks. This section provides detailed instructions for the Project Manager to complete a Procurement Audit.

Step 8-13 – Procurement Audit (Sub – process A)

- **Objective:** To document "lessons learned" from the procurement process for application to future solicitations.

- **Instructions**:
Using the After Action Review (AAR) Document and Process, assess the effectiveness and relevance of the following components of the procurement process:

    - Project scope and requirements as developed
    - Business Review – Department of Procurement and Contracts and Legal
    - Solicitation Process
    - Evaluation Process
    - Negotiation Process
    - Contract Support Documents

- **Estimated Time Duration:**
    - 5– 10 days, depending on project size and scope

- **Tip(s) for Success:**
    - Be sure to notify business owners that original project resources have been released and the business now consults with the project support team (maintenance/operations group) for future assistance.

Conduct Lessons Learned

- Review project past performance. Review the good, bad and the ugly for corrective action
- Discuss improvement opportunities
- Release Team

Technical Case Scenario – The Closing Phase

- ❖ Conducting Lessons Learned

33 Strategies

33 Strategies of Project Management

INITIATION	1 Overview of the Project Initiation Process; 2 Understanding the Strategic Plan; 3 Understanding the authority of the Project Manager; 4 Estimating Qualitative benefits; 5 Understanding the politics and power of the stakeholder; 6 PID scoring framework; 7 EDT presentation meeting
PLANNING	8 Understanding of the PM Cycle; 9 Make or Buy Decision; 10 Procurement Tips and Tricks; 11 Contract Types; 12 The WBS; 13 Network Diagrams; 14 The Critical Path; 15 Milestone Approach; 16 Estimating cost & resources; 17 Designing your PM Strategy; 18 The baseline project schedule; 19 Change Control Process; 20 Quality Assurance Process; 21 The Project Plan; 22 The Kickoff Meeting
EXECUTING	23 Executing the work plan; 24 Evaluating team performance; 25 Holding status meetings; 26 Producing status reports; 27 Action item and Issue logs
MONITOR CONTROL	28 Risk management; 29 Determine variances; 30 Reporting on project performance; 31 Hosting EDT meetings
CLOSING	32 Confirm all deliverables; 33 Conduct lessons learned

Overall PID Process

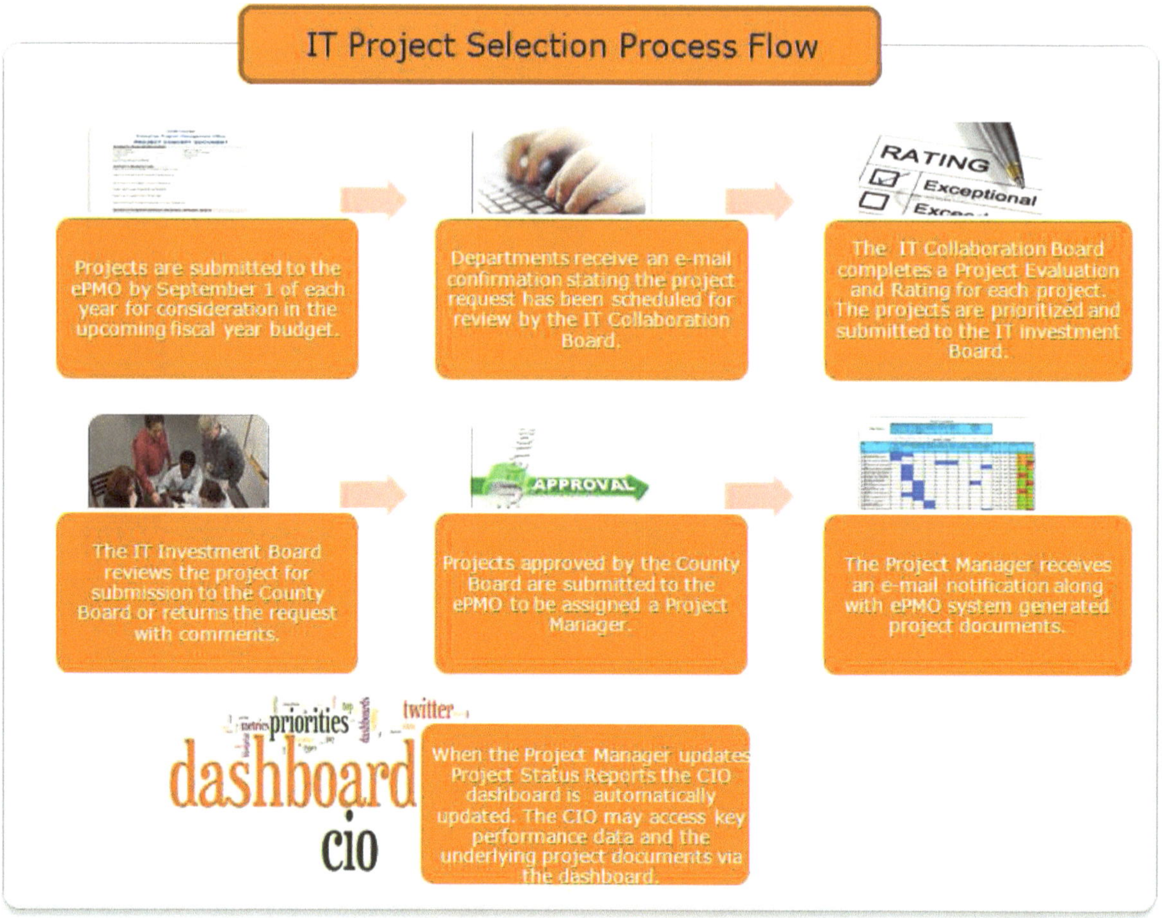

SharePoint PID Process Flow

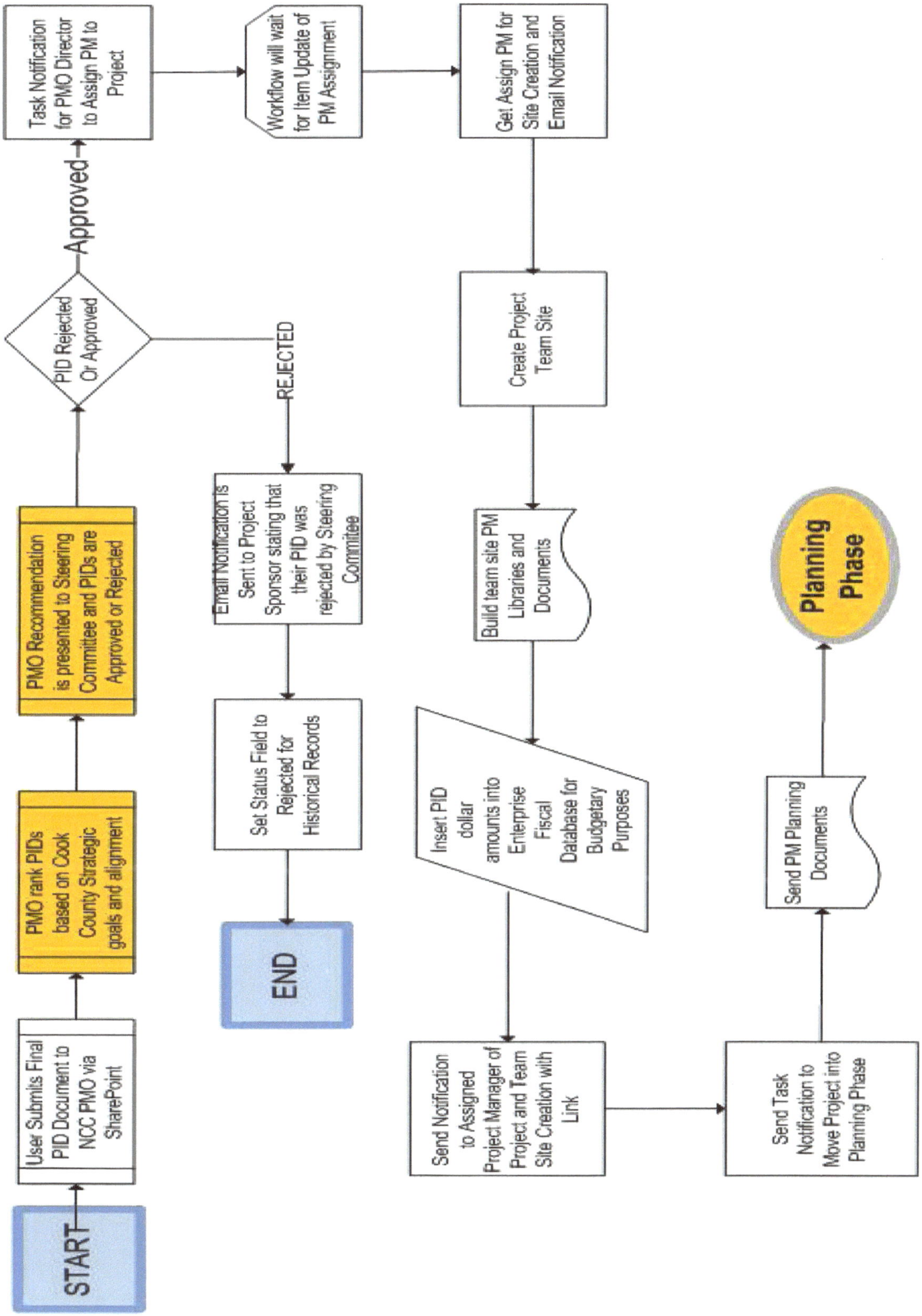

Overall Initiation Process Flow

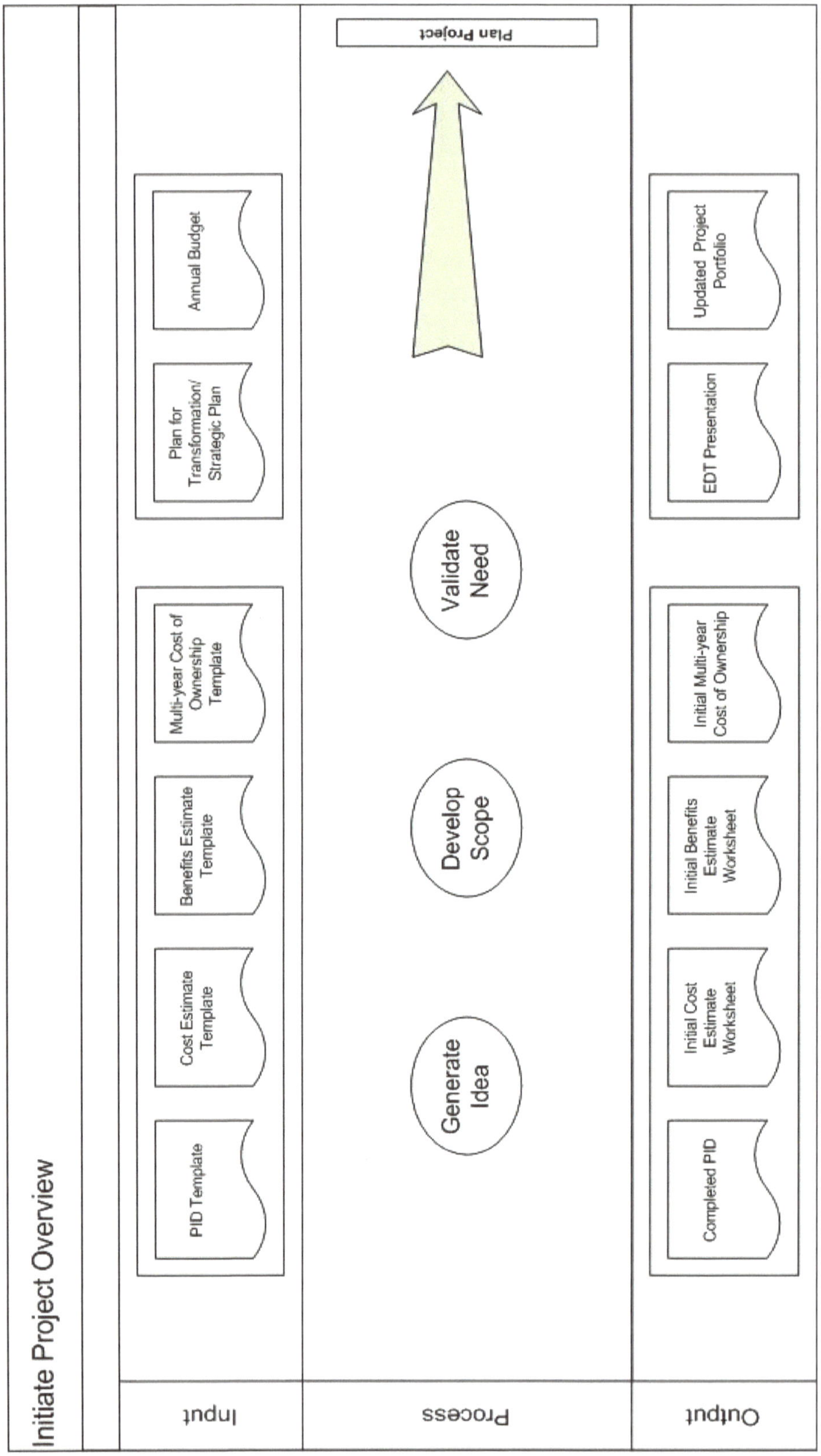

Generate Idea

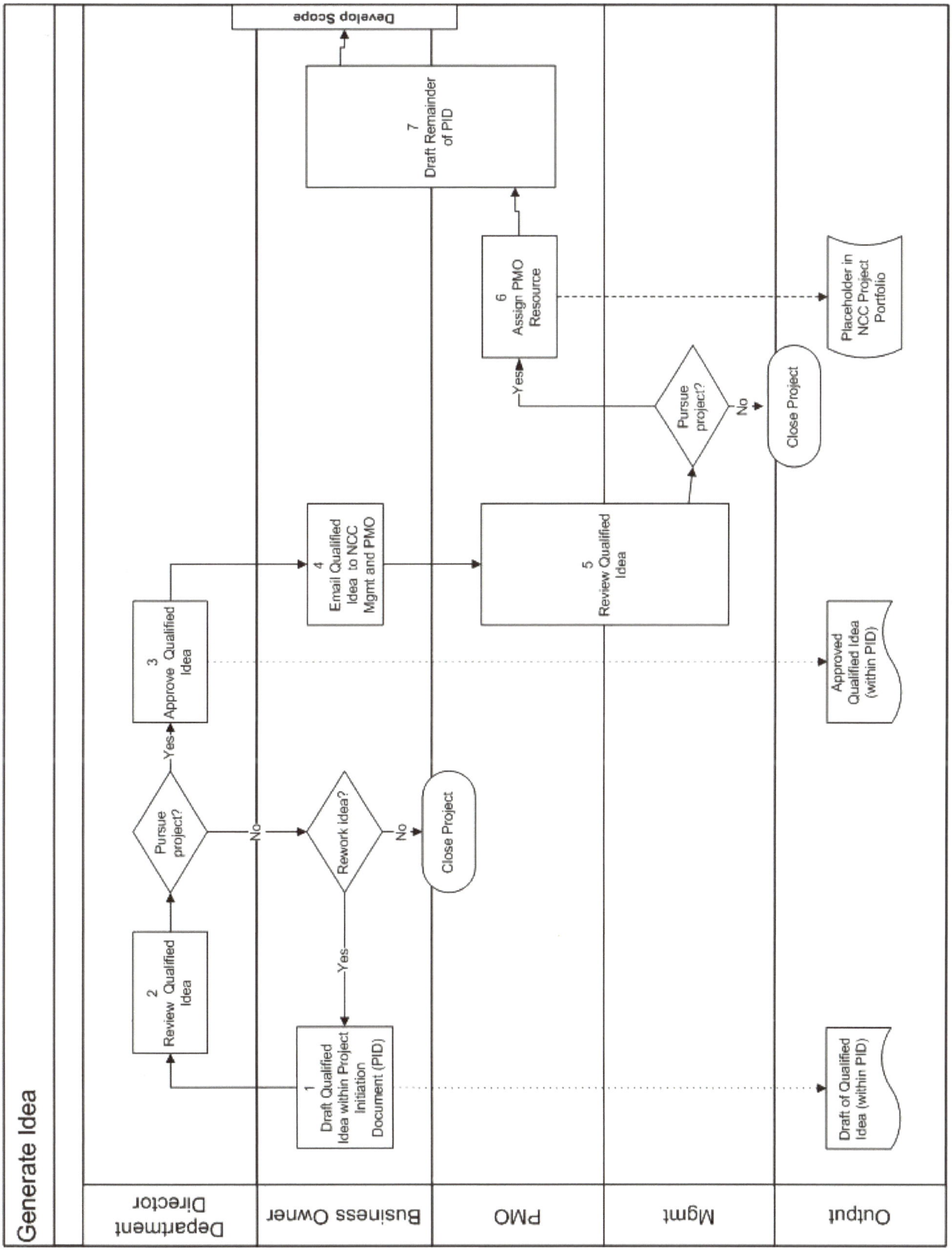

Develop Scope

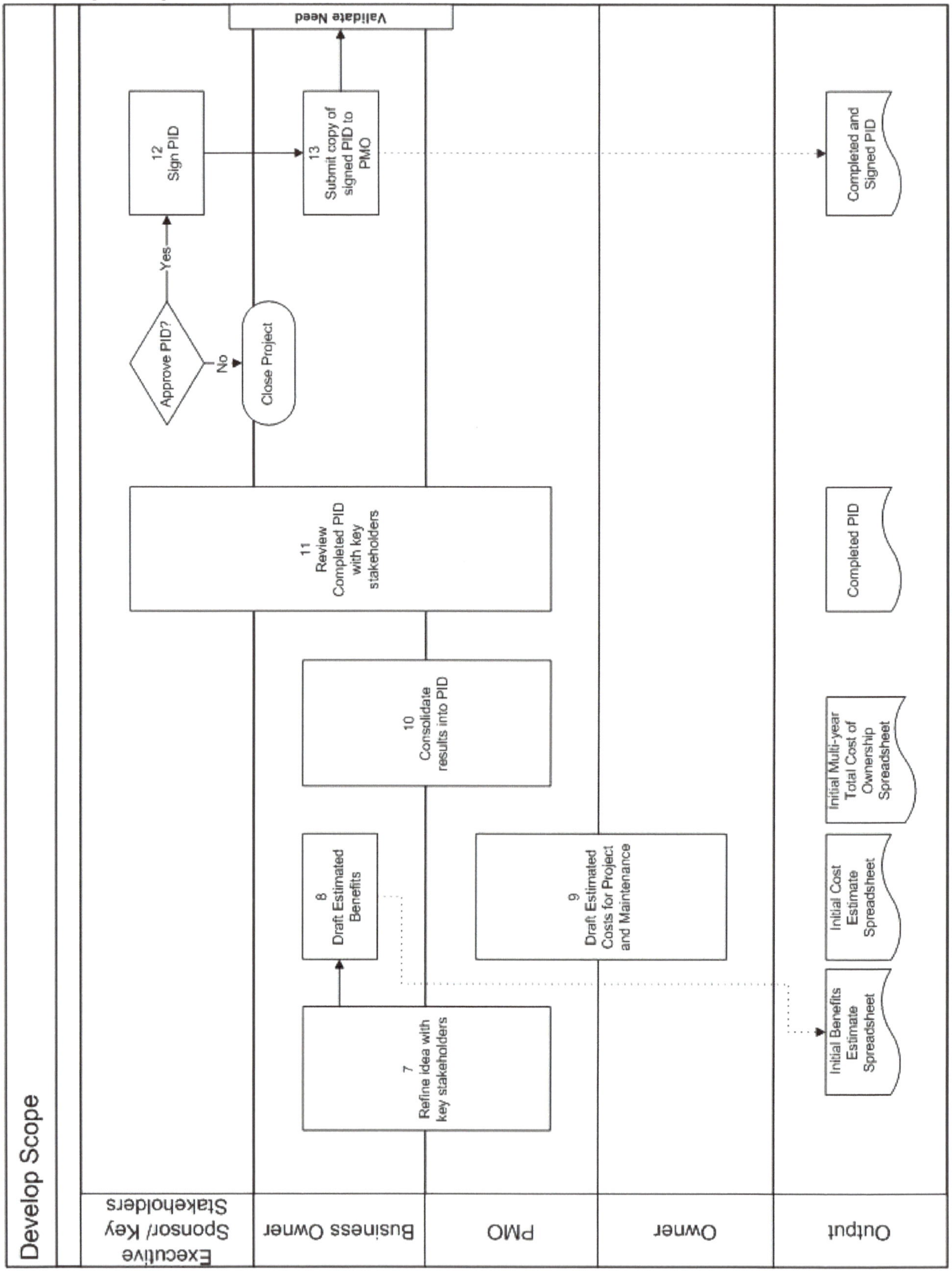

Validate Need

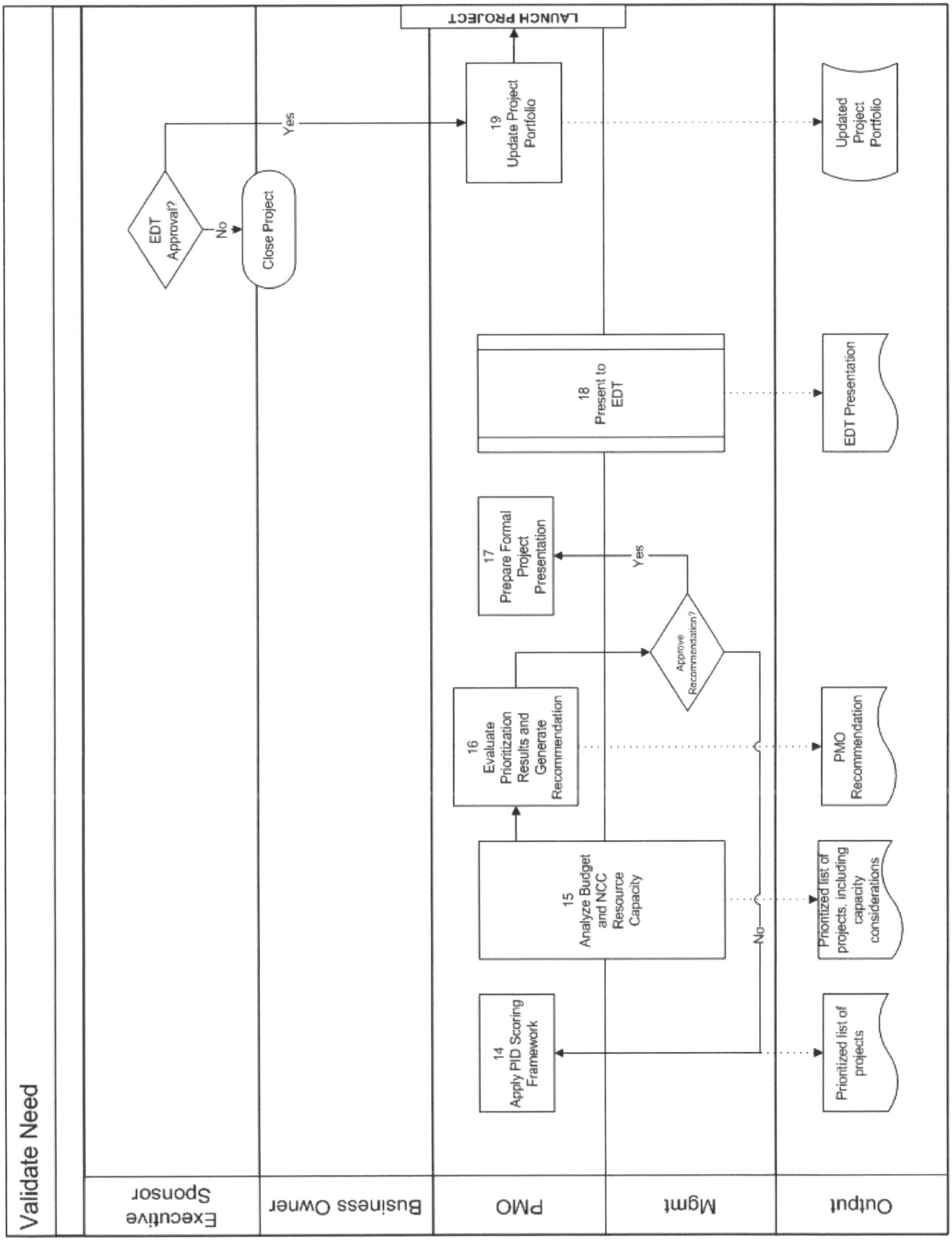

Launch Project

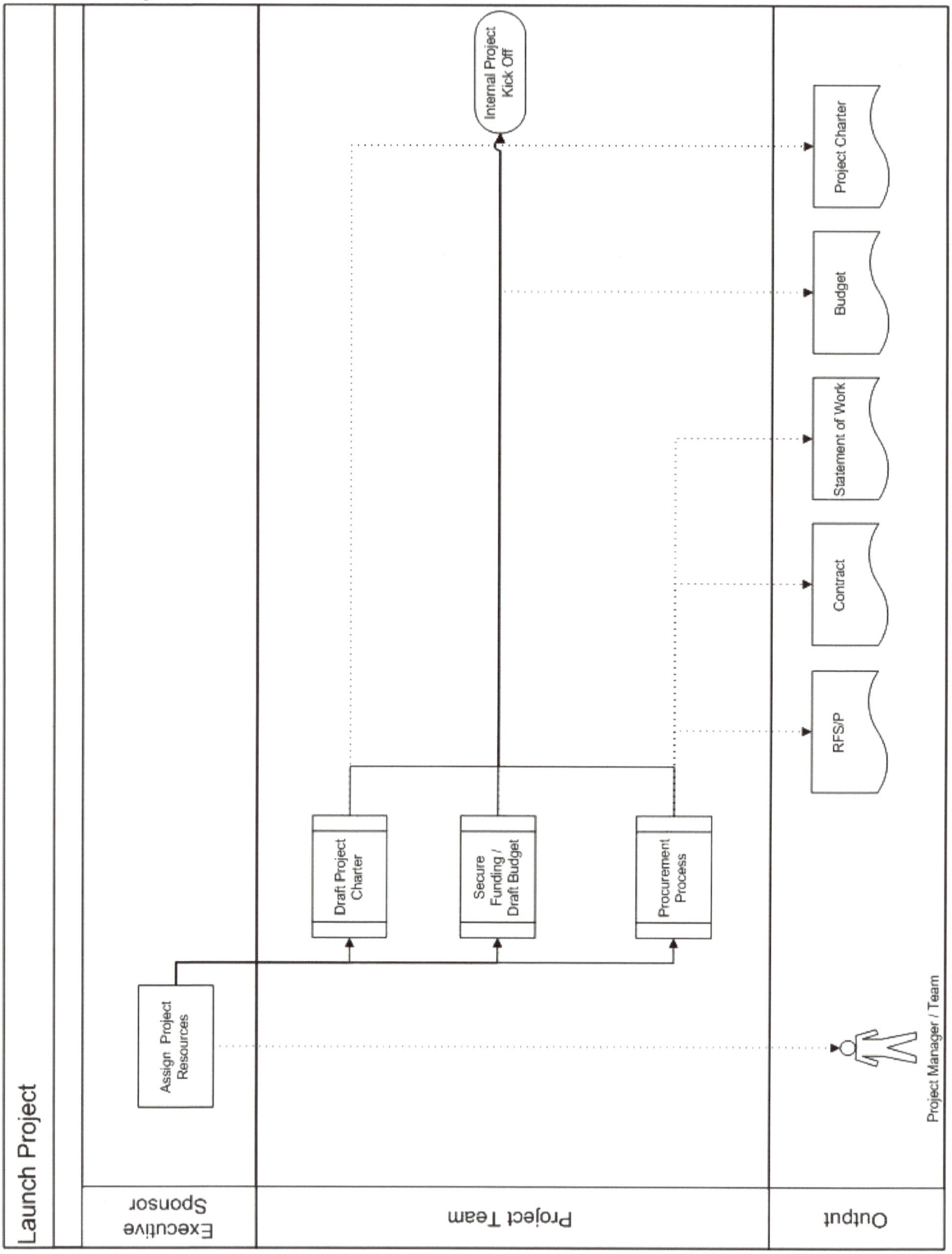

Planning Stage 1

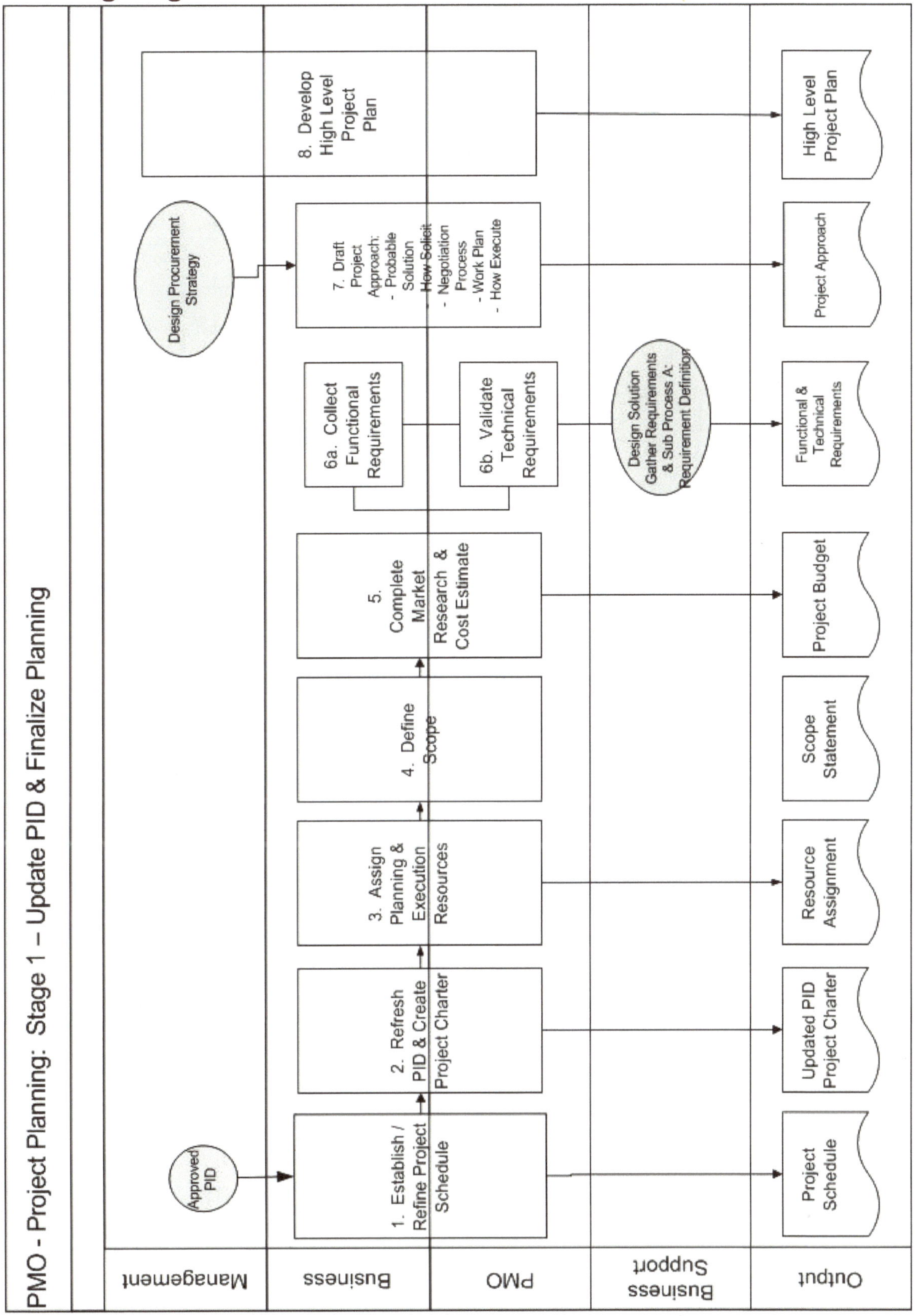

Planning Stage 1.1

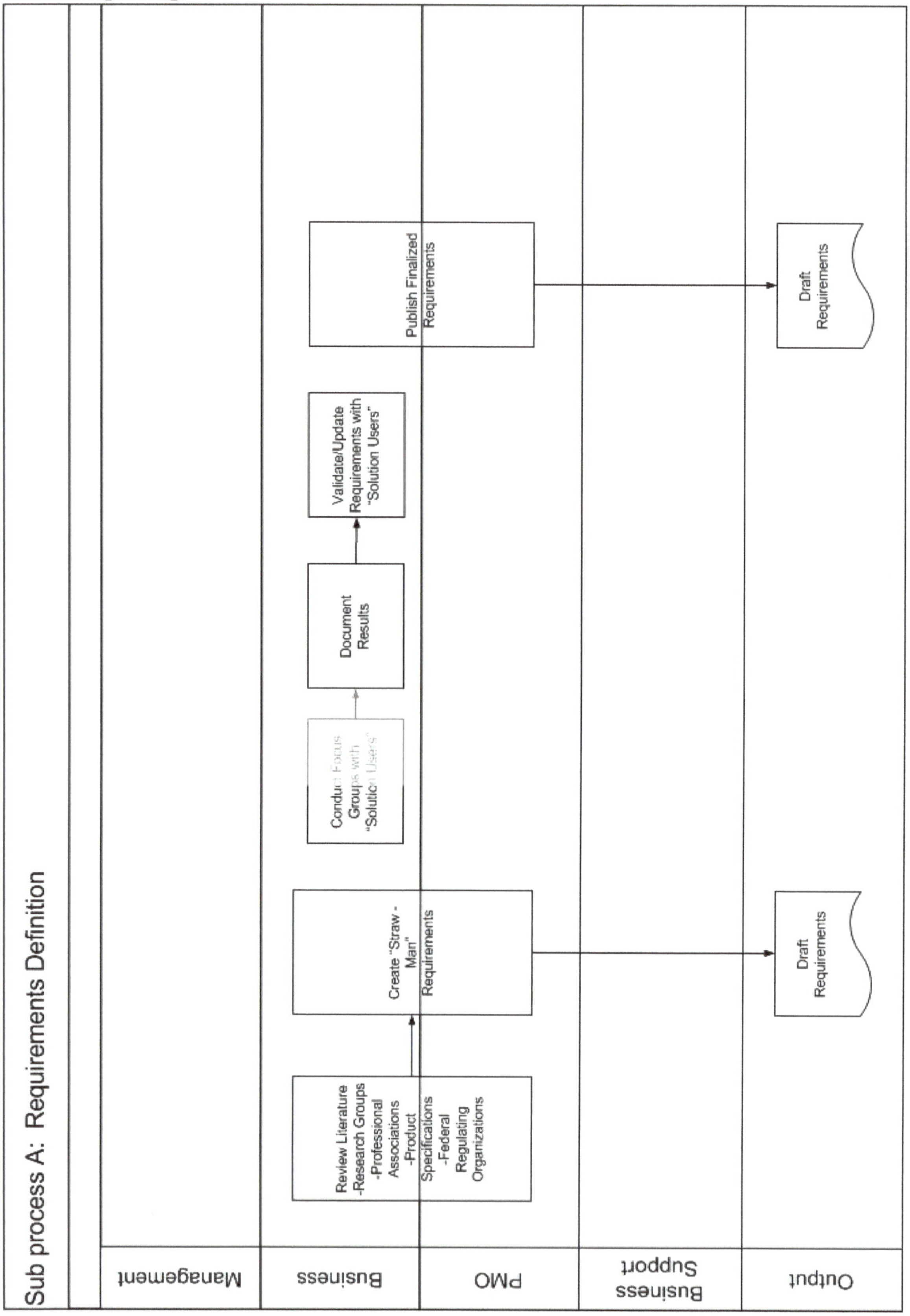

Planning Stage 1.1.1

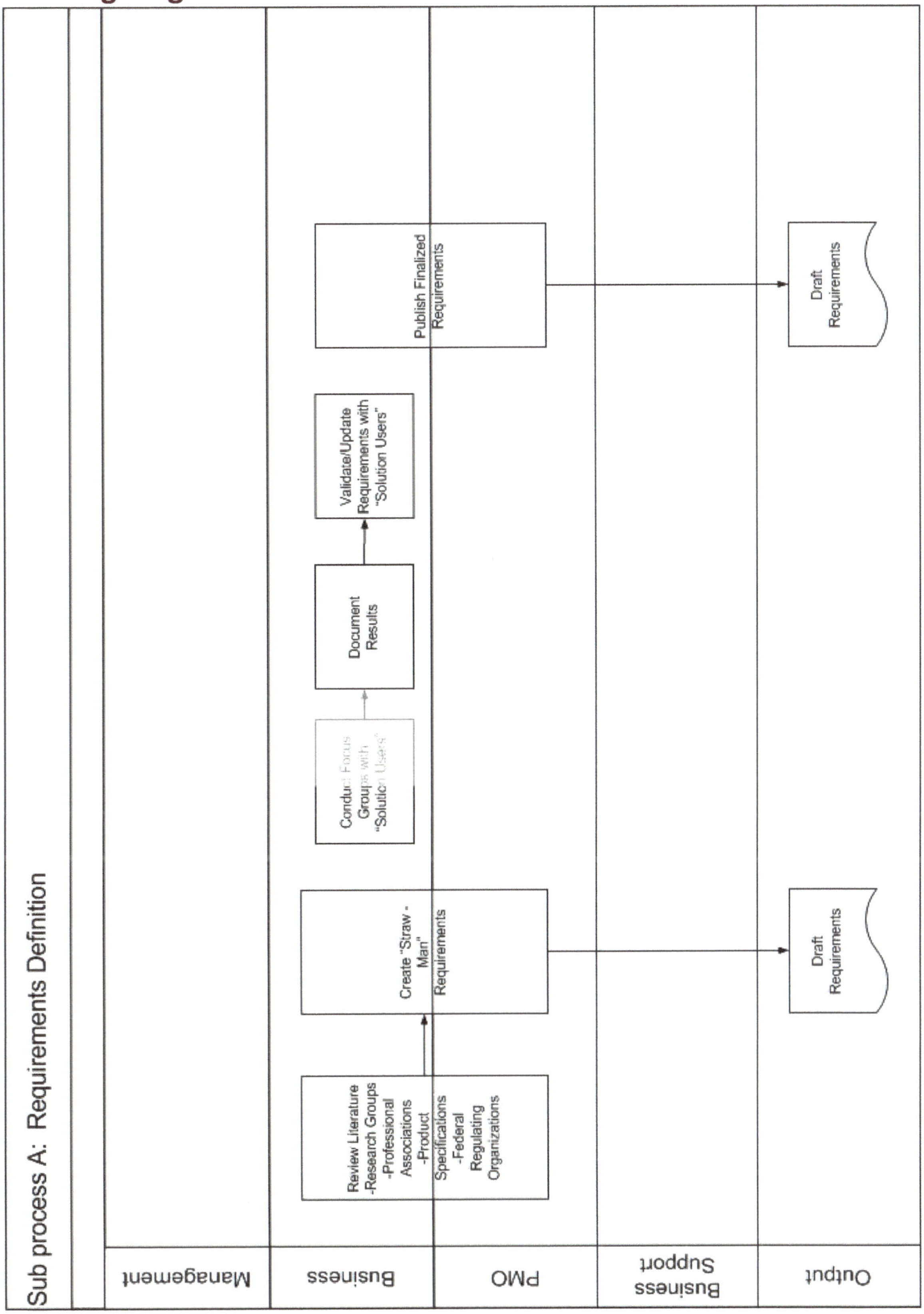

Planning Stage 1.2

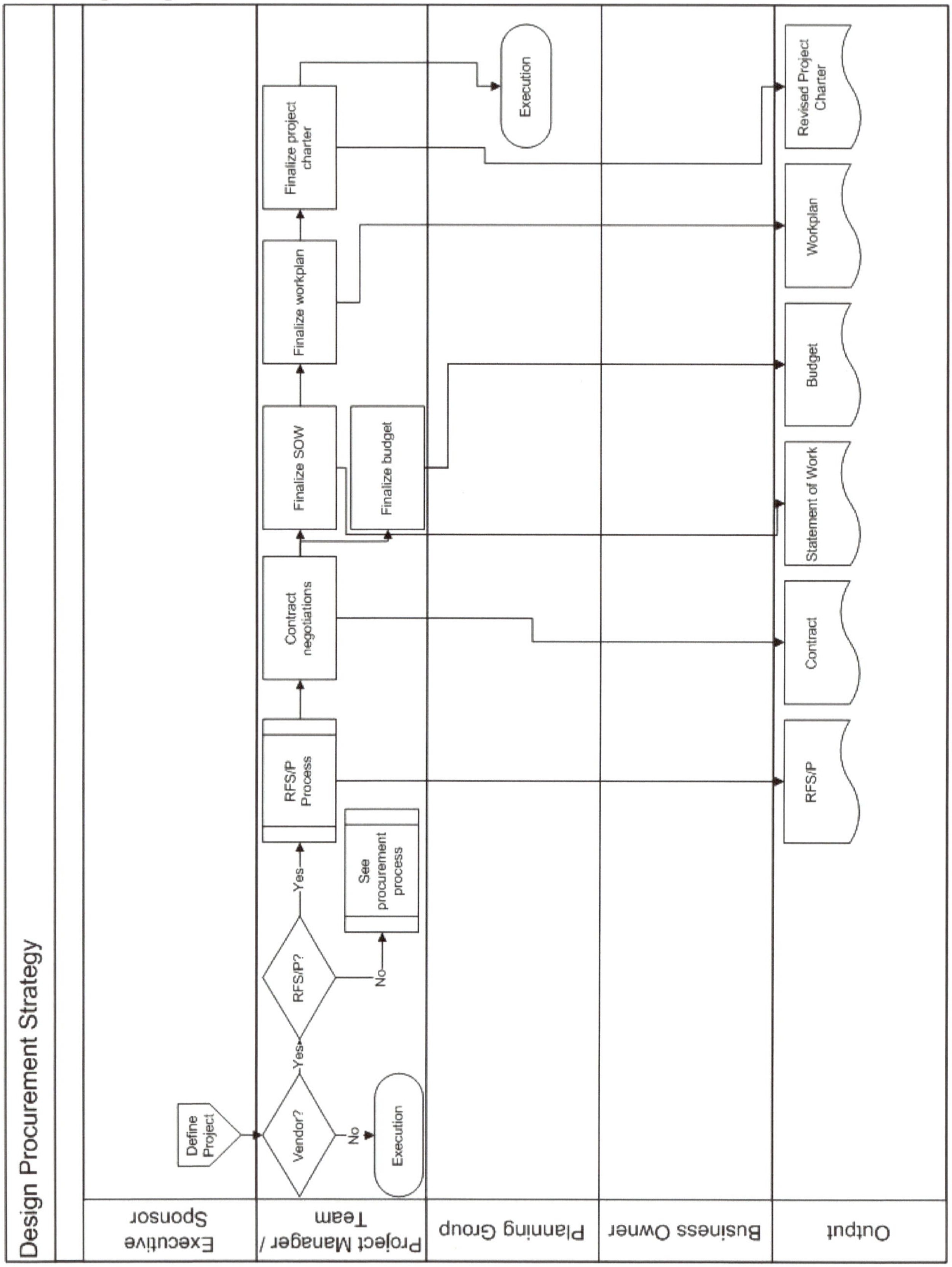

Planning Stage 2.1.2

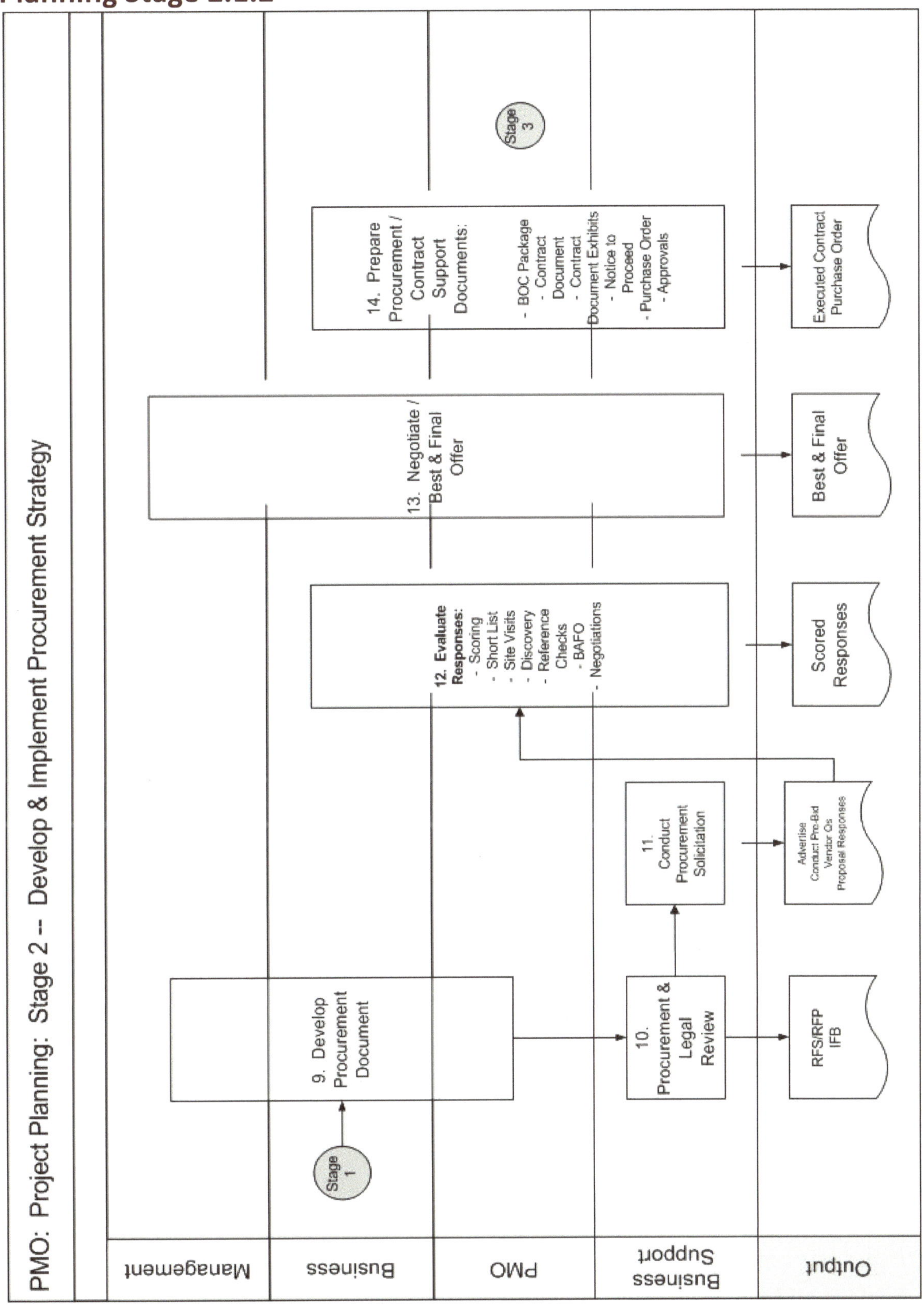

Planning Stage 2.1.2.1

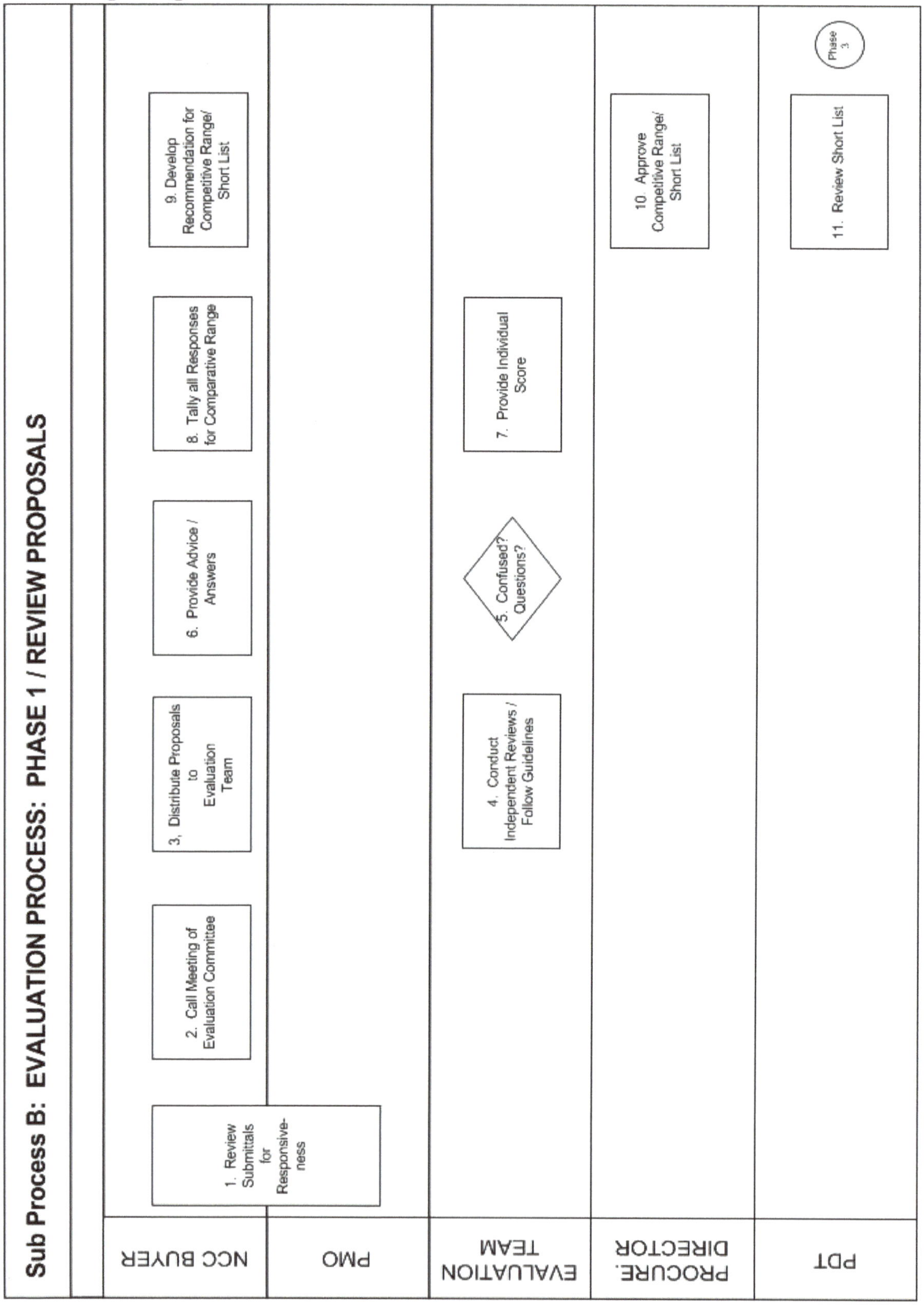

Planning Stage 2.1.2.2

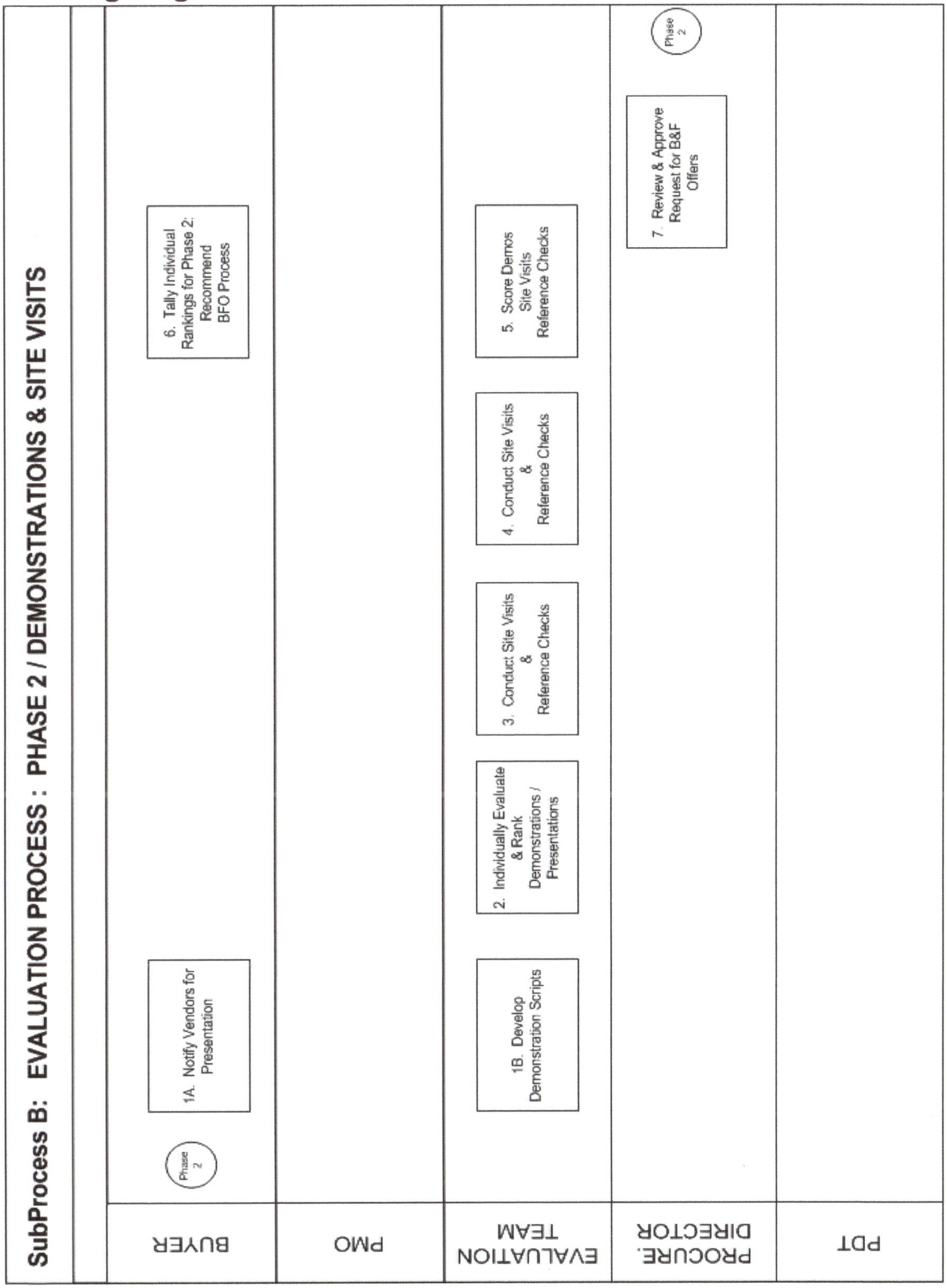

Planning Stage 2.1.2.3

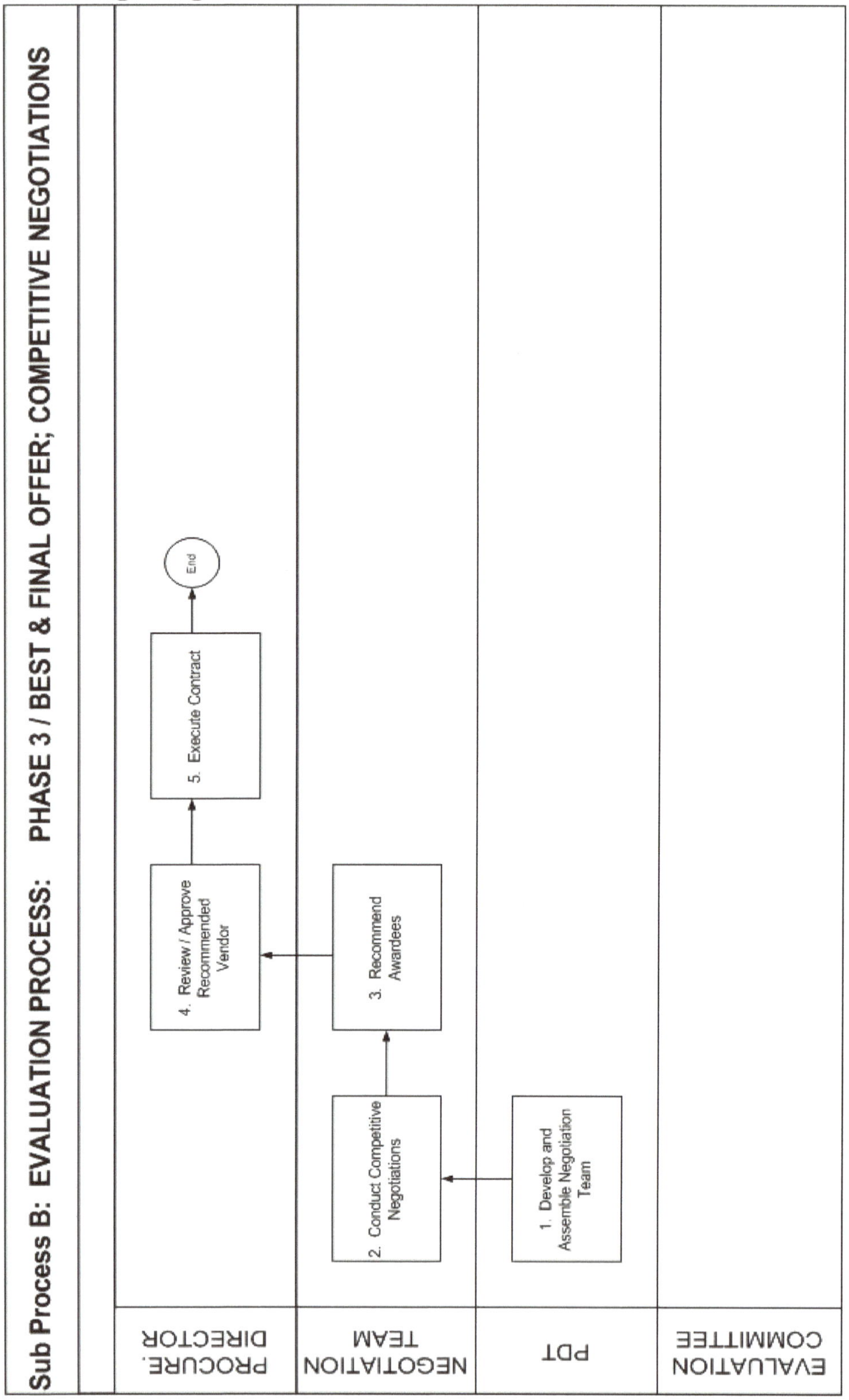

Planning Stage 3.0

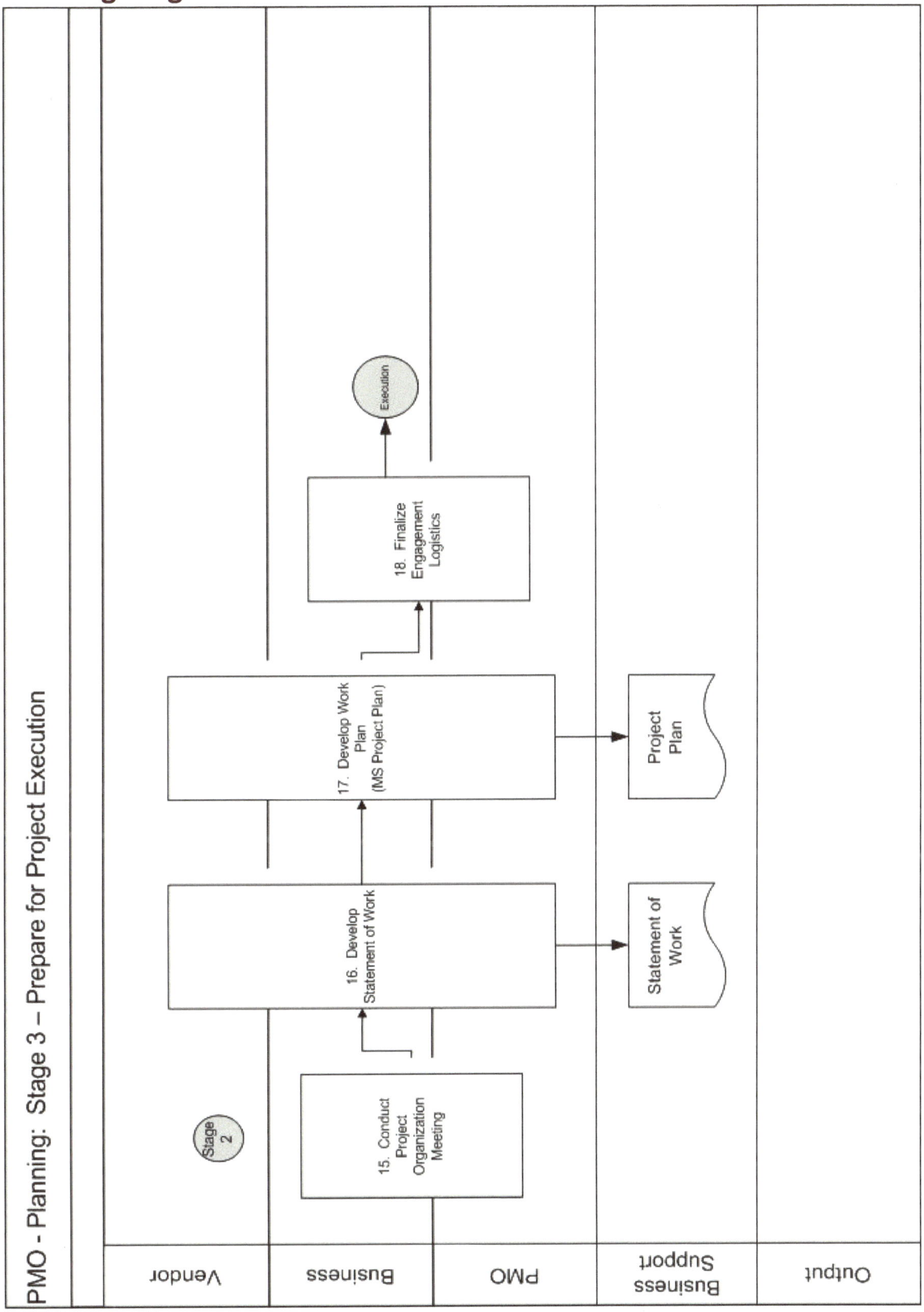

Execution Stage 1.0

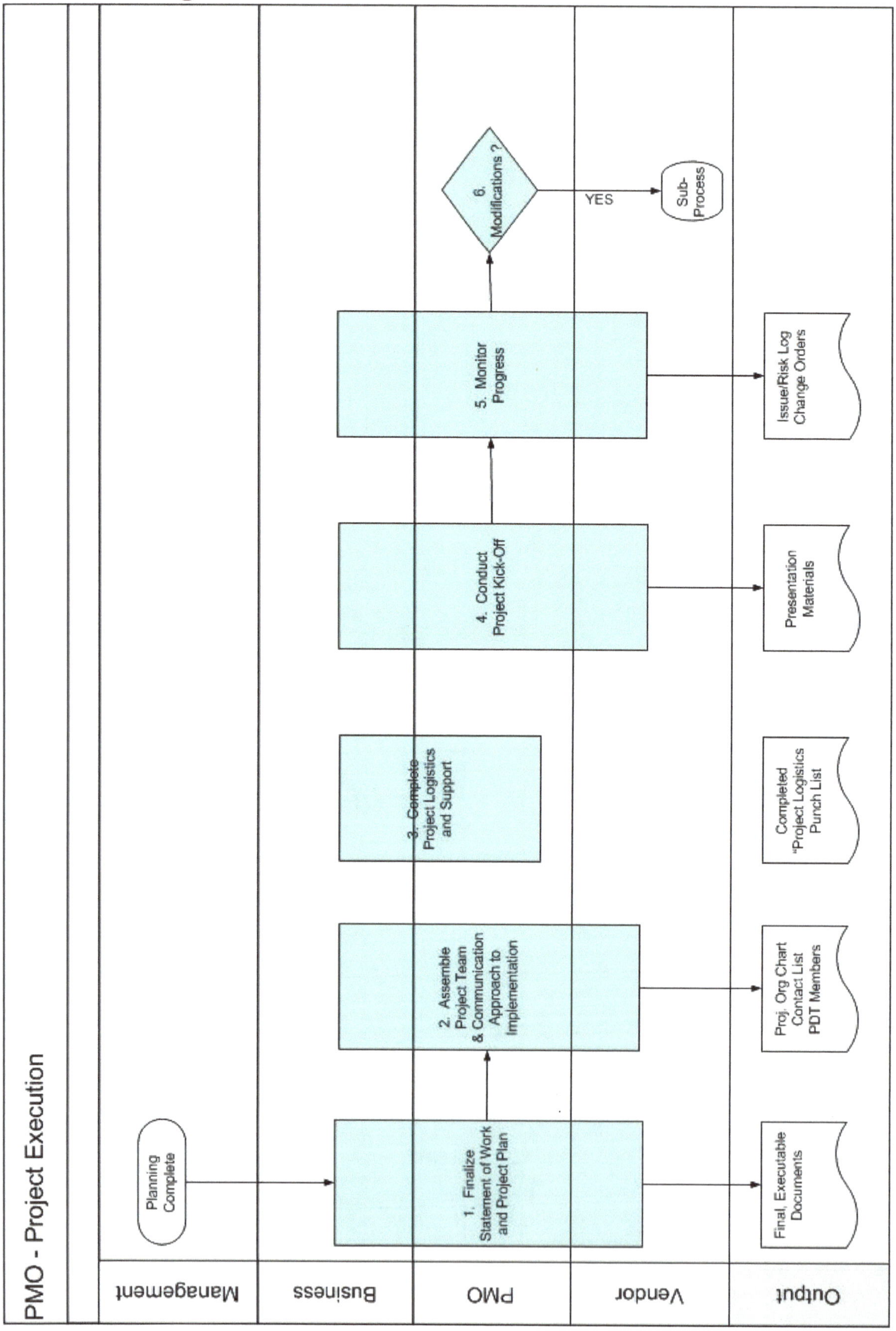

Execution Stage 2.0

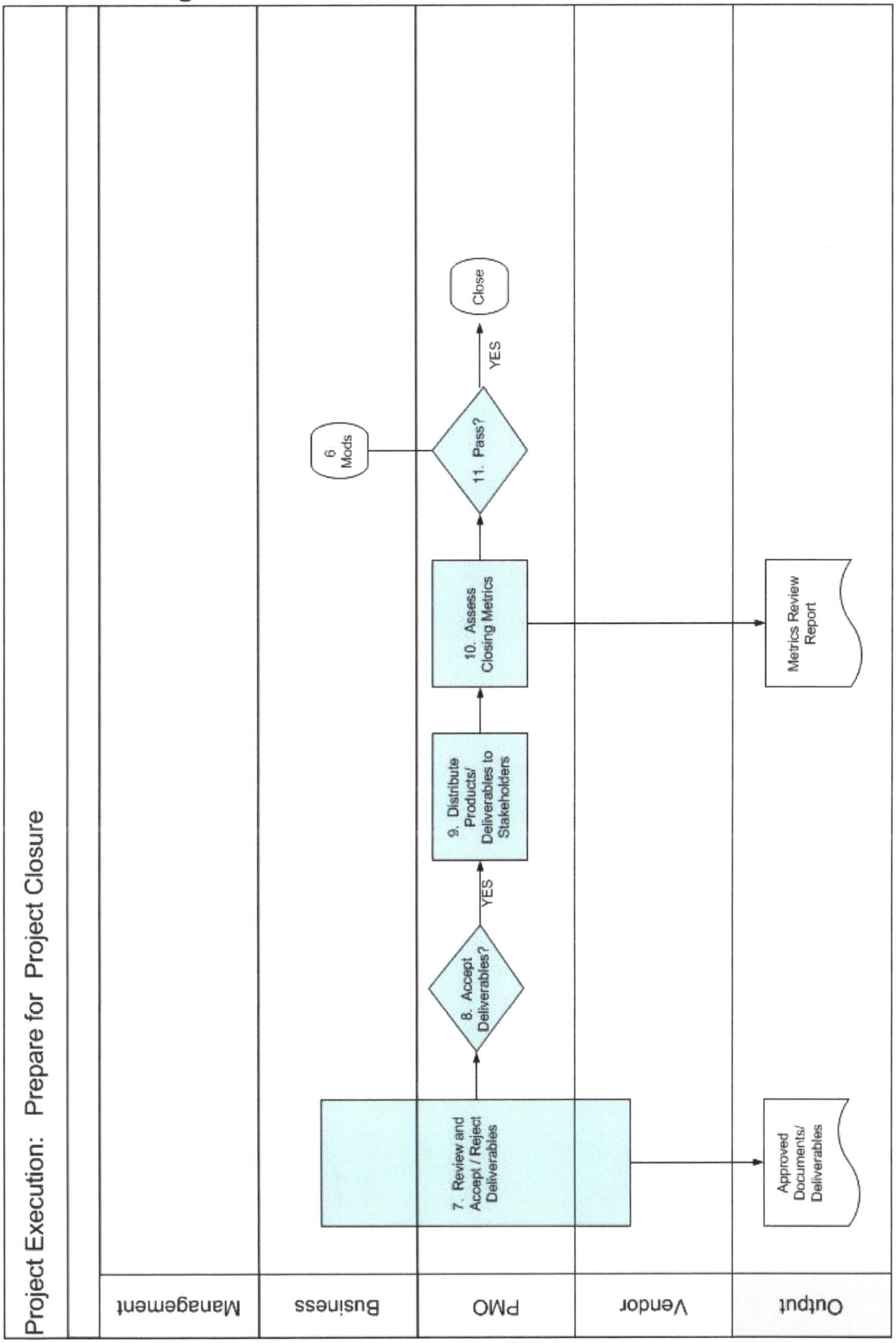

Project Monitor/Control 1.0

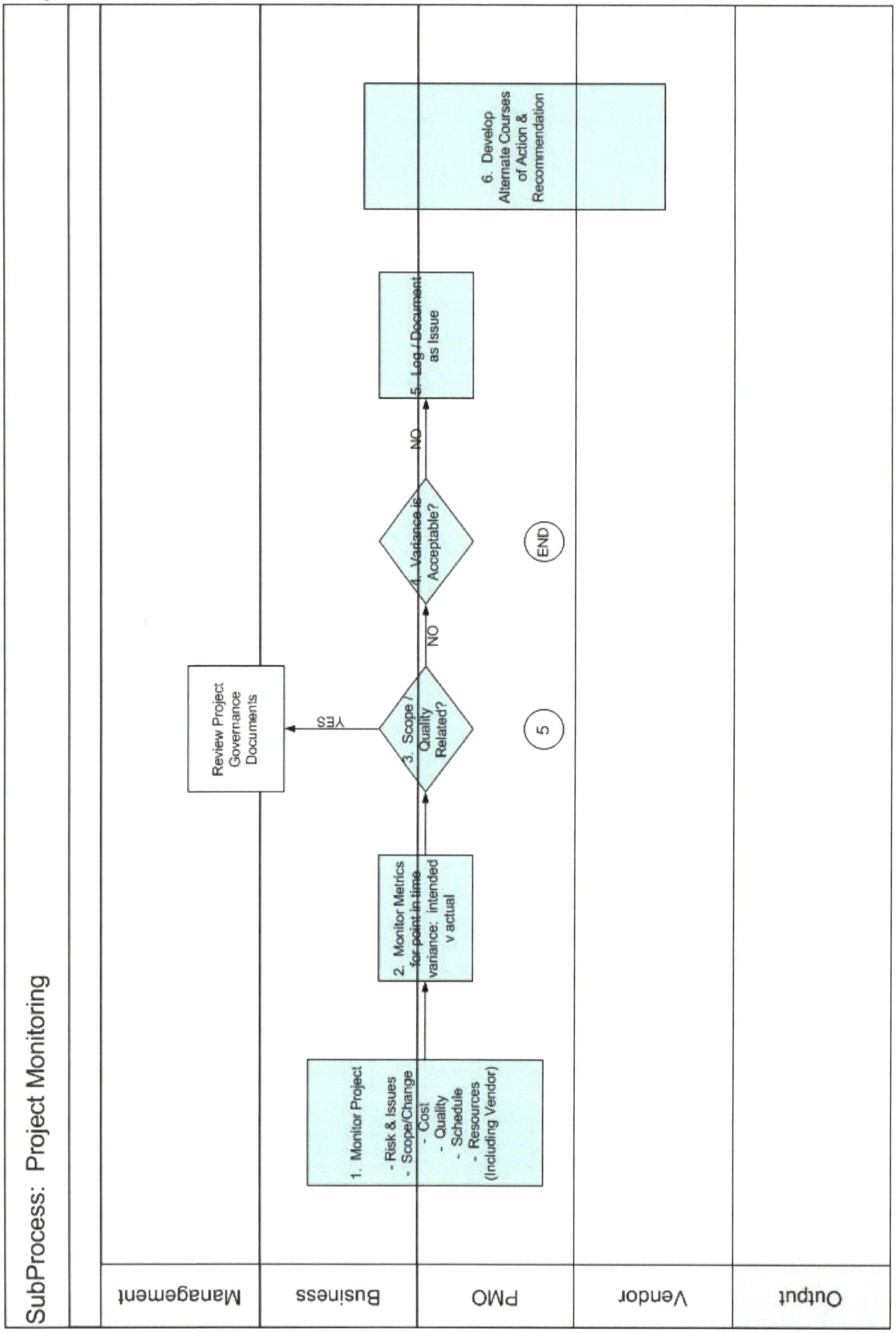

Change Control

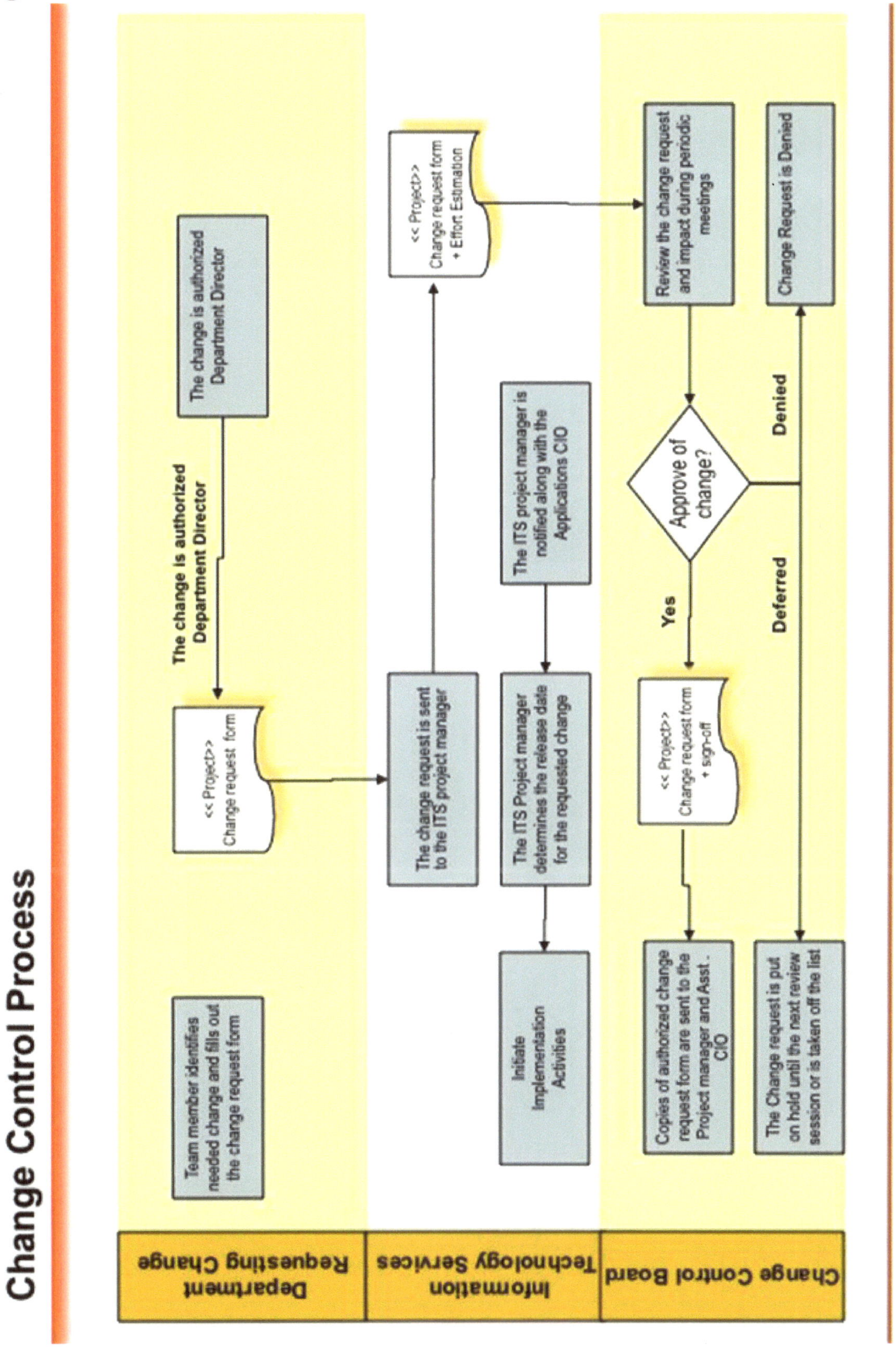

Project Monitor/Control 2.0

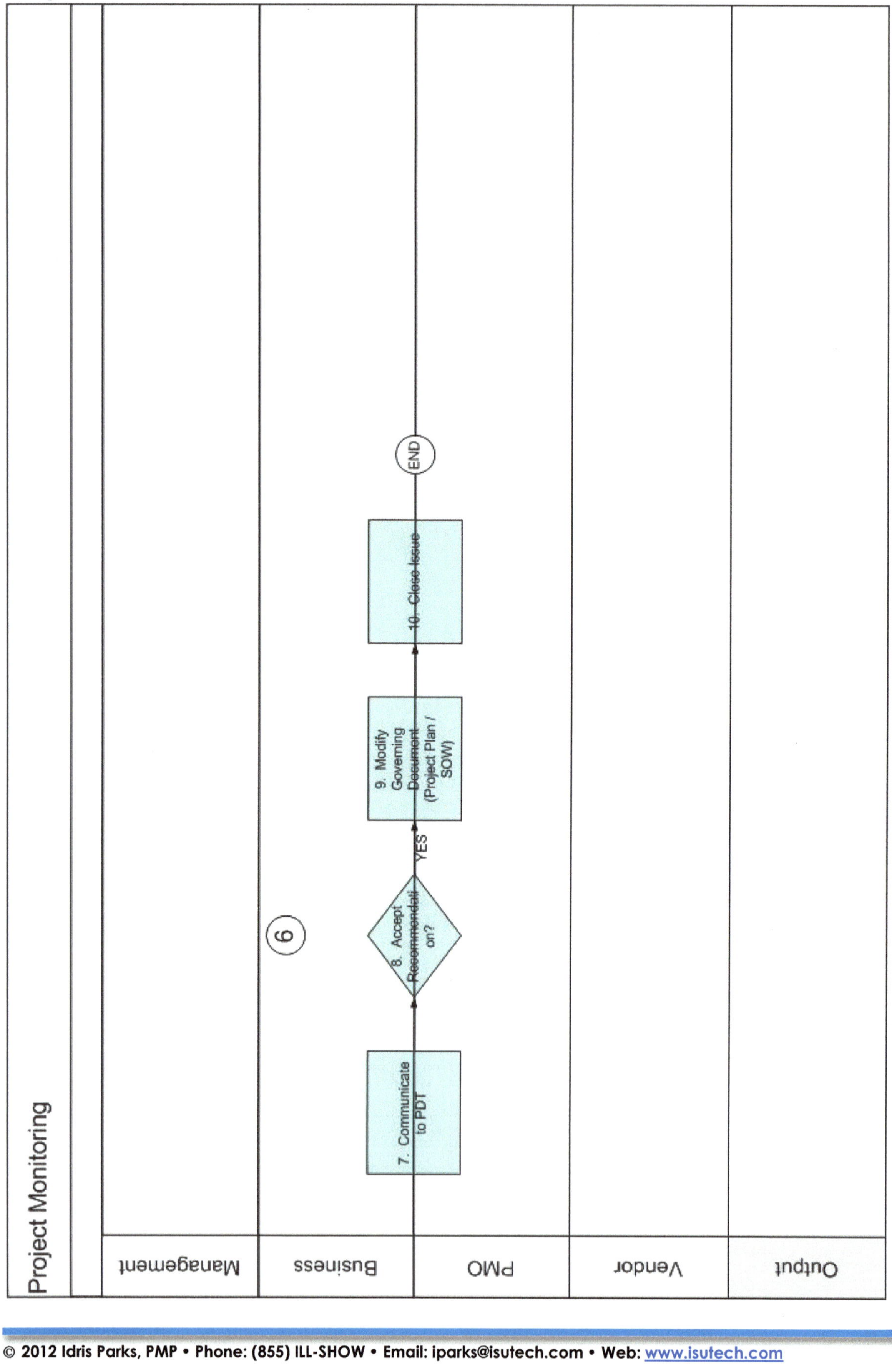

Closure

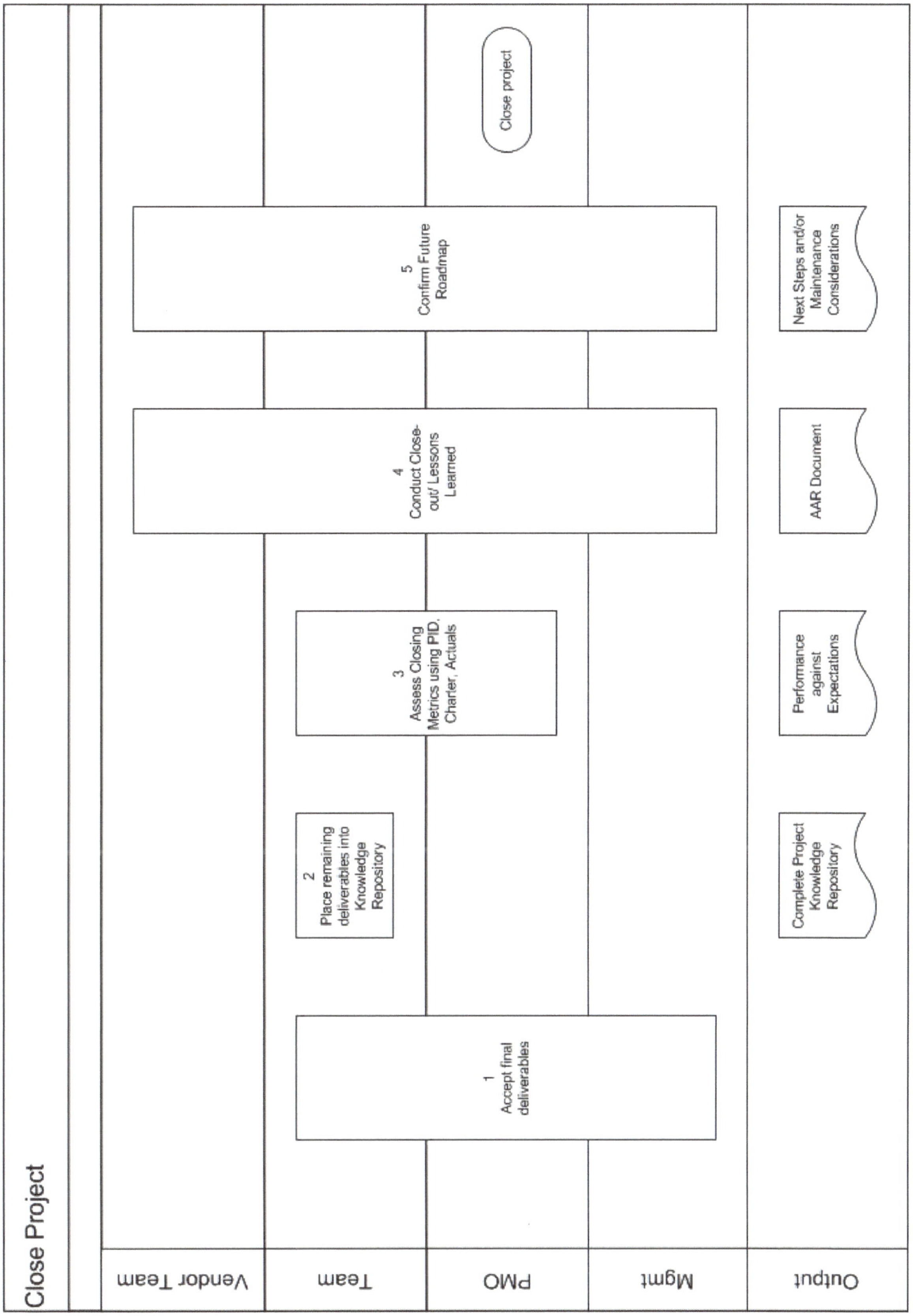

Close Project
Vendor Team
Team
PMO
Mgmt
Output
1
Accept final deliverables
2
Place remaining deliverables into Knowledge Repository
3
Assess Closing Metrics using PID, Charter, Actuals
4
Conduct Close-out/ Lessons Learned
5
Confirm Future Roadmap
Close project
Complete Project Knowledge Repository
Performance against Expectations
AAR Document
Next Steps and/or Maintenance Considerations

Earned Value Reporting

Actual % Complete:
Targeted Milestone:
Budget: $300,000.00

NETWORK UPGRADE PROJECT

START	C									END
Milestones										
WBS	1.2	1.3	1.4.1	1.5	1.6	1.7	1.9.9	5.4	6.0	6.1
Task										
Date	1/1/04	1/2/04	1/3/04	1/4/04	1/5/04	1/6/04	1/7/04	1/8/04	1/9/04	1/10/04
Weight	10	10	10	10	10	10	10	10	10	10
Project Completion	10%	20%	30%	40%	50%	60%	70%	80%	90%	100%
Act % Com.	100%	100%	50%	80%	100%	100%	90%	100%	100%	0%
Weight Dollar $	$30,000	$30,000	$30,000	$30,000	$30,000	$30,000	$30,000	$30,000	$30,000	$300,000
PV	$30,000	$60,000	$90,000	$120,000	$150,000	$180,000	$210,000	$240,000	$270,000	$300,000
EV	$30,000.00	$60,000.00	$75,000.00	$99,000.00	$129,000.00	$159,000.00	$186,000.00	$216,000.00	$246,000.00	$246,000.00
AC	$30,000.00	$60,000.00	$75,000.00	$99,000.00	$129,000.00	$159,000.00	$186,000.00	$216,000.00	$246,000.00	$246,000.00
SV	$0.00	$0.00	($15,000.00)	($21,000.00)	($21,000.00)	($21,000.00)	($24,000.00)	($24,000.00)	($24,000.00)	($54,000.00)
CV	$0.00	$0.00	$0.00	$0.00	$0.00	$0.00	$0.00	$0.00	$0.00	$0.00
SPI	1.00	1.00	0.83	0.83	0.86	0.88	0.89	0.90	0.91	0.82
CPI	1.00	1.00	1.00	1.00	1.00	1.00	1.00	1.00	1.00	1.00
EAC	$300,000.00	$300,000.00	$300,000.00	$300,000.00	$300,000.00	$300,000.00	$300,000.00	$300,000.00	$300,000.00	$300,000.00
ETC	$270,000.00	$240,000.00	$225,000.00	$201,000.00	$171,000.00	$141,000.00	$114,000.00	$84,000.00	$54,000.00	$54,000.00
VAC	$0.00	$0.00	$0.00	$0.00	$0.00	$0.00	$0.00	$0.00	$0.00	$0.00
History EV	$22,500.00	$50,000.00	$80,000.00	$100,000.00	$120,000.00	$180,000.00	$186,000.00	$240,000.00	$230,000.00	$290,000.00
History SPI	0.75	0.83	0.89	0.83	0.80	1.00	0.89	1.00	0.85	0.97

EARNED VALUE GRAPH TO PROJECT SCHEDULE

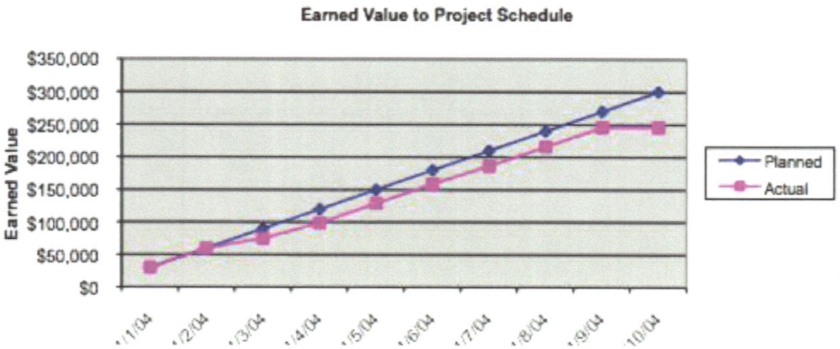

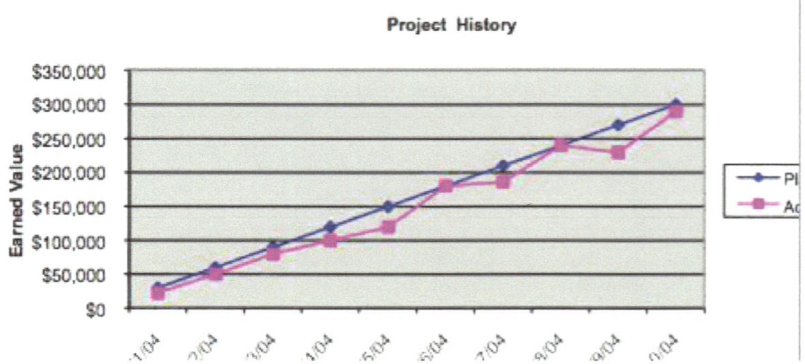

ITS Relocation Project WBS
Date:4/21/12
Revision 1.0

ID		Task Name	Program	Duration	Start	Finish
1		**1 ITS RELOCATION PROGRAM**	**RELOC**	**278.4 days**	**1/2/06**	**1/25/07**
2	✓	**1.1 Vision/Scope (PM Initiation & Planning Phase)**	**RELOC**	**180 days**	**1/2/06**	**9/8/06**
3	✓	1.1.1 Evaluate corporate business objectives	RELOC	60 days	1/2/06	3/24/06
4	✓	1.1.2 Determine technology goals and objectives	RELOC	60 days	1/2/06	3/24/06
5	✓	1.1.3 Formulate preliminary cost/benefit analysis	RELOC	60 days	1/2/06	3/24/06
6	✓	1.1.4 Determine high level project scope	RELOC	60 days	1/2/06	3/24/06
7	✓	1.1.5 Determine major milestones	RELOC	1 day	3/27/06	3/27/06
8	✓	1.1.6 Secure executive sponsorship/funding	RELOC	2 days	3/28/06	3/29/06
9	✓	1.1.7 Develop PDT Benefit VOIP Presentation	RELOC	5 days	3/30/06	4/5/06
10	✓	1.1.8 Create Project Charter	RELOC	1 day	4/6/06	4/6/06
11	✓	1.1.9 Vision/scope complete	RELOC	0 days	4/6/06	4/6/06
12	✓	1.1.10 Create Scope Statement for ITS Relocation Program	RELOC	1 day	4/7/06	4/7/06
13	✓	1.1.11 Approval of Exchange and Network Migration for XYZ	RELOC	10 days	8/8/06	8/21/06
14	✓	1.1.12 Create WBS	RELOC	45 days	4/7/06	6/8/06
15	✓	1.1.13 Create Network Diagram	RELOC	45 days	4/7/06	6/8/06
16	✓	1.1.14 Estimate Time and Cost	RELOC	45 days	4/7/06	6/8/06
17	✓	1.1.15 Determine Critical Path	RELOC	60 days	4/7/06	6/29/06
18	✓	1.1.16 Develop Schedule	RELOC	60 days	4/7/06	6/29/06
19	✓	**1.1.17 Finalize Team and Resource Mangement Plan**	**RELOC**	**5.69 days**	**4/14/06**	**4/21/06**
36	✓	**1.1.18 Develop Budget**	**RELOC**	**63 days**	**4/14/06**	**7/11/06**
44	✓	**1.1.19 Define Communication Strategy**	**RELOC**	**2 days**	**6/21/06**	**6/23/06**
51	✓	**1.1.20 Perform Risk Assessment**	**RELOC**	**2 days**	**6/22/06**	**6/26/06**
58	✓	**1.1.21 Create Procurement Plan**	**RELOC**	**39 days**	**7/18/06**	**9/8/06**
59	✓	1.1.21.1 Create RFQ for VOIP Solution	RELOC	10 days	7/18/06	7/31/06
60	✓	1.1.21.2 Appoval of XYZ Network Migration	RELOC	1 day	8/31/06	8/31/06
61	✓	1.1.21.3 Procure TM Resources for XYZ AD & Exchange Migration	RELOC	6 days	8/14/06	9/8/06
62	✓	1.1.22 Finalizde Project Plan	RELOC	0 days	8/17/06	8/17/06
63	✓	1.1.23 Hold Kickoff Meeting	RELOC	0 days	8/14/06	8/14/06
64		**1.2 Planning (PM Execution Phase)**	**RELOC**	**64 days**	**8/8/06**	**11/3/06**
65	✓	**1.2.1 Needs Assessment of XYZ Computing Environment (XYZ)**	**RELOC**	**10 days**	**8/31/06**	**9/14/06**
66	✓	1.2.1.1 Detail business organizational requirements	RELOC	10 days	9/1/06	9/14/06
67	✓	1.2.1.2 Detail geographic considerations	RELOC	10 days	9/1/06	9/14/06
68	✓	1.2.1.3 Detail key business processes	RELOC	10 days	9/1/06	9/14/06
69	✓	1.2.1.4 Detail information architecture/flow	RELOC	10 days	9/1/06	9/14/06
70	✓	1.2.1.5 Detail current messaging architecture	RELOC	10 days	9/1/06	9/14/06
71	✓	1.2.1.6 Detail current collaboration architecture	RELOC	10 days	9/1/06	9/14/06
72	✓	1.2.1.7 Detail application requirements	RELOC	10 days	9/1/06	9/14/06
73	✓	1.2.1.8 Detail technology architecture	RELOC	10 days	9/1/06	9/14/06
74	✓	1.2.1.9 Detail server hardware and software inventory	RELOC	10 days	9/1/06	9/14/06
75	✓	1.2.1.10 Detail client hardware and software inventory	RELOC	10 days	9/1/06	9/14/06
76	✓	1.2.1.11 Detail current and future information technology standards	RELOC	10 days	9/1/06	9/14/06
77	✓	1.2.1.12 Detail current administrative/service delivery model	RELOC	10 days	9/1/06	9/14/06
78	✓	1.2.1.13 Document current computing environment	RELOC	10 days	9/1/06	9/14/06
79	✓	1.2.1.14 Needs Assessment of XYZ Computing Environment (XYZ) complete	RELOC	0 days	8/31/06	8/31/06
80	✓	**1.2.2 Identify Coexistence Strategies between XYZ and XYZ**	**RELOC**	**2 days**	**9/14/06**	**9/18/06**
81	✓	1.2.2.1 Identify interoperability issues within the company (for example, operating systems supported, topology, protocol)	RELOC	2 days	9/15/06	9/18/06
82	✓	1.2.2.2 Identify coexistence strategies complete	RELOC	0 days	9/14/06	9/14/06
83	✓	1.2.3 Procure Migration Tools for AD & Exchange 2003 Migration	RELOC	5 days	9/1/06	9/7/06
84	✓	1.2.4 Train the team in Windows AD & Exchange 2003 Migration Tool	RELOC	3 days	9/8/06	9/12/06
85	✓	**1.2.5 Planning for Active Directory (XYZ using Migration Tool)**	**RELOC**	**6 days**	**9/14/06**	**9/22/06**
86	✓	1.2.5.1 Review current configuration documents and define a lab model	RELOC	4 days	9/15/06	9/20/06
87	✓	1.2.5.2 Select one or more lab locations	RELOC	4 hrs	9/15/06	9/15/06
88	✓	1.2.5.3 Determine lab space and environmental requirements	RELOC	4 days	9/15/06	9/20/06
89	✓	1.2.5.4 Determine power and network connection requirements	RELOC	4 hrs	9/15/06	9/15/06
90	✓	1.2.5.5 Design and document logical and physical configuration for the lab	RELOC	2 days	9/15/06	9/18/06
91	✓	1.2.5.6 Determine hardware requirements	RELOC	4 hrs	9/15/06	9/15/06
92	✓	1.2.5.7 Determine software requirements, including business applications and tools	RELOC	4 days	9/15/06	9/20/06
93	✓	1.2.5.8 Determine who needs to use the lab	RELOC	2 hrs	9/15/06	9/15/06
94	✓	1.2.5.9 Determine database requirements	RELOC	4 days	9/15/06	9/20/06
95	✓	1.2.5.10 Determine wiring and network tap plans	RELOC	2 hrs	9/15/06	9/15/06
96	✓	1.2.5.11 Acquire hardware, including cables and software	RELOC	2 hrs	9/15/06	9/15/06
97	✓	1.2.5.12 Acquire workspace equipment (for example, desks, chairs, white boards, cork boards, lamps, telephones, and shelving)	RELOC	2 hrs	9/15/06	9/15/06
98	✓	1.2.5.13 Build and configure the network	RELOC	4 days	9/15/06	9/20/06
99	✓	1.2.5.14 Test network connectivity	RELOC	2 hrs	9/15/06	9/15/06
100	✓	1.2.5.15 Build and configure the servers	RELOC	4 days	9/15/06	9/20/06
101	✓	1.2.5.16 Install applications and build databases on the servers	RELOC	6 days	9/15/06	9/22/06
102	✓	1.2.5.17 Install testing and administrative tools	RELOC	4 days	9/15/06	9/20/06
103	✓	1.2.5.18 Build and configure the client computers	RELOC	4 days	9/15/06	9/20/06
104	✓	1.2.5.19 Install applications on the client computers	RELOC	4 days	9/15/06	9/20/06
105	✓	1.2.5.20 Test all the lab components	RELOC	4 days	9/15/06	9/20/06
106	✓	1.2.5.21 Assign a lab manager	RELOC	4 days	9/15/06	9/20/06
107	✓	1.2.5.22 Define a change control process for the lab	RELOC	2 days	9/15/06	9/18/06
108	✓	1.2.5.23 Create, test, and document the lab restore process	RELOC	4 days	9/15/06	9/20/06
109	✓	1.2.5.24 Establish test lab requirement complete	RELOC	0 days	9/14/06	9/14/06
110			**AD**	**14 days**	**9/1/06**	**9/20/06**
111		**1.2.6.1 Plan Active Directory Deployment**	**AD**	**13 days**	**9/1/06**	**9/19/06**
112		**1.2.6.1.1 Determine Active Directory and Domain Namespace**	**AD**	**5 days**	**9/1/06**	**9/7/06**
113	✓	1.2.6.1.1.1 Map business goals to Active Directory features	AD	5 days	9/1/06	9/7/06
114	✓	**1.2.6.1.1.2 Design Active Directory Forest Plan**	**AD**	**5 days**	**9/1/06**	**9/7/06**
115	✓	1.2.6.1.1.2.1 Determine the number of forests for the network	AD	5 days	9/1/06	9/7/06
116	✓	1.2.6.1.1.2.2 Define a forest change control policy	AD	5 days	9/1/06	9/7/06

ID		Task Name	Program	Duration	Start	Finish
117	✓	**1.2.6.1.1.2.3 Document Impact Considerations of Changes to Forest after Deployment**	**AD**	**5 days**	**9/1/06**	**9/7/06**
118	✓	1.2.6.1.1.2.3.1 Define schema change policy	AD	5 days	9/1/06	9/7/06
119	✓	1.2.6.1.1.2.3.2 Define forest to forest trusts	AD	5 days	9/1/06	9/7/06
120	✓	1.2.6.1.1.2.3.3 Define configuration change policy	AD	5 days	9/1/06	9/7/06
121	✓	1.2.6.1.1.2.4 Document forest plan	AD	5 days	9/1/06	9/7/06
122		**1.2.6.1.1.3 Design Active Directory Domain Plan**	**AD**	**5 days**	**9/1/06**	**9/7/06**
123	✓	1.2.6.1.1.3.1 Determine the Number of Domains in Each Forest	AD	5 days	9/1/06	9/7/06
124	✓	**1.2.6.1.1.3.2 Evaluate Domains Model**	**AD**	**5 days**	**9/1/06**	**9/7/06**
125	✓	1.2.6.1.1.3.2.1 Evaluate preserving existing Windows NT 4 domains	AD	5 days	9/1/06	9/7/06
126	✓	1.2.6.1.1.3.2.2 Evaluate physical partitioning considerations	AD	5 days	9/1/06	9/7/06
127	✓	1.2.6.1.1.3.3 Assign a Domain Name System (DNS) name to each domain to create domain hierarchy	AD	5 hrs	9/1/06	9/1/06
128	✓	1.2.6.1.1.3.4 Document impact considerations of changes to domain after deployment	AD	5 days	9/1/06	9/7/06
129	✓	**1.2.6.1.1.4 Design Active Directory Organizational Unit (OU) Plan**	**AD**	**5 days**	**9/1/06**	**9/7/06**
130	✓	1.2.6.1.1.4.1 Define OUs to delegate administration	AD	5 days	9/1/06	9/7/06
131	✓	1.2.6.1.1.4.2 Define OUs to apply Group Policy	AD	5 days	9/1/06	9/7/06
132	✓	1.2.6.1.1.4.3 Document impact considerations of changes to OU structures after deployment	AD	5 days	9/1/06	9/7/06
133		**1.2.6.1.1.5 Design a Site Topology Plan**	**AD**	**5 days**	**9/1/06**	**9/7/06**
134	✓	**1.2.6.1.1.5.1 Define Sites and Site Links Using the Physical Network Topology**	**AD**	**5 days**	**9/1/06**	**9/7/06**
135	✓	1.2.6.1.1.5.1.1 Obtain physical network topology map	AD	5 days	9/1/06	9/7/06
136	✓	1.2.6.1.1.5.1.2 Create site for each local-area network (LAN) or set of LANs connected by high-speed backbone	AD	5 days	9/1/06	9/7/06
137	✓	1.2.6.1.1.5.1.3 Record internet protocol (IP) subnets for each site	AD	5 days	9/1/06	9/7/06
138	✓	**1.2.6.1.1.5.1.4 Define Site Links**	**AD**	**5 days**	**9/1/06**	**9/7/06**
139	✓	1.2.6.1.1.5.1.4.1 Define site connections with site links	AD	5 days	9/1/06	9/7/06
140	✓	1.2.6.1.1.5.1.4.2 Define replication schedules	AD	5 days	9/1/06	9/7/06
141	✓	1.2.6.1.1.5.1.4.3 Define replication intervals	AD	5 days	9/1/06	9/7/06
142	✓	1.2.6.1.1.5.1.4.4 Define replication transports	AD	5 days	9/1/06	9/7/06
143	✓	1.2.6.1.1.5.1.4.5 Define link costs	AD	5 days	9/1/06	9/7/06
144	✓	**1.2.6.1.1.5.2 Define Server Locations Within Sites**	**AD**	**5 days**	**9/1/06**	**9/7/06**
145	✓	**1.2.6.1.1.5.2.1 Define Additional Domain Controllers**	**AD**	**5 days**	**9/1/06**	**9/7/06**
146	✓	1.2.6.1.1.5.2.1.1 Analyze failover requirements	AD	5 days	9/1/06	9/7/06
147	✓	1.2.6.1.1.5.2.1.2 Analyze domain controller client workload	AD	5 days	9/1/06	9/7/06
148	✓	1.2.6.1.1.5.2.2 Define location of global catalog (GC) servers	AD	5 days	9/1/06	9/7/06
149	✓	1.2.6.1.1.5.2.3 Define location of DNS servers	AD	5 days	9/1/06	9/7/06
150	✓	1.2.6.1.1.5.3 Document impact considerations of changes to site topology after deployment	AD	5 hrs	9/1/06	9/1/06
151		**1.2.6.1.2 Evaluate Migration Strategies**	**AD**	**5 days**	**9/8/06**	**9/14/06**
152	✓	1.2.6.1.2.1 Determine your migration roadmap	AD	5 hrs	9/8/06	9/8/06
153	✓	1.2.6.1.2.2 Determine supported upgrade paths	AD	5 days	9/8/06	9/14/06
154	✓	1.2.6.1.2.3 Examine your existing domain structure	AD	5 days	9/8/06	9/14/06
155	✓	1.2.6.1.2.4 Determine the reasons for restructuring domains	AD	5 days	9/8/06	9/14/06
156	✓	1.2.6.1.2.5 Determine when to restructure domains	AD	5 days	9/8/06	9/14/06
157	✓	1.2.6.1.2.6 Determine your strategy for upgrading domain controllers	AD	5 days	9/8/06	9/14/06
158	✓	1.2.6.1.2.7 Determine the order for upgrading domains	AD	5 days	9/8/06	9/14/06
159	✓	1.2.6.1.2.8 Develop your recovery plan	AD	5 days	9/8/06	9/14/06
160	✓	1.2.6.1.2.9 Determine when to move to native mode	AD	5 hrs	9/8/06	9/8/06
161	✓	**1.2.6.1.3 Evaluate Synchronizing Active Directory with Microsoft Exchange Server**	**AD**	**2 days**	**9/15/06**	**9/18/06**
162	✓	1.2.6.1.3.1 Examine your domain structure and Exchange site topology	AD	2 days	9/15/06	9/18/06
163	✓	1.2.6.1.3.2 Review your network for Active Directory Connector (ADC) deployment	AD	2 days	9/15/06	9/18/06
164	✓	1.2.6.1.3.3 Consider specific network requirements	AD	2 days	9/15/06	9/18/06
165	✓	**1.2.6.1.4 Determine which Directory Service (DS) You Will Manage Objects From**	**AD**	**1 day**	**9/19/06**	**9/19/06**
166	✓	1.2.6.1.4.1 Evaluate administration of objects from Active Directory	AD	1 day	9/19/06	9/19/06
167	✓	1.2.6.1.4.2 Evaluate administration of objects from Exchange Server 2000 Directory Service	AD	1 day	9/19/06	9/19/06
168	✓	1.2.6.1.4.3 Define objects for directory synchronization	AD	1 day	9/19/06	9/19/06
169	✓	1.2.6.1.4.4 Map Exchange containers with Active Directory OUs	AD	1 day	9/19/06	9/19/06
170	✓	1.2.6.1.4.5 Design connection agreements	AD	1 day	9/19/06	9/19/06
171	✓	1.2.6.1.4.6 Document your ADC connection plan strategy/standards	AD	1 day	9/19/06	9/19/06
172	✓	1.2.6.1.5 Plan Active Directory deployment complete	AD	0 days	9/18/06	9/18/06
173		**1.2.6.2 Remediate Risk Assessment**	**AD**	**2 days**	**9/18/06**	**9/20/06**
174	✓	1.2.6.2.1 Review risk assessment document	AD	2 days	9/19/06	9/20/06
175	✓	1.2.6.2.2 Identify solutions	AD	2 days	9/19/06	9/20/06
176	✓	1.2.6.2.3 Communicate to project sponsor, senior management, and project members	AD	2 days	9/19/06	9/20/06
177	✓	1.2.6.2.4 Evaluate risk as part of day-to-day project management	AD	2 days	9/19/06	9/20/06
178	✓	1.2.6.2.5 Remediate risk assessment complete	AD	0 days	9/18/06	9/18/06
179	✓	**1.2.6.3 Develop Communications**	**AD**	**2 days**	**9/19/06**	**9/20/06**
180	✓	1.2.6.3.1 Review communications strategy/standards	AD	2 days	9/19/06	9/20/06
181	✓	1.2.6.3.2 Develop communication materials	AD	2 days	9/19/06	9/20/06
182	✓	1.2.6.3.3 Review communications materials	AD	2 days	9/19/06	9/20/06
183	✓	1.2.6.3.4 Approve communications strategy and materials	AD	2 days	9/19/06	9/20/06
184	✓	1.2.6.3.5 Develop communications complete	AD	2 days	9/19/06	9/20/06
185	✓	**1.2.6.4 Develop Education/Training**	**AD**	**2 days**	**9/19/06**	**9/20/06**
186	✓	1.2.6.4.1 Review training strategy/standards	AD	2 days	9/19/06	9/20/06
187	✓	1.2.6.4.2 Develop/acquire training materials	AD	2 days	9/19/06	9/20/06
188	✓	1.2.6.4.3 Review education materials	AD	2 days	9/19/06	9/20/06
189	✓	1.2.6.4.4 Approve education strategy and materials	AD	2 days	9/19/06	9/20/06
190	✓	1.2.6.4.5 Develop education/training complete	AD	2 days	9/19/06	9/20/06
191	✓	1.2.6.5 AD Planning Complete	AD	0 days	9/18/06	9/18/06
192		**1.2.7 Plan Exchange 2003 Development (XYZ using Migration Tool)**	**Ex2003**	**44.6 days**	**8/9/06**	**10/10/06**
193		**1.2.7.1 Identify Detailed Exchange 2003 Architecture**	**Ex2003**	**2 days**	**8/31/06**	**9/4/06**
194	✓	**1.2.7.1.1 Identify Exchange Server Types and Numbers**	**Ex2003**	**2 days**	**9/1/06**	**9/4/06**
195	✓	1.2.7.1.1.1 Identify mailbox servers	Ex2003	2 days	9/1/06	9/4/06
196	✓	1.2.7.1.1.2 Identify public folder servers	Ex2003	2 days	9/1/06	9/4/06
197	✓	1.2.7.1.1.3 Identify connector servers	Ex2003	2 days	9/1/06	9/4/06

ID		Task Name	Program	Duration	Start	Finish
198	✓	**1.2.7.1.1.4 Real-Time Collaboration Servers**	**Ex2003**	**2 days**	**9/1/06**	**9/4/06**
199	✓	1.2.7.1.1.4.1 Identify data conferencing servers	Ex2003	2 days	9/1/06	9/4/06
200	✓	1.2.7.1.1.4.2 Identify video conferencing servers	Ex2003	2 days	9/1/06	9/4/06
201	✓	1.2.7.1.1.4.3 Identify instant messaging servers	Ex2003	2 days	9/1/06	9/4/06
202	✓	1.2.7.1.1.4.4 Identify chat servers	Ex2003	2 days	9/1/06	9/4/06
203	✓	1.2.7.1.2 Identify exchange server types and numbers complete	Ex2003	0 days	8/31/06	8/31/06
204	✓	1.2.7.2 Identify hardware configurations for server types	Ex2003	2 days	9/1/06	9/4/06
205	✓	1.2.7.3 Identify optimal network configuration/location	Ex2003	2 days	9/1/06	9/4/06
206	✓	1.2.7.4 Identify detailed Exchange 2003 architecture complete	Ex2003	0 days	9/4/06	9/4/06
207	✓	**1.2.7.5 Evaluate Exchange Migration Strategies**	**Ex2003**	**2 days**	**9/5/06**	**9/6/06**
208	✓	1.2.7.5.1 Determine your migration roadmap	Ex2003	2 days	9/5/06	9/6/06
209	✓	1.2.7.5.2 Determine supported upgrade paths	Ex2003	2 days	9/5/06	9/6/06
210	✓	1.2.7.5.3 Examine your existing domain structure	Ex2003	2 days	9/5/06	9/6/06
211	✓	1.2.7.5.4 Examine your exchange site structure	Ex2003	2 days	9/5/06	9/6/06
212	✓	1.2.7.5.5 Identify architecture modifications for Windows 2003/Exchange 2003	Ex2003	2 days	9/5/06	9/6/06
213	✓	**1.2.7.6 Mixed Environment Considerations**	**Ex2003**	**2 days**	**9/7/06**	**9/8/06**
214	✓	1.2.7.6.1 Evaluate active directory connector	Ex2003	2 days	9/7/06	9/8/06
215	✓	1.2.7.6.2 Evaluate routing in a mixed environment	Ex2003	2 days	9/7/06	9/8/06
216	✓	1.2.7.6.3 Mixed environment considerations complete	Ex2003	2 days	9/7/06	9/8/06
217	✓	**1.2.7.7 Evaluate Synchronizing Active Directory with Exchange 5.5**	**Ex2003**	**2 days**	**9/11/06**	**9/12/06**
218	✓	1.2.7.7.1 Examine your domain structure and Exchange site topology	Ex2003	2 days	9/11/06	9/12/06
219	✓	1.2.7.7.2 Review your network for Active Directory deployment	Ex2003	2 days	9/11/06	9/12/06
220	✓	1.2.7.7.3 Consider specific network requirements	Ex2003	2 days	9/11/06	9/12/06
221		**1.2.7.8 Determine Which Directory Service You Will Manage Objects From**	**Ex2003**	**2 days**	**9/12/06**	**9/14/06**
222	✓	1.2.7.8.1 Evaluate administration of objects from Active Directory	Ex2003	2 days	9/13/06	9/14/06
223	✓	1.2.7.8.2 Evaluate administration of objects from Exchange Server 5.5 directory service	Ex2003	2 days	9/13/06	9/14/06
224	✓	1.2.7.8.3 Define objects for directory synchronization	Ex2003	2 days	9/13/06	9/14/06
225	✓	1.2.7.8.4 Map Exchange containers with Windows 2000 organizational units (OUs)	Ex2003	2 days	9/13/06	9/14/06
226	✓	1.2.7.8.5 Design connection agreements	Ex2003	2 days	9/13/06	9/14/06
227	✓	1.2.7.8.6 Document your ADC connection plan strategy/standards	Ex2003	2 days	9/13/06	9/14/06
228	✓	1.2.7.8.7 Synchronizing Active Directory with Exchange 5.5 complete	Ex2003	0 days	9/12/06	9/12/06
229		**1.2.7.9 Identify Coexistence Strategies**	**Ex2003**	**3 days**	**9/14/06**	**9/19/06**
230	✓	1.2.7.9.1 Identify interoperability issues within the company (for example, operating systems supported, topology, protocol)	Ex2003	3 days	9/15/06	9/19/06
231	✓	1.2.7.9.2 Identify interoperability issues with the organization's partners (for example, topology, protocol)	Ex2003	3 days	9/15/06	9/19/06
232	✓	1.2.7.9.3 Identify interoperability in Exchange 2003/Exchange 5.5 mixed environments and down level NT 4.0 domains	Ex2003	3 days	9/15/06	9/19/06
233		**1.2.7.9.4 Identify Upgrade Exchange 5.5 Upgrade Scenarios**	**Ex2003**	**3 days**	**9/14/06**	**9/19/06**
234	✓	1.2.7.9.4.1 Identify in-place server upgrade	Ex2003	3 days	9/15/06	9/19/06
235	✓	1.2.7.9.4.2 Move mailbox upgrade	Ex2003	3 days	9/15/06	9/19/06
236	✓	1.2.7.9.4.3 Consolidate servers	Ex2003	3 days	9/15/06	9/19/06
237	✓	1.2.7.9.4.4 Identify upgrade Exchange 5.5 upgrade scenarios complete	Ex2003	0 days	9/14/06	9/14/06
238	✓	**1.2.7.9.5 Identify Interoperability Scenarios**	**Ex2003**	**3 days**	**9/15/06**	**9/19/06**
239	✓	1.2.7.9.5.1 Exchange 2003 in a separate organization from Exchange 5.5	Ex2003	3 days	9/15/06	9/19/06
240	✓	1.2.7.9.5.2 Exchange 2003 in the same organization as Exchange 5.5	Ex2003	3 days	9/15/06	9/19/06
241	✓	**1.2.7.9.5.3 Exchange 2003 in the Same Exchange 5.5 Site**	**Ex2003**	**3 days**	**9/15/06**	**9/19/06**
242	✓	1.2.7.9.5.3.1 Exchange 2003 messaging in an Exchange 5.5 site	Ex2003	3 days	9/15/06	9/19/06
243	✓	1.2.7.9.5.3.2 Exchange 2003 directory in an Exchange 5.5 site	Ex2003	3 days	9/15/06	9/19/06
244	✓	1.2.7.9.5.4 Exchange 2003 in multiple Exchange 5.5 sites	Ex2003	3 days	9/15/06	9/19/06
245	✓	1.2.7.9.6 Identify coexistence strategies complete	Ex2003	0 days	9/14/06	9/14/06
246		**1.2.7.10 Identify Exchange 2003 Connector Strategy**	**Ex2003**	**15 days**	**9/19/06**	**10/10/06**
247	✓	1.2.7.10.1 Connector migration considerations	Ex2003	15 days	9/20/06	10/10/06
248		**1.2.7.10.2 Mail System Connectors**	**Ex2003**	**3 days**	**9/19/06**	**9/22/06**
249	✓	1.2.7.10.2.1 Identify Exchange Lotus Notes connector	Ex2003	3 days	9/20/06	9/22/06
250	✓	1.2.7.10.2.2 Identify Exchange MSMail connector	Ex2003	3 days	9/20/06	9/22/06
251	✓	1.2.7.10.2.3 Identify Exchange Lotus cc:Mail connector	Ex2003	3 days	9/20/06	9/22/06
252	✓	1.2.7.10.2.4 Identify Exchange Novell GroupWise connector	Ex2003	3 days	9/20/06	9/22/06
253	✓	1.2.7.10.2.5 Mail systems connectors complete	Ex2003	0 days	9/19/06	9/19/06
254		**1.2.7.10.3 Legacy Connectors Strategy**	**Ex2003**	**1.5 days**	**9/19/06**	**9/21/06**
255	✓	1.2.7.10.3.1 Exchange-profs	Ex2003	1.5 days	9/20/06	9/21/06
256	✓	1.2.7.10.3.2 Exchange-SNADS	Ex2003	1.5 days	9/20/06	9/21/06
257	✓	1.2.7.10.3.3 Legacy connectors strategy complete	Ex2003	0 days	9/19/06	9/19/06
258	✓	1.2.7.10.4 Identify inter-organizational replication and directory synchronization considerations	Ex2003	1.5 days	9/20/06	9/21/06
259	✓	1.2.7.10.5 Evaluate exchange migration strategies complete	Ex2003	0 days	9/19/06	9/19/06
260	✓	**1.2.7.11 Client Strategy, Standards and Management**	**Ex2003**	**3 days**	**9/20/06**	**9/22/06**
261	✓	1.2.7.11.1 Define client strategy (for example, Outlook, OWA, etc.)	Ex2003	3 days	9/20/06	9/22/06
262	✓	1.2.7.11.2 Define client application requirements based on job function	Ex2003	3 days	9/20/06	9/22/06
263	✓	1.2.7.11.3 Define client configuration restrictions based on job function	Ex2003	3 days	9/20/06	9/22/06
264	✓	1.2.7.11.4 Configure approved client hardware (laptops and desktops)	Ex2003	3 days	9/20/06	9/22/06
265	✓	1.2.7.11.5 Configure basic Outlook 2003/Outlook Web Access user interface options	Ex2003	3 days	9/20/06	9/22/06
266	✓	1.2.7.11.6 Determine multilanguage options	Ex2003	3 days	9/20/06	9/22/06
267	✓	1.2.7.11.7 Determine accessibility options	Ex2003	3 days	9/20/06	9/22/06
268	✓	1.2.7.11.8 Configure applications based on client requirements and administrative guidelines	Ex2003	3 days	9/20/06	9/22/06
269	✓	1.2.7.11.9 Document client strategy/standards	Ex2003	3 days	9/20/06	9/22/06
270		**1.2.7.12 Client Change Configuration Strategy**	**Ex2003**	**2 days**	**9/22/06**	**9/26/06**
271	✓	1.2.7.12.1 Define user and organization change and configuration management needs	Ex2003	2 days	9/25/06	9/26/06
272	✓	1.2.7.12.2 Evaluate and select desired Exchange 2003 change and configuration management features	Ex2003	2 days	9/25/06	9/26/06
273	✓	1.2.7.12.3 Evaluate other applications for software distribution, etc. (for example, SMS, Tivoli)	Ex2003	2 days	9/25/06	9/26/06
274	✓	1.2.7.12.4 Configure server shares and group policy for user data management	Ex2003	2 days	9/25/06	9/26/06
275	✓	1.2.7.12.5 Configure server shares and group policy for user settings management	Ex2003	2 days	9/25/06	9/26/06
276	✓	1.2.7.12.6 Client change configuration strategy complete	Ex2003	0 days	9/22/06	9/22/06
277	✓	1.2.7.12.7 Client strategy, standards, and management complete	Ex2003	0 days	9/22/06	9/22/06
278	✓	**1.2.7.13 Security Considerations**	**Ex2003**	**15 days**	**9/20/06**	**10/10/06**

ID		Task Name	Program	Duration	Start	Finish
279	✓	**1.2.7.13.1 Operational Security**	**Ex2003**	**15 days**	**9/20/06**	**10/10/06**
280	✓	1.2.7.13.1.1 Identify the security risks that apply to your architecture	Ex2003	15 days	9/20/06	10/10/06
281	✓	1.2.7.13.1.2 Assess solutions for identifiable security risks	Ex2003	15 days	9/20/06	10/10/06
282	✓	1.2.7.13.1.3 Determine what part of the user community needs to use strong authentication for interactive or remote access logon	Ex2003	15 days	9/20/06	10/10/06
283	✓	1.2.7.13.1.4 Define policy for enabling remote access services	Ex2003	15 days	9/20/06	10/10/06
284	✓	1.2.7.13.1.5 Develop procedures/communication regarding remote access procedures, including connection methods	Ex2003	15 days	9/20/06	10/10/06
285	✓	1.2.7.13.1.6 Determine the local security policy requirements for different categories of systems on the network	Ex2003	15 days	9/20/06	10/10/06
286	✓	1.2.7.13.1.7 Develop a test plan to verify your common business applications run correctly under properly configured secure systems	Ex2003	15 days	9/20/06	10/10/06
287	✓	1.2.7.13.1.8 Define what additional applications are needed that provide enhanced security features to meet your organization security objectives	Ex2003	15 days	9/20/06	10/10/06
288	✓	1.2.7.13.1.9 State your policies for securing the administrator account and the administration consoles	Ex2003	15 days	9/20/06	10/10/06
289	✓	1.2.7.13.1.10 Identify the situations where you plan to delegate administrator control for specific tasks	Ex2003	15 days	9/20/06	10/10/06
290	✓	1.2.7.13.1.11 Identify your policies regarding auditing, including staffing	Ex2003	15 days	9/20/06	10/10/06
291	✓	1.2.7.13.1.12 Document security strategy/standards	Ex2003	15 days	9/20/06	10/10/06
292	✓	1.2.7.13.1.13 Operational security complete	Ex2003	0 days	10/10/06	10/10/06
293	✓	**1.2.7.14 E-mail Security**	**Ex2003**	**3 days**	**8/9/06**	**8/14/06**
294	✓	**1.2.7.14.1 Basic Types of Security**	**Ex2003**	**3 days**	**8/9/06**	**8/14/06**
295	✓	1.2.7.14.1.1 Consider S/MIME and PGP	Ex2003	3 days	8/9/06	8/14/06
296	✓	1.2.7.14.1.2 Consider message body encryption	Ex2003	3 days	8/9/06	8/14/06
297	✓	1.2.7.14.1.3 Consider digital signatures	Ex2003	3 days	8/9/06	8/14/06
298	✓	1.2.7.14.1.4 Consider key management service	Ex2003	3 days	8/9/06	8/14/06
299	✓	1.2.7.14.1.5 Consider certificate server	Ex2003	3 days	8/9/06	8/14/06
300	✓	1.2.7.14.1.6 Basic types of security complete	Ex2003	0 days	8/14/06	8/14/06
301	✓	**1.2.7.14.2 Security Planning**	**Ex2003**	**3 days**	**8/9/06**	**8/14/06**
302	✓	1.2.7.14.2.1 Consider intracompany	Ex2003	3 days	8/9/06	8/14/06
303	✓	1.2.7.14.2.2 Consider intercompany	Ex2003	3 days	8/9/06	8/14/06
304	✓	1.2.7.14.2.3 Determine trusted third party	Ex2003	3 days	8/9/06	8/14/06
305	✓	1.2.7.14.2.4 Security planning complete	Ex2003	0 days	8/14/06	8/14/06
306	✓	1.2.7.14.3 Security considerations complete	Ex2003	0 days	8/14/06	8/14/06
307	✓	**1.2.7.15 Antivirus Protection Considerations**	**Ex2003**	**3 days**	**8/14/06**	**8/17/06**
308	✓	1.2.7.15.1 Determine backbone infrastructure virus strategy	Ex2003	3 days	8/14/06	8/17/06
309	✓	1.2.7.15.2 Determine local server virus strategy	Ex2003	3 days	8/14/06	8/17/06
310	✓	1.2.7.15.3 Determine desktop virus strategy	Ex2003	3 days	8/14/06	8/17/06
311	✓	1.2.7.15.4 Antivirus protection considerations complete	Ex2003	0 days	8/17/06	8/17/06
312	✓	**1.2.7.16 Mail Enabled Application Compatibility with Exchange 2003**	**Ex2003**	**3 days**	**9/1/06**	**9/5/06**
313	✓	1.2.7.16.1 Review detailed application inventory document	Ex2003	3 days	9/1/06	9/5/06
314	✓	1.2.7.16.2 Consider reducing the number of applications you use and developing desktop standards	Ex2003	3 days	9/1/06	9/5/06
315	✓	1.2.7.16.3 Develop a system for prioritizing applications	Ex2003	3 days	9/1/06	9/5/06
316	✓	1.2.7.16.4 Prioritize the applications by how critical they are to running your business	Ex2003	3 days	9/1/06	9/5/06
317	✓	1.2.7.16.5 Write a test plan, including test methodology, lab and test resource requirements, and schedule	Ex2003	3 days	9/1/06	9/5/06
318	✓	1.2.7.16.6 Develop a test tracking system for capturing and reporting test results	Ex2003	3 days	9/1/06	9/5/06
319	✓	1.2.7.16.7 Schedule test events	Ex2003	3 days	9/1/06	9/5/06
320	✓	1.2.7.16.8 Test applications and record results	Ex2003	3 days	9/1/06	9/5/06
321	✓	1.2.7.16.9 Report on testing progress	Ex2003	3 days	9/1/06	9/5/06
322	✓	1.2.7.16.10 Resolve application incompatibilities	Ex2003	3 days	9/1/06	9/5/06
323	✓	1.2.7.16.11 Application compatibility with Exchange 2003 complete	Ex2003	0 days	9/5/06	9/5/06
324	✓	**1.2.7.17 Terminal Services**	**Ex2003**	**2 days**	**9/6/06**	**9/7/06**
325	✓	1.2.7.17.1 Determine how terminal services benefit the business environment	Ex2003	2 days	9/6/06	9/7/06
326	✓	1.2.7.17.2 Determine licensing requirements	Ex2003	2 days	9/6/06	9/7/06
327	✓	1.2.7.17.3 Document the existing computing environment	Ex2003	2 days	9/6/06	9/7/06
328	✓	1.2.7.17.4 Develop a plan for implementing terminal services including networking, security, and domain structure	Ex2003	2 days	9/6/06	9/7/06
329	✓	1.2.7.17.5 Establish guidelines and standards for server deployment including CPU, storage, and so on	Ex2003	2 days	9/6/06	9/7/06
330	✓	1.2.7.17.6 Document detailed terminal services strategy/standards	Ex2003	2 days	9/6/06	9/7/06
331	✓	1.2.7.17.7 Terminal services complete	Ex2003	0 days	9/7/06	9/7/06
332		**1.2.7.18 Infrastructure Change Configuration Strategy**	**Ex2003**	**3 days**	**9/19/06**	**9/22/06**
333	✓	1.2.7.18.1 Define user and organization change and configuration management needs	Ex2003	3 days	9/20/06	9/22/06
334	✓	1.2.7.18.2 Evaluate and select desired Exchange 2003 change and configuration management features	Ex2003	3 days	9/20/06	9/22/06
335	✓	1.2.7.18.3 Evaluate other applications for software distribution, etc. (for example, SMS, Tivoli)	Ex2003	3 days	9/20/06	9/22/06
336	✓	1.2.7.18.4 Infrastructure change configuration strategy complete	Ex2003	0 days	9/19/06	9/19/06
337	✓	**1.2.7.19 Remediate Risk Assessment**	**Ex2003**	**3 days**	**9/20/06**	**9/22/06**
338	✓	1.2.7.19.1 Review risk assessment document	Ex2003	3 days	9/20/06	9/22/06
339	✓	1.2.7.19.2 Identify solutions	Ex2003	3 days	9/20/06	9/22/06
340	✓	1.2.7.19.3 Communicate to project sponsor, senior management, and project members	Ex2003	3 days	9/20/06	9/22/06
341	✓	1.2.7.19.4 Evaluate risk as part of day-to-day project management	Ex2003	3 days	9/20/06	9/22/06
342	✓	1.2.7.19.5 Remediate risk assessment complete	Ex2003	0 days	9/22/06	9/22/06
343	✓	**1.2.7.20 Develop Communications**	**Ex2003**	**3 days**	**9/20/06**	**9/22/06**
344	✓	1.2.7.20.1 Review communications strategy/standards	Ex2003	3 days	9/20/06	9/22/06
345	✓	1.2.7.20.2 Develop communication materials	Ex2003	3 days	9/20/06	9/22/06
346	✓	1.2.7.20.3 Review communications materials	Ex2003	3 days	9/20/06	9/22/06
347	✓	1.2.7.20.4 Approve communications strategy and materials	Ex2003	3 days	9/20/06	9/22/06
348	✓	1.2.7.20.5 Communication complete	Ex2003	0 days	9/22/06	9/22/06
349	✓	**1.2.7.21 Develop Education/Training**	**Ex2003**	**3 days**	**9/20/06**	**9/22/06**
350	✓	1.2.7.21.1 Review training strategy/standards	Ex2003	3 days	9/20/06	9/22/06
351	✓	1.2.7.21.2 Develop/acquire training materials	Ex2003	3 days	9/20/06	9/22/06
352	✓	1.2.7.21.3 Review education materials	Ex2003	3 days	9/20/06	9/22/06
353	✓	1.2.7.21.4 Approve education strategy and materials	Ex2003	3 days	9/20/06	9/22/06
354	✓	1.2.7.21.5 Develop training complete	Ex2003	0 days	9/22/06	9/22/06
355	✓	1.2.7.22 Development complete	Ex2003	0 days	9/22/06	9/22/06
356	✓	**1.2.8 LAN and WAN Migration**	**LANWAN**	**60 days**	**8/14/06**	**11/3/06**
357	✓	1.2.8.1 Review business goals/direction/vision	LANWAN	0.5 days	8/14/06	8/14/06

ID	ⓘ	Task Name	Program	Duration	Start	Finish
358	✓	**1.2.8.2 Ready Assessmnet**	**LANWAN**	**4 days**	**8/14/06**	**8/17/06**
359	✓	**1.2.8.2.1 Review Current Infrastructure**	**LANWAN**	**0.25 days**	**8/14/06**	**8/14/06**
360	✓	1.2.8.2.1.1 Review hardware environment	LANWAN	2 hrs	8/14/06	8/14/06
361	✓	1.2.8.2.1.2 Review software environment	LANWAN	2 hrs	8/14/06	8/14/06
362	✓	1.2.8.2.1.3 Review communications environment	LANWAN	2 hrs	8/14/06	8/14/06
363	✓	1.2.8.2.1.4 Review connectivity LAN/WAN	LANWAN	2 hrs	8/14/06	8/14/06
364	✓	1.2.8.2.1.5 Review support environment	LANWAN	2 hrs	8/14/06	8/14/06
365	✓	1.2.8.2.1.6 Review geographic factors	LANWAN	2 hrs	8/14/06	8/14/06
366	✓	1.2.8.2.1.7 Review current infrastructure complete	LANWAN	0 days	8/14/06	8/14/06
367	✓	**1.2.8.2.2 Identify Target Areas for Improvement**	**LANWAN**	**4 days**	**8/14/06**	**8/17/06**
368	✓	1.2.8.2.2.1 Identify hardware improvements	LANWAN	4 days	8/14/06	8/17/06
369	✓	1.2.8.2.2.2 Identify software improvements	LANWAN	4 days	8/14/06	8/17/06
370	✓	1.2.8.2.2.3 Identify communications considerations	LANWAN	4 days	8/14/06	8/17/06
371	✓	1.2.8.2.2.4 Identify connectivity LAN/WAN improvements/issues	LANWAN	4 days	8/14/06	8/17/06
372	✓	1.2.8.2.2.5 Identify support environment improvements/additions	LANWAN	4 days	8/14/06	8/17/06
373	✓	1.2.8.2.2.6 Identify mitigation of geographic factors	LANWAN	4 days	8/14/06	8/17/06
374	✓	1.2.8.2.2.7 Identify target areas for improvement	LANWAN	4 days	8/14/06	8/17/06
375	✓	1.2.8.2.3 Define system requirements	LANWAN	4 days	8/14/06	8/17/06
376	✓	1.2.8.2.4 Define target performance metrics	LANWAN	4 days	8/14/06	8/17/06
377	✓	**1.2.8.2.5 Review Current Market Solution Vendors**	**LANWAN**	**2 days**	**8/14/06**	**8/15/06**
378	✓	1.2.8.2.5.1 Hardware vendors	LANWAN	2 days	8/14/06	8/15/06
379	✓	1.2.8.2.5.2 Software vendors	LANWAN	2 days	8/14/06	8/15/06
380	✓	1.2.8.2.5.3 Communications vendors	LANWAN	2 days	8/14/06	8/15/06
381	✓	1.2.8.2.5.4 Design partners	LANWAN	2 days	8/14/06	8/15/06
382	✓	1.2.8.2.5.5 Implementation partners	LANWAN	2 days	8/14/06	8/15/06
383	✓	1.2.8.2.5.6 Ready Assessment Complete	LANWAN	2 days	8/14/06	8/15/06
384	✓	**1.2.8.3 Needs Assessment for LAN/WAN Migration**	**LANWAN**	**60 days**	**8/14/06**	**11/3/06**
385	✓	**1.2.8.3.1 WAN Migration DS3**	**LANWAN**	**60 days**	**8/14/06**	**11/3/06**
386	✓	**1.2.8.3.1.1 Site Survey**	**LANWAN**	**5 days**	**8/14/06**	**8/18/06**
387	✓	1.2.8.3.1.1.1 Visit 333 S. Wasbash	LANWAN	2.5 days	8/14/06	8/16/06
388	✓	1.2.8.3.1.1.2 Visit 4859 S Wabash (SBC)	LANWAN	5 days	8/14/06	8/18/06
389	✓	**1.2.8.3.1.2 Determine Telecommunication Evaluation**	**LANWAN**	**5 days**	**8/14/06**	**8/18/06**
390	✓	1.2.8.3.1.2.1 Determine DeMarc Extension	LANWAN	5 days	8/14/06	8/18/06
391	✓	1.2.8.3.1.2.2 Determine Cable Jumper Requirements	LANWAN	5 days	8/14/06	8/18/06
392	✓	1.2.8.3.1.2.3 Determine Physical Security	LANWAN	5 days	8/14/06	8/18/06
393	✓	1.2.8.3.1.3 Inventory existing equipment	LANWAN	5 days	8/14/06	8/18/06
394	✓	1.2.8.3.1.4 Document Findings and Report for Procurement of CPE LAN/WAN Equipment	LANWAN	15 days	8/14/06	9/1/06
395	✓	**1.2.8.3.1.5 Review XYZ WAN Design Requirements**	**LANWAN**	**5 days**	**8/14/06**	**8/18/06**
396	✓	1.2.8.3.1.5.1 Remote site location WAN requirements	LANWAN	5 days	8/14/06	8/18/06
397	✓	1.2.8.3.1.5.2 Review IP addressing/routing scheme	LANWAN	5 days	8/14/06	8/18/06
398	✓	1.2.8.3.1.5.3 Router/Switch configs requirements	LANWAN	5 days	8/14/06	8/18/06
399	✓	1.2.8.3.1.5.4 XYZ technical interview	LANWAN	5 days	8/14/06	8/18/06
400	✓	**1.2.8.3.1.6 Contract Amendment**	**LANWAN**	**60 days**	**8/14/06**	**11/3/06**
401	✓	1.2.8.3.1.6.1 Revised Bill of Material (BOM)	LANWAN	5 days	8/14/06	8/18/06
402	✓	1.2.8.3.1.6.2 Submit Request for Design (RFD)	LANWAN	5 days	8/14/06	8/18/06
403	✓	1.2.8.3.1.6.3 Acceptance of Rate Letters	LANWAN	5 days	8/14/06	8/18/06
404	✓	1.2.8.3.1.6.4 Forward Rate letters to contract management	LANWAN	5 days	8/14/06	8/18/06
405	✓	1.2.8.3.1.6.5 Contract amendment documentation	LANWAN	5 days	8/14/06	8/18/06
406	✓	1.2.8.3.1.6.6 AT&T contract amendment approved and signed by XYZ	LANWAN	5 days	8/14/06	8/18/06
407	✓	1.2.8.3.1.6.7 Order submission and process for SONET Modification	LANWAN	60 days	8/14/06	11/3/06
408	✓	1.2.8.3.1.6.8 Order submission to Secure 2000 DID Lines	LANWAN	40 days	8/14/06	10/6/06
409	✓	1.2.8.3.1.6.9 Procure Customer Premises Equipment (CPE) Equipment for SONET RELOCATION	LANWAN	40 days	9/4/06	10/27/06
410	✓	1.2.8.3.1.7 Obtain signoff on deliverables for Planning	LANWAN	0 days	8/14/06	8/14/06
411	✓	1.2.8.3.1.8 Secure approval to proceed	LANWAN	0 days	8/14/06	8/14/06
412	✓	**1.2.8.3.1.9 Needs Analysis for Data/Hardware/Backup**	**LANWAN**	**10 days**	**8/14/06**	**8/25/06**
413	✓	**1.2.8.3.1.9.1 Document on worksheet listing of all server information that will relocate to 333 S. Wasbash**	**LANWAN**	**10 days**	**8/14/06**	**8/25/06**
414	✓	1.2.8.3.1.9.1.1 Identify (hostname, physical and virtual Ip address, Gateway,etc.)	LANWAN	10 days	8/14/06	8/25/06
415	✓	1.2.8.3.1.9.1.2 Application + functionality + Dependency per server to business	LANWAN	10 days	8/14/06	8/25/06
416	✓	1.2.8.3.1.9.1.3 Interface documentation label standard	LANWAN	10 days	8/14/06	8/25/06
417	✓	1.2.8.3.1.9.1.4 Server Interface Assignment	LANWAN	10 days	8/14/06	8/25/06
418	✓	1.2.8.3.1.9.1.5 Chassis and Component hardware details	LANWAN	10 days	8/14/06	8/25/06
419	✓	1.2.8.3.1.9.1.6 Maintanance contract status with part(s) covered	LANWAN	10 days	8/14/06	8/25/06
420	✓	1.2.8.3.1.9.1.7 Maintenance contract Number	LANWAN	10 days	8/14/06	8/25/06
421	✓	1.2.8.3.1.9.1.8 Maintenance support 800 number	LANWAN	10 days	8/14/06	8/25/06
422	✓	1.2.8.3.1.9.1.9 List applications form most to least busness critical	LANWAN	10 days	8/14/06	8/25/06
423	✓	1.2.8.3.1.9.1.10 List XYZ administrator/support persons with contact numbers	LANWAN	10 days	8/14/06	8/25/06
424	✓	**1.2.8.3.1.9.2 Backup Data**	**LANWAN**	**10 days**	**8/14/06**	**8/25/06**
425	✓	1.2.8.3.1.9.2.1 Define method on how backup jobs will be moved to new location	LANWAN	10 days	8/14/06	8/25/06
426	✓	1.2.8.3.1.9.2.2 Test Incremental job and document duration required for job	LANWAN	10 days	8/14/06	8/25/06
427	✓	1.2.8.3.1.9.2.3 Restore incremental backup job, verifying positive confirmation of functionality	LANWAN	10 days	8/14/06	8/25/06
428	✓	1.2.8.3.1.9.2.4 Create incremental backup job via Backup System	LANWAN	10 days	8/14/06	8/25/06
429	✓	**1.2.8.3.1.9.3 Backup Hardware**	**LANWAN**	**10 days**	**8/14/06**	**8/25/06**
430	✓	1.2.8.3.1.9.3.1 Identify spare parts available for servers	LANWAN	10 days	8/14/06	8/25/06
431	✓	1.2.8.3.1.9.3.2 Identify spare parts needed (Critical) and contact Manufacture for leadtime	LANWAN	10 days	8/14/06	8/25/06
432	✓	1.2.8.3.1.9.3.3 Consider renewing server maintenance contracts for hardware replacemnet	LANWAN	10 days	8/14/06	8/25/06
433	✓	**1.2.8.3.1.9.4 Lan/Wan Network**	**LANWAN**	**10 days**	**8/14/06**	**8/25/06**
434	✓	1.2.8.3.1.9.4.1 Verify Ip Address schedma for server equipment	LANWAN	10 days	8/14/06	8/25/06
435	✓	1.2.8.3.1.9.4.2 Verify IP address schema for infrastructure equipment	LANWAN	10 days	8/14/06	8/25/06
436	✓	1.2.8.3.1.9.4.3 Verify IP address schema for printers equipment	LANWAN	10 days	8/14/06	8/25/06
437	✓	1.2.8.3.1.9.4.4 Create logical diagram illustration of system connectivity	LANWAN	10 days	8/14/06	8/25/06
438	✓	1.2.8.3.1.9.4.5 Archive/Backup all switch, router firewall and other infrastructure device configurations	LANWAN	10 days	8/14/06	8/25/06

ID		Task Name	Program	Duration	Start	Finish
439	✓	1.2.8.3.1.9.4.6 Develop test plan for post-cutover tests between local network nodes	LANWAN	10 days	8/14/06	8/25/06
440	✓	1.2.8.3.1.9.4.7 Identify spare equipment to be relocated to 333 S. Wabash	LANWAN	10 days	8/14/06	8/25/06
441	✓	1.2.8.3.1.9.4.8 Systematically reboot infrastrucutre deveices to verify stability	LANWAN	10 days	8/14/06	8/25/06
442	✓	1.2.8.3.1.9.4.9 SONET Verification	LANWAN	10 days	8/14/06	8/25/06
443	✓	1.2.8.3.1.9.4.10 Verify PRI installiation	LANWAN	10 days	8/14/06	8/25/06
444	✓	1.2.8.3.1.9.4.11 Verify DID numbers to be ported	LANWAN	10 days	8/14/06	8/25/06
445	✓	1.2.8.4 LAN WAN Needs Assessment and Analysis complete	LANWAN	0 days	8/14/06	8/14/06
446	✓	**1.2.9 Marketing Telecommunication Campaign**	**MARK**	**33 days**	**8/14/06**	**9/27/06**
447	✓	1.2.9.1 Establish targeted vertical markets	MARK	5 days	8/14/06	8/18/06
448	✓	1.2.9.2 Segment by industry or vertical market	MARK	5 days	8/14/06	8/18/06
449	✓	1.2.9.3 Quantify total available market	MARK	5 days	8/14/06	8/18/06
450	✓	1.2.9.4 Define served available market	MARK	5 days	8/14/06	8/18/06
451	✓	1.2.9.5 Budget realistic response factor	MARK	5 days	8/14/06	8/18/06
452	✓	1.2.9.6 Market research complete	MARK	0 days	8/14/06	8/14/06
453	✓	1.2.9.7 Plan for Physical Move of Hardware and User Services (RFP)	MARK	30 days	8/14/06	9/27/06
454	✓	**1.2.10 Needs Assessment of VOIP Requirements**	**VOIP**	**25 days**	**8/8/06**	**9/11/06**
455	✓	1.2.10.1 Selection of IPT Vendor System and Partner	RELOC	10 days	8/8/06	8/21/06
456	✓	1.2.10.2 Meet with Stakeholders to review Corporate and Critial To Quality (CTQ) objectives	VOIP	1 day	8/22/06	8/22/06
457	✓	1.2.10.3 Document VoIP Functional Requirements	VOIP	1 day	8/22/06	8/22/06
458	✓	1.2.10.4 Document current Departmental Telecom Environment (POTS, ISDN, DSL circuits)	VOIP	1 day	8/22/06	8/22/06
459	✓	**1.2.10.5 Document Needs Assessment of Voice and Data Circuits for all sites moving to 333 S. Wabash**	**VOIP**	**15 days**	**8/22/06**	**9/11/06**
460	✓	1.2.10.5.1 Document Circuit type at each location (T1 or DS1,DSL,PRI,BRI,Analog POTS,etc.)	VOIP	5 days	8/22/06	8/28/06
461	✓	1.2.10.5.2 Quanity of each Circuit	VOIP	5 days	8/22/06	8/28/06
462	✓	1.2.10.5.3 Contract Number	VOIP	5 days	8/22/06	8/28/06
463	✓	1.2.10.5.4 Contract term and Termincation Cost	VOIP	5 days	8/22/06	8/28/06
464	✓	1.2.10.5.5 Carrier contact Name and Number	VOIP	5 days	8/22/06	8/28/06
465	✓	1.2.10.5.6 DID Mapping of Current and New Numbers	VOIP	15 days	8/22/06	9/11/06
466	✓	**1.2.10.5.7 Document all voice, fax numbers to be ported to 333 S. Wabash**	**VOIP**	**5 days**	**8/29/06**	**9/4/06**
467	✓	1.2.10.5.7.1 Toll Free Number(s)	VOIP	5 days	8/29/06	9/4/06
468	✓	1.2.10.5.7.2 Document Analog Number(s)	VOIP	5 days	8/29/06	9/4/06
469	✓	**1.2.11 Relocation Move Hardware Planning**	**RELOC**	**30 days**	**8/14/06**	**9/22/06**
470	✓	**1.2.11.1 Departmental Needs Assessment**	**RELOC**	**10 days**	**8/14/06**	**8/25/06**
471	✓	1.2.11.1.1 Network (Switching)	RELOC	10 days	8/14/06	8/25/06
472	✓	1.2.11.1.2 Carrier (POTS, T1, ISDN)	RELOC	10 days	8/14/06	8/25/06
473	✓	**1.2.11.2 Equipment (Services, Application(s) and Servers**	**RELOC**	**10 days**	**8/14/06**	**8/25/06**
474	✓	1.2.11.2.1 System Access	RELOC	10 days	8/14/06	8/25/06
475	✓	**1.2.11.3 Risk Assessment**	**RELOC**	**10 days**	**8/14/06**	**8/25/06**
476	✓	1.2.11.3.1 Data Recovery	RELOC	10 days	8/14/06	8/25/06
477	✓	1.2.11.3.2 System Turn Down	RELOC	10 days	8/14/06	8/25/06
478	✓	1.2.11.3.3 Damage	RELOC	10 days	8/14/06	8/25/06
479	✓	1.2.11.3.4 Replacement	RELOC	10 days	8/14/06	8/25/06
480	✓	**1.2.11.4 Departmental Inventory**	**RELOC**	**10 days**	**8/14/06**	**8/25/06**
481	✓	1.2.11.4.1 Computers	RELOC	10 days	8/14/06	8/25/06
482	✓	1.2.11.4.2 Servers	RELOC	10 days	8/14/06	8/25/06
483	✓	1.2.11.4.3 Fax	RELOC	10 days	8/14/06	8/25/06
484	✓	**1.2.11.5 Adjunct Functionalitites (Departmental)**	**RELOC**	**10 days**	**8/14/06**	**8/25/06**
485	✓	1.2.11.5.1 Remote Access	RELOC	10 days	8/14/06	8/25/06
486	✓	1.2.11.5.2 Remote Services	RELOC	10 days	8/14/06	8/25/06
487	✓	**1.2.11.6 Departmental Relocation Scheduling**	**RELOC**	**10 days**	**8/14/06**	**8/25/06**
488	✓	1.2.11.6.1 XYZ Schedule (December 1, 2006)	RELOC	10 days	8/14/06	8/25/06
489	✓	1.2.11.6.2 XYZ Schedule (January 15, 2007)	RELOC	10 days	8/14/06	8/25/06
490	✓	1.2.11.6.3 Remote Location Schedule	RELOC	10 days	8/14/06	8/25/06
491	✓	1.2.11.6.4 Construction Schedule	RELOC	10 days	8/14/06	8/25/06
492	✓	**1.2.11.7 System Contingencies**	**RELOC**	**10 days**	**8/14/06**	**8/25/06**
493	✓	1.2.11.7.1 Network Partners	RELOC	10 days	8/14/06	8/25/06
494	✓	1.2.11.7.2 Data Recovery	RELOC	10 days	8/14/06	8/25/06
495	✓	1.2.11.7.3 System Replacement	RELOC	10 days	8/14/06	8/25/06
496	✓	1.2.11.8 Business Recovery Considerations	RELOC	10 days	8/14/06	8/25/06
497	✓	1.2.11.9 Procure Moving Company	RELOC	30 days	8/14/06	9/22/06
498	✓	**1.3 Design**		**126.31 days**	**4/21/06**	**10/16/06**
499	✓	**1.3.1 VOIP**	**VOIP**	**126.31 days**	**4/21/06**	**10/16/06**
500	✓	**1.3.1.1 Define the objectives of the converged network**	**VOIP**	**12.5 days**	**9/12/06**	**9/28/06**
501	✓	1.3.1.1.1 Define Ready Assessment Plan	VOIP	12.5 days	9/12/06	9/28/06
502	✓	1.3.1.1.2 Define Dialing Policies	VOIP	12.5 days	9/12/06	9/28/06
503	✓	1.3.1.1.3 Define Telephony requirements	VOIP	12.5 days	9/12/06	9/28/06
504	✓	1.3.1.1.4 Define SLAs	VOIP	12.5 days	9/12/06	9/28/06
505	✓	1.3.1.1.5 Define IVR UML and Database DataMart	VOIP	12.5 days	9/12/06	9/28/06
506	✓	1.3.1.1.6 Define Menu system and Call Routing Flow	VOIP	12.5 days	9/12/06	9/28/06
507	✓	1.3.1.1.7 Define Network VLANS and Subnets for VoIP Topology	VOIP	12.5 days	9/12/06	9/28/06
508	✓	1.3.1.1.8 Review the current Network environment	VOIP	12.5 days	9/12/06	9/28/06
509	✓	1.3.1.1.9 Draft the System Requirements Document	VOIP	12.5 days	9/12/06	9/28/06
510	✓	1.3.1.1.10 Determine the Support Systems and Tools for Network Management	VOIP	12.5 days	9/12/06	9/28/06
511	✓	1.3.1.1.11 Obtain Feedback from Vendors and Collegues	VOIP	12.5 days	9/12/06	9/28/06
512	✓	1.3.1.2 Develop Installation and Testing Plan	VOIP	15 days	9/12/06	10/2/06
513	✓	1.3.1.3 Develop Migration Strategy	VOIP	15 days	9/12/06	10/2/06
514	✓	**1.3.1.4 Design VoIP Network and Dialing Plans**	**VOIP**	**120 days**	**4/21/06**	**10/6/06**
515	✓	1.3.1.4.1 Document VoIP Topology and Network Design		120 days	4/21/06	10/6/06
516	✓	1.3.1.4.2 Document Dialing Plans, SLA(s)		90 days	4/21/06	8/25/06
517	✓	**1.3.1.5 Design IVR UML and DataMart**	**VOIP**	**10 days**	**4/21/06**	**5/5/06**
518	✓	1.3.1.5.1 Document Use Cases	VOIP	10 days	4/21/06	5/5/06
519	✓	1.3.1.5.2 Document Dialing Plans	VOIP	10 days	4/21/06	5/5/06

ID		Task Name	Program	Duration	Start	Finish
520	✓	1.3.1.6 Define and Document IPT Proof of Concept	VOIP	10 days	4/21/06	5/5/06
521	✓	1.3.1.7 Procure all BOM (Bill of Material) for IPT requirements	VOIP	40 days	8/22/06	10/16/06
522	✓	**1.3.2 WAN Migration**	**WANLAN**	**126.31 days**	**4/21/06**	**10/16/06**
523	✓	1.3.2.1 Secure necessary architectural resources	WANLAN	3 days	4/21/06	4/26/06
524	✓	**1.3.2.2 Document exising LAN/WAN IP Adressing Scheme**	**LANWAN**	**10 days**	**4/21/06**	**5/5/06**
525	✓	1.3.2.2.1 Review existing IP Addressing Scheme	LANWAN	10 days	4/21/06	5/5/06
526	✓	1.3.2.2.2 Document existing IP Addressing Scheme	LANWAN	10 days	4/21/06	5/5/06
527	✓	1.3.2.2.3 Needs Assement Complete	LANWAN	10 days	4/21/06	5/5/06
528	✓	1.3.2.2.4 Identify Equipment (BOM) and Purchasing Requirements from Site Review	LANWAN	10 days	4/21/06	5/5/06
529	✓	**1.3.2.3 Preliminary Recommendation Deisgn Documents**	**LANWAN**	**10 days**	**4/21/06**	**5/5/06**
530	✓	1.3.2.3.1 Document existing IP addressing scheme and naming standards	LANWAN	10 days	4/21/06	5/5/06
531	✓	1.3.2.3.2 Develop preliminary IP Scheme design document	LANWAN	10 days	4/21/06	5/5/06
532	✓	1.3.2.3.3 Develop preliminary naming standard design document	LANWAN	10 days	4/21/06	5/5/06
533	✓	1.3.2.3.4 Obtain user feedback/input on design	LANWAN	10 days	4/21/06	5/5/06
534	✓	1.3.2.3.5 Preliminary Recommendation Design Document for Project #2 complete	LANWAN	10 days	4/21/06	5/5/06
535	✓	**1.3.2.4 Detail Solution Design Documents for IP Project**	**LANWAN**	**5 days**	**8/9/06**	**8/15/06**
536	✓	1.3.2.4.1 Develop detail IP Scheme document	LANWAN	5 days	8/9/06	8/15/06
537	✓	1.3.2.4.2 Develop detail naming standards	LANWAN	5 days	8/9/06	8/15/06
538	✓	1.3.2.4.3 Develop On Going Procedures	LANWAN	5 days	8/9/06	8/15/06
539	✓	1.3.2.4.4 Develop Training Recommendation	LANWAN	5 days	8/9/06	8/15/06
540	✓	1.3.2.4.5 XYZ Review Deliverables for IP Project	LANWAN	5 days	8/9/06	8/15/06
541	✓	1.3.2.4.6 Present fidning to project team	LANWAN	5 days	8/9/06	8/15/06
542	✓	1.3.2.4.7 Obtain Signoff on Acceptance of Design deliverable	LANWAN	5 days	8/9/06	8/15/06
543	✓	**1.3.2.5 Draft Preliminary Infrastructure Design Documents**	**LANWAN**	**60 days**	**4/21/06**	**7/14/06**
544	✓	1.3.2.5.1 Preliminary hardware design	LANWAN	60 days	4/21/06	7/14/06
545	✓	1.3.2.5.2 Preliminary software design	LANWAN	60 days	4/21/06	7/14/06
546	✓	1.3.2.5.3 Preliminary communications design	LANWAN	60 days	4/21/06	7/14/06
547	✓	1.3.2.5.4 Preliminary connectivity LAN/WAN design	LANWAN	60 days	4/21/06	7/14/06
548	✓	1.3.2.5.5 Preliminary support environment design	LANWAN	60 days	4/21/06	7/14/06
549	✓	1.3.2.5.6 Draft preliminary infrastructure design document complete	LANWAN	60 days	4/21/06	7/14/06
550	✓	1.3.2.6 Review preliminary design documents	LANWAN	60 days	4/21/06	7/14/06
551	✓	1.3.2.7 Obtain feedback/input on design	LANWAN	60 days	4/21/06	7/14/06
552	✓	**1.3.2.8 Develop Detailed Infrastructure Design Documents**	**LANWAN**	**60 days**	**4/21/06**	**7/14/06**
553	✓	1.3.2.8.1 Develop detailed hardware design	LANWAN	60 days	4/21/06	7/14/06
554	✓	1.3.2.8.2 Develop detailed software design	LANWAN	60 days	4/21/06	7/14/06
555	✓	1.3.2.8.3 Develop detailed communications design	LANWAN	60 days	4/21/06	7/14/06
556	✓	1.3.2.8.4 Develop detailed connectivity LAN/WAN design	LANWAN	60 days	4/21/06	7/14/06
557	✓	1.3.2.8.5 Develop detailed support environment design	LANWAN	60 days	4/21/06	7/14/06
558	✓	1.3.2.8.6 Develop detailed infrastructure design documents complete	LANWAN	60 days	4/21/06	7/14/06
559	✓	1.3.2.9 Align long/short term infrastructure design with business goals	LANWAN	60 days	4/21/06	7/14/06
560	✓	1.3.2.10 Infrastructure Design complete	LANWAN	0 days	7/14/06	7/14/06
561	✓	**1.3.2.11 Finalization/Validation**	**LANWAN**	**10 days**	**4/21/06**	**5/5/06**
562	✓	1.3.2.11.1 Secure resources based upon approved initiatives	LANWAN	10 days	4/21/06	5/5/06
563	✓	1.3.2.11.2 Finalize detailed design based upon budgetary considerations	LANWAN	10 days	4/21/06	5/5/06
564	✓	1.3.2.11.3 Develop detailed implementation strategy	LANWAN	10 days	4/21/06	5/5/06
565	✓	1.3.2.11.4 Validate implementation strategy in test environment	LANWAN	10 days	4/21/06	5/5/06
566	✓	1.3.2.11.5 Review implementation strategy noting other initiatives	LANWAN	10 days	4/21/06	5/5/06
567	✓	1.3.2.11.6 Secure approval to proceed	LANWAN	10 days	4/21/06	5/5/06
568	✓	1.3.2.11.7 Finalization/validation complete	LANWAN	0 days	4/21/06	4/21/06
569	✓	**1.3.2.12 WAN GigaMAN and SONET Design**	**LANWAN**	**23 days**	**8/21/06**	**9/20/06**
570	✓	1.3.2.12.1 Develop Network Diagram for SONET Ring and GigaMAN	LANWAN	3 days	8/21/06	8/23/06
571	✓	1.3.2.12.2 Develop XYZ site contact list for all locations	LANWAN	1 day	8/21/06	8/21/06
572	✓	1.3.2.12.3 Develop IP addressing/routing spreadsheet update	LANWAN	10 days	8/21/06	9/1/06
573	✓	1.3.2.12.4 Develop XYZ communication plan for rollout (Marketing)	LANWAN	10 days	8/21/06	9/1/06
574	✓	**1.3.2.12.5 Gather Testing Requirements**	**LANWAN**	**10 days**	**8/24/06**	**9/6/06**
575	✓	1.3.2.12.5.1 Interview XYZ	LANWAN	10 days	8/24/06	9/6/06
576	✓	1.3.2.12.5.2 Gather main site location testing requirements	LANWAN	10 days	8/24/06	9/6/06
577	✓	**1.3.2.12.6 Gather remote site location testing requirements**	**LANWAN**	**10 days**	**8/24/06**	**9/6/06**
578	✓	1.3.2.12.6.1 Document Testing plan	LANWAN	10 days	8/24/06	9/6/06
579	✓	1.3.2.12.6.2 Create Staging and Testing Plan	LANWAN	10 days	8/24/06	9/6/06
580	✓	1.3.2.12.6.3 Create high level test pilot diagram	LANWAN	10 days	8/24/06	9/6/06
581	✓	1.3.2.12.6.4 Review staging area	LANWAN	10 days	8/24/06	9/6/06
582	✓	1.3.2.12.6.5 Acceptance of Test Plan	LANWAN	10 days	8/24/06	9/6/06
583	✓	**1.3.2.12.7 Develop migration and implementation plan**	**LANWAN**	**10 days**	**9/7/06**	**9/20/06**
584	✓	1.3.2.12.7.1 Document Findings	LANWAN	10 days	9/7/06	9/20/06
585	✓	1.3.2.12.7.2 Document shortfalls and dependencies	LANWAN	10 days	9/7/06	9/20/06
586	✓	1.3.2.12.7.3 Document site readiness requirements	LANWAN	10 days	9/7/06	9/20/06
587	✓	1.3.2.12.7.4 Document physical hardware placement connectivity	LANWAN	10 days	9/7/06	9/20/06
588	✓	1.3.2.12.7.5 Document migration path	LANWAN	10 days	9/7/06	9/20/06
589	✓	1.3.2.12.7.6 Create contingency plan	LANWAN	10 days	9/7/06	9/20/06
590	✓	1.3.2.12.7.7 Acceptance of migration plan	LANWAN	10 days	9/7/06	9/20/06
591	✓	1.3.2.12.7.8 Secure Approval to Proceed	LANWAN	10 days	9/7/06	9/20/06
592	✓	1.3.2.12.7.9 Secure necessary consulting resources for testing	LANWAN	10 days	9/7/06	9/20/06
593	✓	1.3.2.12.7.10 Draft Preliminary Design of network infrastructure	LANWAN	10 days	9/7/06	9/20/06
594	✓	1.3.2.12.7.11 Check Point on Infrastructure facilities requirements	LANWAN	10 days	9/7/06	9/20/06
595	✓	**1.3.2.13 LAN DESIGN**	**LANWAN**	**40 days**	**8/21/06**	**10/16/06**
596	✓	**1.3.2.13.1 Gather Testing Requirements for Relocation and IPT Requirements**	**LANWAN**	**10 days**	**8/22/06**	**9/4/06**
597	✓	1.3.2.13.1.1 Interview at XYZ	LANWAN	10 days	8/22/06	9/4/06
598	✓	1.3.2.13.1.2 DHCP,STATIC,IP DEVICES, User Workstations Requirement Gathering	LANWAN	10 days	8/22/06	9/4/06
599	✓	1.3.2.13.1.3 Gather application testing requirements	LANWAN	10 days	8/22/06	9/4/06
600	✓	1.3.2.13.1.4 XYZ Acceptance of Testing Requirements	LANWAN	10 days	8/22/06	9/4/06

ID		Task Name	Program	Duration	Start	Finish
601	✓	**1.3.2.13.2 Create Test Pilot Network Diagram**	**LANWAN**	**10 days**	**8/21/06**	**9/4/06**
602	✓	1.3.2.13.2.1 Develop test pilot network diagram	LANWAN	10 days	8/22/06	9/4/06
603	✓	1.3.2.13.2.2 XYZ Acceptance of Test Pilot Network Diagram	LANWAN	0 days	8/21/06	8/21/06
604	✓	**1.3.2.13.3 Document Testing Criteria**	**LANWAN**	**10 days**	**8/21/06**	**9/4/06**
605	✓	1.3.2.13.3.1 Develop Testing Methodology Document	LANWAN	10 days	8/22/06	9/4/06
606	✓	1.3.2.13.3.2 Create Test Site Plan	LANWAN	10 days	8/22/06	9/4/06
607	✓	1.3.2.13.3.3 Create Ucase Document for Testing	LANWAN	10 days	8/22/06	9/4/06
608	✓	1.3.2.13.3.4 XYZ acceptance of testing criteria	LANWAN	0 days	8/21/06	8/21/06
609	✓	**1.3.2.13.4 Finalization/Validation**	**LANWAN**	**10 days**	**8/21/06**	**9/4/06**
610	✓	1.3.2.13.4.1 Secure resources based upon approved initiatives	LANWAN	10 days	8/22/06	9/4/06
611	✓	1.3.2.13.4.2 Finalize detailed design of network infrastructure	LANWAN	10 days	8/22/06	9/4/06
612	✓	1.3.2.13.4.3 Obtain signoff on detailed design	LANWAN	10 days	8/22/06	9/4/06
613	✓	1.3.2.13.4.4 Finalization/validation complete	LANWAN	10 days	8/22/06	9/4/06
614	✓	1.3.2.13.4.5 Secure approval to proceed	LANWAN	0 days	8/21/06	8/21/06
615	✓	**1.3.2.13.5 Migration Document (Planning)**	**LANWAN**	**10 days**	**8/22/06**	**9/4/06**
616	✓	1.3.2.13.5.1 Migration Plan/Discovery/GAP Fill	LANWAN	10 days	8/22/06	9/4/06
617	✓	1.3.2.13.5.2 Document Findings	LANWAN	10 days	8/22/06	9/4/06
618	✓	1.3.2.13.5.3 Document Shortfall/Dependencies	LANWAN	10 days	8/22/06	9/4/06
619	✓	1.3.2.13.5.4 Document Assumptions	LANWAN	10 days	8/22/06	9/4/06
620	✓	1.3.2.13.5.5 Document Physical Hardware Placements & Connectivity	LANWAN	10 days	8/22/06	9/4/06
621	✓	1.3.2.13.5.6 Define & Document VLAN/Port Mapping	LANWAN	10 days	8/22/06	9/4/06
622	✓	1.3.2.13.5.7 Obtain Customer Feedback and Signoff	LANWAN	10 days	8/22/06	9/4/06
623	✓	1.3.2.13.5.8 Document Migration Path	LANWAN	10 days	8/22/06	9/4/06
624	✓	1.3.2.13.5.9 Acceptance of Migration Plan Document - DEL. WAN08	LANWAN	10 days	8/22/06	9/4/06
625	✓	1.3.2.13.5.10 End Migration Document Planning	LANWAN	10 days	8/22/06	9/4/06
626	✓	1.3.2.13.5.11 Test Site Identified and begin move	LANWAN	10 days	8/22/06	9/4/06
627	✓	1.3.2.13.5.12 Infrastructure facilities requirements are confirmed	LANWAN	10 days	8/22/06	9/4/06
628	✓	1.3.2.13.6 Procure Equipment for Parralle LAN & WAN Migration	LANWAN	40 days	8/22/06	10/16/06
629	✓	1.3.3 Design Complete	LANWAN	0 days	10/6/06	10/6/06
630		**1.4 Testing**	**VOIP**	**65.6 days**	**9/8/06**	**12/8/06**
631	✓	**1.4.1 Test AD Proof of Concept (POC)**	**AD**	**40.6 days**	**9/8/06**	**11/3/06**
632	✓	**1.4.1.1 Prepare for POC**	**AD**	**5 days**	**9/21/06**	**9/27/06**
633	✓	1.4.1.1.1 Prepare a test plan and checklists based on development/design solutions	AD	5 days	9/21/06	9/27/06
634	✓	1.4.1.1.2 Document features and components to test	AD	5 days	9/21/06	9/27/06
635	✓	1.4.1.1.3 Secure testing personnel	AD	5 days	9/21/06	9/27/06
636	✓	**1.4.1.2 Ensure the Testing Lab Environment Simulates the Proposed Environment**	**AD**	**5 days**	**9/28/06**	**10/4/06**
637	✓	1.4.1.2.1 Configure server hardware and drivers	AD	5 days	9/28/06	10/4/06
638	✓	1.4.1.2.2 Configure services and configurations	AD	5 days	9/28/06	10/4/06
639	✓	1.4.1.2.3 Configure user accounts	AD	5 days	9/28/06	10/4/06
640	✓	1.4.1.2.4 Configure domain structure (simulated domain hierarchy)	AD	5 days	9/28/06	10/4/06
641	✓	1.4.1.2.5 Configure server function/strategy	AD	5 days	9/28/06	10/4/06
642	✓	1.4.1.2.6 Configure mixed environment	AD	5 days	9/28/06	10/4/06
643	✓	1.4.1.2.7 Configure client computer configuration	AD	5 days	9/28/06	10/4/06
644	✓	1.4.1.2.8 Configure network topology and protocols	AD	5 days	9/28/06	10/4/06
645	✓	1.4.1.2.9 Configure network connectivity	AD	5 days	9/28/06	10/4/06
646	✓	1.4.1.2.10 Test server applications running on domain controllers	AD	5 days	9/28/06	10/4/06
647	✓	1.4.1.2.11 Configure remote connectivity	AD	5 days	9/28/06	10/4/06
648	✓	1.4.1.2.12 Configure peripherals	AD	5 days	9/28/06	10/4/06
649	✓	1.4.1.2.13 Configure interoperability with other operating systems (for example, UNIX, mainframe)	AD	5 days	9/28/06	10/4/06
650	✓	1.4.1.2.14 Configure administrative tools	AD	5 days	9/28/06	10/4/06
651	✓	1.4.1.2.15 Configure fault tolerance techniques	AD	5 days	9/28/06	10/4/06
652	✓	1.4.1.2.16 Configure Terminal Services	AD	5 days	9/28/06	10/4/06
653	✓	**1.4.1.3 Deploy POC/Lab Testing Environment**	**AD**	**10 days**	**10/4/06**	**10/18/06**
654	✓	**1.4.1.3.1 Validate Structural Plans**	**AD**	**10 days**	**10/5/06**	**10/18/06**
655	✓	1.4.1.3.1.1 Replication load versus client logon over wide-area network (WAN)	AD	10 days	10/5/06	10/18/06
656	✓	1.4.1.3.1.2 Perform replication topology (end to end replication latency, KCC routing and failover handling)	AD	10 days	10/5/06	10/18/06
657	✓	**1.4.1.3.1.3 Size Domain Controllers**	**AD**	**10 days**	**10/5/06**	**10/18/06**
658	✓	1.4.1.3.1.3.1 Categorize geographical locations and create	AD	10 days	10/5/06	10/18/06
659	✓	1.4.1.3.1.3.2 Standardize on two or three domain controller configurations (high/medium/low-load domain controllers)	AD	10 days	10/5/06	10/18/06
660	✓	**1.4.1.3.1.4 Simulate Load on Domain Controllers**	**AD**	**10 days**	**10/5/06**	**10/18/06**
661	✓	1.4.1.3.1.4.1 Use tools to simulate logon, change, and add operations	AD	10 days	10/5/06	10/18/06
662	✓	1.4.1.3.1.4.2 Collect data from legacy servers and use as baselines	AD	10 days	10/5/06	10/18/06
663	✓	**1.4.1.3.1.5 Test Administration, Management, and Delegation**	**AD**	**2 days**	**10/5/06**	**10/6/06**
664	✓	1.4.1.3.1.5.1 Develop scripts for common tasks	AD	2 days	10/5/06	10/6/06
665	✓	1.4.1.3.1.5.2 Test and improve scripts in lab	AD	2 days	10/5/06	10/6/06
666	✓	**1.4.1.3.1.6 Test Migration**	**AD**	**1 day**	**10/5/06**	**10/5/06**
667	✓	1.4.1.3.1.6.1 Test how account domain restructuring affects user logon, resource access, and application access	AD	1 day	10/5/06	10/5/06
668	✓	1.4.1.3.1.6.2 Test migration procedures	AD	1 day	10/5/06	10/5/06
669	✓	1.4.1.3.1.6.3 Test using real life data (for example, Windows NT 4.0 BDC or Windows 2000 controller created from real domain)	AD	0.5 days	10/5/06	10/5/06
670	✓	**1.4.1.3.1.7 Test Applications**	**AD**	**6.67 days**	**10/5/06**	**10/13/06**
671	✓	1.4.1.3.1.7.1 Create list of business critical applications and assign test owner	AD	6.67 days	10/5/06	10/13/06
672	✓	1.4.1.3.1.7.2 Test whether applications run on Windows	AD	6.67 days	10/5/06	10/13/06
673	✓	1.4.1.3.1.7.3 Test how restructuring affects applications	AD	6.67 days	10/5/06	10/13/06
674	✓	1.4.1.3.2 Analyze results	AD	10 days	10/5/06	10/18/06
675	✓	**1.4.1.3.3 Perform Full-Cycle Risk Assessment**	**AD**	**2 days**	**10/5/06**	**10/6/06**
676	✓	1.4.1.3.3.1 Document lessons learned	AD	2 days	10/5/06	10/6/06
677	✓	1.4.1.3.3.2 Document modifications	AD	2 days	10/5/06	10/6/06
678	✓	1.4.1.3.3.3 Address readiness to proceed to pilot	AD	2 days	10/5/06	10/6/06
679	✓	1.4.1.3.4 Deploy POC complete	AD	0 days	10/4/06	10/4/06
680	✓	1.4.1.3.5 Planning complete	AD	0 days	10/4/06	10/4/06
681	✓	**1.4.1.4 Deployment of POC**	**AD**	**9 days**	**10/19/06**	**10/31/06**

ID	ℹ	Task Name	Program	Duration	Start	Finish
682	✓	**1.4.1.4.1 Deploy Pilot System**	**AD**	**9 days**	**10/19/06**	**10/31/06**
683	✓	**1.4.1.4.1.1 Plan Pilot Deployment**	**AD**	**5 days**	**10/19/06**	**10/25/06**
684	✓	1.4.1.4.1.1.1 Identify pilot scope and objectives	AD	1 day	10/19/06	10/19/06
685	✓	1.4.1.4.1.1.2 Identify pilot groups/individuals/resources/equipment	AD	1 day	10/19/06	10/19/06
686	✓	1.4.1.4.1.1.3 Document resources and tasks	AD	1 day	10/19/06	10/19/06
687	✓	1.4.1.4.1.1.4 Develop communications materials for user community (for example, FAQs, Web site, e-mails)	AD	1 day	10/19/06	10/19/06
688	✓	1.4.1.4.1.1.5 Develop the user support plan	AD	1 day	10/19/06	10/19/06
689	✓	1.4.1.4.1.1.6 Develop the training plan	AD	1 day	10/19/06	10/19/06
690	✓	1.4.1.4.1.1.7 Ensure POC lab is stable	AD	1 day	10/19/06	10/19/06
691	✓	**1.4.1.4.1.1.8 Develop the Rollout Process**	**AD**	**5 days**	**10/19/06**	**10/25/06**
692	✓	1.4.1.4.1.1.8.1 Identify tools and supplies the installer needs	AD	5 days	10/19/06	10/25/06
693	✓	1.4.1.4.1.1.8.2 Identify lists of scripts and their location(s)	AD	5 days	10/19/06	10/25/06
694	✓	1.4.1.4.1.1.8.3 Identify backups to be taken prior to and during deployment	AD	5 days	10/19/06	10/25/06
695	✓	1.4.1.4.1.1.8.4 Document steps for migrating to the new domain structure	AD	5 days	10/19/06	10/25/06
696	✓	1.4.1.4.1.1.8.5 Document steps for performing manual and automated computer upgrades	AD	5 days	10/19/06	10/25/06
697	✓	1.4.1.4.1.1.8.6 Document installer acceptance tests	AD	5 days	10/19/06	10/25/06
698	✓	1.4.1.4.1.1.8.7 Document operational procedures installers and administrators are to perform (resetting permissions, changing passwords, etc.)	AD	5 days	10/19/06	10/25/06
699	✓	1.4.1.4.1.1.8.8 Document steps for backing out if pilot fails	AD	5 days	10/19/06	10/25/06
700	✓	1.4.1.4.1.1.9 Identify known risks and contingency plans	AD	5 days	10/19/06	10/25/06
701	✓	1.4.1.4.1.1.10 Develop rollback plan	AD	5 days	10/19/06	10/25/06
702	✓	**1.4.1.4.1.2 Set up Deployment**	**AD**	**1 day**	**10/26/06**	**10/26/06**
703	✓	1.4.1.4.1.2.1 Communicate with users	AD	1 day	10/26/06	10/26/06
704	✓	1.4.1.4.1.2.2 Conduct user training	AD	1 day	10/26/06	10/26/06
705	✓	1.4.1.4.1.2.3 Ensure support organization is prepared	AD	1 day	10/26/06	10/26/06
706	✓	**1.4.1.4.1.3 Perform Windows NT Domain Upgrade with Active Directory Migration Tool**	**AD**	**3 days**	**10/27/06**	**10/31/06**
707	✓	1.4.1.4.1.3.1 Apply appropriate service packs to servers in source domain	AD	1 day	10/27/06	10/27/06
708	✓	1.4.1.4.1.3.2 Configure two-way trust between source and target domain	AD	2 days	10/27/06	10/30/06
709	✓	**1.4.1.4.1.3.3 Configure Groups**	**AD**	**1 day**	**10/27/06**	**10/27/06**
710	✓	1.4.1.4.1.3.3.1 Add the domain admins global group from the source domain to the administrators local group in the target domain	AD	1 day	10/27/06	10/27/06
711	✓	1.4.1.4.1.3.3.2 Add the admins global group from the target domain to the administrators local group in the source dor	AD	1 day	10/27/06	10/27/06
712	✓	1.4.1.4.1.3.3.3 Create SourceDomain$$$ group	AD	1 day	10/27/06	10/27/06
713	✓	1.4.1.4.1.3.4 Enable auditing appropriately on source and target domains	AD	1 day	10/27/06	10/27/06
714	✓	1.4.1.4.1.3.5 Create administrative shares	AD	1 day	10/27/06	10/27/06
715	✓	1.4.1.4.1.3.6 Grant appropriate user rights	AD	1 day	10/27/06	10/27/06
716	✓	1.4.1.4.1.3.7 Run the Active Directory Migration Tool	AD	3 days	10/27/06	10/31/06
717	✓	**1.4.1.5 Implementation Perform Domain Upgrade / New Installation**	**AD**	**3 days**	**9/8/06**	**9/13/06**
718	✓	**1.4.1.5.1 Build Domain Controllers**	**AD**	**3 days**	**9/8/06**	**9/13/06**
719	✓	1.4.1.5.1.1 Install server as member server	AD	3 days	9/8/06	9/13/06
720	✓	1.4.1.5.1.2 Install DNS with operating system (always use fixed IP addresses)	AD	3 days	9/8/06	9/13/06
721	✓	**1.4.1.5.1.3 Configure Domain Name System (DNS) Clients**	**AD**	**3 days**	**9/8/06**	**9/13/06**
722	✓	1.4.1.5.1.3.1 Verify DNS client points to local server as preferred DNS server and any other DNS server as alternate DNS server	AD	3 days	9/8/06	9/13/06
723	✓	1.4.1.5.1.3.2 Point forest root domain to another forest root domain controller as preferred and local server as alternate DNS server	AD	3 days	9/8/06	9/13/06
724	✓	1.4.1.5.1.3.3 Configure DNS client before running dcpromo	AD	3 days	9/8/06	9/13/06
725	✓	**1.4.1.5.1.3.4 Configure First Domain Controller**	**AD**	**3 days**	**9/8/06**	**9/13/06**
726	✓	1.4.1.5.1.3.4.1 Point to any existing DNS server before running dcpromo	AD	3 days	9/8/06	9/13/06
727	✓	1.4.1.5.1.3.4.2 Reconfigure DNS client after second domain controller is promoted to use second domain controller as preferred DNS controller	AD	3 days	9/8/06	9/13/06
728	✓	1.4.1.5.1.3.5 Verify second root domain controller is promoted	AD	3 days	9/8/06	9/13/06
729	✓	1.4.1.5.1.4 Put in place monitoring software	AD	3 days	9/8/06	9/13/06
730	✓	1.4.1.5.1.5 Move machine into its final location	AD	3 days	9/8/06	9/13/06
731	✓	1.4.1.5.1.6 Promote domain controller	AD	3 days	9/8/06	9/13/06
732	✓	**1.4.1.5.1.7 Run Quality Assurance Tools**	**AD**	**3 days**	**9/8/06**	**9/13/06**
733	✓	1.4.1.5.1.7.1 Check event log	AD	3 days	9/8/06	9/13/06
734	✓	1.4.1.5.1.7.2 Verify using dcdiag	AD	3 days	9/8/06	9/13/06
735	✓	1.4.1.5.1.7.3 Verify using netdiag	AD	3 days	9/8/06	9/13/06
736	✓	1.4.1.5.1.7.4 Verify using repadmin	AD	3 days	9/8/06	9/13/06
737	✓	1.4.1.5.1.8 Consider domain controller prestaging if large number of domain controllers have to be built	AD	3 days	9/8/06	9/13/06
738	✓	**1.4.1.5.2 Delegate DNS Domain For Forest Root (DNS Integration)**	**AD**	**3 days**	**9/8/06**	**9/13/06**
739	✓	**1.4.1.5.2.1 Verify DNS Client (Resolver)**	**AD**	**3 days**	**9/8/06**	**9/13/06**
740	✓	1.4.1.5.2.1.1 Verify on forest root domain controller: Preferred DNS server points to a different computer (should be in the same site or close site)	AD	3 days	9/8/06	9/13/06
741	✓	1.4.1.5.2.1.2 Verify on non-forest root domain controller: Preferred DNS server should be local computer	AD	3 days	9/8/06	9/13/06
742	✓	**1.4.1.5.2.2 Configure DNS Server**	**AD**	**3 days**	**9/8/06**	**9/13/06**
743	✓	1.4.1.5.2.2.1 Create delegation entry for new domain controller	AD	3 days	9/8/06	9/13/06
744	✓	1.4.1.5.2.2.2 Zones will be configured after Active Directory is installed on the domain controller/DNS server	AD	3 days	9/8/06	9/13/06
745	✓	**1.4.1.5.3 Create Forest Root Domain**	**AD**	**3 days**	**9/8/06**	**9/13/06**
746	✓	**1.4.1.5.3.1 Implement Root Domain Best Practices**	**AD**	**3 days**	**9/8/06**	**9/13/06**
747	✓	**1.4.1.5.3.1.1 Configure the First Root Domain Controller**	**AD**	**3 days**	**9/8/06**	**9/13/06**
748	✓	1.4.1.5.3.1.1.1 Manually create _msdcs.<forest-root> DNS domain	AD	3 days	9/8/06	9/13/06
749	✓	1.4.1.5.3.1.1.2 Add DNS delegation entries	AD	3 days	9/8/06	9/13/06
750	✓	1.4.1.5.3.1.1.3 Get monitoring and backup in place	AD	3 days	9/8/06	9/13/06
751	✓	**1.4.1.5.3.1.2 Configure Second Root Domain Controller**	**AD**	**3 days**	**9/8/06**	**9/13/06**
752	✓	1.4.1.5.3.1.2.1 Promote domain controller	AD	3 days	9/8/06	9/13/06
753	✓	1.4.1.5.3.1.2.2 Transfer all domain wide operations master roles	AD	3 days	9/8/06	9/13/06
754	✓	1.4.1.5.3.1.2.3 Get monitoring and backup in place	AD	3 days	9/8/06	9/13/06
755	✓	**1.4.1.5.3.1.3 Configure Additional Root Domain Controllers**	**AD**	**3 days**	**9/8/06**	**9/13/06**
756	✓	1.4.1.5.3.1.3.1 Promote domain controller	AD	3 days	9/8/06	9/13/06
757	✓	1.4.1.5.3.1.3.2 Get monitoring in place	AD	3 days	9/8/06	9/13/06
758	✓	1.4.1.5.3.1.3.3 Do not add GC service (reduces number of replication connections to domain controllers in other doma	AD	3 days	9/8/06	9/13/06

ID	Task Name	Program	Duration	Start	Finish
759	**1.4.1.5.3.1.4 Deploy Forest Root Domain Controllers to All Hubs**	**AD**	**3 days**	**9/8/06**	**9/13/06**
760	**1.4.1.5.3.1.4.1 Create Configuration Data**	**AD**	**3 days**	**9/8/06**	**9/13/06**
761	1.4.1.5.3.1.4.1.1 Add forest data (infrastructure data) to the DS as soon as second domain controller is installed	AD	3 days	9/8/06	9/13/06
762	1.4.1.5.3.1.4.1.2 Add domain data (owned by resource owners, delegated OUs and user/group accounts, resources [servers, shares, printers]) to the DS as soon as second domain controller is installed	AD	3 days	9/8/06	9/13/06
763	**1.4.1.6 Evaluate the Pilot**	**AD**	**3 days**	**11/1/06**	**11/3/06**
764	1.4.1.6.1 Conduct desktop test scenarios	AD	3 days	11/1/06	11/3/06
765	1.4.1.6.2 Conduct server test scenarios	AD	3 days	11/1/06	11/3/06
766	1.4.1.6.3 Conduct third-party application test scenarios	AD	3 days	11/1/06	11/3/06
767	1.4.1.6.4 Conduct custom application test scenarios	AD	3 days	11/1/06	11/3/06
768	1.4.1.6.5 Conduct coexistence test scenarios	AD	3 days	11/1/06	11/3/06
769	1.4.1.6.6 Identify scope changes	AD	3 days	11/1/06	11/3/06
770	1.4.1.6.7 Identify cost factors	AD	3 days	11/1/06	11/3/06
771	1.4.1.6.8 Identify interoperability issues	AD	3 days	11/1/06	11/3/06
772	1.4.1.6.9 Identify unanticipated downtime	AD	3 days	11/1/06	11/3/06
773	**1.4.1.6.10 Perform Post-Pilot Evaluation**	**AD**	**3 days**	**11/1/06**	**11/3/06**
774	1.4.1.6.10.1 Obtain user feedback	AD	3 days	11/1/06	11/3/06
775	1.4.1.6.10.2 Evaluate lessons learned	AD	3 days	11/1/06	11/3/06
776	1.4.1.6.10.3 Modify items as necessary	AD	3 days	11/1/06	11/3/06
777	1.4.1.6.10.4 Document recommendation for next steps	AD	3 days	11/1/06	11/3/06
778	1.4.1.6.10.5 Consider leaving pilot operational for future testing	AD	3 days	11/1/06	11/3/06
779	1.4.1.6.11 Deploy pilot system complete	AD	0 days	11/3/06	11/3/06
780	1.4.1.6.12 Production deployment approved	AD	0 days	11/3/06	11/3/06
781	**1.4.2 Test Exchange 2003 Proof of Concept Lab Machines**	**Ex2003**	**20 days**	**10/10/06**	**11/7/06**
782	**1.4.2.1 Proof of Concept (POC)**	**Ex2003**	**20 days**	**10/11/06**	**11/7/06**
783	**1.4.2.1.1 POC Preparation**	**Ex2003**	**20 days**	**10/11/06**	**11/7/06**
806	1.4.2.2 Perform tests to test plan specification	Ex2003	1.67 days	10/11/06	10/12/06
807	1.4.2.3 Analyze results	Ex2003	20 days	10/11/06	11/7/06
808	**1.4.2.4 Mitigate Results**	**Ex2003**	**20 days**	**10/11/06**	**11/7/06**
809	**1.4.2.4.1 Test Case Problem**	**Ex2003**	**20 days**	**10/11/06**	**11/7/06**
810	1.4.2.4.1.1 Document in proof of concept tracking system	Ex2003	20 days	10/11/06	11/7/06
811	1.4.2.4.1.2 Revise test case	Ex2003	20 days	10/11/06	11/7/06
812	1.4.2.4.1.3 Rerun the test	Ex2003	20 days	10/11/06	11/7/06
813	1.4.2.4.1.4 Document results/changes	Ex2003	20 days	10/11/06	11/7/06
814	1.4.2.4.1.5 Test case problem complete	Ex2003	20 days	10/11/06	11/7/06
815	**1.4.2.4.2 Lab Setup Problem**	**Ex2003**	**20 days**	**10/11/06**	**11/7/06**
816	1.4.2.4.2.1 Document in proof of concept tracking system	Ex2003	20 days	10/11/06	11/7/06
817	1.4.2.4.2.2 Follow lab change control process	Ex2003	20 days	10/11/06	11/7/06
818	1.4.2.4.2.3 Reconfigure lab	Ex2003	20 days	10/11/06	11/7/06
819	1.4.2.4.2.4 Rerun test	Ex2003	20 days	10/11/06	11/7/06
820	1.4.2.4.2.5 Document results/changes	Ex2003	20 days	10/11/06	11/7/06
821	1.4.2.4.2.6 Lab setup problem complete	Ex2003	20 days	10/11/06	11/7/06
822	**1.4.2.4.3 Development/Design Problem**	**Ex2003**	**20 days**	**10/11/06**	**11/7/06**
823	1.4.2.4.3.1 Document in proof of concept tracking system	Ex2003	20 days	10/11/06	11/7/06
824	1.4.2.4.3.2 Escalate development/design issues	Ex2003	20 days	10/11/06	11/7/06
825	1.4.2.4.3.3 Prioritize/risk analysis	Ex2003	20 days	10/11/06	11/7/06
826	1.4.2.4.3.4 Track resolution	Ex2003	20 days	10/11/06	11/7/06
827	1.4.2.4.3.5 Development/design problem complete	Ex2003	20 days	10/11/06	11/7/06
828	1.4.2.4.4 Deploy development solution to proof of concept lab machines complete	Ex2003	20 days	10/11/06	11/7/06
829	**1.4.2.5 Perform Full Cycle Risk Assessment**	**Ex2003**	**20 days**	**10/11/06**	**11/7/06**
830	1.4.2.5.1 Document lessons learned	Ex2003	20 days	10/11/06	11/7/06
831	1.4.2.5.2 Document modifications	Ex2003	20 days	10/11/06	11/7/06
832	1.4.2.5.3 Address readiness to proceed to pilot	Ex2003	20 days	10/11/06	11/7/06
833	1.4.2.5.4 Perform full cycle risk assessment complete	Ex2003	20 days	10/11/06	11/7/06
834	1.4.2.6 Proof of concept complete	Ex2003	20 days	10/11/06	11/7/06
835	**1.4.2.7 Pilot**	**Ex2003**	**20 days**	**10/10/06**	**11/7/06**
836	**1.4.2.7.1 Planning**	**Ex2003**	**20 days**	**10/10/06**	**11/7/06**
837	1.4.2.7.1.1 Identify pilot scope and objectives	Ex2003	20 days	10/11/06	11/7/06
838	1.4.2.7.1.2 Identify pilot groups/individuals/resources/equipment	Ex2003	20 days	10/11/06	11/7/06
839	1.4.2.7.1.3 Document resources and tasks	Ex2003	20 days	10/11/06	11/7/06
840	1.4.2.7.1.4 Develop communications materials for user community (for example, FAQs, Web Site, E-mails)	Ex2003	20 days	10/11/06	11/7/06
841	1.4.2.7.1.5 Develop the user support plan	Ex2003	20 days	10/11/06	11/7/06
842	1.4.2.7.1.6 Develop the training plan	Ex2003	20 days	10/11/06	11/7/06
843	1.4.2.7.1.7 Insure proof of concept lab stable	Ex2003	20 days	10/11/06	11/7/06
844	**1.4.2.7.1.8 Develop the Rollout Process**	**Ex2003**	**20 days**	**10/11/06**	**11/7/06**
845	1.4.2.7.1.8.1 Identify tools and supplies the installer needs	Ex2003	20 days	10/11/06	11/7/06
846	1.4.2.7.1.8.2 Identify lists of scripts and their location	Ex2003	20 days	10/11/06	11/7/06
847	1.4.2.7.1.8.3 Identify backups to be taken prior to/during deployment	Ex2003	20 days	10/11/06	11/7/06
848	1.4.2.7.1.8.4 Document steps for migrating to the new domain structure	Ex2003	20 days	10/11/06	11/7/06
849	1.4.2.7.1.8.5 Document steps for performing manual and automated computer upgrades	Ex2003	20 days	10/11/06	11/7/06
850	1.4.2.7.1.8.6 Document installer acceptance tests	Ex2003	20 days	10/11/06	11/7/06
851	1.4.2.7.1.8.7 Document operational procedures installers and administrators are to perform (for example, resetting permissions, changing passwords, etc.)	Ex2003	20 days	10/11/06	11/7/06
852	1.4.2.7.1.8.8 Document steps for backing out if pilot fails	Ex2003	20 days	10/11/06	11/7/06
853	1.4.2.7.1.8.9 Develop the rollout process complete	Ex2003	20 days	10/11/06	11/7/06
854	1.4.2.7.1.9 Identify known risks and contingency plans for them	Ex2003	20 days	10/11/06	11/7/06
855	1.4.2.7.1.10 Develop rollback plan	Ex2003	20 days	10/11/06	11/7/06
856	1.4.2.7.1.11 Pilot planning complete	Ex2003	0 days	10/10/06	10/10/06
857	**1.4.3 VOIP**		**25 days**	**11/6/06**	**12/8/06**
858	**1.4.3.1 Staging**	**VOIP**	**25 days**	**11/6/06**	**12/8/06**
859	1.4.3.1.1 Stage and Configure all VoIP Equipment	VOIP	5 days	11/6/06	11/10/06
860	1.4.3.1.2 Install Pilot System and Test	VOIP	5 days	11/13/06	11/17/06

ID	ⓘ	Task Name	Program	Duration	Start	Finish
861	✓	1.4.3.1.3 Test POC for VoIP QoS and Call Routing Functionality	VOIP	5 days	11/20/06	11/24/06
862	✓	1.4.3.1.4 Test Proof of Concept for XYZ IVR	VOIP	10 days	11/27/06	12/8/06
863	✓	**1.4.4 LAN AND WAN MIGRATION**	**LANWAN**	**15 days**	**10/17/06**	**11/6/06**
864	✓	**1.4.4.1 Secure necessary resources for staging**	**LANWAN**	**15 days**	**10/17/06**	**11/6/06**
865	✓	1.4.4.1.1 Document Cisco Recommended IOS Software Revisions	LANWAN	10 days	10/17/06	10/30/06
866	✓	1.4.4.1.2 Create Test Environment fron Design Document	LANWAN	10 days	10/17/06	10/30/06
867	✓	1.4.4.1.3 Pre Test Pilot Network	LANWAN	10 days	10/17/06	10/30/06
868	✓	1.4.4.1.4 Select infrastructure component to deploy to testing	LANWAN	10 days	10/17/06	10/30/06
869	✓	1.4.4.1.5 Review deployment team tasks and timeline	LANWAN	10 days	10/17/06	10/30/06
870	✓	1.4.4.1.6 Communicate impact to community	LANWAN	10 days	10/17/06	10/30/06
871	✓	1.4.4.1.7 ID Test User Base - DEL. WAN10	LANWAN	10 days	10/17/06	10/30/06
872	✓	1.4.4.1.8 Logistics to Pilot Network	LANWAN	10 days	10/17/06	10/30/06
873	✓	1.4.4.1.9 Setup Space for Testing	LANWAN	10 days	10/17/06	10/30/06
874	✓	1.4.4.1.10 ID Actual Bodies to Setup Space	LANWAN	10 days	10/17/06	10/30/06
875	✓	1.4.4.1.11 Perform physical move to pilot environment	LANWAN	10 days	10/17/06	10/30/06
876	✓	1.4.4.1.12 Unbox equipment	LANWAN	10 days	10/17/06	10/30/06
877	✓	1.4.4.1.13 Deploy Testing Equipment to Pilot Network from Design Document	LANWAN	10 days	10/17/06	10/30/06
878	✓	1.4.4.1.14 Deploy Test Routers on Piot (Rack & Stack)	LANWAN	10 days	10/17/06	10/30/06
879	✓	1.4.4.1.15 Deploy Test Switches on Piot (Rack & Stack)	LANWAN	10 days	10/17/06	10/30/06
880	✓	1.4.4.1.16 Deploy Test Firewall on Pilot (Rack & Stack)	LANWAN	10 days	10/17/06	10/30/06
881	✓	1.4.4.1.17 Deplot Test DHCP Server on Pilot (Rack & Stack)	LANWAN	10 days	10/17/06	10/30/06
882	✓	1.4.4.1.18 Deploy Test WINS Server on Pilot (Rack & Stack)	LANWAN	10 days	10/17/06	10/30/06
883	✓	1.4.4.1.19 Deploy Test DOMAIN CONTROLLERS on Pilot (Rack & Stack)	LANWAN	10 days	10/17/06	10/30/06
884	✓	1.4.4.1.20 Deploy Test Migrate Printers on Pilot (Rack & Stack)	LANWAN	10 days	10/17/06	10/30/06
885	✓	1.4.4.1.21 Deploy Test Migrate Workstations on Pilot (Rack & Stack)	LANWAN	10 days	10/17/06	10/30/06
886	✓	**1.4.4.1.22 Create test pilot network complete**	**LANWAN**	**10 days**	**10/17/06**	**10/30/06**
887	✓	1.4.4.1.22.1 Configure test routers and switches	LANWAN	10 days	10/17/06	10/30/06
888	✓	1.4.4.1.22.2 Implement VLAN IP Scheme on Test Environment	LANWAN	10 days	10/17/06	10/30/06
889	✓	1.4.4.1.22.3 Test all networking equipment on pilot network using methodology and Ucase - DEL. WAN07	LANWAN	10 days	10/17/06	10/30/06
890	✓	1.4.4.1.22.4 Test all applications on pilot network using methodology and Ucase - DEL. WAN07	LANWAN	10 days	10/17/06	10/30/06
891	✓	1.4.4.1.22.5 Validate migration strategy in test environment	LANWAN	10 days	10/17/06	10/30/06
892	✓	1.4.4.1.22.6 Document Results	LANWAN	10 days	10/17/06	10/30/06
893	✓	1.4.4.1.22.7 Evaluate pilot feedback	LANWAN	10 days	10/17/06	10/30/06
894	✓	1.4.4.1.22.8 Finalize detail deployment strategy	LANWAN	10 days	10/17/06	10/30/06
895	✓	1.4.4.1.22.9 Pilot testing complete - DEL. WAN07	LANWAN	10 days	10/17/06	10/30/06
896	✓	1.4.4.1.22.10 XYZ User Approval	LANWAN	10 days	10/17/06	10/30/06
897	✓	1.4.4.1.22.11 Secure approval to proceed	LANWAN	10 days	10/17/06	10/30/06
898	✓	1.4.4.1.23 Signoff on Test Pilot Completion	LANWAN	10 days	10/17/06	10/30/06
899	✓	1.4.4.1.24 Signoff for detail deployment strategy	LANWAN	10 days	10/17/06	10/30/06
900	✓	**1.4.4.1.25 Staging**	**LANWAN**	**15 days**	**10/17/06**	**11/6/06**
901	✓	1.4.4.1.25.1 Secure necessary resources for implementation	LANWAN	15 days	10/17/06	11/6/06
902	✓	1.4.4.1.25.2 Logistics to Staging Area	LANWAN	15 days	10/17/06	11/6/06
903	✓	1.4.4.1.25.3 Confirm inventory w/ site location	LANWAN	15 days	10/17/06	11/6/06
904	✓	1.4.4.1.25.4 Secure deployment resources	LANWAN	15 days	10/17/06	11/6/06
905	✓	1.4.4.1.25.5 Identify Staging Location Area	LANWAN	15 days	10/17/06	11/6/06
906	✓	1.4.4.1.25.6 ID Equipment to move staging	LANWAN	15 days	10/17/06	11/6/06
907	✓	1.4.4.1.25.7 ID movers to Staging Area	LANWAN	15 days	10/17/06	11/6/06
908	✓	1.4.4.1.25.8 Unbox Equipment	LANWAN	15 days	10/17/06	11/6/06
909	✓	1.4.4.1.25.9 Inventory equipment	LANWAN	15 days	10/17/06	11/6/06
910	✓	1.4.4.1.25.10 Test Equipment	LANWAN	15 days	10/17/06	11/6/06
911	✓	1.4.4.1.25.11 Labeling Equipment with Naming Convention Standard & IP Standard	LANWAN	15 days	10/17/06	11/6/06
912	✓	1.4.4.1.25.12 Document Serial Number	LANWAN	15 days	10/17/06	11/6/06
913	✓	1.4.4.1.25.13 Document Box w/ Location	LANWAN	15 days	10/17/06	11/6/06
914	✓	1.4.4.1.25.14 Unbox Equipment Complete	LANWAN	15 days	10/17/06	11/6/06
915	✓	1.4.4.1.25.15 Configure Routers & Switches & Nokia FW in staging environment - DEL. WAN05	LANWAN	15 days	10/17/06	11/6/06
916	✓	1.4.4.1.25.16 Train deployment resources in deployment methodology	LANWAN	15 days	10/17/06	11/6/06
917	✓	1.4.4.1.25.17 Quality Audit of equipment configurations	LANWAN	15 days	10/17/06	11/6/06
918	✓	1.4.4.1.25.18 Document Testing and On Going Procedures	LANWAN	15 days	10/17/06	11/6/06
919	✓	1.4.4.1.26 LAN/WAN Staging Complete	LANWAN	0 days	11/6/06	11/6/06
920	✓	1.4.4.2 Testing Complete	LANWAN	0 days	11/6/06	11/6/06
921	✓	**1.5 Deployment**		**65.4 days**	**9/27/06**	**12/28/06**
922	✓	**1.5.1 Marketing Campaign**	**MARK**	**10 days**	**9/27/06**	**10/11/06**
923	✓	1.5.1.1 Select initial vertical markets	MARK	2 days	9/28/06	9/29/06
924	✓	1.5.1.2 Issue industry press release	MARK	2 days	9/28/06	9/29/06
925	✓	1.5.1.3 Conduct mass mailing for specific markets	MARK	10 days	9/28/06	10/11/06
926	✓	1.5.1.4 Launch complete	MARK	0 days	9/27/06	9/27/06
927	✓	**1.5.1.5 Post Launch Analysis**	**MARK**	**1 day**	**9/27/06**	**9/28/06**
928	✓	1.5.1.5.1 Enter prospects into customer relationship management database	MARK	1 day	9/28/06	9/28/06
929	✓	1.5.1.5.2 Classify prospects (hot, warm, and cold)	MARK	1 day	9/28/06	9/28/06
930	✓	1.5.1.5.3 Funnel hot prospects to direct sales team	MARK	1 day	9/28/06	9/28/06
931	✓	1.5.1.5.4 Direct warm prospects to inside sales desk	MARK	1 day	9/28/06	9/28/06
932	✓	1.5.1.5.5 Direct cold prospects to telemarketing team	MARK	1 day	9/28/06	9/28/06
933	✓	1.5.1.5.6 Measure response rate	MARK	1 day	9/28/06	9/28/06
934	✓	1.5.1.5.7 Measure success rate by vertical market and customer	MARK	1 day	9/28/06	9/28/06
935	✓	1.5.1.5.8 Determine sales dollars and calculate ROI	MARK	1 day	9/28/06	9/28/06
936	✓	1.5.1.5.9 Compile final counts and summaries	MARK	1 day	9/28/06	9/28/06
937	✓	1.5.1.5.10 Campaign complete	MARK	0 days	9/27/06	9/27/06
938	✓	**1.5.2 LAN AND WAN MIGRATION**	**LANWAN**	**5 days**	**11/6/06**	**11/13/06**
939	✓	1.5.2.1 Pre-Implementation Planning	LANWAN	3 days	11/7/06	11/9/06
940	✓	1.5.2.2 Back up all network devices for SBC 9 sites	LANWAN	3 days	11/7/06	11/9/06
941	✓	1.5.2.3 Planning of Implementation Strategy	LANWAN	3 days	11/7/06	11/9/06

ID		Task Name	Program	Duration	Start	Finish
942	✓	1.5.2.4 Validate Site Contact	LANWAN	3 days	11/7/06	11/9/06
943	✓	1.5.2.5 Move Equipment to 333 S. Wabash Site Location	LANWAN	3 days	11/7/06	11/9/06
944	✓	1.5.2.6 Mount, Cable, Rack & Stack at all SBC Nine	LANWAN	3 days	11/7/06	11/9/06
945	✓	1.5.2.7 Review deployment team tasks and timeline	LANWAN	3 days	11/7/06	11/9/06
946	✓	1.5.2.8 Pre-Implementation Planning Complete	LANWAN	3 days	11/7/06	11/9/06
947	✓	1.5.2.9 Secure Approval to Proceed	LANWAN	3 days	11/7/06	11/9/06
948	✓	1.5.2.10 Logistics	LANWAN	3 days	11/6/06	11/9/06
949	✓	1.5.2.10.1 Secure deployment resources	LANWAN	3 days	11/7/06	11/9/06
950	✓	1.5.2.10.2 Train deployment resources in deployment methodology	LANWAN	3 days	11/7/06	11/9/06
951	✓	1.5.2.10.3 Logistics complete	LANWAN	0 days	11/6/06	11/6/06
952	✓	1.5.2.11 Pilot	LANWAN	5 days	11/6/06	11/13/06
953	✓	1.5.2.11.1 Select infrastructure component to deploy	LANWAN	5 days	11/7/06	11/13/06
954	✓	1.5.2.11.2 Review deployment team tasks and timeline	LANWAN	5 days	11/7/06	11/13/06
955	✓	1.5.2.11.3 Communicate impact to community	LANWAN	5 days	11/7/06	11/13/06
956	✓	1.5.2.11.4 Deploy infrastructure component	LANWAN	5 days	11/7/06	11/13/06
957	✓	1.5.2.11.5 Test infrastructure component	LANWAN	5 days	11/7/06	11/13/06
958	✓	1.5.2.11.6 Release to production/operations environment	LANWAN	5 days	11/7/06	11/13/06
959	✓	1.5.2.11.7 Obtain feedback	LANWAN	5 days	11/7/06	11/13/06
960	✓	1.5.2.11.8 Evaluate pilot feedback	LANWAN	5 days	11/7/06	11/13/06
961	✓	1.5.2.11.9 Pilot complete	LANWAN	0 days	11/6/06	11/6/06
962	✓	1.5.2.12 Determine readiness to proceed	LANWAN	0 days	11/6/06	11/6/06
963	✓	1.5.2.13 Final Deployment	LANWAN	5 days	11/6/06	11/13/06
964	✓	1.5.2.13.1 Review deployment team tasks and timeline	LANWAN	5 days	11/7/06	11/13/06
965	✓	1.5.2.13.2 Communicate impact to community	LANWAN	5 days	11/7/06	11/13/06
966	✓	1.5.2.13.3 Deploy infrastructure components	LANWAN	5 days	11/7/06	11/13/06
967	✓	1.5.2.13.4 Test infrastructure component	LANWAN	5 days	11/7/06	11/13/06
968	✓	1.5.2.13.4.1 Verify MDF able to accept server and equipment	LANWAN	5 days	11/7/06	11/13/06
969	✓	1.5.2.13.4.2 Verify Power to each rack	LANWAN	5 days	11/7/06	11/13/06
970	✓	1.5.2.13.4.3 Verify UPS in installed	LANWAN	5 days	11/7/06	11/13/06
971	✓	1.5.2.13.4.4 Verify UPS is functional	LANWAN	5 days	11/7/06	11/13/06
972	✓	1.5.2.13.4.5 Verify Fiber to MDF and IDF is installed	LANWAN	5 days	11/7/06	11/13/06
973	✓	1.5.2.13.4.6 Corridinate with carrier to forward DID information	TELECOM	5 days	11/7/06	11/13/06
974	✓	1.5.2.13.4.7 Corrdinate with Telco Partner to distribute phone	TELECOM	5 days	11/7/06	11/13/06
975	✓	1.5.2.13.5 Release to production/operations environment	LANWAN	5 days	11/7/06	11/13/06
976	✓	1.5.2.13.6 Obtain feedback	LANWAN	0 days	11/6/06	11/6/06
977	✓	1.5.2.13.7 Final deployment complete	LANWAN	0 days	11/6/06	11/6/06
978	✓	1.5.2.14 Post Implementation Review	LANWAN	1 day	11/6/06	11/7/06
979	✓	1.5.2.14.1 Document lessons learned	LANWAN	1 day	11/7/06	11/7/06
980	✓	1.5.2.14.2 Distribute to team members	LANWAN	1 day	11/7/06	11/7/06
981	✓	1.5.2.14.3 Create software maintenance team	LANWAN	1 day	11/7/06	11/7/06
982	✓	1.5.2.14.4 Post implementation review complete	LANWAN	0 days	11/6/06	11/6/06
983	✓	1.5.3 Deploy Production AD System	AD	27 days	11/14/06	12/21/06
984	✓	1.5.3.1 Perform Windows NT Domain Upgrade	AD	27 days	11/14/06	12/21/06
985	✓	1.5.3.1.1 Prepare OU structure of data owners (It is recommended that a script is developed as this process may have to be repeated up to 100 times.)	AD	4 days	11/14/06	11/20/06
986	✓	1.5.3.1.2 Create New Regional Domain	AD	3 days	11/20/06	11/23/06
987	✓	1.5.3.1.2.1 Create DNS delegation from root domain	AD	1 day	11/20/06	11/21/06
988	✓	1.5.3.1.2.2 Install first domain controller	AD	1 day	11/21/06	11/22/06
989	✓	1.5.3.1.2.3 Configure client to point to itself as primary DNS server and any other DNS server as alternate DNS server	AD	1 day	11/22/06	11/23/06
990	✓	1.5.3.1.3 Restructure Actives	AD	12 days	11/23/06	12/11/06
991	✓	1.5.3.1.3.1 Complete user migration as part of account domain restructuring	AD	2 days	11/23/06	11/27/06
992	✓	1.5.3.1.3.2 Complete global group migration as part of account domain restructuring	AD	2 days	11/27/06	11/29/06
993	✓	1.5.3.1.3.3 Complete migration of user profiles as part of account domain restructuring	AD	2 days	11/29/06	12/1/06
994	✓	1.5.3.1.3.4 Complete migration of Exchange mailbox access as part of account domain restructuring	AD	2 days	12/1/06	12/5/06
995	✓	1.5.3.1.3.5 Complete migration of workstations as part of account domain restructuring	AD	2 days	12/5/06	12/7/06
996	✓	1.5.3.1.3.6 Complete migration of resources as part of account domain restructuring	AD	2 days	12/7/06	12/11/06
997	✓	1.5.3.1.4 Restructure Account Domain	AD	8 days	12/11/06	12/21/06
998	✓	1.5.3.1.4.1 Prepare for Restructuring	AD	8 days	12/11/06	12/21/06
999	✓	1.5.3.1.4.1.1 Install migration tool	AD	1 day	12/11/06	12/12/06
1000	✓	1.5.3.1.4.1.2 Prepare Source and Target Domain	AD	2 days	12/12/06	12/14/06
1001	✓	1.5.3.1.4.1.2.1 Create trust relationship	AD	1 day	12/12/06	12/13/06
1002	✓	1.5.3.1.4.1.2.2 Create group membership	AD	1 day	12/13/06	12/14/06
1003	✓	1.5.3.1.4.1.3 Identify service accounts	AD	1 day	12/14/06	12/15/06
1004	✓	1.5.3.1.4.1.4 Migrate all global groups to target domain	AD	2 days	12/15/06	12/19/06
1005	✓	1.5.3.1.4.1.5 Continue to administer users and groups in the source domain	AD	2 days	12/19/06	12/21/06
1006	✓	1.5.4 Deployment Exchange 2003	Ex2003	5 days	12/21/06	12/28/06
1007	✓	1.5.4.1 Communicate with pilot users	Ex2003	4 hrs	12/21/06	12/21/06
1008	✓	1.5.4.2 Conduct user training	Ex2003	5 days	12/21/06	12/28/06
1009	✓	1.5.4.3 Ensure support organization is prepared	Ex2003	4 days	12/21/06	12/27/06
1010	✓	1.5.4.4 Prepare pilot sites)	Ex2003	2 days	12/21/06	12/25/06
1011	✓	1.5.4.5 Deploy the rollout process	Ex2003	5 days	12/21/06	12/28/06
1012	✓	1.5.4.6 Pilot deployment complete	Ex2003	0 days	12/21/06	12/21/06
1013	✓	1.5.4.7 Evaluate the Pilot	Ex2003	5 days	12/21/06	12/28/06
1014	✓	1.5.4.7.1 Conduct desktop test scenarios	Ex2003	5 days	12/21/06	12/28/06
1015	✓	1.5.4.7.2 Conduct server test scenarios	Ex2003	5 days	12/21/06	12/28/06
1016	✓	1.5.4.7.3 Conduct third-party application test scenarios	Ex2003	5 days	12/21/06	12/28/06
1017	✓	1.5.4.7.4 Conduct custom application test scenarios	Ex2003	5 days	12/21/06	12/28/06
1018	✓	1.5.4.7.5 Conduct coexistence test scenarios	Ex2003	5 days	12/21/06	12/28/06
1019	✓	1.5.4.7.6 Identify scope changes	Ex2003	3 days	12/21/06	12/26/06
1020	✓	1.5.4.7.7 Identify cost factors	Ex2003	2 days	12/21/06	12/25/06
1021	✓	1.5.4.7.8 Identify interoperability issues	Ex2003	3 days	12/21/06	12/26/06
1022	✓	1.5.4.7.9 Identify unanticipated downtime	Ex2003	2 days	12/21/06	12/25/06

ITS Relocation Project WBS
Date:4/21/12
Revision 1.0

ID		Task Name	Program	Duration	Start	Finish
1023	✓	1.5.4.7.10 Pilot test complete	Ex2003	0 days	12/21/06	12/21/06
1024	✓	**1.5.4.8 Post-Pilot Evaluation**	**Ex2003**	**5 days**	**12/21/06**	**12/28/06**
1025	✓	1.5.4.8.1 Obtain user feedback	Ex2003	5 days	12/21/06	12/28/06
1026	✓	1.5.4.8.2 Evaluate lessons learned	Ex2003	2 days	12/21/06	12/25/06
1027	✓	1.5.4.8.3 Modify items as necessary	Ex2003	2 days	12/21/06	12/25/06
1028	✓	1.5.4.8.4 Document recommendation for next steps	Ex2003	2 days	12/21/06	12/25/06
1029	✓	1.5.4.8.5 Post-pilot evaluation complete	Ex2003	0 days	12/21/06	12/21/06
1030	✓	1.5.4.9 Pilot complete	Ex2003	0 days	12/21/06	12/21/06
1031	✓	**1.5.4.10 Deployment**	**Ex2003**	**5 days**	**12/21/06**	**12/28/06**
1032	✓	**1.5.4.10.1 Communications**	**Ex2003**	**2 days**	**12/21/06**	**12/25/06**
1033	✓	1.5.4.10.1.1 Review communications strategy document	Ex2003	2 days	12/21/06	12/25/06
1034	✓	1.5.4.10.1.2 Start communications	Ex2003	4 hrs	12/21/06	12/21/06
1035	✓	1.5.4.10.1.3 Communications complete	Ex2003	0 days	12/21/06	12/21/06
1036	✓	**1.5.4.10.2 Education/Training**	**Ex2003**	**5 days**	**12/21/06**	**12/28/06**
1037	✓	1.5.4.10.2.1 Review education/training strategy document	Ex2003	1 day	12/21/06	12/22/06
1038	✓	1.5.4.10.2.2 Conduct administrative training	Ex2003	5 days	12/21/06	12/28/06
1039	✓	1.5.4.10.2.3 Conduct user training	Ex2003	5 days	12/21/06	12/28/06
1040	✓	1.5.4.10.2.4 Education/training complete	Ex2003	0 days	12/21/06	12/21/06
1041	✓	**1.5.5 VoIP**	**VOIP**	**10 days**	**12/11/06**	**12/22/06**
1042	✓	1.5.5.1 Install Production System and Execute Test Plan	VOIP	10 days	12/11/06	12/22/06
1043	✓	1.5.5.2 Gain Approval to Proceed	VOIP	0 days	12/22/06	12/22/06
1044	✓	**1.6 Implementation**	**AD**	**25 days**	**12/21/06**	**1/25/07**
1045	✓	**1.6.1 Execute AD Migration**	**AD**	**5 days**	**12/21/06**	**12/28/06**
1046	✓	1.6.1.1 Run Service Account Wizard	AD	5 days	12/21/06	12/28/06
1047	✓	1.6.1.2 Create manageable batch of users (for example, 100 users)	AD	5 days	12/21/06	12/28/06
1048	✓	**1.6.1.3 Migrate Batch of Users (with SIDs in SIDHistory)**	**AD**	**5 days**	**12/21/06**	**12/28/06**
1049	✓	1.6.1.3.1 Enable target account	AD	5 days	12/21/06	12/28/06
1050	✓	1.6.1.3.2 Expire source account (for example, in 7 days)	AD	5 days	12/21/06	12/28/06
1051	✓	1.6.1.3.3 Notify users of new passwords	AD	5 days	12/21/06	12/28/06
1052	✓	1.6.1.4 Migrate local user profiles (if applicable)	AD	5 days	12/21/06	12/28/06
1053	✓	1.6.1.5 Re-migrate all global groups	AD	5 days	12/21/06	12/28/06
1054	✓	1.6.1.6 Continue to make all changes to global group memberships in the source domain	AD	5 days	12/21/06	12/28/06
1055	✓	1.6.1.7 Make changes to user accounts in the domain where account is active (like Remote Access Service [RAS] permission)	AD	5 days	12/21/06	12/28/06
1056	✓	**1.6.1.8 Clean-up Account Domain**	**AD**	**5 days**	**12/21/06**	**12/28/06**
1057	✓	1.6.1.8.1 Freeze creation of new accounts in the source domain	AD	5 days	12/21/06	12/28/06
1058	✓	1.6.1.8.2 Re-migrate all global groups	AD	5 days	12/21/06	12/28/06
1059	✓	1.6.1.8.3 Start administering in the target domain only	AD	5 days	12/21/06	12/28/06
1060	✓	1.6.1.8.4 Switch source domain into maintenance mode	AD	5 days	12/21/06	12/28/06
1061	✓	1.6.1.8.5 Keep at least two domain controllers online until all migration operations have finished	AD	5 days	12/21/06	12/28/06
1062	✓	1.6.1.8.6 Decommission domain when done	AD	5 days	12/21/06	12/28/06
1063	✓	1.6.1.8.7 Make backup tape of Passive Directory Connector	AD	5 days	12/21/06	12/28/06
1064	✓	**1.6.1.9 Migrate Resource Domain**	**AD**	**5 days**	**12/21/06**	**12/28/06**
1065	✓	**1.6.1.9.1 Prepare to Restructure Resource Domains**	**AD**	**5 days**	**12/21/06**	**12/28/06**
1066	✓	1.6.1.9.1.1 Create account for migration in resource domains	AD	5 days	12/21/06	12/28/06
1067	✓	1.6.1.9.1.2 Verify account is a member of domain administrators	AD	5 days	12/21/06	12/28/06
1068	✓	1.6.1.9.2 Create target OUs	AD	5 days	12/21/06	12/28/06
1069	✓	1.6.1.9.3 Establish trust relationships between resource and target domains	AD	5 days	12/21/06	12/28/06
1070	✓	1.6.1.9.4 Identify and migrate service accounts	AD	5 days	12/21/06	12/28/06
1071	✓	**1.6.1.9.5 Restructure Resource Domain**	**AD**	**5 days**	**12/21/06**	**12/28/06**
1072	✓	1.6.1.9.5.1 Migrate workstations	AD	5 days	12/21/06	12/28/06
1073	✓	1.6.1.9.5.2 Migrate member servers	AD	5 days	12/21/06	12/28/06
1074	✓	1.6.1.9.5.3 Clone shared local groups	AD	5 days	12/21/06	12/28/06
1075	✓	1.6.1.9.5.4 Migrate domain controllers	AD	5 days	12/21/06	12/28/06
1076	✓	1.6.1.9.6 Decommission Windows NT 4.0 domains	AD	5 days	12/21/06	12/28/06
1077	✓	**1.6.1.10 Upgrade from Windows 2000 Domain**	**AD**	**5 days**	**12/21/06**	**12/28/06**
1078	✓	1.6.1.10.1 Apply appropriate Windows 2000 service packs	AD	5 days	12/21/06	12/28/06
1079	✓	1.6.1.10.2 Check upgrade compatibility of domain	AD	5 days	12/21/06	12/28/06
1080	✓	1.6.1.10.3 Obtain required permissions	AD	5 days	12/21/06	12/28/06
1081	✓	**1.6.1.10.4 Prepare Schema Master**	**AD**	**5 days**	**12/21/06**	**12/28/06**
1082	✓	1.6.1.10.4.1 Backup schema master	AD	5 days	12/21/06	12/28/06
1083	✓	1.6.1.10.4.2 Disconnect schema master	AD	5 days	12/21/06	12/28/06
1084	✓	1.6.1.10.4.3 Run adprep /forestprep on schema master	AD	5 days	12/21/06	12/28/06
1085	✓	1.6.1.10.4.4 Use dcdiag and other tools to verify success	AD	5 days	12/21/06	12/28/06
1086	✓	**1.6.1.10.5 Prepare Infrastructure Operations Master**	**AD**	**5 days**	**12/21/06**	**12/28/06**
1087	✓	1.6.1.10.5.1 Backup infrastructure operations master	AD	5 days	12/21/06	12/28/06
1088	✓	1.6.1.10.5.2 Run adprep/domainprep on infrastructure operations master	AD	5 days	12/21/06	12/28/06
1089	✓	1.6.1.10.5.3 Wait for replication to complete	AD	5 days	12/21/06	12/28/06
1090	✓	1.6.1.10.6 Upgrade domain controllers	AD	5 days	12/21/06	12/28/06
1091	✓	1.6.1.10.7 Upgrade Active Directory clients (Windows 98, Windows 95, Windows NT)	AD	5 days	12/21/06	12/28/06
1092	✓	**1.6.1.11 Convert to Windows Server 2003 Native Mode**	**AD**	**5 days**	**12/21/06**	**12/28/06**
1093	✓	1.6.1.11.1 Ensure all domain controllers are on Windows Server 2003	AD	5 days	12/21/06	12/28/06
1094	✓	1.6.1.11.2 Raise functional level of forests to Windows Server 2003	AD	5 days	12/21/06	12/28/06
1095	✓	1.6.1.11.3 Raise functional level of domains to Windows Server 2003	AD	5 days	12/21/06	12/28/06
1096	✓	1.6.1.11.4 Create forest to forest trusts	AD	5 days	12/21/06	12/28/06
1097	✓	1.6.1.11.5 Configure universal group membership caching	AD	5 days	12/21/06	12/28/06
1098	✓	1.6.1.11.6 Create saved queries for commonly run searches	AD	5 days	12/21/06	12/28/06
1099	✓	1.6.1.12 Deploy production system complete	AD	0 days	12/21/06	12/21/06
1100	✓	1.6.1.13 Deployment complete	AD	0 days	12/21/06	12/21/06
1101	✓	**1.6.1.14 Post-Implementation Review**	**AD**	**5 days**	**12/21/06**	**12/28/06**
1102	✓	1.6.1.14.1 Post-implementation monitoring, mailbox migrations	AD	5 days	12/21/06	12/28/06
1103	✓	1.6.1.14.2 Obtain user feedback	AD	5 days	12/21/06	12/28/06

ITS Relocation Project WBS
Date:4/21/12
Revision 1.0

ID		Task Name	Program	Duration	Start	Finish
1104	✓	1.6.1.14.3 Evaluate lessons learned	AD	5 days	12/21/06	12/28/06
1105	✓	1.6.1.14.4 Modify items as necessary	AD	5 days	12/21/06	12/28/06
1106	✓	1.6.1.14.5 Establish ongoing infrastructure planning team	AD	5 days	12/21/06	12/28/06
1107	✓	1.6.1.14.6 Sharing of post-implementation feedback	AD	5 days	12/21/06	12/28/06
1108	✓	1.6.1.14.7 Post-implementation review complete	AD	5 days	12/21/06	12/28/06
1109	✓	1.6.1.15 Microsoft Active Directory deployment complete	AD	5 days	12/21/06	12/28/06
1110	✓	**1.6.2 Implement the Exchange 2003 Architecture**	**Ex2003**	**20 days**	**12/28/06**	**1/25/07**
1111	✓	1.6.2.1 Review migration strategy/standards document	Ex2003	15 days	12/28/06	1/18/07
1112	✓	1.6.2.2 Restructure/build new architecture	Ex2003	15 days	12/28/06	1/18/07
1113	✓	1.6.2.3 Domain migration complete	Ex2003	15 days	12/28/06	1/18/07
1114	✓	**1.6.2.4 Active Directory**	**Ex2003**	**20 days**	**12/28/06**	**1/25/07**
1115	✓	**1.6.2.4.1 Synchronizing Active Directory with Exchange 5.5**	**Ex2003**	**20 days**	**12/28/06**	**1/25/07**
1116	✓	1.6.2.4.1.1 Review ADC connection plan strategy/standards	Ex2003	20 days	12/28/06	1/25/07
1117	✓	1.6.2.4.1.2 Set up connection agreements	Ex2003	20 days	12/28/06	1/25/07
1118	✓	1.6.2.4.1.3 Test connection agreement configurations	Ex2003	20 days	12/28/06	1/25/07
1119	✓	1.6.2.4.1.4 Determine a schedule for directory synchronization	Ex2003	20 days	12/28/06	1/25/07
1120	✓	1.6.2.4.1.5 Synchronizing Active Directory with Exchange 5.5 complete	Ex2003	20 days	12/28/06	1/25/07
1121	✓	1.6.2.4.2 Install/configure clients	Ex2003	20 days	12/28/06	1/25/07
1122	✓	1.6.2.4.3 Test	Ex2003	20 days	12/28/06	1/25/07
1123	✓	1.6.2.4.4 Migrate XYZ mailboxes over to XYZ Windows 2003 Cluster	Ex2003	20 days	12/28/06	1/25/07
1124	✓	1.6.2.4.5 Migrate Distrubion List	Ex2003	20 days	12/28/06	1/25/07
1125	✓	1.6.2.4.6 Migrate XYZ Workstations over to THEXYZ.NET Domain	Ex2003	20 days	12/28/06	1/25/07
1126	✓	1.6.2.5 Deployment complete	Ex2003	0 days	12/28/06	12/28/06
1127	✓	**1.6.2.6 Post-Implementation Review**	**Ex2003**	**2 days**	**12/28/06**	**1/1/07**
1128	✓	1.6.2.6.1 Obtain user feedback	Ex2003	2 days	12/28/06	1/1/07
1129	✓	1.6.2.6.2 Evaluate lessons learned	Ex2003	2 days	12/28/06	1/1/07
1130	✓	1.6.2.6.3 Modify items as necessary	Ex2003	2 days	12/28/06	1/1/07
1131	✓	1.6.2.6.4 Establish ongoing planning team	Ex2003	2 days	12/28/06	1/1/07
1132	✓	1.6.2.6.5 Post-implementation review complete	Ex2003	0 days	12/28/06	12/28/06
1133	✓	1.6.2.7 Microsoft Exchange 2003 deployment template complete	Ex2003	0 days	12/28/06	12/28/06
1134	✓	**1.6.3 VOIP**	**VOIP**	**12 days**	**12/25/06**	**1/9/07**
1135	✓	1.6.3.1 Execute VOIP Migration Plan and Schedule	VOIP	12 days	12/25/06	1/9/07
1136	✓	**1.6.4 Relocation Deployment**	**RELOC**	**5 days**	**1/9/07**	**1/16/07**
1137	✓	1.6.4.1 Execute Relocation Migration Plan	RELOC	0 days	1/9/07	1/9/07
1138	✓	**1.6.4.2 System Disconnect - Legal & ITS**	**RELOC**	**5 days**	**1/10/07**	**1/16/07**
1139	✓	1.6.4.2.1 System Packaging	RELOC	5 days	1/10/07	1/16/07
1140	✓	1.6.4.2.2 System Shipping	RELOC	5 days	1/10/07	1/16/07
1141	✓	**1.6.4.3 System Reconnect- Legal & ITS**	**RELOC**	**5 days**	**1/10/07**	**1/16/07**
1142	✓	1.6.4.3.1 System Unpacking	RELOC	5 days	1/10/07	1/16/07
1143	✓	1.6.4.3.2 System Deployment	RELOC	5 days	1/10/07	1/16/07
1144	✓	1.6.4.3.3 System Testing (Network, Hardware, Software, WAN)	RELOC	5 days	1/10/07	1/16/07
1145	✓	1.6.5 Relocation GO LIVE	RELOC	0 days	1/16/07	1/16/07
1146	✓	**1.6.6 Closeout**	**RELOC**	**1 day**	**1/17/07**	**1/17/07**
1147	✓	**1.6.6.1 Post Implementation Audit Preparation Process**	**RELOC**	**1 day**	**1/17/07**	**1/17/07**
1148	✓	**1.6.6.1.1 Phase I**	**RELOC**	**1 day**	**1/17/07**	**1/17/07**
1149	✓	1.6.6.1.1.1 Meeti with PDT to review all Project Deliverables and Timeline	RELOC	1 day	1/17/07	1/17/07
1150	✓	1.6.6.1.1.2 Review Contract	RELOC	1 day	1/17/07	1/17/07
1151	✓	1.6.6.1.1.3 Review Budget and Payments	RELOC	1 day	1/17/07	1/17/07
1152	✓	1.6.6.2 Prepare Lesson Learned	RELOC	1 day	1/17/07	1/17/07
1153	✓	1.6.6.3 Hold Closeout Meeting with Project Team	RELOC	1 day	1/17/07	1/17/07
1154	✓	1.6.6.4 Release Resources	RELOC	1 day	1/17/07	1/17/07

www.ingramcontent.com/pod-product-compliance
Lightning Source LLC
LaVergne TN
LVHW070947210926
848482LV00002B/120